ANNUAL EDITIONS

Anthropology 10/11

Thirty-Third Edition

EDITOR

Elvio Angeloni

Pasadena City College

Elvio Angeloni received his BA from UCLA in 1963, his MA in anthropology from UCLA in 1965, and his MA in communication arts from Loyola Marymount University in 1976. He has produced several films, including *Little Warrior,* winner of the Cinemedia VI Best Bicentennial Theme, and *Broken Bottles,* shown on PBS. He served as an academic adviser on the instructional television series *Faces of Culture.* He received the Pasadena City College Outstanding Teacher Award in 2006. He is also the academic editor of *Annual Editions: Physical Anthropology, Classic Edition Sources: Anthropology,* co-editor of *Rountable Viewpoints Physical Anthropology* and co-editor of *Annual Editions: Archaeology.* His primary area of interest has been indigenous peoples of the American Southwest.

The McGraw·Hill Companies

ANNUAL EDITIONS: ANTHROPOLOGY, THIRTY-THIRD EDITION

Published by McGraw-Hill, a business unit of The McGraw-Hill Companies, Inc., 1221 Avenue of the Americas, New York, NY 10020.

Annual Editions is published by the **Contemporary Learning Series** group within the McGraw-Hill Higher Education division.

1 2 3 4 5 6 7 8 9 0 QPD/QPD 0 9

ISBN 978–0–07–812782–3
MHID 0–07–812782–3
ISSN 1091–613X

Managing Editor: *Larry Loeppke*
Senior Managing Editor: *Faye Schilling*
Developmental Editor: *Debra Henricks*
Editorial Coordinator: *Mary Foust*
Editorial Assistant: *Cindy Hedley*
Production Service Assistant: *Rita Hingtgen*
Permissions Coordinator: *Lenny J. Behnke*
Senior Marketing Manager: *Julie Keck*
Senior Marketing Communications Specialist: *Mary Klein*
Marketing Coordinator: *Alice Link*
Project Manager: *Joyce Watters*
Design Specialist: *Tara McDermott*
Production Supervisor: *Sue Culbertson*
Cover Graphics: *Kristine Jubeck*

Compositor: Laserwords Private Limited
Cover Image: © Brand X Pictures/Punchstock (inset); © Digital Vision/Punchstock (background)

Library in Congress Cataloging-in-Publication Data
Main entry under title: Annual Editions: Anthropology. 2010/2011.
1. Anthropology—Periodicals. I. Angeloni, Elvio, *comp.* II. Title: Anthropology.
658'.05

www.mhhe.com

ditors/Academic Advisory Board

bers of the Academic Advisory Board are instrumental in the final selection of articles for each edition of ANNUAL EDITIONS. review of articles for content, level, and appropriateness provides critical direction to the editors and staff. We think that you will heir careful consideration well reflected in this volume.

NUAL EDITIONS: Anthropology 10/11

d Edition

TOR

Angeloni
dena City College

ADEMIC ADVISORY BOARD MEMBERS

Preface

In publishing ANNUAL EDITIONS we recognize the enormous role played by the magazines, newspapers, and journals of the public press providing current, first-rate educational information in a broad spectrum of interest areas. Many of these articles are appropriate for studen researchers, and professionals seeking accurate, current material to help bridge the gap between principles and theories and the real wor These articles, however, become more useful for study when those of lasting value are carefully collected, organized, indexed, and reproduc in a low-cost format, which provides easy and permanent access when the material is needed. That is the role played by ANNUAL EDITION

This thirty-third edition of *Annual Editions: Anthropology* contains a variety of articles on contemporary issues in social and cultural anthropology. In contrast to the broad range of topics with minimum depth that is typical of standard textbooks, this anthology provides an opportunity to read firsthand accounts by anthropologists of their own research. In allowing scholars to speak for themselves about the issues in which they are experts, we are better able to understand the kind of questions anthropologists ask, the ways in which they ask them, and how they go about searching for answers. Indeed, where there is disagreement among anthropologists, this format allows the readers to draw their own conclusions. Given the very broad scope of anthropology—in time, space, and subject matter—the present collection of highly readable articles has been selected according to a certain criteria. The articles have been chosen from both professional and nonprofessional publications for the purpose of supplementing standard textbooks that are used in introductory courses. Some of the articles are considered classics in the field, while others have been selected for their timely relevance.

Included in this volume are a number of features that are designed to make it useful for students, researchers, and professionals in the field of anthropology. While the articles are arranged along the lines of broadly unifying themes, the *Topic Guide* can be used to establish specific reading assignments tailored to the needs of a partic course of study. Other useful features include the *T of Contents* abstracts, which summarize each article present key concepts in bolditalics. In addition, each is preceded by an overview, which provides a backgr for informed reading of the articles, emphasizes cr issues, and presents *key points to consider.* Finally *Internet Reference* section can be used to further ex the topics online.

Annual Editions: Anthropology 10/11 will con to be updated annually. Those involved in producin volume wish to make the next one as useful and effe as possible. Your criticism and advice are always come. Please fill out the postage-paid article rating on the last page of the book and let us know your ions. Any anthology can be improved. This continu be—annually.

Elvio Ang

E

evangeloni@gmai

ontents

UNIT 1
Anthropological Perspectives

UNIT 2
Culture and Communication

concepts in bold italics are developed in the article. For further expansion, please refer to the Topic Guide.

UNIT 3
The Organization of Society and Culture

Unit Overview

The concepts in bold italics are developed in the article. For further expansion, please refer to the Topic Guide.

UNIT 4
Other Families, Other Ways

UNIT 5
Gender and Status

e concepts in bold italics are developed in the article. For further expansion, please refer to the Topic Guide.

UNIT 6
Religion, Belief, and Ritual

The concepts in bold italics are developed in the article. For further expansion, please refer to the Topic Guide.

UNIT 7
Sociocultural Change

concepts in bold italics are developed in the article. For further expansion, please refer to the Topic Guide.

Correlation Guide

The *Annual Editions* series provides students with convenient, inexpensive access to current, carefully selected articles from the public press. **Annual Editions: Anthropology 10/11** is an easy-to-use reader that presents articles on important topics such as *cultural diversity, languag social relationships,* and many more. For more information on *Annual Editions* and other *McGraw-Hill Contemporary Learning Series* titles, vi www.mhhe/cls.com.

This convenient guide matches the units in **Annual Editions: Anthropology 10/11** with the corresponding chapters in three of our best-sellin McGraw-Hill Anthropology textbooks by Kottak and Lavenda/Schultz.

Annual Editions: Anthropology 10/11	Cultural Anthropology, 13/e by Kottak	Mirror for Humanity: A Concise Introduction to Cultural Anthropology, 7/e by Kottak	Core Concepts in Cultur Anthropology, 4/e by Lavenda/Schultz
Unit 1: Anthropological Perspectives	**Chapter 1:** What Is Anthropology? **Chapter 2:** Culture **Chapter 3:** Theory and Methods in Cultural Anthropology **Chapter 4:** Applying Anthropology	**Chapter 1:** What Is Anthropology? **Chapter 3:** Ethics and Methods **Chapter 12:** Applying Anthropology	**Chapter 1:** Anthropology **Chapter 2:** Culture **Chapter 12:** Theory in Cultura Anthropology
Unit 2: Culture and Communication	**Chapter 2:** Culture **Chapter 5:** Language and Communication **Chapter 6:** Ethnicity and Race	**Chapter 2:** Culture **Chapter 4:** Language and Communication **Chapter 11:** Ethnicity and Race	**Chapter 2:** Culture **Chapter 3:** Language **Chapter 4:** Culture and the Individual
Unit 3: The Organization of Society and Culture	**Chapter 11:** Families, Kinship, and Descent **Chapter 13:** Arts, Media, and Sports	**Chapter 7:** Families, Kinship, and Descent **Chapter 13:** Global Issues Today	**Chapter 6:** The Dimensions of Social Organization **Chapter 8:** Economic Anthropology **Chapter 9:** Relatedness: Kinship and Descent
Unit 4: Other Families, Other Ways	**Chapter 10:** Marriage **Chapter 11:** Families, Kinship, and Descent	**Chapter 7:** Families, Kinship, and Descent	**Chapter 9:** Relatedness: Kinship and Descent **Chapter 10:** Marriage and Far
Unit 5: Gender and Status	**Chapter 9:** Gender	**Chapter 8:** Gender	**Chapter 7:** Political Anthropo
Unit 6: Religion, Belief, and Ritual	**Chapter 8:** Political Systems **Chapter 12:** Religion **Chapter 15:** Global Issues Today	**Chapter 6:** Political Systems **Chapter 9:** Religion **Chapter 13:** Global Issues Today	**Chapter 7:** Political Anthropo **Chapter 5:** Expressive Cultur Religion, Worldview, and Art
Unit 7: Sociocultural Change	**Chapter 7:** Making a Living **Chapter 14:** The World System and Colonialism **Chapter 15:** Global Issues Today	**Chapter 5:** Making a Living **Chapter 10:** The World System and Colonialism **Chapter 13:** Global Issues Today	**Chapter 8:** Economic Anthropology **Chapter 11:** Globalization

opic Guide

ɔpic guide suggests how the selections in this book relate to the subjects covered in your course. You may want to use the topics listed on pages to search the Web more easily.

the following pages a number of websites have been gathered specifically for this book. They are arranged to reflect the units of this Annual ɪs reader. You can link to these sites by going to *http://www.mhcls.com*.

he articles that relate to each topic are listed below the bold-faced term.

ulturation

. Before: The Sixties
. Yanomamo
. Playing Indian at Halftime: The Controversy over American Indian Mascots, Logos, and Nicknames in School-Related Events
. Who Needs Love!: In Japan, Many Couples Don't
. Shamanisms: Past and Present
. Understanding Islam
. The Arrow of Disease
. The Price of Progress
. Seeing Conservation through the Global Lens
. What Native Peoples Deserve

ression

. Yanomamo
. . . . but What If It's a Girl?
. Rising Number of Dowry Deaths in India
. Understanding Islam
. The Arrow of Disease
. What Native Peoples Deserve

uism

. Eating Christmas in the Kalahari
. Ties That Bind

d care

Sick of Poverty
Death without Weeping
. Where Fat Is a Mark of Beauty
. . . . but What If It's a Girl?

dren

. Playing Indian at Halftime: The Controversy over American Indian Mascots, Logos, and Nicknames in School-Related Events
Sick of Poverty
. Death without Weeping
Where Fat Is a Mark of Beauty
. . . . but What If It's a Girl?

munication

. Whose Speech Is Better?
. Lost for Words
. Do You Speak American?
Fighting for Our Lives
Expletive Deleted
I Can't Even Open My Mouth: Separating Messages from Metamessages in Family Talk
Shakespeare in the Bush
At a Loss for Words
Ties That Bind
Playing Indian at Halftime: The Controversy over American Indian Mascots, Logos, and Nicknames in School-Related Events
Understanding Islam

ss-cultural experience

Eating Christmas in the Kalahari
Yanomamo
5. Whose Speech Is Better?
11. Shakespeare in the Bush
13. The Inuit Paradox
15. Playing Indian at Halftime: The Controversy over American Indian Mascots, Logos, and Nicknames in School-Related Events
18. Death without Weeping
19. Arranging a Marriage in India
25. Shamanisms: Past and Present
27. Understanding Islam

Cultural change

4. Yanomamo
7. Do You Speak American?
12. At a Loss for Words
13. The Inuit Paradox
20. Who Needs Love!: In Japan, Many Couples Don't
23. . . . but What If It's a Girl?
24. Rising Number of Dowry Deaths in India
25. Shamanisms: Past and Present
31. Why Can't People Feed Themselves?
32. The Arrow of Disease
33. The Price of Progress
34. Of Ice and Men
35. Inundation
36. Isolation
37. Seeing Conservation through the Global Lens
38. What Native Peoples Deserve

Cultural diversity

5. Whose Speech Is Better?
7. Do You Speak American?
15. Playing Indian at Halftime: The Controversy over American Indian Mascots, Logos, and Nicknames in School-Related Events
19. Arranging a Marriage in India
21. The Berdache Tradition
25. Shamanisms: Past and Present
27. Understanding Islam
37. Seeing Conservation through the Global Lens

Cultural identity

5. Whose Speech Is Better?
13. The Inuit Paradox
15. Playing Indian at Halftime: The Controversy over American Indian Mascots, Logos, and Nicknames in School-Related Events
22. Where Fat Is a Mark of Beauty
26. The Adaptive Value of Religious Ritual
27. Understanding Islam
38. What Native Peoples Deserve

Cultural relativity

2. Eating Christmas in the Kalahari
5. Whose Speech Is Better?
6. Lost for Words
7. Do You Speak American?
13. The Inuit Paradox
19. Arranging a Marriage in India
27. Understanding Islam

Ecology and society
13. The Inuit Paradox
17. When Brothers Share a Wife
31. Why Can't People Feed Themselves?
32. The Arrow of Disease
33. The Price of Progress
34. Of Ice and Men
35. Inundation
36. Isolation
37. Seeing Conservation through the Global Lens

Economic systems
16. Sick of Poverty
17. When Brothers Share a Wife
18. Death without Weeping
23. . . . but What If It's a Girl?
24. Rising Number of Dowry Deaths in India
31. Why Can't People Feed Themselves?
32. The Arrow of Disease
33. The Price of Progress
37. Seeing Conservation through the Global Lens

Ethnocentrism
2. Eating Christmas in the Kalahari
15. Playing Indian at Halftime: The Controversy over American Indian Mascots, Logos, and Nicknames in School-Related Events
19. Arranging a Marriage in India
27. Understanding Islam
29. Body Ritual among the Nacirema

Ethnographic fieldwork
1. Before: The Sixties
2. Eating Christmas in the Kalahari
3. Tricking and Tripping: Fieldwork on Prostitution in the Era of AIDS
4. Yanomamo
6. Lost for Words

Family systems
17. When Brothers Share a Wife
18. Death without Weeping
19. Arranging a Marriage in India
20. Who Needs Love!: In Japan, Many Couples Don't
22. Where Fat Is a Mark of Beauty
23. . . . but What If It's a Girl?
24. Rising Number of Dowry Deaths in India

Gender
17. When Brothers Share a Wife
20. Who Needs Love!: In Japan, Many Couples Don't
21. The Berdache Tradition
23. . . . but What If It's a Girl?

Healing
25. Shamanisms: Past and Present
29. Body Ritual among the Nacirema

Health
13. The Inuit Paradox
16. Sick of Poverty
18. Death without Weeping
22. Where Fat Is a Mark of Beauty
25. Shamanisms: Past and Present
29. Body Ritual among the Nacirema
31. Why Can't People Feed Themselves?
32. The Arrow of Disease
33. The Price of Progress

Hunter-gatherers
13. The Inuit Paradox

Industrial Change
12. At a Loss for Words
38. What Native Peoples Deserve

Kinship
17. When Brothers Share a Wife
18. Death without Weeping
20. Who Needs Love!: In Japan, Many Couples Don't
22. Where Fat Is a Mark of Beauty
24. Rising Number of Dowry Deaths in India

Language
5. Whose Speech Is Better?
6. Lost for Words
7. Do You Speak American?
8. Fighting for Our Lives
9. Expletive Deleted
10. I Can't Even Open My Mouth: Separating Messages from Metamessages in Family Talk
11. Shakespeare in the Bush
12. At a Loss for Words
15. Playing Indian at Halftime: The Controversy over American Indian Mascots, Logos, and Nicknames in School-Related Events
27. Understanding Islam

Marriage systems
17. When Brothers Share a Wife
18. Death without Weeping
19. Arranging a Marriage in India
20. Who Needs Love!: In Japan, Many Couples Don't
22. Where Fat Is a Mark of Beauty
23. . . . but What If It's a Girl?
24. Rising Number of Dowry Deaths in India

Medicine
16. Sick of Poverty
25. Shamanisms: Past and Present
29. Body Ritual among the Nacirema

Participant observation
1. Before: The Sixties
2. Eating Christmas in the Kalahari
3. Tricking and Tripping: Fieldwork on Prostitution in the Era of AIDS
6. Lost for Words
11. Shakespeare in the Bush

Patriarchy
20. Who Needs Love!: In Japan, Many Couples Don't

Political systems
16. Sick of Poverty
17. When Brothers Share a Wife
18. Death without Weeping
27. Understanding Islam
31. Why Can't People Feed Themselves?
32. The Arrow of Disease
33. The Price of Progress
37. Seeing Conservation through the Global Lens
38. What Native Peoples Deserve

Poverty
16. Sick of Poverty
18. Death without Weeping
31. Why Can't People Feed Themselves?

ɹals

xuality

cial change

cial equality

Social relationships

Violence

Internet References

The following Internet sites have been selected to support the articles found in this reader. These sites were available at the time of publication. However, because websites often change their structure and content, the information listed may no longer be available. We invite you to visit *http://www.mhcls.com* for easy access to these sites.

Annual Editions: Anthropology 10/11

General Sources

American Anthropologist Association

http://www.aaanet.org

Check out this site—the home page of the American Anthropology Association—for general information about the field of anthropology as well as access to a wide variety of articles.

Anthropology Links

http://anthropology.gmu.edu/

George Mason University's Department of Anthropology website provides a number of interesting links.

Latin American Studies

http://www.library.arizona.edu/search/subjects/

Click on Latin American Studies to access an extensive list of resources—links to encyclopedias, journals, indexes, almanacs, and handbooks, and to the Latin American Network Information Center and Internet Resources for Latin American Studies.

A Sociological Tour through Cyberspace

http://www.trinity.edu/~mkearl/anthro.html

This is an excellent starting point for anthropological resources, using links.

The Royal Anthropological Institute of Great Britain and Ireland (RAI)

www.therai.org.uk/

The world's longest established scholarly association dedicated to the furtherance of anthropology in its broadest and most inclusive sense.

Web Resources for Visual Anthropology

http://www.usc.edu/dept/elab/urlist/index.html

This UR-List offers a mouse-click selection of web resources by cross-indexing 375 anthropological sites according to 22 subject categories.

UNIT 1: Anthropological Perspectives

Archaeology and Anthropology Computing and Study Skills

http://www.isca.ox.ac.uk/index.html

Consult this site of the Institute of Social and Cultural Anthropology to learn about ways to use the computer as an aid in conducting fieldwork, methodology, and analysis.

Kalahari

http://abbott-infotech.co.za/index-kalahari.html

With maps, photographs, and links, this website offers descriptions of the desert, the vegetation, the animals and the people who have lived in the Kalahari.

The Institute for Intercultural Studies

http://www.interculturalstudies.org/main.html

Established by Margaret Mead, the institute is directed by her daughter, Mary Catherine Bates. With links, it promotes accessibility to Mead's work as well as that of several of her associates, including Franz Boas, Ruth Benedict, and Gregory Bateson.

Introduction to Anthropological Fieldwork and Ethnography

http://web.mit.edu/dumit/www/syl-anth.html

This class outline can serve as an invaluable resource for conducting anthropological fieldwork. Addressing such topics as *The Interview and Power Relations in the Field,* the site identifies many important books and articles for further reading.

Theory in Anthropology

http://www.indiana.edu/~wanthro/theory.htm

These web pages cover subdisciplines within anthropology, changes perspectives over time, and prominent theorists, reflecting 30 years dramatic changes in the field.

UNIT 2: Culture and Communication

Center for Nonverbal Studies

http://www.library.kent.edu/resource.php?id=2800

This site is from a private, non-profit research center with links to rel news stories.

Exploratorium Magazine: "The Evolution of Languages

http://www.exploratorium.edu/exploring/language

Where did languages come from and how did they evolve? This educational site explains the history and origin of language. You can also investigate words, word stems, and the similarities of different languages.

Hypertext and Ethnography

http://www.umanitoba.ca/anthropology

Presented by Brian Schwimmer of the University of Manitoba, this site will be of great value to people who are interested in culture and communication. Schwimmer addresses such topics as multivocality complex symbolization.

International Communication Association

http://www.icahdq.org/

The I.C.A. sponsors conferences and publishes books and journals having to do with cross-cultural communication.

Intute: Social Sciences

http://www.intute.ac.uk/socialsciences/cgi-bin/browse.pl?id=12

This site provides links to linguistic associations, journals, and links to we and data bases dedicated to the preservation and study of languages.

Language Extinction

http://www.colorado.edu/iec

"An often overlooked fact in the ecological race against environmen extinction is that many of the world's languages are disappearing at an alarming rate." This article investigates language extinction and i possible consequences.

Language and Culture

http://anthro.palomar.edu/language/default.htm

This is a good introduction to the subject of linguistics and includes related websites.

Nonverbal Behavior

http://www.usal.es/~nonverbal/researchcenters.htm

This site is the gateway to links to all other sites having to do with nonverbal behavior and communication. The site includes links to publications, research centers, experiments, and conferences.

Showcase Anthropology

http://www.anthropology.wisc.edu

Examples of documents that make innovative use of the web as a tool for "an anthropology of the future"—one consisting of multimedi representations in a nonlinear and interactive form—are provided o website.

nternet References

IT 3: The Organization of Society d Culture

.erns of Subsistence

/anthro.palomar.edu/subsistence/default.htm

is site contains good summaries of subsistence practices, from aging to intensive agriculture, as well as the effects of the consequent reases in such areas as population, warfare, and disease. There are o related websites cited.

thsonian Institution Website

//www.si.edu

oking through this site, which provides access to many of the ormous resources of the Smithsonian, will give a sense of the scope anthropological inquiry today.

iology Guy's Anthropology Links

//www.trinity.edu/~mkearl/anthro.html

s list of anthropology resources on the web is suggested by a ciology professor at Trinity University and includes cultures of Asia, ica, the Middle East; Aztecan, Mayan, and aboriginal cultures; sections Mythology, Folklore, Legends, and Archaeology; plus much more.

IT 4: Other Families, Other Ways

nged Marriages

//women3rdworld.miningco.com/cs/arrangedmarriage/

's site, provided by ABOUT, contains a number of papers on arranged rriages. It also has links to other related women's issues, subjects, and ıms.

ship and Social Organization

//www.umanitoba.ca/anthropology

ship, marriage systems, residence rules, incest taboos, and cousin rriages are explored in this kinship tutorial.

and Marriage

//anthro.palomar.edu/marriage/default.htm

s is a good cross-cultural survey of marriage customs, residence rules d the treatment of homosexuality. Related websites are included.

dding Traditions and Customs

//worldweddingtraditions.com/

rriage customs are summarized for every region of the world.

IT 5: Gender and Status

obo Sex and Society

//songweaver.com/info/bonobos.html

s site includes a *Scientific American* article discussing a primate's navior that challenges traditional assumptions about male supremacy uman evolution.

1 Research

//www.amnesty.org/ailib/intcam/femgen/fgm1.htm

dicated to research pertaining to Female Genital Mutilation (FGM), this presents a variety of perspectives: psychological, cultural, sexual, nan rights, and so on.

M Home Page-Online Mendelian Inheritance in Man

//www.nslij-genetics.org/search_omim.html

s National Center for Biotechnology Information database is a catalog uman genes and genetic disorders. It contains text, pictures, and erence information.

ections on Sinai Bedouin Women

//www.sherryart.com/women/bedouin.html

Social anthropologist Ann Gardner tells something of her culture shock while first living with a Sinai Bedouin family as a teenager. She provides links to sites about organization of society and culture, particularly with regard to women.

Women Watch

http://www.un.org/womenwatch/about/

As part of the United Nations, Women Watch serves as a conduit for information and resources on the promotion of gender equality and empowerment throughout the world.

UNIT 6: Religion, Belief, and Ritual

Anthropology Resources Page

http://www.usd.edu/anth/

Many topics can be accessed from this University of South Dakota website. Repatriation and reburial are just two.

Apologetics Index

http://www.apologeticsindex.org/site/index-c/

This site offers resources on religious cults, sects, religions and doctrines.

Magic and Religion

http://anthro.palomar.edu/religion/default.htm

This site deals with the various aspects of folk religion and magic along with related Internet links.

Yahoo: Society and Culture: Death

http://dir.yahoo.com/Society_and_Culture/Death_and_Dying/

This Yahoo site has an extensive index to diverse issues related to how different people approach death, such as beliefs about euthanasia, reincarnation, and burial.

UNIT 7: Sociocultural Change

Association for Political and Legal Anthropology

http://www.aaanet.org/apla/index.htm

As a branch of the American Anthropological Association, this organization supports workshops, lectures, and publications having to do with issues of contemporary importance in the fields of political and legal anthropology, such as nationalism, colonialism, and post-colonial public spheres, multiculturalism and globalism.

Human Rights and Humanitarian Assistance

http://www.etown.edu/vl/humrts.html

Through this site you can conduct research into a number of human rights topics and issues affecting indigenous peoples in the modern era.

The Indigenous Rights Movement in the Pacific

http://www.inmotionmagazine.com/pacific.html

This article addresses issues that pertain to the problems of the Pacific Island peoples as a result of U.S. colonial expansion in the Pacific and Caribbean 100 years ago.

Murray Research Center

http://www.radcliffe.edu/murray_redirect/index.php

This site promotes the use of existing social science data to explore human development in the context of social change.

RomNews Network—Online

http://www.romnews.com/community/index.php

This is a website dedicated to news and information for and about the Roma (European Gypsies). Visit here to learn more about their culture and the discrimination they constantly face.

WWW Virtual Library: Indigenous Studies

http://cwis.org/wwwvl/indig-vl.html

This site presents resources collected by the Center for World Indigenous Studies (CWIS) in Africa, Asia, and the Middle East, Central and South America, Europe, and the Pacific.

World Map

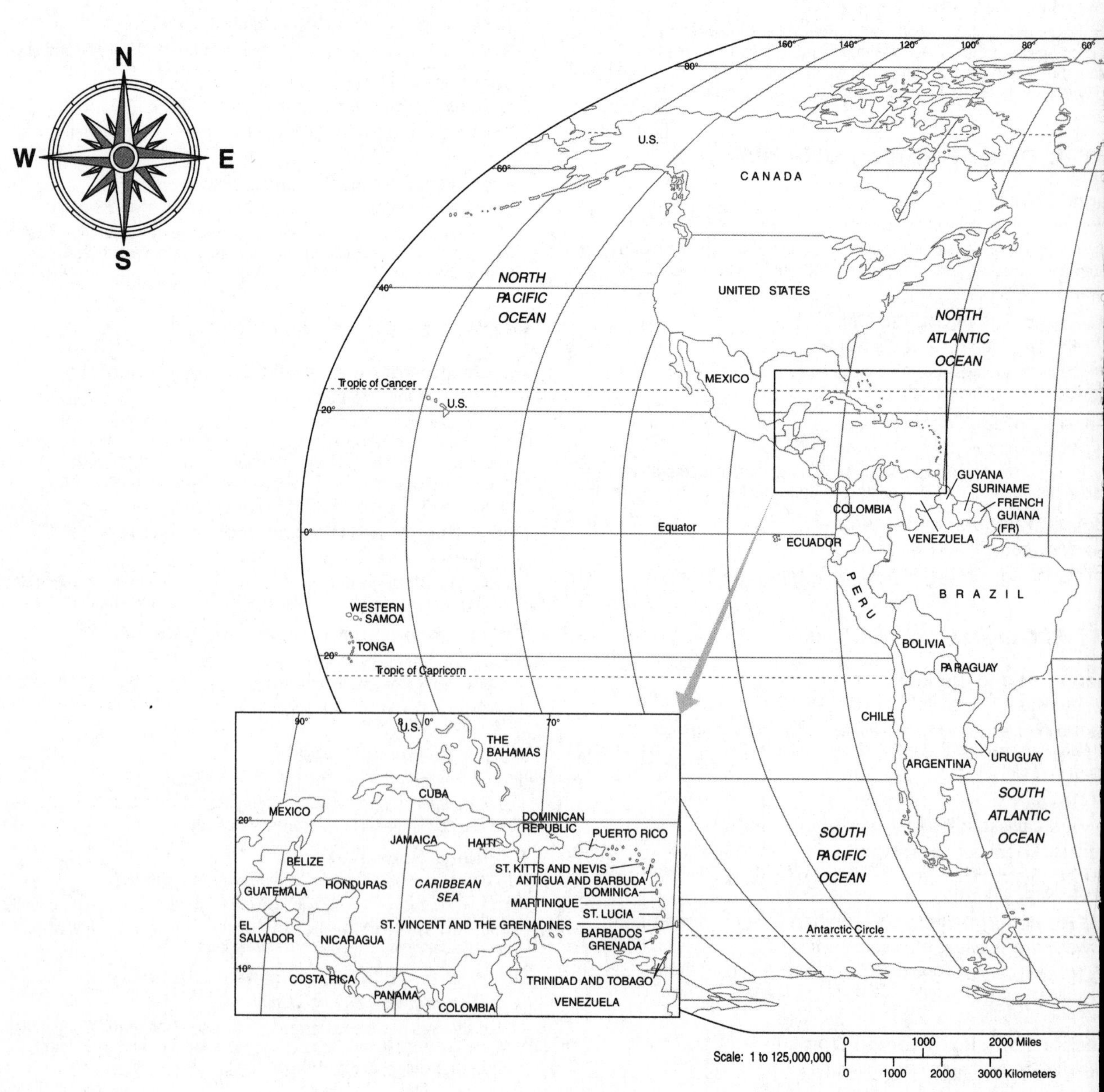
N
S
W
E
U.S.
CANADA
NORTH PACIFIC OCEAN
UNITED STATES
NORTH ATLANTIC OCEAN
MEXICO
Tropic of Cancer
U.S.
GUYANA
SURINAME
FRENCH GUIANA (FR)
COLOMBIA
Equator
ECUADOR
VENEZUELA
PERU
BRAZIL
WESTERN SAMOA
TONGA
BOLIVIA
PARAGUAY
Tropic of Capricorn
CHILE
ARGENTINA
URUGUAY
SOUTH ATLANTIC OCEAN
SOUTH PACIFIC OCEAN
Antarctic Circle
U.S.
THE BAHAMAS
MEXICO
CUBA
DOMINICAN REPUBLIC
PUERTO RICO
JAMAICA
HAITI
BELIZE
ST. KITTS AND NEVIS
ANTIGUA AND BARBUDA
GUATEMALA
HONDURAS
CARIBBEAN SEA
DOMINICA
MARTINIQUE
ST. LUCIA
EL SALVADOR
ST. VINCENT AND THE GRENADINES
BARBADOS
NICARAGUA
GRENADA
COSTA RICA
TRINIDAD AND TOBAGO
PANAMA
COLOMBIA
VENEZUELA
Scale: 1 to 125,000,000
0 1000 2000 Miles
0 1000 2000 3000 Kilometers

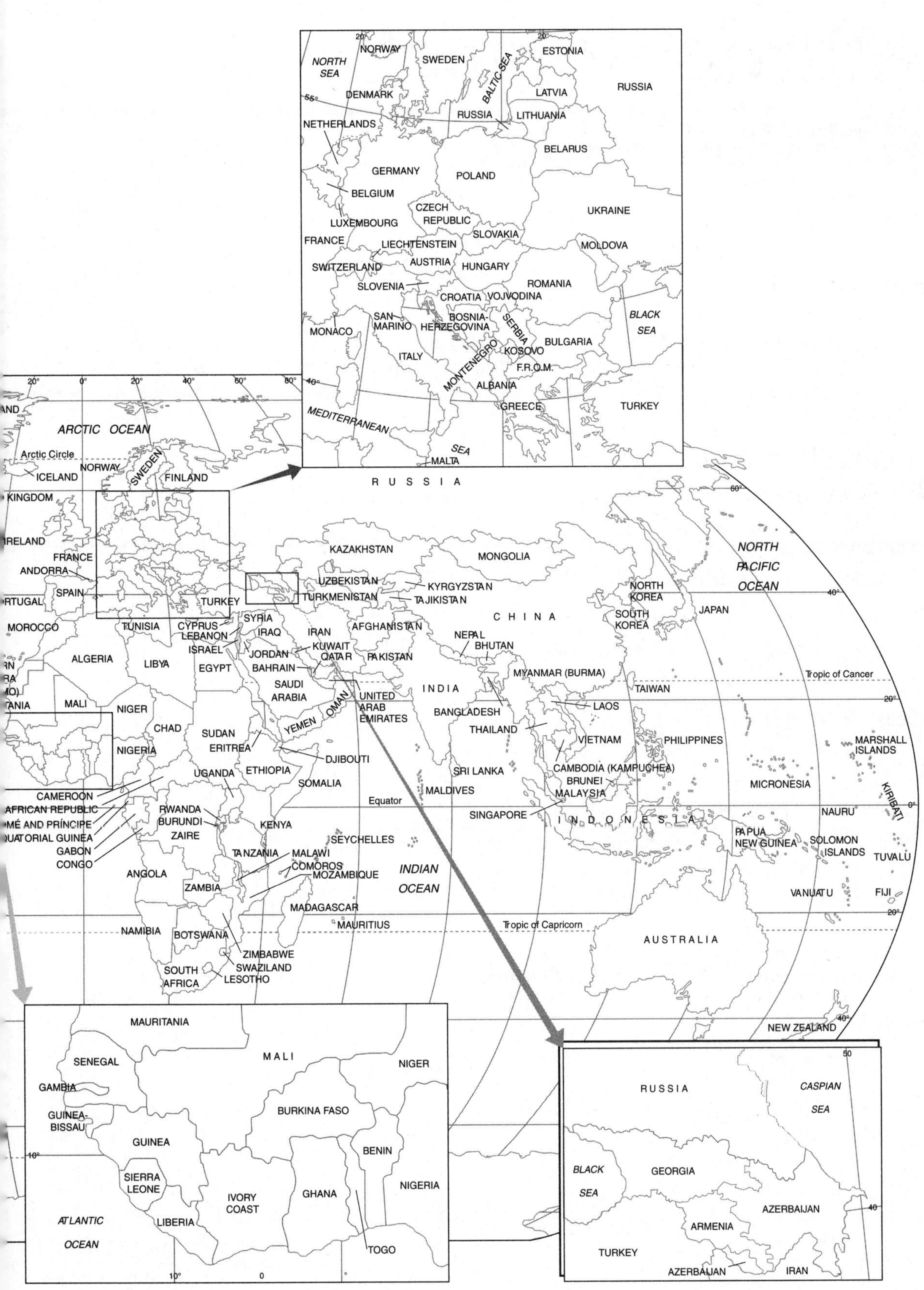
NORTH SEA
NORWAY
SWEDEN
BALTIC SEA
ESTONIA
RUSSIA
DENMARK
LATVIA
RUSSIA
LITHUANIA
NETHERLANDS
BELARUS
GERMANY
POLAND
BELGIUM
CZECH REPUBLIC
UKRAINE
LUXEMBOURG
SLOVAKIA
FRANCE
LIECHTENSTEIN
MOLDOVA
AUSTRIA
SWITZERLAND
HUNGARY
SLOVENIA
ROMANIA
CROATIA
VOJVODINA
SAN MARINO
BOSNIA-HERZEGOVINA
SERBIA
BLACK SEA
MONACO
BULGARIA
KOSOVO
ITALY
MONTENEGRO
F.R.O.M.
ALBANIA
TURKEY
GREECE
MEDITERRANEAN SEA
MALTA
ARCTIC OCEAN
Arctic Circle
ICELAND
NORWAY
SWEDEN
FINLAND
KINGDOM
IRELAND
FRANCE
ANDORRA
SPAIN
TURKEY
MOROCCO
TUNISIA
CYPRUS
LEBANON
ISRAEL
SYRIA
IRAQ
JORDAN
ALGERIA
LIBYA
EGYPT
MALI
NIGER
CHAD
SUDAN
ERITREA
NIGERIA
ETHIOPIA
DJIBOUTI
SOMALIA
UGANDA
CAMEROON
RWANDA
BURUNDI
ZAIRE
KENYA
GABON
CONGO
TANZANIA
MALAWI
COMOROS
MOZAMBIQUE
ANGOLA
ZAMBIA
MADAGASCAR
MAURITIUS
NAMIBIA
BOTSWANA
ZIMBABWE
SWAZILAND
SOUTH AFRICA
LESOTHO
SEYCHELLES
RUSSIA
KAZAKHSTAN
MONGOLIA
UZBEKISTAN
KYRGYZSTAN
TURKMENISTAN
TAJIKISTAN
IRAN
AFGHANISTAN
KUWAIT
QATAR
BAHRAIN
PAKISTAN
SAUDI ARABIA
UNITED ARAB EMIRATES
YEMEN
OMAN
CHINA
NEPAL
BHUTAN
INDIA
MYANMAR (BURMA)
BANGLADESH
THAILAND
LAOS
VIETNAM
SRI LANKA
MALDIVES
CAMBODIA (KAMPUCHEA)
BRUNEI
MALAYSIA
SINGAPORE
INDONESIA
Equator
INDIAN OCEAN
Tropic of Capricorn
NORTH KOREA
SOUTH KOREA
JAPAN
TAIWAN
PHILIPPINES
NORTH PACIFIC OCEAN
Tropic of Cancer
MARSHALL ISLANDS
MICRONESIA
KIRIBATI
NAURU
PAPUA NEW GUINEA
SOLOMON ISLANDS
TUVALU
VANUATU
FIJI
AUSTRALIA
NEW ZEALAND
MAURITANIA
SENEGAL
MALI
NIGER
GAMBIA
GUINEA-BISSAU
BURKINA FASO
GUINEA
BENIN
SIERRA LEONE
IVORY COAST
GHANA
NIGERIA
LIBERIA
TOGO
ATLANTIC OCEAN
RUSSIA
CASPIAN SEA
BLACK SEA
GEORGIA
AZERBAIJAN
ARMENIA
TURKEY
AZERBAIJAN
IRAN

UNIT 1

Anthropological Perspectives

Unit Selections

1. **Before: The Sixties,** Conrad Phillip Kottak
2. **Eating Christmas in the Kalahari,** Richard Borshay Lee
3. **Tricking and Tripping: Fieldwork on Prostitution in the Era of AIDS,** Claire E. Sterk
4. **Yanomamo,** Leslie E. Sponsel

Key Points to Consider

- What are some of the unique research strategies of anthropological fieldwork?
- How can anthropologists who become personally involved with a community through participant observation maintain their objectivity as scientists?
- What kinds of ethical obligations do fieldworkers have toward their informants?
- In what ways do the results of fieldwork depend on the kind of questions asked?
- What lessons can be learned about one's own culture by going to the field?

Student Website

www.mhcls.com

Internet References

Archaeology and Anthropology Computing and Study Skills
http://www.isca.ox.ac.uk/index.html

Kalahari
http://abbott-infotech.co.za/index-kalahari.html

The Institute for Intercultural Studies
http://www.interculturalstudies.org/main.html

Introduction to Anthropological Fieldwork and Ethnography
http://web.mit.edu/dumit/www/syl-anth.html

Theory in Anthropology
http://www.indiana.edu/~wanthro/theory.htm

at least a century, the goals of anthropology have been scribe societies and cultures throughout the world and to are and contrast the differences and similarities among Anthropologists study in a variety of settings and situa- ranging from small hamlets and villages to neighborhoods corporate offices of major urban centers throughout the . They study hunters and gatherers, peasants, farmers, leaders, politicians, and bureaucrats. They examine reli- life in Latin America as well as revolutionary movements.

herever practicable, anthropologists take on the role of cipant observer." Through active involvement in the life of people, they hope to gain an insider's perspective with- acrificing the objectivity of the trained scientist. Sometimes onditions for achieving such a goal seem to form an st insurmountable barrier, but anthropologists call on per- nce, adaptability, and imagination to overcome the odds st them.

e diversity of focus in anthropology means that it is ear- ed less by its particular subject matter than by its perspec- Although the discipline relates to both the biological and sciences, anthropologists know that the boundaries drawn een disciplines are highly artificial. For example, while in y it is possible to examine only the social organization of ily unit or the organization of political power in a nation- in reality it is impossible to separate the biological from the , from the economic, from the political. The explanatory ective of anthropology, as the articles in this unit demon- , is to seek out interrelationships among all these factors.

e first three articles in this section illustrate varying kinds of rch strategies employed by anthropologists as they take on le of "participant observer." Conrad Phillip Kottak's essay, ult on Paradise," shows the hardships imposed by certain cal conditions as well as the "culture shock" experienced as lt of "being away," that is, cut off from the world-at-large. chard Borshay Lee, in "Eating Christmas in the Kalahari," to realize that his behavior conveyed a certain attitude patible with the values of his hosts. In the process, he ed an important lesson about how these hunter-gatherers been able to survive for so long under conditions which ould consider marginal at best. Then, there is "Tricking ripping: Fieldwork on Prostitution in the Era of AIDS," in Claire E. Sterk describes the problems, both professional ersonal, involved in trying to understand the precarious of prostitutes on the urban streets of America. The final in this unit, "Yanomamo," deals with the ethical obliga- anthropologists have toward the people they are studying.

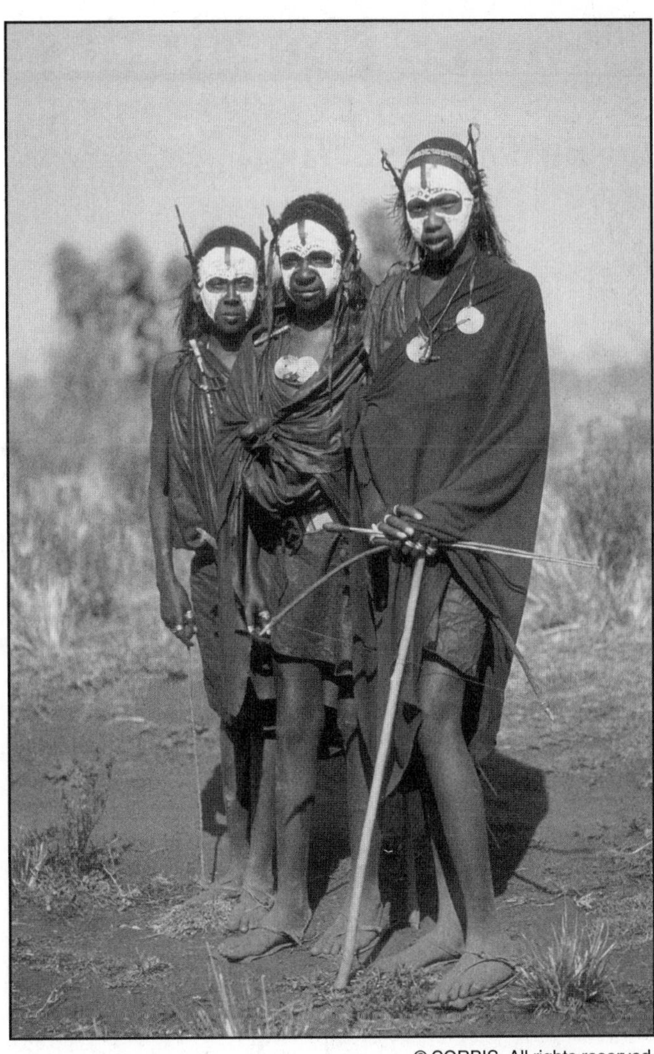

This has become especially important as outside forces increasingly impinge upon and alter the cultures anthropologists claim to respect and wish no harm.

Much is at stake in these discussions as we attempt to achieve a more objective understanding of the diversity of peoples' ways. After all, the purpose of anthropology is not only to describe and explain, but also to develop a special vision of the world in which cultural alternatives (past, present, and future) can be measured against one another and used as guides for human action.

Article 1

Before: The Sixties

CONRAD PHILLIP KOTTAK

It Began by Accident

This is a story of change, but it didn't start out to be that. It began by accident. I first lived in Arembepe during the (North American) summer of 1962. That was between my junior and senior years at New York City's Columbia College (of Columbia University), where I was majoring in anthropology. I went to Arembepe as a participant in a now defunct program designed to give undergraduates an experience in ethnography—the firsthand study of local culture and social life. The program's cumbersome title, the Columbia-Cornell-Harvard-Illinois Summer Field Studies Program in Anthropology, reflected participation by four universities, each with a different field station. The other field sites were in Peru, Mexico, and Ecuador. The area around Salvador, Brazil, had just been chosen for the Columbia field station.

The field team leader was Professor Marvin Harris, who was later to become my adviser and doctoral dissertation committee chair during my graduate work in anthropology at Columbia University, which began in 1963. Also in Salvador that year was Professor Charles Wagley, another Columbia anthropologist, who had worked with Harris and others to establish the program. Through their links with Bahian social scientists, Harris and Wagley chose two villages that were anthropologically interesting but close enough to Salvador to maintain contact with the undergraduates. The two communities lay along the same road. Abrantes, the agricultural village, nearer to Salvador, was the district seat for Arembepe, the more remote fishing village. Liking the coast, I preferred Arembepe, where I was assigned, with fellow team member David Epstein. Harris arranged for us to rent the dilapidated summer house of a city man who sometimes vacationed in Arembepe.

Meanwhile, Professor Wagley's daughter, Betty, a Barnard College student also majoring in anthropology, arrived to spend the summer with her parents in Salvador. She went with us to visit Abrantes and Arembepe and decided she also wanted to do fieldwork in the latter. Betty arranged lodging with a local woman, but since David and I had hired a cook, she ate with us and shared the cost of food and supplies. Betty's mother was Brazilian, and Betty, herself born in Brazil, is bilingual in Portuguese (her first language). This made her more adept at fieldwork than either David or I was. She was also kind enough to translate for us many times.

Having taught anthropology now for more than 30 ye realize how unusual my first field experience was. Most a pologists begin fieldwork, which is required for the doct after a few years of graduate study and not as underg ates. They usually choose the part of the world they w work in and the topic they will investigate there. For exa my own longest ethnographic project came just after g ate school. Having taken courses about several world ar became particularly interested in Madagascar, a large off the southeast coast of Africa. I read as much as I about the cultures of Madagascar. I focused on a probl the social implications of an economic change, the expans irrigated agriculture—that I could investigate there.

With Arembepe, by contrast, someone else—the direct the field program—selected the area, even the village, fc I didn't have time to do the extensive background readin normally precedes fieldwork. Nor did I have much time to the language I would be using in the field.

Although I didn't control the initial choice of Aremb *did* decide to keep on studying it, particularly when, by it was evident that Arembepe had changed more rapidly i than two decades than some places change in centuries. L tudinal (long-term, ongoing) fieldwork during that transf tion is the basis of this book.

Most of my preparation for my 1962 fieldwork wa prefield seminar that Harris offered at Columbia and a seminar about ethnographic field methods taught by Pro Lambros Comitas. In Harris's class, students talked abo kinds of research we planned to do when we got to Brazil ris urged us to do microprojects, focusing on limited aspe community life that we could investigate easily in three m The program's founders didn't intend our work to be tradi holistic ethnography—intensive study of all aspects of life through long-term residence and participant observ Comitas's seminar, on the other hand, had introduced techniques used in long-term, in-depth ethnography. One problems in doing fieldwork in Arembepe in 1962 was th flict between my wish to do a holistic study and the prog preference for a microproject.

The program's goals were modest. I now realize that th realistic, because we were novices. Harris and the other ers wanted us to get our feet wet—to see if we liked fiel

(Conrad P. Kottak)

always got stuck at least once." The road to Arembepe, ing through the district seat, Abrantes, in 1964.

gh to pursue a career in cultural anthropology. Our experi- would also prepare us for later, longer fieldwork. As train- or our microprojects, our prefield seminar assignment was rite a library research paper on the topic we planned to tigate in Brazil.

arris suggested I study race relations, which already had ge literature. Comparisons of race relations in Brazil and Jnited States are appropriate because both countries have a age of slavery. In both there has been considerable mixture ropeans, Africans, and Native Americans. For the seminar, d extensively. I learned the main differences between the of race in Brazil and the United States and wrote a research r on my findings. Harris and I later worked out a specific project on Brazilian racial classification, which I discuss in this chapter.

lthough I prepared myself to investigate Brazilian race ions, my preparation in Brazilian Portuguese was insuf- nt. Language was my biggest barrier in the field. I had r been abroad and had no experience speaking a for- language: high school (Latin) and college (German) had y taught me how to read one. As a result, I spent most e summer of 1962 asking Brazilians to repeat everything said to me. This led Arembepeiros to call me a *papagaio* ot)—because I could only echo words that someone else originated. I discovered that it's difficult to gain much ht into native social life when you can't converse as well ive-year-old can.

e Sixties

ne 1962, when I first set eyes on Arembepe, the 55- neter trip from Salvador was neither simple nor sure. It three hours in a vehicle with four-wheel drive. Located t 13 degrees south of the equator and at sea level, Arem- is never cold, but June and July are rainy, making travel ult. The clay-surfaced road was usually muddy, and we ys got stuck at least once in any round trip. The task of getting our heavy jeep station wagon unstuck usually required a work group of field team members and a dozen helpful onlookers.

Sand, lagoons, and more sand came after the mud. After heavy rains, crossing the freshwater lagoons that bordered Arembepe on the west made the jeep seem like a motorboat. High water washed onto the cabin floor and sometimes stalled the engine. After the lagoons came the dunes, with closely planted coconut trees—posing another traffic hazard. Making it into the village required finding another vehicle's tracks and flooring the accelerator. Once, as a frustrating drive out seemed over, I pulled up in front of the house I was renting to find that the brakes had failed. Frantic pumping kept me from crashing through the kitchen wall.

But Arembepe was worth the trip. I can't imagine a more beautiful field setting. The village was strung along a narrow strip of land (less than a kilometer) between ocean and lagoons. It was more spectacular than any South Sea island I later visited. Arembepe's houses—brightly painted in tones of blue, pink, purple, and orange—stood under lofty coconut palms. To the east, stretches of smooth white sand and protected swimming areas alternated with jagged rocks and churning Atlantic waves. On a sunny day in August, Arembepe was alive with color: the green-blue hues of ocean and lagoons, orange-red of brick and roof tiles, pinks and blues of houses, greens of palms, and white of sand. Colorful fishing boats anchored evenings and Sundays in the port, just east of the central square and the small, white Roman Catholic chapel. The harbor is formed by a rugged, partially submerged reef. Each morning the boats rowed through its narrow channels, then raised their sun-bleached sails to travel to their destinations for the day.

The conjunction of natural beauty with the middle-class appeal of a quaint fishing village had already drawn a handful of tourists and summer residents to Arembepe in 1962. Still, the poor quality of the road made it a hard trip even in summer, the dry season (December to February). Only a few residents of the capital—mainly middle-class and lower-middle-class people—had summer homes in Arembepe. Limited bus service began in 1965, but it brought few visitors until the road was improved in 1970.

Poverty and poor public health were blights that made Arembepe—despite the title of this book—something less than paradise. In theory, Arembepeiros got their drinking water from Big Well, a tiny settlement 2 kilometers away. An entrepreneur who lived there made money selling barrels of water in Arembepe. When well water wasn't readily available, villagers sometimes drank water from the freshwater lagoon. Some mothers even used lagoon water in the powdered milk they mixed for their children. Considering these traditional uses of water—and that the bushes where villagers relieved themselves were on the edge of the lagoon, which rose in the rainy season—it's easy to understand why children suffered from intestinal disorders and extreme malnutrition (the latter partly caused by parasites in their bodies).

(Conrad P. Kottak)

During the 1960s, as we approached Arembepe, the clay road yielded to sand.

Malinowski and Microprojects

I entered this romantic yet imperfect setting as a fledgling ethnographer with ambitious goals and a huge linguistic impediment. Two dimensions of my work in Arembepe bear discussion here. One involves my scientific and professional aims. The second has to do with my personal reactions to an alien setting. First the scientific goals.

As a conscientious anthropology major, I wanted to put the lessons from my classes into practice. I wanted to do the things that Bronislaw Malinowski describes as the ethnographer's work in the first chapter of his classic *Argonauts of the Western Pacific,* a field study of fishers and traders in Melanesia.

I often compared my experiences with Malinowski's. Even our field settings struck me as similar. He had also worked in a tropical South Sea setting (the Trobriand Islands). Though Arembepe is on the mainland, the phrase "South Sea island" kept running through my head. Reading Malinowski's description of the moment when the ethnographer set foot upon a beach reminded me of my own situation. I imagined myself in his sandals. Like me, Malinowski initially had trouble communicating with local people. "I was quite unable to enter any more detailed or explicit conversation with them at first. I knew well that the best remedy for this was to collect concrete data, and accordingly I took a village census, wrote down genealogies, drew up plans and collected the terms of kinship" (Malinowski 1961, p. 5).

I was eager to do those things that Malinowski had done, especially to census the village. But field leader Harris discouraged me, offering another lesson: Before I could gather the detailed and accurate data that ethnography demands, I needed to build rapport; people would have to get to know and trust me. I would have to convince them I wasn't dangerous and that it wouldn't be to their disadvantage to answer my questions. Furthermore, I didn't yet know enough about village life to devise pertinent questions to ask during a census. Accordingly, but regretfully, I put the census on hold and set about building rapport. David Epstein and Betty Wagley, my companions field, were doing the same thing.

How does one build rapport? "Get to know the men," vin told me. To do this I started joining the fishermen fo evening bath in the lagoon. I had my first doubts about th dom of this participant observation when I accidentally ted a floating piece of donkey dung (I like to think I ider the correct mammal) during my third bath. I gave up l bathing when I learned of the lagoon system's infestati schistosomes—liver flukes. After that, I was careful to the lagoon. I followed the advice of public health offici rub exposed body parts with alcohol whenever I came int tact with lagoon water. Arembepeiros found these preca laughable: Not to worry, they said—small fish in the lago the liver flukes (and germs in general).

If the lagoon was now off-limits, there was still the c stoop, where each evening, after the fleet had returned, bat been taken, and the day's main meal consumed, men would to talk. This was male territory. Among females, only smal and old women dared approach. David and I would sit a to talk. My Portuguese was rudimentary. Still, villagers t questions my way. They were curious about the United S but their questions were hardly scintillating: "Were there els in the United States?" "Elephants?" "Monkeys?" They through a litany of animals they had seen on the lottery t people brought back from Salvador. "Look! Up in the sky. jet from the United States heading for Rio," they observed other night, reflecting the airline's schedule. Whenever, arduous mental rehearsal, I found the words to ask a qu about Arembepe, I'd get an incomprehensible reply, follow some such query as "Have you ever seen a bear, Conrado?"

"Bear, bear," I parroted.

"Parrot, parrot," they guffawed.

"Yes, I have seen a bear. I have seen a bear in a zoo."

Rapport building was fascinating indeed.

Visions of Malinowski danced in my head as I ca resent this kind of activity as a waste of time. I was eager something "more scientific." The microproject that Harri I had planned involved testing a difference between race tions in Brazil and the United States. In the United States of descent determines racial identity. If an American ha black (African-American) parent and one white one, he or assigned, automatically at birth and without regard for ph appearance, to the black race. In Brazil, it seemed that s factors determine racial identity and that no descent rule ates. Since, however, no one had systematically demons that Brazil lacks such a rule, we decided that a geneticall phenotypically (physically) mixed community like Aren would be a good place to test it.

When an automatic descent rule operates, full sil belong to the same group. Thus in the United States, fu lings can't belong to different races. In Arembepe, we s to find full siblings who were physically very different, if they were assigned to different races. We found three s with widely varying skin shades, hair types, and facial fea After we photographed them, I finally got to do something

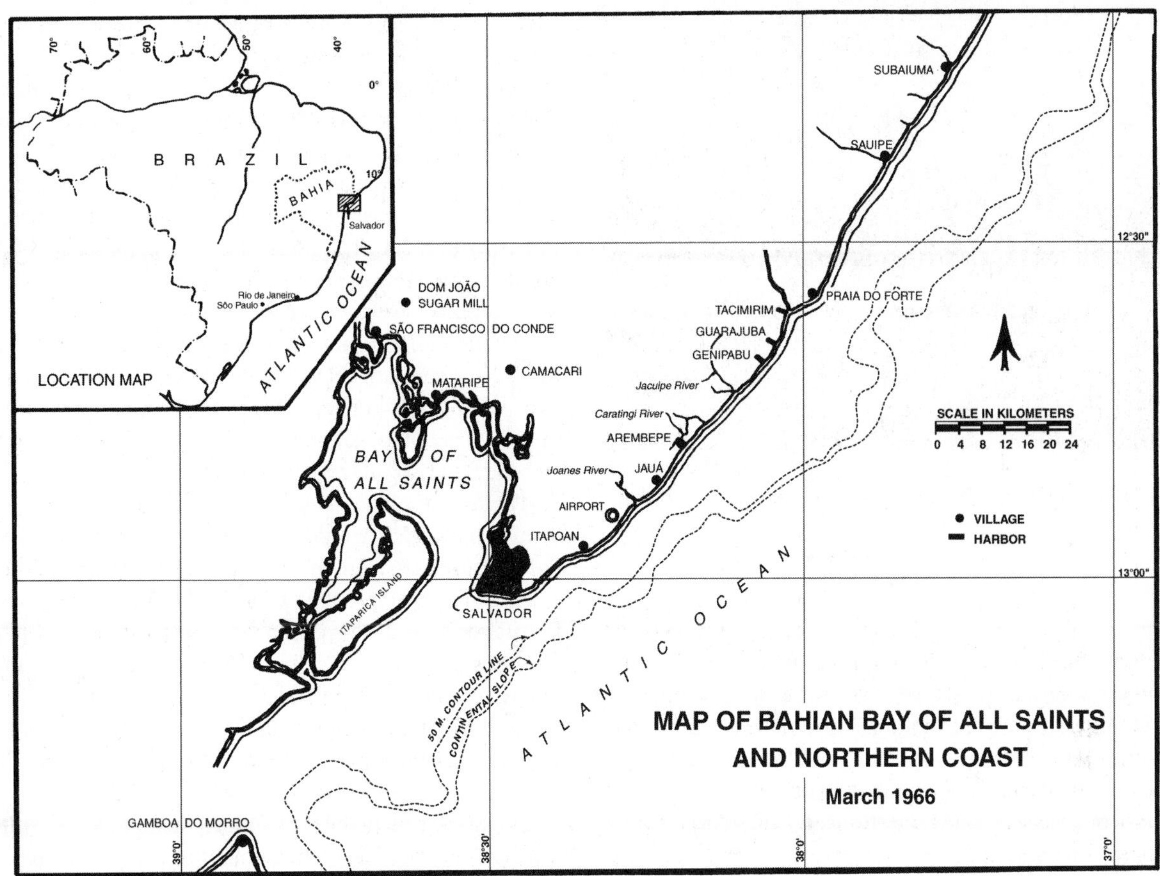

ɛnging than reporting on North American animals. I chose ple of 100 villagers and showed the photo of the sisters to king them to tell me each girl's race. Sure enough, I found nany different terms were used, that in Brazil full siblings belong to different races.

ɛw questions about race emerged from that first survey. We ed another set of questions, based on drawings of individuals contrasted phenotypically. By questioning another sample lagers, I found that Arembepeiros used many more racial (over 40) than had previously been reported for a Brazil- mmunity. They also used them inconsistently, so that the term used for another person might vary from day to day, ght even self-identification. By the time my three months embepe were up, I was fluent in Brazilian racial termi- y, and Harris and I had the basis for a couple of journal s. Although I still felt guilty that I hadn't managed to do a owskian census, I did think I'd accomplished something first field experience.

work again in Brazil, I knew I'd have to improve my Por- se. I could get only so far talking about race relations. I the next summer (1963) taking an intensive course in Bra- Portuguese at Columbia University while another field lived in Arembepe. Also in the summer of 1963, Betty y and I, whose romance had begun under Arembepe's full , got married; and I began graduate school in the fall.

I was delighted, the following spring, to be offered the job of assistant leader of the 1964 field team. I returned to Arembepe in June 1964 determined to do my census. And not just a census. By then I had studied more anthropology, and my Portuguese had improved dramatically. I felt I was ready to do a full-fledged interview schedule (a kind of questionnaire). Peter Gorlin, who now holds a Ph.D. in anthropology and an M.D. degree, was an undergraduate field team member stationed in Jauá, the next village south of Arembepe. Peter had read Malinowski, too; he was also eager to use Malinowski's "method of concrete, statistical documentation" (1961, p. 24), to satisfy the ethnographer's "fundamental obligation of giving a complete survey of the phenomena, and not of picking out the sensational [and] the singular" (1961, p. 11).

I was ready to do a survey of all the households in Arembepe, and Peter wanted to do the same thing in Jauá. But we needed an instrument. Our team leader, the renowned Bahian physician and anthropologist Thales de Azevedo, supplied us with one— an interview schedule that had been used in southern Bahia. We revised the schedule for the fishing villages and had it printed.

An *interview schedule* differs from a standard questionnaire in that the ethnographer talks directly, face to face, with informants, asks the questions, and writes down the answers. Questionnaire procedures, which sociologists routinely use, tend to be more indirect and impersonal; often the respondent fills

(Courtesy Jerald T. Milanich)

The beautiful, microbe-infested, freshwater lagoon that borders Arembepe to the west, at sundown.

in the form. Sociologists normally work with literate people, who can fill out the answer sheets or questionnaire forms themselves. Anthropologists, by contrast, haven't usually worked in places where most people are literate, so we have to record the answers ourselves.

Because we are in charge of pacing, we can choose to digress temporarily from the scheduled questions to follow up intriguing bits of information that emerge in the interview. Thus the ethnographer can keep interviews open-ended and exploratory while asking a basic set of questions, to gather comparable, quantifiable information. I learned as much about Arembepe from the open-ended questioning as I did from the formal queries.

Our interviews in Arembepe illustrate still another difference between the research techniques of anthropologists and sociologists. Because sociologists normally deal with large populations, such as the United States, they must use *sampling techniques,* which enable them to make inferences about a larger group from a detailed study of a smaller one. We didn't need to do sampling in Arembepe, because it was small enough for us to do a total sample—that is, to complete the schedule with all the households there—159 of them.

A final contrast between cultural anthropology and sociology is worth mentioning. Sociologists often distribute their questionnaires by mail or hire research assistants to administer, code, and analyze them. Ethnographers, by contrast, work right in the community, where they encounter a series of real-world obstacles. My main problem as I interviewed in Arembepe wasn't the few villagers who slammed doors in my face or even the droopy-nosed kids who used my pants as a handkerchief. My problem was fleas. I recall my third or fourth interview, in a sand-floored hut. Asking my questions to a dozen smiling members of an extended family, I began to itch in places I was embarrassed to scratch. I made it to the end of the form, but I didn't tarry for open-ended inquiry. Instead I ran home, through the house, out the back door, right into the harbor at high tide. I let the salt water burn into my flea wounds. Fleas bot most of us, especially Betty, that summer. The remedy fc men was to wear pants and sprinkle our cuffs with flea po We managed to interview in almost all Arembepe's househ despite the predatory sand fleas.

Our interview schedule was eight pages long. We asked tions (for each household member) about age, gender, identity, diet, job, religious beliefs and practices, educa political preferences, possessions, consumption patterns ownership of livestock, boats, coconut trees, land, and fa I encouraged Peter not to do a microproject but to follo Malinowskian path I'd wanted to tread. He did it with gus two months he'd finished the schedule with all the house in Jauá. He hiked up the beach to spend August helping and me finish the interviewing in Arembepe.

There are advantages, I now realize, in both mode brief fieldwork. A microproject is easily manageable holds out the promise of a modest research paper. The hc Malinowskian approach is also valuable. I'm convince Portuguese would have improved much more if I'd don interview schedule the first summer, rather than limitin talk to rapport building and race relations. Peter Gorlin's with the schedule in Jauá and Arembepe in 1964 helpe improve his Portuguese much more quickly than I had in 1962.

Doing the schedule had an added benefit I didn't fully re in 1964: It got at least one member of the field team into home in Arembepe. Years later I was to hear from many v ers that they remembered those visits warmly. Our ques asked in their homes, had communicated our personal in and showed we didn't look down on Arembepeiros.

I found the people of Arembepe to be open, warm, anc pitable, much less wary of outsiders than the Betsileo of M gascar, whom I studied for 14 months in 1966–1967. Arembepeiros welcomed us to their homes and gladly ans our questions. Only a handful played hard to get, slan windows and doors as we approached, telling neighbor wouldn't answer our questions. I had to settle for ske information about them and could only make estimates o incomes and consumption patterns, using public inforn and behavior. Fortunately (since the 1964 data are the for much of the detailed comparison between Arembe the 1960s and later), fewer than a dozen households, sca throughout the village, refused to let us do the schedule.

The interview schedule wasn't the only thing I did in A bepe in 1964. Soon after my arrival, I met an excellent in ant, Alberto, whose name figures prominently in the stor follows. Then a 40-year-old fisherman, Alberto was the brother of our cook. He felt free to visit our house almost night, and he was eager to teach me about the fishing inc I also got information about fishing by talking to fisherme fish marketers on the beach and by going out in several including that of Tomé, Arembepe's most successful boa tain and owner. Tomé's name, too, is a prominent one in A bepe's recent history.

(Conrad P. Kottak)

field team members Peter Gorlin (second from left) and Bressler with their host family in Jauá, the fishing village ;outh of Arembepe. Note the range of physical variation ıg the local people.

1965 I had my third chance to study Arembepe. The results alyzing the interview schedules and my information on g had been so promising that both Marvin Harris and I felt might, with another summer of fieldwork, amass sufficient o write my doctoral dissertation about Arembepe, which I 'his time Betty and I weren't part of a field team but on our A graduate fellowship and grant supported my work, and was still cheap in cash-poor Arembepe. In summer 1965 I followed the Malinowskian plan, but I already had much of ıtistical and observational data needed for the "firm, clear e" of my community's organization and the "anatomy of ture" (Malinowski 1961, p. 24).

ıat I needed now was flesh for the skeleton. So I spent the er of 1965 gathering data on the "imponderabilia of actual . collected through minute, detailed observations . . . made le by close contact with native life" (Malinowski 1961, . By this time, I didn't really have to harken back to owski to know that although I had the bare bones, I still d to find out more about local opinions, values, and feel- to listen to stories, examine cases, and gather intimate, details about everyday life. Like Napoleon Chagnon, the pal ethnographer of the Yanomamo Indians of Venezuela, v "how much I enjoyed reading monographs that were led with real people, that described real events, and that me sweat and tears, some smells and sentiments mingled he words" (Chagnon 1977, p. xi). I wanted to add such sions—feeling tones—to my ethnography of Arembepe.

Vas an Alien Place

were some of my professional goals and research methods. er part of ethnography is more personal. No matter how ive and scientific they fancy themselves, anthropologists t mechanical measuring instruments. We are inevitably *participant* observers, taking part in—and by so doing modifying, no matter how slightly—the phenomena we are investigating and trying to understand. Not recording machines but people, anthropologists grow up in particular cultural traditions, possess idiosyncratic personality traits and experiences, have their own motivations, impressions, values, and reactions. Nor are our informants alike; we come to appreciate them differently. Some we never appreciate; an occasional one we detest.

Raised in one culture, curious about others, anthropologists still experience culture shock, especially on the first field trip. *Culture shock* refers to the whole set of feelings about being in an alien setting and the resulting reactions. It is a chilly, creepy feeling of alienation, of being without some of the most ordinary, trivial—and therefore basic—cues of one's culture of origin.

As I planned to set off for Brazil in 1962, I couldn't know how naked I would feel without the cloak of my language and culture. My sojourn in Arembepe would be my first trip outside the United States. I was an urban boy who had grown up in Atlanta, Georgia, and New York City. I had little experience with rural life in my country, none with Latin America, and I had received only minimal training in the Portuguese language.

New York City direct to Salvador, Bahia, Brazil. Just a brief stopover in Rio de Janeiro; a longer visit would be a reward at the end of fieldwork. As our plane approached tropical Salvador, I couldn't believe the whiteness of the sand. "That's not snow, is it?" I remarked to a fellow field team member. Marvin Harris had arranged our food and lodging at the Paradise Hotel, overlooking Bahia's magnificent, endlessly blue, All Saints' Bay. My first impressions of Bahia were of smells—alien odors of ripe and decaying mangoes, bananas, and passion fruit—and of swatting ubiquitous flies. There were strange concoctions of rice, black beans, and gobs of unidentified meats and floating pieces of skin. Coffee was strong and sugar crude. Every table top had containers for toothpicks and manioc (cassava) flour, to sprinkle, like parmesan cheese, on anything one might eat. I remember oatmeal soup and a slimy stew of beef tongue in tomatoes. At one meal a disintegrating fish head, eyes still attached, but barely, stared up at me as its body floated in a bowl of bright orange palm oil. Bearing my culture's don't-drink-the-water complex, it took me a few days to discover that plain mineral water quenched thirst better than the gaseous variety. Downstairs from the hotel was the Boite Clock, a nightclub whose rhythmic bossa nova music often kept us from sleeping.

I only vaguely remember my first day in Arembepe. Unlike ethnographers who have studied remote tribes in the tropical forests of South America or the highlands of New Guinea, I didn't hike or ride a canoe for days to arrive at my field site. Arembepe wasn't isolated compared with those places—only compared with every place *I'd* ever been. My first contact with Arembepe was just a visit, to arrange lodging. We found the crumbling summer house of a man who lived in Salvador and arranged to rent it and have it cleaned. We hired Dora, a 25-year-old unmarried mother of two, to cook for us, and another woman to clean house and do our laundry. My first visit to Arembepe didn't leave much of an impression. I knew I'd still have a few more days at the Paradise Hotel, with a real toilet and shower, before having to rough it in the field.

Back in the city, using her fluency in Brazilian language and culture, Betty Wagley bargained for our cots, pots, pans, flashlights, and other supplies. I don't remember our actual move to Arembepe or who accompanied us. Harris had employed a chauffeur; we stopped to deposit some field team members in Abrantes. I do recall what happened when we got to Arembepe. A crowd of children pursued our car through the sand and streets until we parked in front of our house, near the central square. We spent our first few days with children following us everywhere. For weeks we had little daytime privacy. Kids watched our every move through our living room window. Sometimes one made an incomprehensible remark. Usually they just stood there. Occasionally they would groom one another's hair, chewing on the lice they found.

Outcasts from an urban culture, David and I locked our doors. Once he went into Salvador while I stayed the night alone.

"Conrado's scared," said Dora, our cook. "He's afraid of the *bichos* [beasts, real and imaginary] outside." There was really nothing to be afraid of, she assured me. A dangerous *bicho* had never bothered anyone in Arembepe; most people didn't even have locks on their doors.

The sounds, sensations, sights, smells, and tastes of life in Arembepe slowly grew familiar. I grew accustomed to this world without Kleenex, where globs of mucus drooped from the noses of village children whenever a cold passed through. A world where, seemingly without effort, women with gracefully swaying hips carried 18-liter kerosene cans of water on their heads, where boys sailed kites and sported at catching houseflies in their bare hands, where old women smoked pipes, storekeepers offered *cachaça* (common rum) at nine in the morning, and men played dominoes on lazy afternoons when there was no fishing. I was in a world where life was oriented toward water—the sea, where men fished, and the lagoon, where women communally washed clothing, dishes, and their bodies.

Arembepe was a compact village, where the walls of most houses touched those of their neighbors. Privacy was a scarce commodity. No wonder villagers didn't lock their doors—who could steal anything and have it stay a secret? Young lovers found what privacy they could at night.

Even more dramatically than in other places without electricity, Arembepe's night life was transformed when the moon was full. Reflected everywhere by the sand and water, moonlight turned the village by night into almost day. Young people strolled in the streets and courted on the beach. Fishermen sought octopus and "lobster" (Atlantic crayfish) on the reef. Accustomed to the electrified, artificial pace of city life, I was enchanted by the moonlight and its effect on this remote village. Moonless nights impressed me, too. For the first time I could understand how the Milky Way got its name. Only in a planetarium had I seen a sky so crammed with stars. Looking south, distant Salvador's electric lights just barely dimmed the white stars against the coal-black sky, and for the first time I could view the Southern Cross in its magnificence.

Even a devout astrologer would have been impressed the extent to which activities were governed by the phases moon. This was a slower and more natural epoch in Aremb history than the years that were to follow. People awakened sunrise and went to bed early. Moonlight and a calm sea pe ted occasional nighttime fishing, but the pattern was for the to leave in the early morning and return in the late after Boats usually went out five or six days a week; as Chris Arembepeiros took Sunday as a day of rest. But generall in Arembepe followed the availability of natural light an passing of day and night.

Another force of nature, the weather, influenced the rh of life. My visits to Arembepe were during the season of rai rough seas. Sailboats were vulnerable to high winds and st weather, and it was dangerous to negotiate the narrow cha in the rocky reef when racing home to escape a sudden s Storms usually lasted no more than a week, but I remembe three-week lull, in 1964. People speculated incessantly when the weather would improve; they had no access to we reports. Villagers lamented that they couldn't work. Even they began to complain of hunger. Cattle were brought in farms to be butchered and sold, but many households we poor to buy beef. Villagers said they were hungry for fis something with flesh to complement a diet of coffee, suga manioc flour. The weather even forced us to let up on our viewing. Our schedule had a whole section on diet—the q ties of various foods that people bought or ate per day, or month. We felt embarrassed asking people what they normal or good times when they were starving for protei indeed, for all items whose purchase required cash.

The tropical rainy season meant constant high humi perfect climate for molds. My black leather dress shoes t white with mildew. Peter Gorlin had bought a navy blue dry suit before his trip to Bahia in 1964. Since we attende formal affairs in Salvador, Peter let his suit hang in a robe in Jauá until he finally needed it. Discovering, a few before a party, that it was covered with mildew, Peter ch into a Salvador hotel, took a shower with his suit on, la and rinsed it, wore it to the party, and dripped dry for th few hours.

The tile roofs of the houses we rented in Arembepe never very effective in keeping the moisture (and bats Whenever it rained, we had to avoid the large leaks, bu was no place we could be completely dry. One rainy day the three-week fishing lull, Dora told us that lately, smelli moist walls of her wattle-and-daub (stick-and-mud) hut, s remembered her craving as a child to lick, even eat, dir the mud walls. Arembepeiros sometimes did eat earth, sh us. This geophagy may have been a symptom of iron defi in lean times.

I can summarize my feelings about living in Aremb the 1960s by saying that I had a profound sense of being In those days, almost no one except a fish buyer from Sa ever drove a car into Arembepe. I felt cut off from the Only a few villagers owned radios, which rarely brough

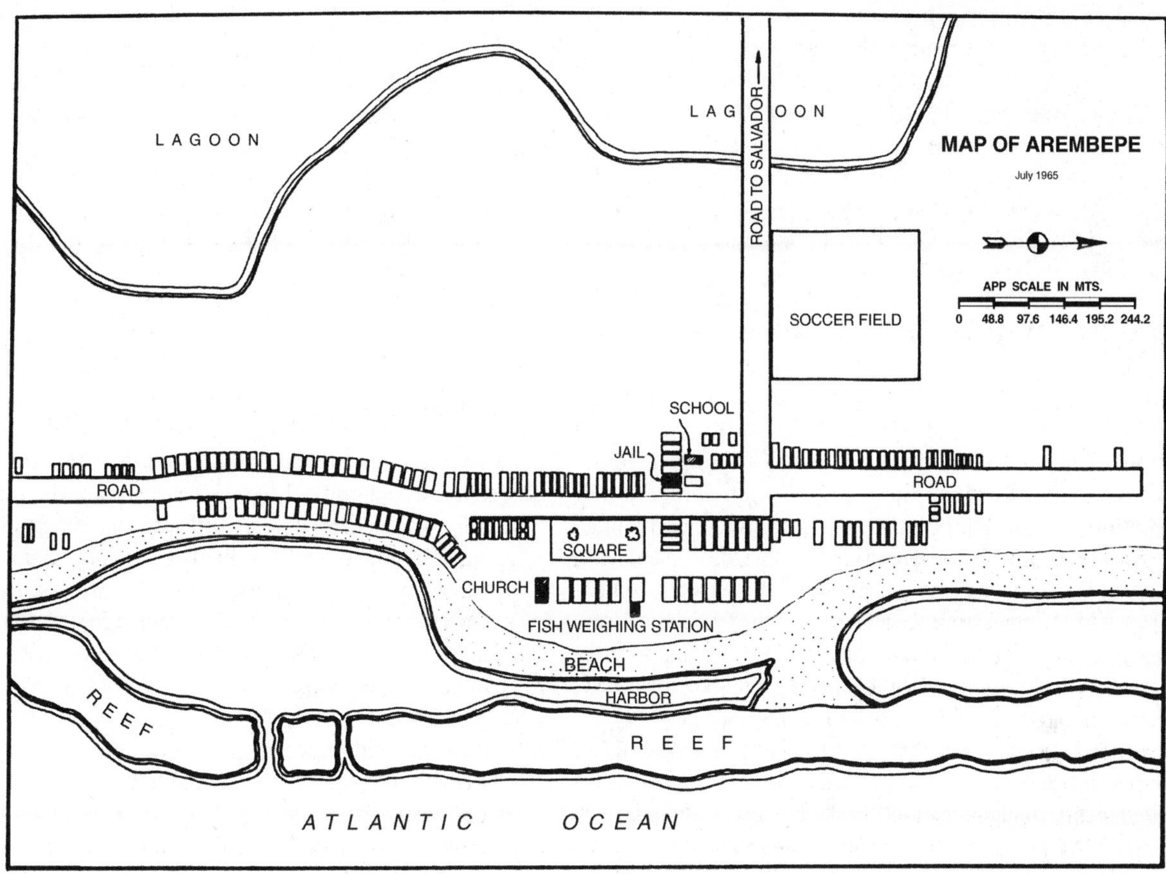

: rest of the world anyway. I pored over every word of s Latin American edition on each visit to Salvador. We times planned our trips into Salvador to coincide with the ne new *Time* came out.

en for Betty Wagley Kottak, a Brazilian (of dual nation-, Arembepe was unfamiliar. It was far removed from the stication, social stratification, and style consciousness of e Janeiro and São Paulo, which she knew well. Betty had exposed to much of Brazil's "Great Tradition" (to use t Redfield's term for the culture of literate, mainly urban, but not the "little traditions" of its peasants and rural For both of us, then, as for the other field team members, bepe provided a strong contrast with all previous settings lives.

hink that our work in Arembepe also gave us a better standing of rural America as recently as the 1930s and 1940s. Then, in many isolated pockets, especially among the poor, night life still went on by candle and lantern. This was before business, government, and media had fully introduced rural folk to the industrial world's vast inventory of benefits and costs.

We learned firsthand about the habits and values of Arembepeiros, how they tried to make ends meet, how they dealt with fortune and adversity. We got to know many people as individuals and as friends. Characters like Alberto, Dora, and Tomé, whose words, stories, and experiences are laced through this chronicle of a changing Arembepe, are much more to me than informants. They are people I value as I do my friends and special colleagues in the United States. Yet they are the kind of people that few outsiders will ever have a chance to meet. The anthropologist's special obligation is to tell their story for them.

Article 2

Eating Christmas in the Kalahari

RICHARD BORSHAY LEE

The !Kung Bushmen's knowledge of Christmas is third-hand. The London Missionary Society brought the holiday to the southern Tswana tribes in the early nineteenth century. Later, native catechists spread the idea far and wide among the Bantu-speaking pastoralists, even in the remotest corners of the Kalahari Desert. The Bushmen's idea of the Christmas story, stripped to its essentials, is "praise the birth of white man's god-chief"; what keeps their interest in the holiday high is the Tswana-Herero custom of slaughtering an ox for his Bushmen neighbors as an annual goodwill gesture. Since the 1930's, part of the Bushmen's annual round of activities has included a December congregation at the cattle posts for trading, marriage brokering, and several days of trance-dance feasting at which the local Tswana headman is host.

As a social anthropologist working with !Kung Bushmen, I found that the Christmas ox custom suited my purposes. I had come to the Kalahari to study the hunting and gathering subsistence economy of the !Kung, and to accomplish this it was essential not to provide them with food, share my own food, or interfere in any way with their food-gathering activities. While liberal handouts of tobacco and medical supplies were appreciated, they were scarcely adequate to erase the glaring disparity in wealth between the anthropologist, who maintained a two-month inventory of canned goods, and the Bushmen, who rarely had a day's supply of food on hand. My approach, while paying off in terms of data, left me open to frequent accusations of stinginess and hard-heartedness. By their lights, I was a miser.

The Christmas ox was to be my way of saying thank you for the cooperation of the past year; and since it was to be our last Christmas in the field, I determined to slaughter the largest, meatiest ox that money could buy, insuring that the feast and trance-dance would be a success.

Through December I kept my eyes open at the wells as the cattle were brought down for watering. Several animals were offered, but none had quite the grossness that I had in mind. Then, ten days before the holiday, a Herero friend led an ox of astonishing size and mass up to our camp. It was solid black, stood five feet high at the shoulder, had a five-foot span of horns, and must have weighed 1,200 pounds on the hoof. Food consumption calculations are my specialty, and I quickly figured that bones and viscera aside, there was enough meat—at least four pounds—for every man, woman, and child of the 150 Bushmen in the vicinity of /ai/ai who were expected at the feast.

Having found the right animal at last, I paid the Herer (\$56) and asked him to keep the beast with his herd until C mas day. The next morning word spread among the peopl the big solid black one was the ox chosen by /ontah (my I man name; it means, roughly, "whitey") for the Christmas That afternoon I received the first delegation. Ben!a, an ou ken sixty-year-old mother of five, came to the point slowl

"Where were you planning to eat Christmas?"

"Right here at /ai/ai," I replied.

"Alone or with others?"

"I expect to invite all the people to eat Christmas with

"Eat what?"

"I have purchased Yehave's black ox, and I am goi slaughter and cook it."

"That's what we were told at the well but refused to b it until we heard it from yourself."

"Well, it's the black one," I replied expansively, alth wondering what she was driving at.

"Oh, no!" Ben!a groaned, turning to her group. "They right." Turning back to me she asked, "Do you expect us that bag of bones?"

"Bag of bones! It's the biggest ox at /ai/ai."

"Big, yes, but old. And thin. Everybody knows there's nc on that old ox. What did you expect us to eat off it, the hor

Everybody chuckled at Ben!a's one-liner as they w away, but all I could manage was a weak grin.

That evening it was the turn of the young men. They came t our evening fire. /gaugo, about my age, spoke to me man-to-

"/ontah, you have always been square with us," he "What has happened to change your heart? That sack o and bones of Yehave's will hardly feed one camp, let alc the Bushmen around ai/ai." And he proceeded to enumera seven camps in the /ai/ai vicinity, family by family. "Pe you have forgotten that we are not few, but many. Or a too blind to tell the difference between a proper cow and wreck? That ox is thin to the point of death."

"Look, you guys," I retorted, "that is a beautiful anima I"m sure you will eat it with pleasure at Christmas."

"Of course we will eat it; it's food. But it won't fill us the point where we will have enough strength to dance. W eat and go home to bed with stomachs rumbling."

t night as we turned in, I asked my wife, Nancy: "What
ı think of the black ox?"
ooked enormous to me. Why?"
ll, about eight different people have told me I got gypped;
ox is nothing but bones."
hat's the angle?" Nancy asked. "Did they have a better
sell?"
, they just said that it was going to be a grim Christmas
e there won't be enough meat to go around. Maybe I'll
independent judge to look at the beast in the morning."
ht and early, Halingisi, a Tswana cattle owner, appeared
camp. But before I could ask him to give me his opinion
ave's black ox, he gave me the eye signal that indicated a
ntial chat. We left the camp and sat down.
tah, I'm surprised at you: you've lived here for three
nd still haven't learned anything about cattle."
t what else can a person do but choose the biggest, strong-
nal one can find?" I retorted.
ok, just because an animal is big doesn't mean that it has
of meat on it. The black one was a beauty when it was
r, but now it is thin to the point of death."
ll I've already bought it. What can I do at this stage?"
ught it already? I thought you were just considering it.
ou'll have to kill it and serve it, I suppose. But don't
much of a dance to follow."
spirits dropped rapidly. I could believe that Ben!a and
just might be putting me on about the black ox, but Hal-
eemed to be an impartial critic. I went around that day
as though I had bought a lemon of a used car.
he afternoon it was Tomazo's turn. Tomazo is a fine
a top trance performer . . . and one of my most reliable
ants. He approached the subject of the Christmas cow as
my continuing Bushman education.
friend, the way it is with us Bushmen," he began, "is
love meat. And even more than that, we love fat. When
t we always search for the fat ones, the ones dripping
yers of white fat: fat that turns into a clear, thick oil in the
g pot, fat that slides down your gullet, fills your stomach
es you a roaring diarrhea," he rhapsodized.
feeling as we do," he continued, "it gives us pain to be
such a scrawny thing as Yehave's black ox. It is big, yes,
doubt its giant bones are good for soup, but fat is what
lly crave and so we will eat Christmas this year with a
heart."
prospect of a gloomy Christmas now had me worried, so
Tomazo what I could do about it.
ok for a fat one, a young one . . . smaller, but fat. Fat
to make us *//gom* ('evacuate the bowels'), then we will
oy."
suspicions were aroused when Tomazo said that he hap-
o know of a young, fat, barren cow that the owner was
to part with. Was Tomazo working on commission, I
ed? But I dispelled this unworthy thought when we
ched the Herero owner of the cow in question and found
had decided not to sell.

The scrawny wreck of a Christmas ox now became the talk of the /ai/ai water hole and was the first news told to the outlying groups as they began to come in from the bush for the feast. What finally convinced me that real trouble might be brewing was the visit from u!au, an old conservative with a reputation for fierceness. His nickname meant spear and referred to an incident thirty years ago in which he had speared a man to death. He had an intense manner; fixing me with his eyes, he said in clipped tones:

"I have only just heard about the black ox today, or else I would have come here earlier. /ontah, do you honestly think you can serve meat like that to people and avoid a fight?" He paused, letting the implications sink in. "I don't mean fight you, /ontah; you are a white man. I mean a fight between Bushmen. There are many fierce ones here, and with such a small quantity of meat to distribute, how can you give everybody a fair share? Someone is sure to accuse another of taking too much or hogging all the choice pieces. Then you will see what happens when some go hungry while others eat."

The possibility of at least a serious argument struck me as all too real. I had witnessed the tension that surrounds the distribution of meat from a kudu or gemsbok kill, and had documented many arguments that sprang up from a real or imagined slight in meat distribution. The owners of a kill may spend up to two hours arranging and rearranging the piles of meat under the gaze of a circle of recipients before handing them out. And I also knew that the Christmas feast at /ai/ai would be bringing together groups that had feuded in the past.

Convinced now of the gravity of the situation, I went in earnest to search for a second cow; but all my inquiries failed to turn one up.

The Christmas feast was evidently going to be a disaster, and the incessant complaints about the meagerness of the ox had already taken the fun out of it for me. Moreover, I was getting bored with the wisecracks, and after losing my temper a few times, I resolved to serve the beast anyway. If the meat fell short, the hell with it. In the Bushmen idiom, I announced to all who would listen:

"I am a poor man and blind. If I have chosen one that is too old and too thin, we will eat it anyway and see if there is enough meat there to quiet the rumbling of our stomachs."

On hearing this speech, Ben!a offered me a rare word of comfort. "It's thin," she said philosophically, "but the bones will make a good soup."

At dawn Christmas morning, instinct told me to turn over the butchering and cooking to a friend and take off with Nancy to spend Christmas alone in the bush. But curiosity kept me from retreating. I wanted to see what such a scrawny ox looked like on butchering and if there *was* going to be a fight, I wanted to catch every word of it. Anthropologists are incurable that way.

The great beast was driven up to our dancing ground, and a shot in the forehead dropped it in its tracks. Then, freshly cut branches were heaped around the fallen carcass to receive the meat. Ten men volunteered to help with the cutting. I asked /gaugo to make the breast bone cut. This cut, which begins the butchering process for most large game, offers easy access for removal of the viscera. But it also allows the hunter to spot-check the amount of fat on the animal. A fat game animal carries a white layer up to an inch thick on the chest, while in a thin one, the knife will quickly cut to bone. All eyes fixed on his hand as /gaugo, dwarfed by the great carcass, knelt to the breast. The first cut opened a pool of solid white in the black skin. The second and third cut widened and deepened the creamy white. Still no bone. It was pure fat; it must have been two inches thick.

"Hey /gau," I burst out, "that ox is loaded with fat. What's this about the ox being too thin to bother eating? Are you out of your mind?"

"Fat?" /gau shot back, "You call that fat? This wreck is thin, sick, dead!" And he broke out laughing. So did everyone else. They rolled on the ground, paralyzed with laughter. Everybody laughed except me; I was thinking.

I ran back to the tent and burst in just as Nancy was getting up. "Hey, the black ox. It's fat as hell! They were kidding about it being too thin to eat. It was a joke or something. A put-on. Everyone is really delighted with it!"

"Some joke," my wife replied. "It was so funny that you were ready to pack up and leave /ai/ai."

If it had indeed been a joke, it had been an extraordinarily convincing one, and tinged, I thought, with more than a touch of malice as many jokes are. Nevertheless, that it was a joke lifted my spirits considerably, and I returned to the butchering site where the shape of the ox was rapidly disappearing under the axes and knives of the butchers. The atmosphere had become festive. Grinning broadly, their arms covered with blood well past the elbow, men packed chunks of meat into the big cast-iron cooking pots, fifty pounds to the load, and muttered and chuckled all the while about the thinness and worthlessness of the animal and /ontah's poor judgment.

We danced and ate that ox two days and two nights; we cooked and distributed fourteen potfuls of meat and no one went home hungry and no fights broke out.

But the "joke" stayed in my mind. I had a growing feeling that something important had happened in my relationship with the Bushmen and that the clue lay in the meaning of the joke. Several days later, when most of the people had dispersed back to the bush camps, I raised the question with Hakekgose, a Tswana man who had grown up among the !Kung, married a !Kung girl, and who probably knew their culture better than any other non-Bushman.

"With us whites," I began, "Christmas is supposed to be the day of friendship and brotherly love. What I can't figure out is why the Bushmen went to such lengths to criticize and belittle the ox I had bought for the feast. The animal was perfectly good and their jokes and wisecracks practically ruined the holiday for me."

"So it really did bother you," said Hakekgose. "Well, that's the way they always talk. When I take my rifle and go hunting with them, if I miss, they laugh at me for the rest of the day. But even if I hit and bring one down, it's no better. To them, the kill is always too small or too old or too thin; and as we sit down on the kill site to cook and eat the liver, they keep grumbling, even with their mouths full of meat. They say things like, 'Oh this is awful! What a worthless animal! Whatever made me think that this Tswana rascal could hunt!' "

"Is this the way outsiders are treated?" I asked.

"No, it is their custom; they talk that way to each other too. Go and ask them."

/gaugo had been one of the most enthusiastic in making me feel bad about the merit of the Christmas ox. I sought him out first.

"Why did you tell me the black ox was worthless, when you could see that it was loaded with fat and meat?"

"It is our way," he said smiling. "We always like to fool people about that. Say there is a Bushman who has been hunting. He must not come home and announce like a braggard, 'I have killed a big one in the bush!' He must first sit down in silence until I or someone else comes up to his fire and asks, 'What did you see today?' He replies quietly, 'Ah, I'm no good for hunting. I saw nothing at all [pause] just a little tiny one.' Then I smile to myself," /gaugo continued, "because I know he has killed something big."

"In the morning we make up a party of four or five people to cut up and carry the meat back to the camp. When we arrive at the kill we examine it and cry out, 'You mean to say you have dragged us all the way out here in order to make us carry home your pile of bones? Oh, if I had known it was this thin I wouldn't have come.' Another one pipes up, 'People, to think I gave up a nice day in the shade for this. At home we may be hungry but at least we have nice cool water to drink.' If the horns are big, someone says, 'Did you think that somehow you were going to boil down the horns for soup?'

"To all this you must respond in kind. 'I agree,' you say, 'this one is not worth the effort; let's just cook the liver for strength and leave the rest for the hyenas. It is not too late to hunt today and even a duiker or a steenbok would be better than this mess.'

"Then you set to work nevertheless; butcher the animal, carry the meat back to the camp and everyone eats," /gaugo concluded.

Things were beginning to make sense. Next, I went to Tomazo. He corroborated /gaugo's story of the obligatory insults over a kill and added a few details of his own.

"But," I asked, "why insult a man after he has gone to all that trouble to track and kill an animal and when he is going to share the meat with you so that your children will have something to eat?"

"Arrogance," was his cryptic answer.

"Arrogance?"

"Yes, when a young man kills much meat he comes to think of himself as a chief or a big man, and he thinks of the rest of us as his servants or inferiors. We can't accept this. We refuse one who boasts, for someday his pride will make him kill somebody. So we always speak of his meat as worthless. This way we cool his heart and make him gentle."

"But why didn't you tell me this before?" I asked Tomazo with some heat.

:ause you never asked me," said Tomazo, echoing the
that has come to haunt every field ethnographer.

pieces now fell into place. I had known for a long time situations of social conflict with Bushmen I held all the was the only source of tobacco in a thousand square and I was not incapable of cutting an individual off for operation. Though my boycott never lasted longer than ays, it was an indication of my strength. People resented sence at the water hole, yet simultaneously dreaded my . In short I was a perfect target for the charge of arro- nd for the Bushmen tactic of enforcing humility.

d been taught an object lesson by the Bushmen; it had om an unexpected corner and had hurt me in a vulnera- . For the big black ox was to be the one totally generous, ng act of my year at /ai/ai, and I was quite unprepared reaction I received.

read it, their message was this: There are no totally gen- cts. All "acts" have an element of calculation. One black ghtered at Christmas does not wipe out a year of careful lation of gifts given to serve your own ends. After all, an animal and share the meat with people is really no more than Bushmen do for each other every day and with far less fanfare.

In the end, I had to admire how the Bushmen had played out the farce—collectively straight-faced to the end. Curiously, the episode reminded me of the *Good Soldier Schweik* and his marvelous encounters with authority. Like Schweik, the Bushmen had retained a thorough-going skepticism of good intentions. Was it this independence of spirit, I wondered, that had kept them culturally viable in the face of generations of contact with more powerful societies, both black and white? The thought that the Bushmen were alive and well in the Kalahari was strangely comforting. Perhaps, armed with that independence and with their superb knowledge of their environment, they might yet survive the future.

Richard Borshay Lee is a full professor of anthropology at the University of Toronto. He has done extensive fieldwork in southern Africa, is coeditor of *Man the Hunter* (1968) and *Kalahari Hunter-Gatherers* (1976), and author of *The !Kung San: Men, Women, and Work in a Foraging Society.*

Article 3

Tricking and Tripping

Fieldwork on Prostitution in the Era of AIDS

CLAIRE E. STERK

Students often think of anthropological fieldwork as requiring travel to exotic tropical locations, but that is not necessarily the case. This reading is based on fieldwork in the United States—on the streets in New York City as well as Atlanta. Claire Sterk is an anthropologist who works in a school of public health and is primarily interested in issues of women's health, particularly as it relates to sexual behavior. In this selection, an introduction to a recent book by the same title, she describes the basic fieldwork methods she used to study these women and their communities. Like most cultural anthropologists, Sterk's primary goal was to describe "the life" of prostitution from the women's own point of view. To do this, she had to be patient, brave, sympathetic, trustworthy, curious, and nonjudgmental. You will notice these characteristics in this selection; for example, Sterk begins her book with a poem written by one of her informants. Fieldwork is a slow process, because it takes time to win people's confidence and to learn their language and way of seeing the world. In this regard, there are probably few differences between the work of a qualitative sociologist and that of a cultural anthropologist (although anthropologists would not use the term "deviant" to describe another society or a segment of their own society).

Throughout the world, HIV/AIDS is fast becoming a disease found particularly in poor women. Sex workers or prostitutes have often been blamed for AIDS, and they have been further stigmatized because of their profession. In reality, however, entry into prostitution is not a career choice; rather, these women and girls are themselves most often victims of circumstances such as violence and poverty. Public health officials want to know why sex workers do not always protect their health by making men wear condoms. To answer such questions, we must know more about the daily life of these women. The way to do that, the cultural anthropologist would say, is to ask and to listen.

As you read this selection, ask yourself the following questions:

- What happens when Sterk says, "I'm sorry for you" to one of her informants? Why?
- Why do you think fieldwork might be a difficult job?
- Do you think that the fact that Sterk grew up in Amsterdam, where prostitution is legal, affected her research?
- Which of the six themes of this work, described at the end of the article, do you think is most important?

One night in March of 1987 business was slow. hanging out on a stroll with a group of street tutes. After a few hours in a nearby diner/coffe we were kicked out. The waitress felt bad, but she need table for some new customers. Four of us decided to sit car until the rain stopped. While three of us chatted abo Piper wrote this poem. As soon as she read it to us, the co tion shifted to more serious topics—pimps, customers, cc many hassles of being a prostitute, to name a few. We d that if I ever finished a book about prostitution, the book start with her poem.

This book is about the women who work in the low elons of the prostitution world. They worked in the stre other public settings as well as crack houses. Some o women viewed themselves primarily as prostitutes, number of them used drugs to cope with the pressures life. Others identified themselves more as drug users, a main reason for having sex for money or other goods support their own drug use and often the habit of the partner. A small group of women interviewed for thi had left prostitution, and most of them were still strug integrate their past experiences as prostitutes in their lives.

The stories told by the women who participated project revealed how pimps, customers, and others s police officers and social and health service providers them as "fallen" women. However, their accounts also their strengths and the many strategies they developed lenge these others. Circumstances, including their dr often forced them to sell sex, but they all resisted the that they might be selling themselves. Because they e in an illegal profession, these women had little statu working conditions were poor, and their work was cally and mentally exhausting. Nevertheless, many described the ways in which they gained a sense of over their lives. For instance, they learned how to m late pimps, how to control the types of services and le time bought by their customers, and how to select cus While none of these schemes explicitly enhanced thei ing conditions, they did make the women feel stron better about themselves.

this book, I present prostitution from the point of view women themselves. To understand their current lives, it ecessary to learn how they got started in the life, the vari- rocesses involved in their continued prostitution careers, nk between prostitution and drug use, the women's inter- ıs with their pimps and customers, and the impact of the epidemic and increasing violence on their experiences. I xamined the implications for women. Although my goal o present the women's thoughts, feelings, and actions in own words, the final text is a sociological monograph com- by me as the researcher. Some women are quoted more others because I developed a closer relationship with them, se they were more able to verbalize and capture their cir- ances, or simply because they were more outspoken.

e Sample

ata for this book are qualitative. The research was con- d during the last ten years in the New York City and ta metropolitan areas. One main data source was partici- observation on streets, in hotels and other settings known rostitution activity, and in drug-use settings, especially that allowed sex-for-drug exchanges. Another data source n-depth, life-history interviews with 180 women ranging from 18 to 59 years, with an average age of 34. One in vomen was African-American and one in three white; the ning women were Latina. Three in four had completed school, and among them almost two-thirds had one or years of additional educational training. Thirty women raduated from college.

rty women worked as street prostitutes and did not use . On average, they had been prostitutes for 11 years. Forty n began using drugs an average of three years after they working as prostitutes, and the average time they had d as prostitutes was nine years. Forty women used drugs erage of five years before they became prostitutes, and average they had worked as prostitutes for eight years. ıer forty women began smoking crack and exchanging r crack almost simultaneously, with an average of four in the life. Twenty women who were interviewed were stitutes.

mments on Methodology

I tell people about my research, the most frequent ques- am asked is how I gained access to the women rather what I learned from the research. For many, prostitution unusual topic of conversation, and many people have ssed surprise that I, as a woman, conducted the research. g my research some customers indeed thought I was a ng woman, a fact that almost always amuses those who bout my work. However, few people want to hear stories the women's struggles and sadness. Sometimes they ask ons about the reasons why women become prostitutes. of the time, they are surprised when I tell them that the tutes as well as their customers represent all layers of y. Before presenting the findings, it seems important to discuss the research process, including gaining access to the women, developing relationships, interviewing, and then leaving the field.[1]

Locating Prostitutes and Gaining Entree

One of the first challenges I faced was to identify locations where street prostitution took place. Many of these women worked on strolls, streets where prostitution activity is concentrated, or in hotels known for prostitution activity. Others, such as the crack prostitutes, worked in less public settings such as a crack house that might be someone's apartment.

I often learned of well-known public places from professional experts, such as law enforcement officials and health care providers at emergency rooms and sexually transmitted disease clinics. I gained other insights from lay experts, including taxi drivers, bartenders, and community representatives such as members of neighborhood associations. The contacts universally mentioned some strolls as the places where many women worked, where the local police focused attention, or where residents had organized protests against prostitution in their neighborhoods.

As I began visiting various locales, I continued to learn about new settings. In one sense, I was developing ethnographic maps of street prostitution. After several visits to a specific area, I also was able to expand these maps by adding information about the general atmosphere on the stroll, general characteristics of the various people present, the ways in which the women and customers connected, and the overall flow of action. In addition, my visits allowed the regular actors to notice me.

I soon learned that being an unknown woman in an area known for prostitution may cause many people to notice you, even stare at you, but it fails to yield many verbal interactions. Most of the time when I tried to make eye contact with one of the women, she quickly averted her eyes. Pimps, on the other hand, would stare at me straight on and I ended up being the one to look away. Customers would stop, blow their horn, or wave me over, frequently yelling obscenities when I ignored them. I realized that gaining entree into the prostitution world was not going to be as easy as I imagined it. Although I lacked such training in any of my qualitative methods classes, I decided to move slowly and not force any interaction. The most I said during the initial weeks in a new area was limited to "how are you" or "hi." This strategy paid off during my first visits to one of the strolls in Brooklyn, New York. After several appearances, one of the women walked up to me and sarcastically asked if I was looking for something. She caught me off guard, and all the answers I had practiced did not seem to make sense. I mumbled something about just wanting to walk around. She did not like my answer, but she did like my accent. We ended up talking about the latter and she was especially excited when I told her I came from Amsterdam. One of her friends had gone to Europe with her boyfriend, who was in the military. She understood from her that prostitution and drugs were legal in the Netherlands. While explaining to her that some of her friend's impressions were incorrect, I was able to show off some of my knowledge about prostitution. I mentioned that I was interested in prostitution and wanted to write a book about it.

Despite the fascination with my background and intentions, the prostitute immediately put me through a Streetwalker 101 test, and apparently I passed. She told me to make sure to come back. By the time I left, I not only had my first conversation but also my first connection to the scene. Variations of this entry process occurred on the other strolls. The main lesson I learned in these early efforts was the importance of having some knowledge of the lives of the people I wanted to study, while at the same time refraining from presenting myself as an expert.

Qualitative researchers often refer to their initial connections as gatekeepers and key respondents. Throughout my fieldwork I learned that some key respondents are important in providing initial access, but they become less central as the research evolves. For example, one of the women who introduced me to her lover, who was also her pimp, was arrested and disappeared for months. Another entered drug treatment soon after she facilitated my access. Other key respondents provided access to only a segment of the players on a scene. For example, if a woman worked for a pimp, [she] was unlikely . . . to introduce me to women working for another pimp. On one stroll my initial contact was with a pimp whom nobody liked. By associating with him, I almost lost the opportunity to meet other pimps. Some key respondents were less connected than promised—for example, some of the women who worked the street to support their drug habit. Often their connections were more frequently with drug users and less so with prostitutes.

Key respondents tend to be individuals central to the local scene, such as, in this case, pimps and the more senior prostitutes. Their function as gatekeepers often is to protect the scene and to screen outsiders. Many times I had to prove that I was not an undercover police officer or a woman with ambitions to become a streetwalker. While I thought I had gained entree, I quickly learned that many insiders subsequently wondered about my motives and approached me with suspicion and distrust.

Another lesson involved the need to proceed cautiously with self-nominated key respondents. For example, one of the women presented herself as knowing everyone on the stroll. While she did know everyone, she was not a central figure. On the contrary, the other prostitutes viewed her as a failed streetwalker whose drug use caused her to act unprofessionally. By associating with me, she hoped to regain some of her status. For me, however, it meant limited access to the other women because I affiliated myself with a woman who was marginal to the scene. On another occasion, my main key respondent was a man who claimed to own three crack houses in the neighborhood. However, he had a negative reputation, and people accused him of cheating on others. My initial alliance with him delayed, and almost blocked, my access to others in the neighborhood. He intentionally tried to keep me from others on the scene, not because he would gain something from that transaction but because it made him feel powerful. When I told him I was going to hang out with some of the other people, he threatened me until one of the other dealers stepped in and told him to stay away. The two of them argued back and forth, and finally I was free to go. Fortunately, the dealer who had spoken u me was much more central and positively associated wit local scene. Finally, I am unsure if I would have had succ gaining entrance to the scene had I not been a woman.

Developing Relationships and Trust

The processes involved in developing relationships in res situations amplify those involved in developing relationsh general. Both parties need to get to know each other, be aware and accepting of each other's roles, and engage reciprocal relationship. Being supportive and providing p cal assistance were the most visible and direct ways for the researcher to develop a relationship. Throughout the I have given countless rides, provided child care on num occasions, bought groceries, and listened for hours to s that were unrelated to my initial research questions. Grad my role allowed me to become part of these women's live to build rapport with many of them.

Over time, many women also realized that I was un ested in being a prostitute and that I genuinely was inte in learning as much as possible about their lives. Many fel tered that someone wanted to learn from them and that the knowledge to offer. Allowing women to tell their storie engaging in a dialogue with them probably were the single important techniques that allowed me to develop relatior with them. Had I only wanted to focus on the questions in mind, developing such relationships might have been difficult.

At times, I was able to get to know a woman only aft pimp endorsed our contact. One of my scariest experi occurred before I knew to work through the pimps, an such man had some of his friends follow me on my way one night. I will never know what plans they had in mind f because I fortunately was able to escape with only a few br Over a year later, the woman acknowledged that her pim gotten upset and told her he was going to teach me a less

On other occasions, I first needed to be screened by o and managers of crack houses before the research coul tinue. Interestingly, screenings always were done by a ma if the person who vouched for me was a man himself. the women also were cautious, the ways in which they ch me out tended to be much more subtle. For example, them would tell me a story, indicating that it was a secret another person on the stroll. Although I failed to realize the time, my field notes revealed that frequently after conversation, others would ask me questions about relate ics. One woman later acknowledged that putting out suc ries was a test to see if I would keep information confide

Learning more about the women and gaining a better standing of their lives also raised many ethical questions. N book told me how to handle situations in which a pimp a woman, a customer forced a woman to engage in unv sex acts, a customer requested unprotected sex from a who knew she was HIV infected, or a boyfriend had re ctations regarding a woman's earnings to support his drug . I failed to know the proper response when asked to engage egal activities such as holding drugs or money a woman had n from a customer. In general, my response was to explain I was there as a researcher. During those occasions when ures became too severe, I decided to leave a scene. For ple, I never returned to certain crack houses because pimps continued to ask me to consider working for them.

ver time, I was fortunate to develop relationships with peo- ho "watched my back." One pimp in particular intervened if rceived other pimps, customers, or passersby harassing me. so was the one who gave me my street name: Whitie (indi- g my racial background) or Ms. Whitie for those who disre- ed me. While this was my first street name, I subsequently others. Being given a street name was a symbolic gesture of otance. Gradually, I developed an identity that allowed me both an insider and an outsider. While hanging out on the s and other gathering places, including crack houses, I had al with some of the same uncomfortable conditions as the itutes, such as cold or warm weather, lack of access to a rest , refusals from owners for me to patronize a restaurant, and urse, harassment by customers and the police.

articipated in many informal conversations. Unless pushed so, I seldom divulged my opinions. I was more open with eelings about situations and showed empathy. I learned ly that providing an opinion can backfire. I agreed that one women was struggling a lot and stated that I felt sorry for Vhile I meant to indicate my "genuine concern for her, she that I felt sorry for her because she was a failure. When inally, after several weeks, talked with me again, I was o explain to her that I was not judging her, but rather felt erned for her. She remained cynical and many times asked or favors to make up for my mistake. It took me months e I felt comfortable telling her that I felt I had done enough hat it was time to let go. However, if she was not ready, eeded to know that I would no longer go along. This was f many occasions when I learned that although I wanted to ate my work as a researcher, that I wanted people to like ust me, I also needed to set boundaries.

ainy and slow nights often provided good opportunities for participate in conversations with groups of women. Popu- oics included how to work safely, what to do about condom ow to make more money. I often served as a health educa- d a supplier of condoms, gels, vaginal douches, and other ine products. Many women were very worried about the epidemic. However, they also were worried about how to condom when a customer refused to do so. They worried ularly about condom use when they needed money badly onsequently, did not want to propose that the customer use or fear of rejection. While some women became experts at ng" their customers use a condom—for example, "by hid- in their mouth prior to beginning oral sex—others would condoms to please me but never pull one out. If a woman IV positive and I knew she failed to use a condom, I faced hical dilemma of challenging her or staying out of it.

veloping trusting relationships with crack prostitutes was difficult. Crack houses were not the right environment for informal conversations. Typically, the atmosphere was tense and everyone was suspicious of each other. The best times to talk with these women were when we bought groceries together, when I helped them clean their homes, or when we shared a meal. Often the women were very different when they were not high than they were when they were high or craving crack. In my conversations with them, I learned that while I might have observed their actions the night before, they themselves might not remember them. Once I realized this, I would be very careful to omit any detail unless I knew that the woman herself did remember the event.

In-Depth Interviews

All interviews were conducted in a private setting, including women's residences, my car or my office, a restaurant of the women's choice, or any other setting the women selected. I did not begin conducting official interviews until I developed relationships with the women. Acquiring written informed consent prior to the interview was problematic. It made me feel awkward. Here I was asking the women to sign a form after they had begun to trust me. However, often I felt more upset about this technicality than the women themselves. As soon as they realized that the form was something the university required, they seemed to understand. Often they laughed about the official statements, and some asked if I was sure the form was to protect them and not the school.[2] None of the women refused to sign the consent form, although some refused to sign it right away and asked to be interviewed later.

In some instances the consent procedures caused the women to expect a formal interview. Some of them were disappointed when they saw I only had a few structured questions about demographic characteristics, followed by a long list of open-ended questions. When this disappointment occurred, I reminded the women that I wanted to learn from them and that the best way to do so was by engaging in a dialogue rather than interrogating them. Only by letting the women identify their salient issues and the topics they wanted to address was I able to gain an insider's perspective. By being a careful listener and probing for additional information and explanation, I as the interviewer, together with the women, was able to uncover the complexities of their lives. In addition, the nature of the interview allowed me to ask questions about contradictions in a woman's story. For example, sometimes a woman would say that she always used a condom. However, later on in the conversation she would indicate that if she needed drugs she would never use one. By asking her to elaborate on this, I was able to begin developing insights into condom use by type of partner, type of sex acts, and social context.

The interviewer becomes much more a part of the interview when the conversations are in-depth than when a structured questionnaire is used. Because I was so integral to the process, the way the women viewed me may have biased their answers. On the one hand, this bias might be reduced because of the extent to which both parties already knew each other; on the other, a woman might fail to give her true opinion and reveal her actions if she knew that these went against the interviewer's opinion. I suspected that some women played down the ways in which their pimps manipulated them once they knew that I was not too fond of these men. However, some might have taken more time to explain the relationship with their pimp in order to "correct" my image.

My background, so different from that of these women, most likely affected the nature of the interviews. I occupied a higher socioeconomic status. I had a place to live and a job. In contrast to the nonwhite women, I came from a different racial background. While I don't know to what extent these differences played a role, I acknowledge that they must have had some effect on this research.

Leaving the Field

Leaving the field was not something that occurred after completion of the fieldwork, but an event that took place daily. Although I sometimes stayed on the strolls all night or hung out for several days, I always had a home to return to. I had a house with electricity, a warm shower, a comfortable bed, and a kitchen. My house sat on a street where I had no fear of being shot on my way there and where I did not find condoms or syringes on my doorstep.

During several stages of the study, I had access to a car, which I used to give the women rides or to run errands together. However, I will never forget the cold night when everyone on the street was freezing, and I left to go home. I turned up the heat in my car, and tears streamed down my cheeks. I appreciated the heat, but I felt more guilty about that luxury than ever before. I truly felt like an outsider, or maybe even more appropriate, a betrayer.

Throughout the years of fieldwork, there were a number of times when I left the scene temporarily. For example, when so many people were dying from AIDS, I was unable to ignore the devastating impact of this disease. I needed an emotional break.

Physically removing myself from the scene was common when I experienced difficulty remaining objective. Once I became too involved in a woman's life and almost adopted her and her family. Another time I felt a true hatred for a crack house owner and was unable to adhere to the rules of courteous interactions. Still another time, I got angry with a woman whose steady partner was HIV positive when she failed to ask him to use a condom when they had sex.

I also took temporary breaks from a particular scene by shifting settings and neighborhoods. For example, I would invest most of my time in women from a particular crack house for several weeks. Then I would shift to spending more time on one of the strolls, while making shorter and less frequent visits to the crack house. By shifting scenes, I was able to tell people why I was leaving and to remind all of us of my researcher role.

While I focused on leaving the field, I became interested in women who had left the life. It seemed important to have an understanding of their past and current circumstances. I knew some of them from the days when they were working, but identifying others was a challenge. There was no gathering place for ex-prostitutes. Informal networking, advertisements in newspapers, and local clinics and community settings all me to reach twenty of these women. Conducting interv with them later in the data collection process prepared me t specific questions. I realized that I had learned enough the life to know what to ask. Interviewing ex-prostitutes prepared me for moving from the fieldwork to writing.

It is hard to determine exactly when I left the field. It s like a process that never ends. Although I was more physi removed from the scene, I continued to be involved while lyzing the data and writing this book. I also created opp nities to go back, for example, by asking women to giv feedback on parts of the manuscript or at times when I ex enced writer's block and my car seemed to automatically itself to one of the strolls. I also have developed other res projects in some of the same communities. For example, a project on intergenerational drug use and a gender-sp intervention project to help women remain HIV negative brought me back to the same population. Some of the w have become key respondents in these new projects, whil ers now are members of a research team. For example, Bet of the women who has left prostitution, works as an out worker on another project.

Six Themes in the Ethnograph of Prostitution

The main intention of my work is to provide the reader a perspective on street prostitution from the point of vi the women themselves. There are six fundamental aspe the women's lives as prostitutes that must be considered first concerns the women's own explanations for their inv ment in prostitution and their descriptions of the va circumstances that led them to become prostitutes. Thei ries include justifications such as traumatic past experie especially sexual abuse, the lack of love they experienc children, pressures by friends and pimps, the need for c and most prominently, the economic forces that pushed into the life. A number of women describe these justific as excuses, as reflective explanations they have develope becoming a prostitute.

The women describe the nature of their initial experiences, often involved alienation from those outside the life. They als the differences in the processes between women who work as tutes and use drugs and women who do not use drugs.

Although all these women work either on the street or in use settings, their lives do differ. My second theme is a typ that captures these differences, looking at the women's prost versus drug-use identities. The typology distinguishes amo streetwalkers, women who work strolls and who do not use (b) hooked prostitutes, women who identify themselves ma prostitutes but who upon their entrance into the life also bega drugs; (c) prostituting addicts, women who view themselves as drug users and who became prostitutes to support their drug and (d) crack prostitutes, women who trade sex for crack.

typology explains the differences in the women's strat-
or soliciting customers, their screening of customers, of sex acts, and bargaining for services. For example, etwalkers have the most bargaining power, while such appears to be lacking among the crack prostitutes.

prostitutes work in a vacuum. The third theme is the pimps, a label that most women dislike and for which efer to substitute "old man" or "boyfriend." Among the one finds entrepreneur lovers, men who mainly employ alkers and hooked prostitutes and sometimes prostitut-icts. Entrepreneur lovers engage in the life for business . They treat the women as their employees or their prop-d view them primarily as an economic commodity. The ıccessful a woman is in earning them money, the more t it is for that woman to leave her entrepreneur pimp. t prostituting addicts and some hooked prostitutes work ver pimp, a man who is their steady partner but who also f their earnings. Typically, such pimps employ only one . The dynamics in the relationship between a prostitute lover pimp become more complex when both partners gs. Drugs often become the glue of the relationship.

many crack prostitutes, their crack addiction serves as a ew plan to exchange sex for crack when they first begin often several weeks or months pass before a woman who sex for crack realizes that she is a prostitute.

orically, society has blamed prostitutes for introducing sex-ansmitted diseases into the general population. Similarly, s them scapegoats for the spread of HIV/AIDS. Yet their nd customers are not held accountable. The fourth theme in ropological study of prostitution is the impact of the AIDS ic on the women's lives. Although most are knowledgeable IIV risk behaviors and the ways to reduce their risk, many ceptions exist. The women describe the complexities of n use, especially with steady partners but also with paying ers. Many women have mixed feelings about HIV testing, ing how to cope with a positive test result while no cure is le. A few of the women already knew their HIV-infected nd the discussion touches on their dilemmas as well.

fifth theme is the violence and abuse that make common nces in the women's lives. An ethnography of prostitution low the women to describe violence in their neighborhoods as well as violence in prostitution and drug-use settings. The most common violence they encounter is from customers. These men often assume that because they pay for sex they buy a woman. Apparently, casual customers pose more of a danger than those who are regulars. The types of abuse the women encounter are emotional, physical, and sexual. In addition to customers, pimps and boyfriends abuse the women. Finally, the women discuss harassment by law enforcement officers.

When I talked with the women, it often seemed that there were no opportunities to escape from the life. Yet the sixth and final theme must be the escape from prostitution. Women who have left prostitution can describe the process of their exit from prostitution. As ex-prostitutes they struggle with the stigma of their past, the challenges of developing a new identity, and the impact of their past on current intimate relationships. Those who were also drug users often view themselves as ex-prostitutes and recovering addicts, a perspective that seems to create a role conflict. Overall, most ex-prostitutes find that their past follows them like a bad hangover.

Notes

1. For more information about qualitative research methods, see, for example, Patricia Adler and Peter Adler, *Membership Roles in Field Research* (Newbury Park: Sage, 1987); Michael Agar, *The Professional Stranger* (New York: Academic Press, 1980) and *Speaking of Ethnography* (Beverly Hills: Sage, 1986); Howard Becker and Blanche Geer, "Participant Observation and Interviewing: A Comparison," *Human Organization* 16 (1957): 28–32; Norman Denzin, *Sociological Methods: A Sourcebook* (Chicago: Aldine, 1970); Barney Glaser and Anselm Strauss, *The Discovery of Grounded Theory: Strategies for Qualitative Research* (Chicago: Aldine, 1967); Y. Lincoln and E. Guba, *Naturalistic Inquiry* (Beverly Hills: Sage, 1985); John Lofland, "Analytic Ethnography: Features, Failings, and Futures," *Journal of Contemporary Ethnography* 24 (1996): 30–67; and James Spradley, *The Ethnographic Interview* (New York: Holt, Rinehart and Winston, 1979) and *Participant Observation* (New York: Holt, Rinehart and Winston, 1980).
2. For a more extensive discussion of informed consent procedures and related ethical issues, see Bruce L. Berg, *Qualitative Research Methods for the Social Sciences,* 3rd edition, Chapter 3: "Ethical Issues" (Boston: Allyn and Bacon, 1998).

Yanomamo

LESLIE E. SPONSEL

As one of the most famous of all cultures in anthropology and beyond, the Yanomami are ethnographic celebrities. They are a large population of indigenous people living in a vast area of some 192,000 square kilometers in the Amazon rain forest. The heart of their homeland is the Sierra Parima, part of the Guyana Highlands, the mountainous divide between the watersheds of the two most famous rivers of the Amazon region, the Orinoco and the Amazon itself. Their territory overlaps the border between northwestern Brazil and southeastern Venezuela. Some 21,000 Yanomami reside in 363 scattered communities that range in size from 30 to 90 individuals with a few reaching more than 200 in size. Although very little archaeological research has been conducted in the area, two other independent lines of evidence, linguistics and blood group genetics, indicate that the Yanomami have been a separate population for 2,000 years. Their language remains classified as independent, unrelated to any others on the continent of South America.

Surely among the reasons for their survival for millennia is one of the most outstanding attributes that distinguishes this unique culture, reciprocity. It is a pivotal social principle applied in almost every aspect of their daily life, and most commonly through kindness, sharing, cooperation, and camaraderie. However, this principle is also applied in resolving disputes, occasionally even through violence between individuals, groups, or villages. In various ways reciprocity extends beyond ordinary life to their relationships with the spiritual component of their world as well. For example, every Yanomami hunter has a counterpart in the form of an animal spirit in the forest that he cannot kill without seriously endangering himself. The unity, interconnectedness, and interdependence of all life is a fundamental tenet of the religion and philosophy of the Yanomami, another expression of reciprocity.

The Yanomami world is intensely intimate, socially and ecologically. Traditionally people dwell together in a big, palm leaf thatched, communal, round house with a large open central plaza. Their egalitarian society is structured primarily along lines of kinship. In this communal shelter, the hammocks of each nuclear or extended family are arranged around a hearth along the back perimeter. Each village is relatively autonomous politically with a charismatic headman who can lead only by persuasion in developing a consensus. There is no chief or other authority uniting more than one community, let alone Yanomami society as a whole, although alliances with several ot lages are common for economic, social, and political pu In Yanomami society the units of residence, kinship, and are not isomorphic, but overlap in diverse, complex, ar ways. This dynamic is mirrored by the subsistence ec that entails almost daily forays into the surrounding fo gardening, hunting, fishing, and gathering. Accordingl viduals accumulate an extensive detailed knowledge of t ogy of their habitat from such regular intimate experien

Yanomami society successfully adapted to the divers *firme* (interfluvial) forest ecosystems within its territory millennia. They developed an ecologically sustainable in terms of their low population density; limited inte material culture; high mobility; rotational subsistence omy; environmental knowledge; and worldview, valu attitudes. They practice a rotational system of land and r use not only in their shifting or swidden farming, but their hunting, fishing, and gathering. The last three ac emphasize extensive trekking several times a year wh may camp in the forest for a week to a month or so at Their environmental knowledge includes well over a h species of wild plants that they use for food, medicin other purposes. Furthermore, their worldview, values, a tudes usually help promote respect for nature. For instan have a system of extensive prohibitions on consuming animal species, some of which apply to everyone in th munity whereas others are specific to individual circums These food taboos reduce pressure on prey species. Thu millennia of use the forest and its wildlife remain inta sustainability of traditional Yanomami society is no rc illusion.

The ancestral homeland of the Yanomami is a region biological diversity in several respects: tropical rain for systems; altitudinal zonation and other variations in c soils, and biota from lowlands to highlands; *tepuis;* and *Tepuis,* or *inselbergs,* are isolated tabletop mountains like islands of biological evolution with relatively high endemicity. *Refugia* are areas of relict forest survivin periods of wet and dry climatic oscillations during the cene. For environmentalists and others concerned with A nian ecosystems and biological diversity, the optimum re conservation would be the continued survival and welfar Yanomami and other indigenous societies.

til recently, Yanomami territory was also a refuge in two respects, political and cultural. The Yanomami may have ted to the core of their territory in the Sierra Parima to e slave raids from adjacent Carib neighbors during the ial period. They are one of the unique indigenous cultures ning in the Amazon, part of the cultural diversity of this n that is increasingly endangered through serious viola- of the human rights of the indigenous peoples by some ists, miners, ranchers, government agents, military, mis- ries, anthropologists, tourists, and other foreigners.

though not generally recognized, the Yanomami in Brazil Venezuela have been influenced in varying ways and es for centuries at least indirectly by Western "civiliza- and sometimes even by direct contact on the margins of erritory. However, only since the 1970s have they progres- become an endangered people, first as the result of the ruction of the Northern Perimeter highway that penetrated ilometers into the southern portion of their traditional ter- , and since the mid-1980s by the invasion of tens of thou- of illegal gold miners, initially in Brazil, and then more tly also hundreds infiltrating into Venezuela. This cannot beled with euphemisms such as cultural contact, accultura- cultural change, or even catastrophic cultural change— clearly in effect it amounts to ecocide, ethnocide, and ide.

e of the most serious threats of all to the Yanomami in ast two decades has been placer mining, although mainly azil. It is conducted on the land surface by washing away al sediments along river and stream banks with high- ure hoses and through dredging the bottom of rivers. causes deforestation, game depletion and displacement, versity reduction, mercury and other pollution, river and n bank destruction and siltation, and fishery degradation. stence and sport hunting by gold miners, and noise from nes and gold mining machinery all combine to degrade abitat of game and fish as well as deplete and displace their ations. Obviously this has deleterious effects on the ani- rotein resources, nutrition, health, and disease resistance al Yanomami communities. Some Yanomami go hungry ven beg for food from the miners, something unknown in raditional society. For the first time, Yanomami are experi- g poverty and inequality. Other detrimental new practices troduced such as alcohol abuse and prostitution. Conse- ly, every aspect of Yanomami society, culture, and ecology ffect attacked at all levels.

roduced disease is certainly the most serious immediate to all Yanomami. In Brazil, at least 15% of the Yanomami ation has already died, mostly as a result of epidemic ses introduced by the gold miners: tuberculosis, venereal ses, and even AIDS. The incidence of previously exist- seases, such as malaria and onchocerciasis (African river ness), has markedly increased as well. Although this medi- nergency has long been recognized, and was even pre- in advance of the earlier road construction, the Brazilian enezuelan governments have consistently failed to provide ate medical assistance for the Yanomami. However, the s of the Pro-Yanomami Commission in Brazil together with the French organization called Doctors Without Borders have brought more medical assistance to some Yanomami communities. Unfortunately, there are no comparable efforts in Venezuela, although the situation appears to be less dire.

There have been homicides and even mass murders of Yanomami by gold miners that were subsequently investigated and documented. For instance, the Hashimu massacre involved a series of events from June through August of 1993. The 12 victims included women, children, and elderly. Several of the bodies were mutilated and some even decapitated.

The miners have brought prostitution that spreads diseases. They have also introduced trade goods that can trigger competition and aggression among Yanomami. They have even given Yanomami shotguns, perhaps to win over friends in areas where they mine. The negative effects on the Yanomami of venereal disease, competition for trade goods, and shotguns may sometimes be inadvertent, or sometimes even intentional.

Although the number of miners in Yanomami territory has declined substantially in recent years from a high of around 40,000 in 1987, there are still regular invasions each dry season. Moreover, changes in the national and regional economies, increases in the price of gold, or discoveries of new kinds of minerals could easily and quickly lead to catastrophic explosions of the mining population at any time in the future with grave consequences for the Yanomami.

Since the 1980s, the territory of the Yanomami nation in the country of Brazil has been turned, in effect, into killing fields because of the illegal invasion of many thousands of gold miners with a multitude of negative health, social, and environmental consequences. However, this disturbing human tragedy is not simply an inadvertent result of the activity of the miners and those who support and profit from their activity. It is also clearly the direct result of the failure of the state and provincial governments of Brazil and Venezuela to adequately protect and promote the human rights of the Yanomami, even though both countries have joined in numerous international agreements on human rights and also have significant protections specified in their own constitutions and laws. After decades of a mixture of governmental apathy, incompetence, corruption, and even complicity, all of which is well documented in numerous sources, the Yanomami are an endangered society. They will continue to be threatened, unless the international community marshals a much more concerted, systematic, forceful, and sustained initiative on their behalf.

Anthropologists are part of the international community, and some, such as those who are members of the American Anthropological Association, are supposed to follow a formal code of professional ethics that assigns first priority to the welfare of the host community in research. Furthermore, anthropologists have knowledge of some 500 years of recurrent historical trends in situations in which Western "civilization" made war against indigenous societies. From a diversity of sources the profession also has access to substantial specific knowledge about Yanomami culture and ecology as well as the continuing crisis they suffer. Anthropology in the United States and other countries has its own organizations and contacts with relevant governmental and nongovernmental organizations. In short, anthropologists already possess sufficient knowledge to act on behalf of social and environmental justice for the Yanomami. Yet, with few outstanding exceptions, anthropologists individually and collectively have been grossly negligent in this regard.

By now more than three-dozen anthropologists have worked with thc Yanomami in various areas and ways for widely different lengths of time. For instance, the eminent Yanomami ethnographer, Jacques Lizot, actually lived with them for more than a quarter of a century. By now more than 60 books have been published about the Yanomami, albeit with diverse approaches, coverage, quality, and accuracy. With so many different anthropologists publishing this much on the Yanomami for more than a century, it is feasible to compare accounts to identify points of agreement, presumably indicative of ethnographic reality, and other points of disagreement, reflecting the individual ethnographer's interpretation, idiosyncrasies, biases, and other phenomena. For example, only a couple of these dozens of authors are obsessed with the violence in Yanomami society to the extent of exaggeration and distortion as well as to the neglect of the violence committed by outsiders against the Yanomami: Ettore Biocca and Napoleon Chagnon. Another important consideration that has yet to receive much systematic research attention is the fact that there is tremendous variation in the geography, ecology, economy, culture, and history among the some 363 Yanomami villages scattered over the enormous area of 192,000 square kilometers. Communities are located from the Orinoco lowlands into the Guyana Highlands within an altitudinal range of 250 to 1,200 meters above sea level.

It is also feasible to identify historical trends in Yanomami studies (Yanomamalogy). The orientation of anthropological research among the Yanomami has evolved to emphasize more humanitarian, applied, and advocacy work in recent decades. Starting in the late 18th century, various explorers and naturalists like Alexander von Humboldt published anecdotal accounts of brief encounters with the Yanomami. Much later this stage was followed, during the 1960s and 1970s, by salvage ethnography, an attempt to systematically describe as much about Yanomami culture and life as possible. This was guided by the assumption that, as a supposedly "primitive" people surviving from a previous stage of cultural evolution, the Yanomami were destined for extinction in the face of civilization and "progress," or at least for profound cultural change through acculturation and assimilation. The first comprehensive ethnography on the Yanomami was published by Louis Cocco in 1971 after he had lived with them as a Salesian missionary for 15 years. Already at this time there was enough research on the Yanomami by various investigators to allow Cocco to include a whole section on the history of Yanomami studies.

During the 1980s, research on the Yanomami in Venezuela became more problem-oriented, much of it focusing on the causes of their so-called warfare and related issues. Actually the most intense form of Yanomami inter-village aggression is more akin to the famous blood feud between the Hatfield and McCoy families in the Appalachian Mountains between Kentucky and Virginia from 1882 to 1890. In any case, the extended debate about the causes of aggression in Yanomami society was over competing sociobiological and ecological explanations proposed mainly by Napoleon Chagnon and Marvin H[illegible] respectively. Until Brian Ferguson's subsequent metic[illegible] ethno-historical research, the Yanomami were falsely trea[illegible] some kind of a pristine isolate. In addition, the consequ[illegible] on aggression and other aspects of their society of the m[illegible] ment of some villages to the lowlands in pursuit of trade [illegible] and other Western resources were mostly ignored. Further[illegible] there is no scientific or other justification in affording [illegible] nal aggression in Yanomami society so much attention [illegible] largely, if not entirely, ignoring aggressive external force[illegible] clearly threaten their survival, welfare, and rights as f[illegible] human beings.

Simultaneously in Brazil, however, with the dire consequ[illegible] of road construction and then mining in the southern ter[illegible] of the Yanomami, research in that country shifted in em[illegible] sis from basic to applied and advocacy work as exemplifi[illegible] the heroic efforts of anthropologists like Bruce Albert, [illegible] Goodwin Gomez, Alcida Ramos, and Kenneth Taylor, a[illegible] others. In Venezuela, where the situation was not as grav[illegible] urgent, basic research persisted. However, the controvers[illegible] the allegations of serious violations of professional ethic[illegible] of the human rights of the Yanomami on the part of Nap[illegible] Chagnon and associates made in Patrick Tierney's controv[illegible] book in late 2000 have aroused increased concern with [illegible] responsibility and relevance in anthropological research ir[illegible] Venezuela and Brazil. Accordingly, many no longer consi[illegible] justifiable to collect scientific data merely to feed careeris[illegible] the vague promise of contributing to human knowledge. [illegible] egocentric work not only dehumanizes the host communi[illegible] which the research is conducted, but the researcher as wel[illegible] Yanomami and the profession deserve far better.

Fortunately, the Yanomami themselves are increa[illegible] working to sustain their self-determination and other h[illegible] rights, territorial integrity, and ethnic identity, as well as tc[illegible] their own medical, educational, political, and other need[illegible] instance, one of their leaders, Davi Kopenawa Yanomam[illegible] traveled internationally to publicize their situation and [illegible] He has addressed organizations such as the British Ho[illegible] Commons and the United Nations. Some schools in Yano[illegible] communities in Brazil are teaching computer literacy [illegible] equipment provided by donations raised by Cultural Su[illegible] Inc. It may well be just a matter of time before there are [illegible] Yanomami trained as anthropologists documenting thei[illegible] culture and critically assessing what others have pub[illegible] about their society. Thus, although Yanomami face many [illegible] ous threats because of the failures of the state and prov[illegible] governments of Brazil and Venezuela in protecting and ac[illegible] ing their human rights, they are not merely passive victi[illegible] cultural contact and change, but increasingly active age[illegible] struggling to determine their own future. The only anachr[illegible] is those racist and ethnocentric outsiders who continue tc[illegible] them as primitive, worthy only as a source of scientific da[illegible] not of voicing their own opinions—including opinions [illegible] anthropologists. The Yanomami are neither noble nor ig[illegible] savages, but rather they are fellow human beings with a di[illegible] tive culture. Indeed, the word *Yanomami* simply means h[illegible] being.

ferences

sky, R. (2005). *Yanomami: The fierce controversy and what we an learn from it.* Berkeley, CA: University of California Press.

on, N. A. (1997). *Yanomamo.* New York: Harcourt Brace College.

, L. (1972). *Iyewei-Teri: Quince años entre los Yanomamos* Fifteen years among the Yanomamos]. Caracas, Venezuela: ibreria Editorial Salesiana.

son, R. B. (1995). *Yanomami warfare: A political history.* Santa e, NM: School of American Research Press.

Lizot, J. (1985). *Tales of the Yanomami: Daily life in the Venezuelan forest.* New York: Cambridge University Press.

Ramos, A. R. (1995). *Sanuma memories: Yanomami ethnography in times of crisis.* Madison, WI: University of Wisconsin Press.

Rocha, J. (1999). *Murder in the rain forest: The Yanomami, the gold miners, and the Amazon.* London, UK: Latin American Bureau.

Smole, W. J. (1976). *The Yanomama Indians: A cultural geography.* Austin, TX: University of Texas Press.

Tierney, P. (2001). *Darkness in El Dorado: How scientists and journalists devastated the Amazon.* New York: W. W. Norton & Co.

UNIT 2

Culture and Communication

Unit Selections

Key Points to Consider

- In what sense are all languages "equal"?
- How can language restrict our thought processes?
- Should the monitors of the English language, such as teachers and dictionaries, be prescriptive or descriptive?
- What is the relationship between a people's language, culture, and interaction with their environment?
- How has the "argument culture" affected the way we conduct ourselves vis-à-vis others?
- Why do some people swear? Why are some such words more effective than others?
- In what ways is communication difficult in a cross-cultural situation?
- Why should we care about the disappearance of languages?
- How has this section enhanced your ability to communicate more effectively?

Student Website

www.mhcls.com

Internet References

Center for Nonverbal Studies
http://www.library.kent.edu/resource.php?id=2800

Exploratorium Magazine: "The Evolution of Languages"
http://www.exploratorium.edu/exploring/language

Hypertext and Ethnography
http://www.umanitoba.ca/anthropology

International Communication Association
http://www.icahdq.org/

Intute: Social Sciences
http://www.intute.ac.uk/socialsciences/cgi-bin/browse.pl?id=120052

Language Extinction
http://www.colorado.edu/iec

Language and Culture
http://anthro.palomar.edu/language/default.htm

Nonverbal Behavior
http://www.usal.es/~nonverbal/researchcenters.htm

Showcase Anthropology
http://www.anthropology.wisc.edu

hropologists are interested in all aspects of human behav-
l how they interrelate. Language is a form of such behavior , primarily verbal behavior) and, therefore, worthy of Although it changes over time, language is patterned and d down from one generation to the next through learning, stinct. In keeping with the idea that language is, integral nan social interactions, it has long been recognized that n communication through language is, by its nature, dif- from the communication found among other animals. al to this difference is the fact that humans communicate ctly, with symbols that have meaning independent of mediate sensory experiences of either the sender or the er of the message. Thus, for instance, humans are able to the future and the past and not just the present.

cent experiments have shown that anthropoid apes can be a small portion of Ameslan or American Sign Language. It e remembered, however, that their very rudimentary abil- to be tapped by painstaking human effort, and that the of difference between apes and humans serves only to asize the peculiar need of humans for, and development guage.

t as the abstract quality of symbols lifts our thoughts d immediate sense perception, it also inhibits our ability to about and convey the full meaning of our personal experi- No categorical term can do justice to its referents—the of forms to which the term refers. The degree to which an obstacle to clarity of thought and communication to the degree of abstraction involved in the symbols. ord "chair," for instance, would not present much difficulty, t has objective referents. However, consider the trouble ve in thinking and communicating with words whose refer- e not tied to immediate sense perception—words such as om," "democracy," and "justice." Deborah Tannen's dis- n of the "argument culture" (in "Fighting for Our Lives") is example of this. At best, the likely result is symbolic con- an inability to think or communicate in objectively defin- ymbols. At worst, language may be used to purposefully ate.

elated issue has to do with the fact that languages differ what is relatively easy to express within the restrictions r particular vocabularies and grammatical structure (see or Words" by Kate Douglas). Thus, although a given lan- may not have enough words to cope with a new situation ew field of activity, the typical solution is to invent words orrow them. In this way, it has been claimed that any lan- can be used to say anything. This point is challenged,

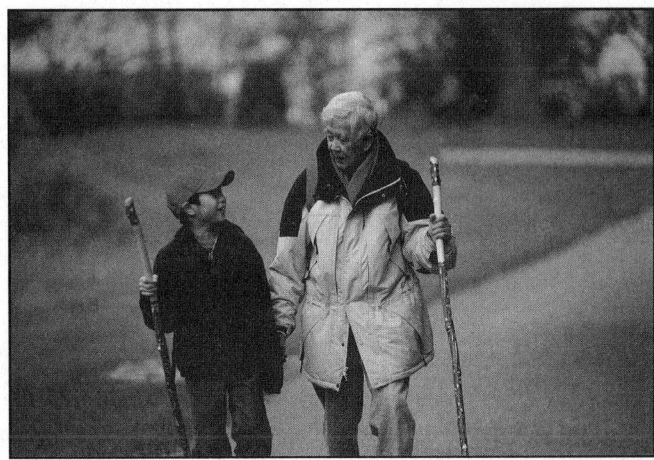

however, by Laura Bohannan's attempt to convey the "true" meaning of Shakespeare's *Hamlet* to the West African Tiv (see "Shakespeare in the Bush"). Much of her task was devoted to finding the most appropriate words in the Tiv language to convey her Western thoughts. At least part of her failure was due to the fact that some of the words just don't exist in the native language, and her inventions were unacceptable to the Tiv.

In a somewhat different manner, both Donna Jo Napoli in "Whose Speech Is Better?" and Deborah Tannen, in "I Can't Even Open My Mouth," point out that there are subtleties to language that cannot be found in a dictionary and whose meaning can only be interpreted in the context of the social situation. In fact, Robert MacNeil shows in "Do You Speak American?" that linguistic diversity within the United States is alive and well and, in spite of the homogenizing effects of the mass media, is actually on the increase. Even when it comes to swear words, which are obviously not the subject of formal instruction in any culture, humans are incorrigibly inventive (see "Expletive Deleted").

Finally, it is the richness and variety of expressions in the languages of the world that cause us to lament the passing of so many of them (see "At a Loss for Words" by Sarah Grey Thomason).

In summary, the articles in this unit show how symbolic confusion may occur between individuals or groups; they illustrate the beauty and wonder inherent in this uniquely human form of communication we call "language;" and they demonstrate the tremendous potential of recent research to enhance effective communication among all of us.

Whose Speech Is Better?

Donna Jo Napoli

Not all speakers of a given language speak the same way. You've noticed speech variations on television. Maybe you've seen the movie *My Fair Lady,* in which Henry Higgins believes that the Queen's English is the superior language of England (and, perhaps, of the world). So the question arises, whose speech is better? And this question is subsumed under the larger question of whether any language is intrinsically superior to another.

Before facing this issue, though, we need to face another matter. Consider these utterances:

Would you mind if I borrowed that cushion for a few moments?

Could I have that pillow for a sec?

Give me that, would you?

All of these utterances could be used to request a pillow.

Which one(s) would you use in addressing a stranger? If you use the first one, perhaps you sense that the stranger is quite different from you (such as a much older person or a person with more stature or authority). Perhaps you're trying to show that you're polite or refined or not a threat. Pay attention to the use of the word "cushion" instead of "pillow." Pillows often belong behind our heads, typically in bed. If you wanted to avoid any hint of intimacy, you might choose to use the word "cushion" for what is clearly a pillow.

Consider the third sentence. It's harder for some people to imagine using this one with a stranger. When I help to renovate urban housing for the poor with a group called Chester Community Improvement Project and I am pounding in nails next to some guy and sweat is dripping off both our brows, I have no hesitation in using this style sentence. With the informality of such a sentence, I'm implying, or perhaps trying to bring about, a sense of comradery.

Of course, it's easy to imagine a scene in which you could use the second sentence with a stranger.

Which one(s) would you use in addressing someone you know well? Again, it could be all three. But now if you use the first one, you might be insulting the addressee. It's not hard to think of a scenario in which this sentence carries a nasty tone rather than a polite one. And you can describe scenarios for the second and third sentences easily.

The point is that we command different registers of language. We can use talk that is fancy or ordinary or extremely informal, and we can choose which register to use in which situations to get the desired effect. So we have lots of variation in o speech in the ways we phrase things (syntax) and the w use (lexicon vocabulary).

Other variation in an individual's speech involves rules (phonology). Say the third sentence aloud severa playing with different ways of saying it. Contrast "gi to "gimme" and "would you" to "wudja." When we say in a sequence, sometimes we contract them, but even word can be said in multiple ways. Say the word "interes several sentences, imagining scenarios that differ in fo Probably your normal (or least marked) pronunciation h syllables: "in-tres-ting." But maybe it has four, and if they are probably "in-er-es-ting."

The pronunciation that is closest to the spelling ("in ting") is more formal and, as a result, is sometimes u humor (as in "very in-ter-es-ting," with a noticeably flair to the pronunciation of "very" or with a drawn-ou "very").

So you have plenty of variation in your own speech, ter who you are, and the more different speech comm you belong to, the more variation you will have. With my er's relatives, I will say, for example, "I hate lobsters any whereas with other people I'm more likely to say, "I ha sters these days." This particular use of "anymore" is co to people from certain geographical areas (the North and Midland, meaning the area from Philadelphia westward t southern Pennsylvania, northern West Virginia, Ohio, I and Illinois to the Mississippi River) but not to peopl other places, who may not even understand what I mea my sister, I used to say, "Ain't nobody gonna tell me do," but I'd never say that to my mother or to other people I was trying to make a sociolinguistic point. This kind signaled for us a comradery outside of the socioeconomi my mother aspired to. In a speech to a convention of lib recently, I said, "That had to change, for I, like you, do n a charmed life," but I'd probably never say that in conve to anyone—it's speech talk. Also, think about the langua use in e-mail and contrast it to your job-related writin example.

Although we cannot explicitly state the rules of o guage, we do choose to use different rules in different co We happily exploit variation, which we encounter in range, from simple differences in pronunciation and voca ɔre marked differences that involve phrasing and sentence ture. When the differences are greater and more numer- we tend to talk of dialects rather than just variations. Thus ınguages of upper class and lower class Bostonians would ably be called variations of American English, whereas the ıages of upper class and lower class Londoners (Queen's ish versus Cockney) would probably be called dialects ritish English. When the dialects are so different as to be ally incomprehensible and/or when they gain a cultural or ical status, we tend to talk of separate languages (such as ch versus Spanish).

here's one more point I want to make before we return to riginal question. I often ask classes to play the game of tel- ne in the following way. We line up twenty-one chairs, and nteers sit on them. Then I whisper in the middle person's erhaps something very simple, such as "Come with me to tore." The middle person then whispers the phrase into the of people on both sides, and the whisper chain goes on to end of the line. Finally, the first and twenty-first persons loud what they heard.

ext we do the same experiment but this time with a sen- that's a little more tricky, perhaps something such as "Why se white shoes for winter sports?" Then we do the experi- with a sentence in a language that the first whisperer (who en not me at this point) speaks reasonably well and might be iar to some of the twenty-one people in the chairs—perhaps thing such as *La lune, c'est magnifique* (which in French s "the moon is wonderful"). Finally, we do the experiment a sentence whispered initially by a native speaker of a lan- e that none of the twenty-one people speak.

pically, the first and twenty-first persons do not come up the same results. Furthermore, the distance between them s greater with each successive experiment.

rt of the problem is in the listening. We don't all hear s the same way. When we haven't heard something clearly, k people to repeat what they said. But sometimes we don't e we haven't heard something clearly, until our inappro- response is corrected. At times the other person doesn't ct us and the miscommunication remains, leading to vari- ther difficulties.

rt of the problem in the experiment is in the repeating. may say, "My economics class is a bore," and you begin econd word with the syllable "eek." I might repeat the nce but use my pronunciation of the second word, which d begin with "ek." If you speak French well, you might say nifique" quite differently from me. In high school or col- language classes, the teacher drilled the pronunciation of n words over and over—but some people never mimicked r satisfaction. A linguist told me a story about a little girl introduced herself as "Litha." The man she was introducing lf to said, "Litha?" The child said, "No, Litha." The man "Litha?" The child said, "No, no. Litha. Li-tha." The man "Lisa?" The child smiled and said, "Right." Repetitions are xact and lead to change.

nperfections in hearing and repeating are two of the rea- that language must change over time. When the Romans marched into Gaul and into the Iberian peninsula and northeastward into what is now Romania, they brought large populations who stayed and spoke a form of street Latin. But over time, the street Latin in Gaul developed into French; that in the Iberian Peninsula developed into Portuguese along the west and Spanish along the east and central portions; that in Romania developed into Romanian. Moreover, the street Latin spoken in the original community on the Italian peninsula changed as well, developing into Italian.

Other factors (besides our imperfections in hearing and in repeating sounds) can influence the speed with which language changes and the ways in which it changes—but the fact is that living languages necessarily change. They always have and they always will.

Many political groups have tried to control language change. During the French Revolution, a controlling faction decided that a standard language would pave the way for unity. Parish priests, who were ordered to survey spoken language, found that many dialects were spoken in different geographic areas, and many of them were quite distinct from the dialect of Paris. Primary schools in every region of France were established with teachers proficient in the Parisian dialect. The effect of this educational reform was not significant until 1881, when state education became free and mandatory, and the standard dialect (that is, Parisian) took hold more firmly. Still, the geographic dialects continued, though weakened, and most important, the standard kept changing. Standard French today is different from the Parisian dialect of 1790. In addition, new varieties of French have formed, as new subcultures have appeared. Social dialects persist and/or arise even when geographic dialects are squelched. Change is the rule in language, so variation will always be with us.

Now we can ask whose speech is better. This is a serious question because our attitudes about language affect how we treat speakers in personal, as well as in business and professional, situations. In what follows I will use the term "standard American English" (a term riddled with problems, which will become more and more apparent as you read)—the variety that we hear in news reports on television and radio. It doesn't seem to be strongly associated with any particular area of the country, although those who aren't from the Midwest often call it midwestern. This variety is also more frequently associated with the middle class than with the lower class, and it is more frequently associated with whites than with other races.

A few years ago a white student from Atlanta, Georgia, recorded herself reading a passage of James Joyce both in standard American English pronunciation and in her Atlanta pronunciation. She then asked strangers (adults of varying ages who lived in the town of Swarthmore, Pennsylvania) to listen to the two readings and answer a set of questions she had prepared. She did not tell the strangers that the recordings were made by a single person (nor that they were made by her). Without exception, the strangers judged the person who read the passage with standard English pronunciation as smarter and better educated, and most of them judged the person who read the passage with Atlanta pronunciation as nicer and more laid-back. This was just a small, informal study, but its findings are consistent with those of larger studies.

Studies have shown that prejudice against certain varieties of speech can lead to discriminatory practices. For example, Professor John Baugh of Stanford University directed a study of housing in which he used different English pronunciations when telephoning people who had advertised apartments for rent. In one call he would use standard American pronunciation; in another, African-American; in another, Latino. (He is African American, but he grew up in the middle class in Los Angeles with many Latino friends. He can sound white, African American, or Latino, at will.) He said exactly the same words in every call, and he controlled for the order in which he made the calls (i.e., sometimes the Latino pronunciation would be used first, sometimes the African-American, and sometimes the standard). He asked if the apartments were still available. More were available when he used the standard pronunciation. Thus it is essential that we examine carefully the question of "better" with regard to language variety.

When I knock on a door and my friend inside says, "Who's there?" I'm likely to answer, "It's me," but I don't say, "It's I" (or, even more unlikely for me, "It is I"). Do you? If you do, do you say that naturally, that is, not self-consciously? Or do you say it because you've been taught that that's the correct thing to say? If you do it naturally, your speech contains an archaism—a little fossil from the past. We all have little fossils. I say, "I'm different from you." Most people today would say, "I'm different than you." My use of "from" after "different" was typical in earlier generations, but it's not typical today. Some of us hold onto archaisms longer than others, and even the most linguistically innovative of us probably have some. So don't be embarrassed by your fossils: They're a fact of language.

But if you say "It's I" self-consciously because you've been taught that that's correct, what does "correct" mean in this situation? If that's what most people used to say but is not what most people say today, you're saying it's correct either because you revere the past (which many of us do) or because you believe that there's a rule of language that's being obeyed by "It's I" and being broken by "It's me."

I'm going to push the analysis of just this one contrast—"It's I" versus "It's me"—quite a distance because I believe that many relevant issues about how people view language will come out of the discussion. Consider the former reason for preferring "It's I," that of revering the past. Many people have this reason for using archaic speech patterns and for preferring that others use them. For some reason, language is treated in a unique way here. We certainly don't hold up the past as superior in other areas, for example, mathematics or physics. So why do some of us feel that changes in language are evidence of decay?

If it were true that the older way of saying something were better simply because it's older, your grandparents spoke better than your parents and your great-grandparents spoke better than your grandparents and so on. Did Chaucer speak a form of English superior to that spoken by Shakespeare? Shall we go further back than Chaucer for our model? There is no natural stopping point. We can go all the way to prehistoric times if we use "older" as the only standard for "better."

The latter reason—believing that "It's I" obeys a rule "It's me" breaks—is more defensible, if it is indeed Defenders of the "It's I" school of speech point out that the verb "be" the elements on both sides of it are grammati equivalent—so they should naturally have the same case.

I've used a linguistic term here: "case." To understand review it), look at these Hungarian sentences:

Megnézhetem a szobát?

Van rádió a szobában?

Hol a szoba?

May I see the room?

Is there a radio in the room?

Where's the room?

I have translated the sentences in a natural way rather word by word. Can you pick out the word in each sen that means "room"? I hope you chose *szobát, szobában, szoba.* These three forms can be thought of as variants o same word. The difference in form is called case marking. books on Hungarian typically claim that a form like *szo* used when the word is the subject of the sentence, a form *szobát* when the word is the direct object, and a form *szobában* when the word conveys a certain kind of loc (comparable to the object of the preposition "in" in Eng So a word can have various forms—various cases—base how it is used in the sentence.

English does not have different case forms for nouns the exception of genitive nouns, such as "boy's" in "the book"). So in the English translations of the Hungarian tences above, the word "room" was invariable. How English does have different case forms for pronouns:

I like tennis.

That tennis racket is mine.

Everyone likes me.

These three forms indicate the first-person singular "mine," and "me." They distinguish subjects ("I") from tives ("mine") from everything else ("me").

Now let's return to "It's I." Must elements on either si "be" be equivalent? In the following three sentences, diff syntactic categories are on either side of "be" (here "NP" s for "noun phrase"):

Bill is tall

Bill is off his rocker.

Bill is to die for.

NP "be" AP

NP "be" PP

NP "be" VP

"Tall" is an adjective (here, an adjective phrase, AP). "C a preposition, and it's part of the prepositional phrase (PP his rocker." "To die for" is a verb phrase (VP). Thus the tw ments that flank "be" do not have to be equivalent in cate ill, in the sentence "It's I," the elements that flank "be" oth pronouns ("It" and "I"), so maybe these elements are valent in this sentence. Let's test that claim by looking at ment. Verbs agree with their subject in English, whether subject precedes or follows them:

hn's nice.

John nice?

ut "be" in our focus sentence agrees with the NP to its left, its right:

's I.

t am I.

o one would say "It am I." Therefore, the NP to the right e" is not the subject of the sentence, which means that the flanking "be" are not equivalent—"It" is the subject, but not.

erhaps you think that the equivalency that matters here has with meaning, not with syntax. Let's pursue that: Do "It" I" have equivalent meaning in "It's I"? Notice that you can say:

t's you."

fact, the slot after "It's" can be filled by several different ouns. "It" in these sentences is not meaningful; it is simply ce holder, just as in sentences about time and weather:

's four o'clock.

's hailing.

ut "I" is meaningful because it refers to a person (the ker). Therefore, "It" and "I" are not equivalent in meaning sentence "It's I."

sum, it's not clear that the elements on either side of "be" sentence "It's I" are equivalent in any linguistic way. We conclude something even stronger. We noted that "It" in sentences is the subject and that the pronoun following a of "be" is not the subject. But the pronoun following "be" o not a genitive. Given the pronoun case system of English ssed above, we expect the pronoun to take the third form "elsewhere" form), which is "me," not "I." In other words, ase system would lead us to claim that "It's me" is thc matical sentence.

m not saying "It's I" is ungrammatical. I want to show that ssue may not be as clean-cut as you might have thought. d, the conclusion I come to is that more than one case m is at play here. Those who say "It's me" are employing ar case rules. But those who say "It's I" have a special rule for certain sentences that contain "be." The impor-oint is that both sets of speakers have rules that determine they say. Their speech is systematic; they are not speaking mly.

at is the key issue of this whole chapter. When we consider tion in language, we must give up the idea of errors and t the idea of patterns. Some people produce one pattern use they are following one set of rules; other people pro- a different pattern because they are following a different set of rules. (For several different types of language variations in English, visit the websites of the West Virginia Dialect Project: http://www.as.wvu.edu/dialect.) From a linguistic perspective, asking whose speech is better would amount to asking whose system is better. But what standards do we have for evaluating systems? What standards do you, as a speaker of the language, employ when you judge between varieties of speech? To answer that question, consider variation in your own speech. Do you consider some varieties better than others? And which ones? If you're like most people, you consider formal or polite speech to be better. But that standard concerns behavior in society—behavior that may reveal or perhaps even determine one's position. We tend to think that the speech of those who hold cultural, economic, or other social power is better, but this has little to do with linguistic structure. Now ask yourself what standards you are using to judge the speech of others.

Such questions often boil down to your politics (who do you esteem?) or to your experience (what are you familiar with?) but not to your grammatical rules. Consider the common claim that some varieties of speech are lazy. Try to find a recording of English speech that you consider lazy. Now mimic it. Some people are good at mimicking the speech of others, but accurately mimicking the speech of anyone else (anyone at all) takes a good ear, good control over the parts of your body that produce speech, and mostly a grasp of the sound rules that are being used. So the speech you thought was lazy wasn't lazy at all. Rather, different rules are being employed in different varieties of speech. What makes each variety distinct from others is its inventory of rules.

Consider learning a foreign language. People who feel confident about their ability to speak and to understand a foreign language in a classroom often visit a place where that language is spoken, only to find that no one is speaking the classroom variety. One of the big differences is usually speed: Ordinary speech can be quite rapid. Again, some claim that fast speech is sloppy, but fast speech is notoriously hard to mimic. It is typically packed with sound rules, so it takes more experience with the language to master all the rules and to be able to produce fast speech.

Among American speakers a common misconception is that British speech is superior to American speech. Part of this belief follows from reverence of the past, already discussed. Part of it follows from the misperception that American upper class speech is closer to British speech—so British speech is associated with high society and with politeness. In fact, the speech of the British changed over time, just as the speech of the American colonialists changed over time. Therefore, modern British speech is not, in general, closer to older forms of English than American speech is. Pockets of conservative varieties of English occur both in the British Isles and in the United States, but most varieties on either side of the Atlantic Ocean have changed considerably. Also, British society is stratified, just as American society is, and not all British speech is either upper class or polite.

Linguists claim that all varieties of a language—all dialects and all languages, for that matter—are equal linguistic citizens. Linguists have recognized that all languages are systematic, obeying certain universal principles regarding the organization and interaction of sounds, the ways we build words and phrases and sentences, and how we code meaning. However, this doesn't mean that all language is esthetically equal. I can recognize a beautiful line in a poem or a story, as I'm sure you can (though we might not agree). But that beautiful line might be in archaic English, formal contemporary English, ordinary contemporary English, very informal contemporary English, African-American Atlanta English, Italian-American Yonkers English, Philadelphia gay English, Chinese-American Seattle English, or so many others. Within our different varieties of speech, we can speak in ways that affect people's hearts or resonate in their minds, or we can speak in ways that are unremarkable. These are personal (esthetic or political) choices.

Some possible effects of the goal of the English only movement (EOM) of minimizing certain language variations in the United States [exist]. But even if English were declared the official language of the United States, variation would not be wiped out. What would be threatened is the richness of the range of variation most speakers are exposed to. Once that exposure is lost, Americans might start thinking that English is a superior language simply because they would no longer hear other languages being spoken by people they know personally and respect. They might become severely provincial in their linguistic attitudes, and given the necessity of global respect these days, such provincialism could be dangerous.

The fact that variation in language is both unavoidable and sometimes the result of esthetic and political choices does not mean that educational institutions should not insist that children master whatever variety of language has been deemed the standard—just for purely practical reasons. There's little doubt that linguistic prejudice is a reality. The adult who cannot speak and write the standard variety may encounter a range of difficulties, from finding suitable employment to achieving social advancement.

At the same time, all of us—and educational institutions, in particular—should respect all varieties of language and show that respect in relevant ways. Look at one notorious controversy: In 1996 the school board in Oakland, California, declared Ebonics to be the official language of the district's African-American students. Given funding regulations for bilingual education in that time and place, this decision had the effect of allowing the school district to use funds set aside for bilingual education to teach their African-American children in Ebonics, as well as in the standard language.

The debate was particularly hot, I believe, because of the sociological issues involved. Many people thought that Ebonics should be kept out of the classroom purely because the dialect was associated with race. Some of these people were African Americans who did not want their children to be disadvantaged by linguistic prejudice; they were afraid that teaching in Ebonics would exaggerate racial linguistic prejudice rather than redress it. Many good books written about the Ebonics controversy for the general public look at the issue from a variety of perspectives (see the suggested readings). But from a linguistic perspective, the issue is more a question of bilingual (or bidialectal) education than anything else.

In sum, variation in language is something we all partic in, and, as a linguist and a writer, I believe it's somethin should revel in. Language is not a monolith, nor can it be should it be, given the complexity of culture and the fac language is the fabric of culture. Some of us are more elo than others, and all of us have moments of greater or lesse quence. But that range in eloquence is found in every lang every dialect, and every variety of speech.

Further Reading on Variation

Andersson, L. G., and P. Trudgill. 1990. *Bad language.* Cambrid Blackwell.

Baron, D. 1994. *Guide to home language repair.* Champaign, Ill. National Council of Teachers of English.

Baugh, J. 1999. *Out of the mouths of slaves.* Austin: University c Texas Press.

Biber, D., and E. Finegan. 1997. *Sociolinguistic perspectives on register.* Oxford: Oxford University Press.

Cameron, D. 1995. *Verbal hygiene.* London: Routledge.

Carver, C. 1989. *American regional dialects: A word geography.* Arbor: University of Michigan Press.

Coulmas, F. 1998. *Handbook of sociolinguistics.* Cambridge: Blackwell.

Fasold, R. 1984. *The sociolinguistics of society.* New York: Blackwell.

Finegan, E. 1980. *Attitudes toward language usage.* New York: Teachers College Press.

Fishman, J. 1968. *Readings in the sociology of language.* Paris: Mouton.

Herman, L. H., and M. S. Herman. 1947. *Manual of American dialects for radio, stage, screen, and television.* New York: Davis.

Hock, H., and B. Joseph. 1996. *An introduction to historical anc comparative linguistics.* Berlin: Mouton de Gruyter.

Labov, W. 1972. *The logic of nonstandard English in language c social context: Selected readings.* Compiled by Pier Paolo Giglioli. Baltimore Md.: Penguin.

Labov, W. 1972. *Sociolinguistic patterns.* Philadelphia: Universi Pennsylvania Press.

LeClerc, F., Schmitt, B. H., and Dube, L. 1994, May. Foreign branding and its effects on product perceptions and attitude *Journal of Marketing Research,* 31: 263–270.

Lippi-Green, R. 1997. *English with an accent.* New York: Routl

McCrum, R., W. Cran, and R. MacNeil. 1986. *The story of Engl* New York: Viking Penguin.

Millward, C. M. 1989. *A biography of the English language.* Or Fla.: Holt, Rinehart and Winston.

Milroy, J., and L. Milroy. 1991. *Authority in language,* 2nd ed. London: Routledge.

Moss, B., and K. Walters. 1993. Rethinking diversity: Axes of difference in the writing classroom. In L. Odell, ed., *Theor practice in the teaching of writing: Rethinking the disciplir* Carbondale: Southern Illinois University Press.

Peyton, J., S. McGinnis, and D. Ranard, eds. 2001. *Heritage languages in America: Preserving a national resource* (fro Delta Systems, phone 800–323–8270), Arlington, Va.

Romaine, S. 1994. *Language in society: An introduction to sociolinguistics.* Oxford: Oxford University Press.

er, K., and H. Giles, eds. 1979. *Social markers in speech.* New York: Cambridge University Press.

nan, C. R., G. R. Tucker, and W. Lambert. 1972. The effects of speech style and other attributes on teachers' attitudes toward pupils. *Language and Society,* 1: 131–42.

R. L. 1994. *Language change.* London: Routledge.

eich, U. [1953] 1968. *Languages in contact.* The Hague: Mouton.

am, W. 1991. *Dialects and American English.* Englewood Cliffs, N.J.: Prentice Hall.

am, W., and N. Schilling-Estes. 1998. *American English—ialects and variation.* Oxford: Blackwell.

rther Reading on Ebonics

, C. 1994. Enhancing the delivery of services to black special education students from non-standard English backgrounds. Final Report. University of Maryland, Institute for the Study of Exceptional Children and Youth. (Available through ERIC Document Reproduction Service. Document No. ED 370 377.)

, C., D. Christian, and O. Taylor. 1999. *Making the connection: Language and academic achievement among African American students.* Washington, D.C. and McHenry, Ill.: Center for Applied Linguistics and Delta Systems.

, C., W. Wolfram, and J. Detwyler. 1993. Language differences: A new approach for special educators. *Teaching Exceptional Children,* 26, no. (1): 44–47.

, C., W. Wolfram, J. Detwyler, and B. Harry. 1993. Confronting dialect minority issues in special education: Reactive and proactive perspectives. In *Proceedings of the Third National Research Symposium on Limited English Proficient Student Issues: Focus on Middle and High School Issues,* 2: 737–62. U.S. Department of Education, Office of Bilingual Education and Minority Languages Affairs. (Available through ERIC Document Reproduction Service. Document No. ED 356 673.)

, J. C., and R. W. Shuy, eds. 1969. Teaching black children to read. Available as reprints from the University of Michigan, Ann Arbor (313-761-4700).

, J. 2000. *Beyond Ebonics.* New York: Oxford University Press.

Christian, D. 1997. Vernacular dialects and standard American English in the classroom. ERIC Minibib. Washington, D.C.: ERIC Clearinghouse on Languages and Linguistics. (This minibibliography cites seven journal articles and eight documents related to dialect usage in the classroom. The documents can be accessed on microfiche at any institution with the ERIC collection, or they can be ordered directly from EDRS.)

Dillard, J. L. 1972. *Black English: Its history and use in the U.S.* New York: Random House.

Fasold, R. W. 1972. Tense marking in black English: A linguistic and social analysis. Available as reprints from the University of Michigan, Ann Arbor (313-761-4700).

Fasold, R. W., and R. W. Shuy, eds. 1970. *Teaching standard English in the inner city.* Washington, D.C.: Center for Applied Linguistics.

Wiley, T. G. 1996. The case of African American language. In *Literacy and language diversity in the United States,* pp. 125–32. Washington, D. C.: Center for Applied Linguistics and Delta Systems.

Wolfram, W. 1969. A sociolinguistic description of Detroit Negro speech. Available as reprints from the University of Michigan, Ann Arbor (313-761-4700).

Wolfram, W. 1990, February. Incorporating dialect study into the language arts class. *ERIC Digest.* Available from the ERIC Clearinghouse on Languages and Linguistics, Center for Applied Linguistics, 4646 40th Street NW, Washington, D.C. 20016-1859, (202-362-0700).

Wolfram, W. 1994. Bidialectal literacy in the United States. In D. Spencer, ed., *Adult biliteracy in the United States,* pp. 71–88. Washington, D.C.: Center for Applied Linguistics and Delta Systems.

Wolfram, W., and C. Adger. 1993. *Handbook on language differences and speech and language pathology: Baltimore City public schools.* Washington, D.C.: Center for Applied Linguistics.

Wolfram, W., C. Adger, and D. Christian. 1999. Dialects in schools and communities. Mahwah, N.J.: Erlbaum.

Wolfram, W., and N. Clarke, eds. 1971. *Black-white speech relationships.* Washington, D.C.: Center for Applied Linguistics.

Lost for Words

Kate Douglas

They've no myths, no numbers or colours and few words for past or present. No wonder the Pirahã people defy our most cherished ideas about language.

"How was your world created?" asks the young anthropologist in Portuguese. He awaits the translation into Pirahã. "The world is created," replies one of the assembled men in his own language. "Tell me how your god made all this." the anthropologist presses on. "All things are made," comes the answer. The interview lurches on for a few more minutes, until suddenly, the question-and-answer session is overtaken by a deluge of excited banter as the assembled Pirahã vie to be heard.

"I've cracked it," says the anthropologist as he hands his tape recording to Dan Everett a few weeks later. "Here is the Pirahã creation myth." Everett is dubious. In the past three decades, the linguist from the University of Manchester, UK, has spent a total of seven years living with the Pirahã in the Amazon rainforest and is one of just three outsiders, along with his ex-wife and a missionary who spent time with them in the 1960s and 1970s, who is fluent in their language. He has long maintained that they are among the few people on Earth who have not devised a story to explain their existence. Others, including this particular anthropologist, find the idea difficult to accept.

Everett listens to the tape. After the short, stilted exchange, he hears some bright spark in the crowd point out that this guy asking them odd questions doesn't know their language, so he will need to get help from Everett to translate the tapes. "Hello, Dan!" comes a chorus of Pirahã voices. "How are you?" "When will we see you?" "When you come, bring us some matches." "And bananas." "And whisky." And so on. Nice try, but no creation myth here.

The lack of mythology is just one small aspect of why the Pirahã are so fascinating to anthropologists. According to Everett, they also have virtually no notion of time, and seem to live entirely in the moment. There is no creative storytelling and no oral history beyond two generations. They have no art except the crude line drawings they use to depict figures from their spirit world.

They are among the least materialistic people in the world, with very few possessions and little desire to attain more. They also have the simplest kinship system yet recorded: the language only has specific terms for "son" and "daughter." Past that, they talk in general terms about older and younger generations.

Pirahã culture is remarkably resistant to change. These ple continue to be monolingual and maintain their tradi way of life despite more than 200 years of regular contac outsiders.

Until recently, the Pirahã were best known among lin because of debates over whether their language has any for colours, and the fact that it has no number terms. though, they have hit the scientific big time with the pu tion last year of a controversial paper by Everett. In it he issue with some of the most influential ideas in lingu In particular, he argues that the Pirahã's peculiar lan is shaped not by some innate language instinct, as man guists attest, but by their extraordinary culture. What's he says that Pirahã language and culture hold fundan lessons in what it means to be human (Current Anthrop vol 46, p 621).

There are around 350 Pirahã people, living along a kilometre stretch of the Maici river in the south-west of B Amazonas state. Their lifestyle has much in common with indigenous Amazonian hunter-gatherers, but what really out the Pirahã is their attitude to life. They are very laid- accepting things as they are, not fretting about the futur taking great pleasure in life. Above all, these are a peopl live for the moment.

For the Pirahã this is not simply an "alternative" philos it is deeply ingrained in their culture, and—Everett argue their language. "They confine their talk to subjects th within their own immediate experience," he says. And this and-now approach is reflected in their vocabulary and gra which largely inhibits talk of abstract concepts and gene tions (see "Sing It to Me").

This immediate and literal way of seeing the world fit the Pirahã's apparent lack of a creation myth, but it see odds with one of the most important aspects of their eve life. They believe in an elaborate spirit world, which tak form of something like parallel universes, with evil spirits iting their own realms above and below the Earth. It may suspiciously mystical for a culture supposed to lack myth but Everett notes that the Pirahã's relationship with their world is remarkably practical. They claim to have direct e ence of some of the evil spirits—a notion made only too him during his early days in the Amazon when he was a one night and asked to ward off an evil spirit nearby. Ma lly into the jungle, he soon heard the low growl of the ": a prowling panther.

Pirahã also use spirits to make sense of the bad things appen to them. If someone inexplicably falls ill, for exam-ey might conclude that he has stepped on a "bad" leaf orted into the jungle by an evil spirit from its own world. rsely, if a wound heals, they will say that the damaged as been exchanged with a spirit for a good one. "You get icture of lots of mutilated spirits wandering around out ' says Everett.

en there is the counting—or lack of it. Back in 1980, Everett was living in the Amazon with his then wife and hree children, the Pirahã came asking for evening classes. said they wanted to learn to count so that they would know er they were being cheated by the outsiders who came to villages by riverboat to trade for Brazil nuts and other for-oduce. Each evening for eight months, enthusiastic men omen sat down with Everett's entire family to learn, in uese, the rudiments of numeracy. Then one day they sud-decided to abandon the classes, saying that they could master numbers—in fact, in all that time, not one of them arned to count to 10 or even to add 1 and 1.

ading lessons, which took place at around the same time, with similar results. After much tuition the villagers suc-d in reading together, and out loud, the word bigí, which ground or sky in Pirahã. "They immediately all laughed," tt recalls. "I asked what was so funny. They answered that hey had just said sounded like their word for 'sky'. I said ndeed it did because it was their word. They reacted by that if that is what we were trying to teach them, they d us to stop: 'we don't write our language'." Bemused, tt asked why they had come. "Their motivation turned out hat it was fun to be together and I made popcorn."

me linguists have interpreted the Pirahã people's inability n to count as support for the idea that the language we shapes the way we think. This was proposed in the 1930s njamin Whorf when he was at Yale University, and has e accepted by most linguists in recent years. Since the language has no number words, they argue, its speakers able to learn how to count in another language.

't Count, Won't Count

tt sees things differently. In his paper in Current Anthropol-e argues that it is their culture, not their language that con-the Pirahã's ability to count. The language, says Everett, words for numbers—and indeed any abstract concept that es quantification, such as colour and time, because of the e's emphasis on referring only to immediate, personal ences. It isn't that Pirahã are incapable of thinking in a at allows counting; rather, argues Everett, they don't like coerced or to be told that there is only one correct way to ngs. For example, they are perfectly capable of drawing ght line when they want to make a spirit stick figure, but ould not learn to write the number 1 consistently. What's although they clearly like the camaraderie of lessons, they do not value western knowledge, and actively oppose its introduction to their lives. So while Whorfians say that language shapes cognition, Everett believes that Pirahã culture shapes their language and the way they think.

If that weren't enough, Everett also argues that the Pirahã language is the final nail in the coffin for Noam Chomsky's hugely influential theory of universal grammar. Although this has been modified considerably since its origins in the 1960s, most linguists still hold to its central idea, which is that the human mind has evolved an innate capacity for language and that all languages share certain universal forms that are constrained by the way that we think.

One important example of this universal structure is known as embedding—the stacking of clauses within a single sentence. In English we can say "I think [clause 1] John wants to leave [clause 2]". In Pirahã, however, there is no embedding and every sentence refers to a single event. So the literal translation of this sentence would split it into two separate parts: "My saying [Pirahã has no word for 'think']. John intend-leaves." Chomsky and others argue that embedding in language is what allows "recursion" in thought—the ability to build complex ideas by using some thoughts as subparts of others. Yet Everett suspects

Sing It to Me

In theory, Pirahã is a simple language. With only seven consonants and three vowels, the Pirahã women's dialect has the smallest number of speech sounds, or "phonemic inventory", of any language. The men, who speak a slightly different dialect, use an eighth consonant, making their inventory the next smallest—tied with Hawaiian and Rotokas, which is spoken in Papua New Guinea. Each sentence refers to just one event, and the language has the simplest known set of pronouns, with no plurals, not even a distinction between "I" and "we".

Pirahã lacks words for abstract concepts such as numbers and colours, so that speakers cannot talk about things that are beyond their immediate experience. The language lacks quantification terms such as "all", "each", "every", "most", and "some". And there is no perfect tense—no way of saying "I have eaten", for example.

Despite the seeming simplicity of Pirahã, it is fiendishly difficult to learn. The patterns of stress and intonation are highly complex, allowing speakers to express the same syllable in five different ways. Many words have a variety of meanings depending on the inflection—which can be extremely difficult for an outsider to tune in to. Linguist Dan Everett, who has spent years learning the language, also describes how the Pirahã people convert everyday speech into song, using a characteristic exaggeration of the tones in their language, together with a transformation of some of the consonant sounds into others. "The Pirahã people communicate almost as much by singing, whistling, and humming as they do using consonants and vowels," he notes.

that the Pirahã are capable of recursion even though they lack embedding—an idea that he and others will test later this year.

More fundamentally, Everett says, Pirahã challenges Chomskian theory at its roots. "Hypotheses such as universal grammar are inadequate to account for the Pirahã facts," he says in his Current Anthropology paper, "because they assume that language evolution has ceased to be shaped by the social life of the species." And that isn't the case with Pirahã. Their grammar, he argues, does not come exclusively from any universal mental templates—if such templates exist at all. Rather, they must learn their culture to learn their grammar. He himself only became fluent in Pirahã after years of living alongside them.

Perhaps unsurprisingly, Everett has his detractors. Linguist Brent Berlin from the University of Georgia in Athens calls it an "overstatement" to describe Pirahã as the only language without numbers. Others question the idea that this culture has no words for colours, pointing out that there are expressions such as "blood-like". Stephen Levinson from the Max Planck Institute for Psycholinguistics in Nijmegen, the Netherlands, complains that Everett's central proposition that "Pirahã live in the present" is too vague a notion upon which to hang all these ideas about their culture and language. He also argues that Everett has misinterpreted the Whorfian idea that language shapes thought, by failing to recognise that language is a part of culture.

There is some support for Everett's stance against Chomsky, however. Michael Tomasello from the Max Planck Institute of Evolutionary Anthropology in Leipzig, Germany, says: "Universal grammar was a good try, and it really was not so implausi the time it was proposed, but since then we have learnec about many different languages, and they simply do not f universal cookie cutter." Even experts who support Wh ideas are sympathetic to Everett's central message, that we understand language and culture in isolation from one ano

While debate continues, Everett has already succeec one goal—of drawing attention to the Pirahã. Bright youn students are queuing up to do fieldwork with him in Brazi year, some of the world's top linguists will also visit the to investigate, among other things, the connections be speech and song and between language and cognition. are keen to disprove Everett's conclusions about the P and he seems ready for a tussle. He argues that his theori testable—but only by someone who can speak Pirahã flu and that will require a big investment of time.

What Everett really fears is that time may be running c the Pirahã. The good news is that their culture has so fa vived outside influences—indeed, their enthusiasm for co relations with outsiders means the group has a healthy g diversity. "You are a member if you speak the language ar the lifestyle," says Everett. Yet despite this, he worries abo ever more intrusive presence of settlers, diseases, alcoh the inexorably changing world. "This way of life work well because things are constant. If major change come strategy will fall apart," he says. "I fear that if it does hap will happen very quickly."

o You Speak American?

'ell, butter my butt and call me a biscuit"; a documentary the English language, as spoken in the U.S., is airing on PBS.

BERT MACNEIL

n Columbus Avenue in New York, a young waitress approaches our table and asks, "How are you guys doin'?" My wife and I are old enough to be her grandparents, but we you guys" to her. Today, in American English, guys can be guys, or grandmothers. Girls call themselves guys, even dudes. For ile, young women scorned the word girls, but that is cool again, ably because African-American women use it and it can be real —even empowering—to whites to borrow black talk, like the cool. It is empowering to gay men to call themselves queer, a hated homophobic term, but now used to satirize the whole ng scene of gender attitudes in the TV reality show, "Queer for the Straight Guy." As society changes, so does language, American society has changed enormously in recent decades. over, when new norms are resented or feared, language often target of that fear or resentment.

ow we use the English language became a hot topic during the s, and it remains so today—a charged ingredient in the culture as intensely studied and disputed as any other part of our soci- That is appropriate because nothing is more central to our iden- nd sense of who we are and where we belong. "Aside from a n's physical appearance, the first thing someone will be judged how he or she talks," maintains linguist Dennis Baron.

any feel that the growing informality of American life, the t from fixed standards, ("the march of casualization," *The New Times* recently called it)—in clothing, manners, sexual mores— lected in our language and is corrupting it. They see schools bout teaching grammar and hear nonstandard forms accepted in lcasting, newspapers, politics, and advertising. They believe the n "Winston tastes good like a cigarette should" is so embedded national psyche that few Americans would now balk at the f "like" (instead of "as") because that usage is fast becoming ew standard. They hate such changes in the language and they ir for our culture.

thers, however, believe language is thriving—as inventive and ous as English was in the time of the Elizabethans—and they merican English as the engine driving what is now a global age.

his deep disagreement is one of the issues explored in a survey ucer William Cran and I recently completed and a three-hour mentary, "Do You Speak American?"

We address the controversies, issues, anxieties, and assumptions swirling around language today—some highly emotional and political. Why are black and white Americans speaking less and less like each other? We explain. Does Hispanic immigration threaten the English language? We do not think so. Is our exposure to national media wiping out regional differences and causing us all to speak the same? We think not. Is the language really in serious decline? Well, we have quite a debate about that.

The people who believe so are known as prescriptivists: those who want us to obey prescribed rules of grammar. They do not mind being called curmudgeons and they alternate between pleasure and despair—pleasure in correcting their fellow citizens: despair that they cannot stop the language from going to hell in our generation.

The Prince of Prescriptivists

One of the leading curmudgeons of our time—he has been called the Prince of Prescriptivists—is John Simon, theater critic for *New York Magazine,* and he comes to do battle in "Do You Speak American?" Simon sees the language today as "unhealthy, poor, sad, depressing, and probably fairly hopeless." In the foreword to a new book, *The Dictionary of Disagreeable English,* he writes: "No damsel was ever in such distress, no drayhorse more flogged, no defenseless child more drunkenly abused than the English language today."

The enemies for Simon are the descriptivists, those content to describe language as it actually is used. They include the editors of great dictionaries who, Simon charges, have grown dangerously permissive, abandoning advice on what is correct and what is not. He calls descriptivist linguists "a curse on their race."

One such individual is Jesse Sheidlower, American editor of the august *Oxford English Dictionary.* Does he believe the language is being ruined by the great informality of American life? "No, it is not being ruined at all," he replies. Sheidlower believes that Simon and other language conservatives actually are complaining that linguists and dictionary writers no longer are focused on the language of the elite. They look at the old days and say, "Well, everything used to be very proper, and now we have all these bad words and people are being careless, and so forth." In fact, he insists people always have spoken that way. "It's just that you didn't hear them because the media would only report on the language of the educated upper middle class," Sheidlower points out. "Nowadays . . . we see the language of other groups, of other social groups, of other income levels, in a way that we never used to.

"Language change happens and there's nothing you can do about it." To which Simon replies, "Maybe change is inevitable—maybe. Maybe dying from cancer is also inevitable, but I don't think we should help it along."

Helping it along, to Simon, would mean surrendering to the word "hopefully," one of his pet peeves. "To say, 'Hopefully it won't rain tomorrow'—who, or what, is filled with hope? Nothing. So you have to say, 'I hope it won't rain tomorrow.' But you can say, 'I enter a room hopefully,' because you are the vessel for that hopefulness."

Sheidlower replies that modern computer databases make it possible to check texts back over the centuries: "We see that 'hopefully' is not in fact very new. . . . It goes back hundreds of years, and it has been very common even in highly educated speech for much of the time."

This battle—the stuff of angry skirmishes in books, magazines, and seminars—is only one part of what makes our language news today. Other findings may surprise many people because they challenge widely held popular conceptions, or misconceptions, about the language.

Our study took the form of a journey starting in the Northeast, down to the mid-Atlantic states, west to the Great Lakes, Midwest, Appalachia, then toward the South, through Louisiana, Texas, and California into the Pacific Northwest. In linguistic terms, we traveled through the main dialect areas of the nation. Professional linguists, students of the science of language, were the key to our understanding of the forces changing the language as rapidly as the society has changed in the past 50 years.

While computers, information technology, globalization, digital communications, and satellites have revolutionized how we work, equally potent revolutions have occurred concerning the home, family structure and marriage, sexual mores, the role of women, race relations, and the rise of teenagers as a major consumer and marketing force. With this has come alterations in our public manners, eating habits, clothing, and tolerance of different lifestyles—all of which have been swept by a tide of informality.

Linguists Spring into Action

Observing how these rapid social changes have altered our language have been the linguists, whose new branch of the social sciences really came into its own in the 1960s, followed more recently by sociolinguistics, the study of how language and society interact. They have produced a body of fascinating research that usually is couched in technical language difficult for non-linguists to understand. Dozens of linguists have lent their skills to help us translate their findings, and marry their scholarship to our sampling of the actual speech of ordinary Americans in all its variety, vitality, and humor, drawn from the widest social spectrum. They include waitresses, cowboys, hip-hop artists, Marine drill sergeants, Border Patrol agents, Mexican immigrants, Cajun musicians, African-American and Hispanic broadcasters, and Silicon Valley techies (who try to make computers talk like real people), as well as writers and editors, teachers and teenagers, surfers and snowboarders, actors and screenwriters, and presidents and politicians.

Did they all sound the same? One of the most common assumptions is that our total immersion in the same mass media is making us all speak in a similar manner. Not true, claim the linguists are not talking more alike, but less.

One of the enduring themes in American life is the pu national against regional interests and regret for local distinc ness erased in the relentless march of uniformity. It surface the song "Little Boxes" by Pete Seeger, about people put little boxes of identical houses made of "ticky tacky" and all come out the same. Today, with more and more national chising of basic elements—food, mobile homes, clothing, hc recreation—the U.S. can seem like one giant theme park lessly reduplicated, the triumph of the cookie cutter culture its distinctive art form, the national TV commercial.

Paradoxically, however, language is one fundamental aspect c cultural identity in which growing homogenization is a myth. W some national trends are apparent, regional speech difference only thrive, in some places they are becoming more distinctive. I differences, pride, and identity with place are asserting thems strongly, perhaps as instinctive resistance to the homogenizing f of globalization. One remarkable example is the speech of u African-Americans, which is diverging from standard mainst English. After decades of progress in civil rights, and the grow a large and successful black middle class, African-American sp in our big cities dramatically is going its own way.

Two linguists, Guy Bailey, provost of the University of Tex San Antonio, and Patricia Cukor-Avila of the University of N Texas at Denton have documented this. For 18 years, they have stu a small community in East Central Texas they named "Springv which appears to live in a time warp from a century ago, wh was the center for local cotton sharecroppers, black and white. remains now but the original general store. During the late 1 the Works Progress Administration recorded the voices of el blacks, some former slaves, some the children of slaves.

One of them, Laura Smalley, was born to a slave mother. Sh nine at the time of Emancipation in 1863. She told how the owner kept them ignorant of Lincoln's Proclamation for six mo "An' I thought ol' master was dead, but he wasn'. . . . He'd bee to the war an' come back. All the niggers gathered aroun' to s master again. You know, an' ol' master didn' tell, you know, the free. . . . They worked there, I think now they say they worked six months after that, six months. And turn them loose on the 1 June. That's why, you know, they celebrate that day. Colored celebrates that day."

Black and White Dialects

Reviewing the speech of Smalley and others, the linguists taken by how similar it was to the speech of rural whites o time and place, but now dissimilar to the speech of blacks t Features characteristic of modern black speech, what linguist African-American vernacular English—such as the invariant as in "they 'be' working," or the deleted copular, leaving o auxiliary verb in "they working"—were absent.

Here are samples of modern speech of African-America large cities:

> "When the baby be sleep, and the othe' kids be at school, a my husband be at work, then . . . I might can finally sit down

> "She told David they Mama had went to Chicago to see h sister and her sister's new baby."

ese examples show the invariant "be," and the construction "had ' Bailey and Cukor-Avila say that these features did not exist in speech before World War II. They conclude that, after the great tion to the North from World War I to the 1970s, blacks were gated in urban ghettoes, had less contact with whites than they places like Springville, and their speech began to develop new es, as all human speech does when people are separated cultur- nd have little communication.

is has serious consequences in efforts to reduce the school ut rate among blacks. Not only white teachers, but many n-American instructors, despise the "street talk" or "slang" y call it, and often treat the children as if they were stupid educable. In 1979, a Federal judge in Detroit ruled that an Arbor, Mich., school, ironically named after Martin Luther Jr., was discriminating against black kids because of their age and ordered the school to remedy it. Yet, the prejudice on elsewhere. In 1997, Oakland schools tried to get black h recognized not as a dialect of English but a separate lan- , Ebonics, to qualify for Federal money to teach English as nd language. That backfired amid furious protests nationally black and white educators.

hat is shocking to linguists is the manner in which newspaper columnists excoriate black English, using such as "gibberish." In the linguistic community, black sh is recognized as having its own internal consistency and natical forms. It certainly is not gibberish (which means hing unintelligible) because it works effectively for commu- on within the urban community.

e of the first to give black English this measure of respect was m Labov of the University of Pennsylvania, who testified at ate hearing during the Ebonics furor in 1997: "This African- ican vernacular English . . . is not a set of slang words, or a m set of grammatical mistakes, but a well-formed set of rules mmar and pronunciation that is capable of conveying com- ogic and reasoning."

linguists, the fault lies not in a particular dialect, but in what des others bring to it. Steve Harvey, an African-American osts the most popular morning radio show in Los Angeles, s: "I speak good enough American. You know, I think there's ons of speaking American. I don't think there's any one set because America's so diverse." He added, "You do have to ingual in this country, which means you can be very adept ng, but you also have to be adept at getting through the job iew."

w, without fanfare, some Los Angeles schools have been try- more sympathetic approach to help minority students become ual—by teaching them the differences between African- ican Language, as they call it, and Mainstream American h. We visited PS 100 in Watts to watch fifth-graders play a ardy"-like game in which they won points for "translating" entences as "Last night we bake cookies."

er: "What language is it in?"

nt: "AAL."

er: "It is in African-American Language. What linguistic ture is in AAL?"

nt: "Past-tense marker-ed."

Teacher: "Past-tense marker-ed. That's cool! And how do you code-switch it to Mainstream American English?"

Student: "Last night we baked cookies."

Teacher: "You got five hundred more points." Big cheers from the kids.

So, four decades after the passage of landmark legislation outlawing racial discrimination, the news is that it blatantly survives in language. Columnists would not dream of describing other attributes of being African-American with epithets like "gibberish." They could, however, get away with it in writing about black language, which remains a significant barrier to success in school and ultimately in the job market and housing—pathways to the American dream.

Ironically, as much as it is despised, black English is embraced and borrowed by whites, especially young whites in thrall to the appeal of hip hop music. There are divergences just as dramatic within the English of white Americans. Around the Great Lakes, people are making what Labov believes are "revolutionary changes in the pronunciation of short vowels that have remained relatively stable in the language for a thousand years."

Labov is director of an effort to determine the boundaries of different dialects within American speech. Traditionally, that was achieved by comparing distinctive local or regional words people used for every day things. One surviving example is the different terms for the long sandwich that contains cold cuts, cheese, and lettuce—a grinder in some parts of New England; a wedge in Rhode Island: a spuky in Boston; a hero in New York; a hoagie in Philadelphia; a submarine in Ohio and farther west. By drawing lines around places where each term is used, linguists can form maps of dialect areas. Many such regional terms are dying out because old craft skills are replaced by products marketed nationally. Labov leads a new method in which the different ways people pronounce words are recorded with colored dots on a map of the U.S. Connecting the dots produces the Atlas of North American English.

Labov and his colleagues found startling pronunciation changes in cities such as Chicago, Cleveland, and Detroit and New York State's Rochester and Syracuse. On a computer in his office in Philadelphia, we heard a woman say the word "black," then the complete phrase: "Old senior citizens living on one 'black,' and it was apparent that she was pronouncing "block" like "black." Similarly, another woman mentions what sounds like "bosses." The full sentence reveals she means "buses:" "I can vaguely remember when we had 'bosses' with the antennas on top."

When one vowel changes, so do the neighboring ones: "caught" shifts toward "cot," "cot" toward "cat," "cat" toward "kit" or "keeyat." Labov thinks these changes are quite important. "From our point of view as linguists, we want to understand why people should become more different from each other. We're all watching the same radio and television; we live side by side. And it's important to recognize that people don't always want to behave in the same way."

Labov has a theory that, behind changes like these, are women, the primary transmitters of language. Traditionally enjoying less economic power than men, women rely on the symbolic power offered by words. Labov believes women are more apt than men to adopt "prestige forms" of language and symbols of nonconformism—new or "stigmatized forms" that can acquire a kind of "covert prestige." Labov writes that women are quicker and more forceful in employing the new social symbolism, whatever it may be. Working on his landmark study, "The Principles of Linguistic Change," he identifies a particular type of woman—working class, well-established in her community—who takes pleasure in being nonconformist and is strong enough to influence others. He sees parallels between leadership in fashion and language change. Most young women are alert to novelty in fashion; some have the confidence to embrace it and the natural authority to induce others to follow.

These are mysterious forces working on our language from underneath, as it were, and producing startling changes that, far from homogenizing our speech, actually create more diversity. Despite all the forces of global and national uniformity in products and trends, Americans clearly still want to do their own thing linguistically. An example is Pittsburgh, where the local dialect, or Pittsburghese, is celebrated, constantly talked about, and made a commodity. They know themselves as "Yinzers," from "yinz," the plural of "you," or "you ones." They use "slippy" for "slippery"; "red up" means to "tidy up"; and "anymore" as in "'Anymore,' there's so many new buildings you can't tell which is which." In downtown Pittsburgh—pronounced "dahntahn"—the question, "Did you eat yet?" sounds like "Jeet jet?" If you haven't, the response is, "No, 'jew?'"

Barbara Johnstone, a linguist from Pittsburgh, thinks the pride in their local speech is a way for Pittsburghers to talk about who they are and what it means to live there. People treasure their local accents, because where they come from, or where they feel they belong, still does matter. In the words of California linguist, Carmen Fought, "People want to talk like the people they want to be like." This contradicts the common assumption that media exposure is making everyone sound the same.

Local Accents Prevail

Yet, amusingly, people often are quite unaware of how their own speech sounds to others. Linguists we met were full of stories about people in Texas or coastal North Carolina with strong local accents who were convinced they sounded like Walter Cronkite. It happened to me. I grew up in the Canadian province of Nova Scotia, so fascinated with words that I called a memoir of my childhood *Wordstruck*. Even in my own family, I often heard the same words said differently. My grandfather, from Nova Scotia's south shore, said "garridge" while his daughter, my mother, said "gar-aghe."

Until I first came to the U.S. in 1952, I was unaware how different my speech was even from that of neighboring New England. I was 21 and (briefly, thank God!) an aspiring actor, thrilled to be working in a summer theater in Massachusetts. The first time I stepped on to the stage and opened my mouth, the director said, "You can't talk like that." I was stunned, not knowing until that moment that I was pronouncing "out" to rhyme with "oat," and "about" with "aboat"—still the common Nova Scotian pronunciation. Anxious not to close any career doors, I immediately began trying to modify the "oat" sound, but 50 years later, when I am tired or back with my brothers in Canada, I still slip into the pronunciations I grew up with.

What appears to be the determining force in whether reg dialects survive or disappear is not media influence, but rath movements of people. We talked to John Coffin, a lobsterm South Freeport, Me. Once a quiet fishing and ship-building h but now a bustling outlet shopping center, the town has attrac many new visitors and residents that Coffin fears the Maine w speaking—with its characteristic "ayeh" for "yes"—is disap ing: "I think in this area it's going to be a lost thing," and that r him sad. "I'd like to think my children and grandchildren tal way, whether people laugh at you, wherever we go—whateve people laugh at his Maine accent? "Oh, yes, lots of times. W was in the military, they made fun of me wicked."

"Wicked" is a typical Maine word, meaning "very," "wicked' good."

This homogenizing trend is obvious on some of the island Ocrakoke, off the coast of North Carolina, home of the Hoi Tc people who pronounce "high tide" as "hoi toid." These island become meccas for individuals from elsewhere building va homes, displacing locals and their dialect.

Still, the national media are having some effect: Labov not sound changes that have spread nationally, probably from C nia. One is the vowel in "do," which increasingly sounds like " Labov calls it "oo-fronting"; the sound is produced more to th of the mouth. You also hear it in the word "so," which sounc "so-ew." Another trend, more noticeable among young wome also some men, is a rising inflection at the ends of sentences, ing statements such as "The bus station is around *the corner*" like a query. One of the regions where "oo-fronting" is comr the South, where there are changes just as dramatic as those North. Southern ghosts do not say "boo," but "bew."

The most prevalent shift is that Southerners increasing pronouncing the "r" at the ends of words such as father. I this is due to the large migration of Northerners to Southe ies. Partly it is the historic decline in influence of the c Southern areas that once boasted the great slave-holding p tion culture, and the kind of r-less pronunciation we asso with languid belles posing in hoop skirts on the porches o bellum houses. This advancing "r" marks the growing pr of what linguists call Inland Southern, the speech deriving Appalachia. That pattern goes back to the earliest days of settlement, when people from parts of England who did nc nounce "r" settled the coastal areas, while the Scots-Irish, s from Northern Ireland who spoke with a strong "r," move the hills of Appalachia because the easily-cultivated coasta already was taken.

Their speech has been given a huge boost by the rise of country no longer a regional craze, but a national phenomenon. Those wh country," wherever they come from, "talk country" and "talkin' cc has become a kind of default way of speaking informal Americ considered easygoing and friendly. Pres. George W. Bush has r his trademark, with no disadvantage politically because, like him, many Americans say, "Howya doin'? Doin' fine!" and they are nc particular than he is about making subject agree with verb in se such as, "There's no negotiations with North Korea."

The economic rise of the South has had another startling So many Americans have moved into the South and Southw happily adopted Southernisms—such as "y'all" and "fixin' t

uncing "I" as "all," not the Northern "eye-ee"—that more Amer-
now speak some variety of Southern than any other dialect. That
conclusion of linguist John Fought, who believes that, as the
ation shift to the Sun Belt continues, "In time, we should expect
' southern to become accepted as standard American speech."
at news will come as a shock to Northerners conditioned over
ations to despise Southern talk, considering it evidence of stu-
and backwardness. In the film "Sweet Home Alabama," the
ol' boy played by Josh Lucas says to his Northernized wife,
Witherspoon, "Just because I talk slow, doesn't mean I'm
." The context leads the audience to believe him.
e comedian Jeff Foxworthy still fills huge theaters North and
with his hilarious routine ridiculing Southern speech and
ern attitudes towards it. He kills them with his list of South-
vords:'"

ay-o-naise. Man, a's a lotta people here tonight,"

rinal. I told my brother, 'You're in a lotta trouble when
ddy gets home."

'ichadidja. Hey, you didn't bring your track with you, did
u?"

rthern attitudes to Southerners may be ameliorating slightly,
ly because it no longer is uncool in Northern cities to like
y music and the culture that goes with it. Yet, an ingrained
of the prestige of some dialects and scorn for others is very
alive. Linguist Dennis Preston of Michigan State University
ent years studying the prejudices Americans have concerning
different from their own. He joined us on a train west from
elphia, demonstrating his regular technique. Establishing
rapport with other passengers, he got them to mark on a map
U.S. where they thought people spoke differently. Almost
t exception, they circled the South and New York to locate
rst English. Referring to New York, a Pennsylvania woman
reston contemptuously, "They say waader!" Preston asked,
do you say?" "Water!" she declared proudly.

istinct New York Voice

n, though, detects another emotion creeping in beneath the
and that is pleasure. People may think Southern or New York
is not good, but they find them charming, and that must be
an effect of media exposure, for instance, to the sympathetic
ork characters in the TV series "Law and Order." Linguists
that broadcasting and the movies help all Americans under-
different dialects, perhaps appreciating the diversity in our
. Moreover, no matter how they themselves speak, Americans
understand the language of network broadcasters, which is
sest thing to an overall American standard. That standard
es with the speech that Preston's subjects inevitably identify
best American speech—that of the Midwest—because it has
vest regional features.

That Midwest standard is relevant to the cutting edge of computer research in Silicon Valley. There is heavy investment in efforts to make computers speak like us and understand us. The researchers believe they will achieve that in 10 to 15 years but it is an incredible challenge.

What these efforts demonstrate is how infinitely complex our language and understanding of it is, how meaning turns on the subtlest changes in intonation, how vast any computer data base must be to catch all the nuances we take for granted. How do you program a computer to avoid those charming errors in context which foreigners make in perfectly grammatical sentences? For instance, a sign in an Egyptian hotel states: "Patrons need have no anxiety about the water. It has all been passed by the management." Or, this in a Swiss hotel: "Due to the impropriety of entertaining guests of the opposite sex in the bedrooms, it is suggested that the lobby be used for this purpose."

The effort to make computers understand speech raises other questions about the future of language. Will the technology, and the business imperatives behind it, create an irresistible drive toward more standard speech? If so, which accents or varieties of American speech will that leave out? Whom will it disenfranchise because of their dialect—African-Americans, Hispanics, Cajuns in Louisiana? A couple of years ago, the police chief of Shreveport, La., complained that the computer voice-recognition system used to route nonemergency calls did not understand the local accent. Researchers point out, however, that if you speak like someone from the Midwest, computers will understand you.

The emerging technology is irresistible for business. When United Airlines introduced a computerized voice-recognition system for flight information–replacing live bodies—it saved a reported $25,000,000. As these systems become more sophisticated, a lot of companies will want them to replace expensive warm bodies. Inevitably, more and more of our lives will involve talking to and being understood by computers. Being understood will be increasingly important. Will the technology work to reinforce existing linguistic stereotypes—about your race, ethnicity, gender, or where you live—or help to break them down? Will we have to talk as computers would like us to in order for them to obey us?

During the California portion of filming "Do You Speak American?" I drove a car equipped with an elaborate voice-recognition system. I speak a version of standard broadcast American English, and I tried to enunciate clearly. Occasionally, it worked, but often it did not and the car kept saying, "Pardon me? Pardon me?" and I gave it up.

Everything in the American experience, each new frontier encountered—geographical, spiritual, technological—has altered our language. What kind of a frontier are we crossing by teaching computers our most fundamental human skill, that of the spoken word?

Robert MacNeil, former co-anchor of PBS's Emmy Award-winning "MacNeil/Lehrer NewsHour," is a member of the Television Academy Hall of Fame and the author of several books.

Fighting for Our Lives

Deborah Tannen, PhD

This is not another book about civility. "Civility" suggests a superficial, pinky-in-the-air veneer of politeness spread thin over human relations like a layer of marmalade over toast. This book is about a pervasive warlike atmosphere that makes us approach public dialogue, and just about anything we need to accomplish, as if it were a fight. It is a tendency in Western culture in general, and in the United States in particular, that has a long history and a deep, thick, and far-ranging root system. It has served us well in many ways but in recent years has become so exaggerated that it is getting in the way of solving our problems. Our spirits are corroded by living in an atmosphere of unrelenting contention—an argument culture.

The argument culture urges us to approach the world—and the people in it—in an adversarial frame of mind. It rests on the assumption that opposition is the best way to get anything done: The best way to discuss an idea is to set up a debate; the best way to cover news is to find spokespeople who express the most extreme, polarized views and present them as "both sides"; the best way to settle disputes is litigation that pits one party against the other; the best way to begin an essay is to attack someone; and the best way to show you're really thinking is to criticize.

Our public interactions have become more and more like having an argument with a spouse. Conflict can't be avoided in our public lives any more than we can avoid conflict with people we love. One of the great strengths of our society is that we can express these conflicts openly. But just as spouses have to learn ways of settling their differences without inflicting real damage on each other, so we, as a society, have to find constructive ways of resolving disputes and differences. Public discourse requires *making* an argument for a point of view, not *having* an argument—as in having a fight.

The war on drugs, the war on cancer, the battle of the sexes, politicians' turf battles—in the argument culture, war metaphors pervade our talk and shape our thinking. Nearly everything is framed as a battle or game in which winning or losing is the main concern. These all have their uses and their place, but they are not the only way—and often not the best way—to understand and approach our world. Conflict and opposition are as necessary as cooperation and agreement, but the scale is off balance, with conflict and opposition overweighted. In this book, I show how deeply entrenched the argument culture is, the forms it takes, and how it affects us every day—sometimes in useful ways, but often creating more problems than it solves, causing
rather than avoiding damage. As a sociolinguist, a social
tist, I am trained to observe and explain language and
in human relations, and that is my biggest job here. Bu
also point toward other ways for us to talk to each other
things done in our public lives.

The Battle of the Sexes

My interest in the topic of opposition in public discourse
sified in the years following the publication of *You Jus*
Understand, my book about communication between
and men. In the first year I appeared on many television an
shows and was interviewed for many print articles in news
and magazines. For the most part, that coverage was ext
fair, and I was—and remain—indebted to the many jou
who found my ideas interesting enough to make them
to viewers, listeners, and readers. But from time to time—
often than I expected—I encountered producers who insi
setting up a television show as a fight (either between t
and me or between another guest and me) and print jou
who made multiple phone calls to my colleagues, trying
someone who would criticize my work. This got me th
about what kind of information comes across on shows
articles that take this approach, compared to those that ap
topics in other ways.

At the same time, my experience of the academic wo
had long been my intellectual home began to change.
most part, other scholars, like most journalists, were w
ing and respectful in their responses to my work, even
disagreed on specific points or had alternative views
gest. But about a year after *You Just Don't Understand* b
a best-seller—the wheels of academia grind more slow
those of the popular press—I began reading attacks on m
that completely misrepresented it. I had been in acade
over fifteen years by then, and had valued my interacti
other researchers as one of the greatest rewards of ac
life. Why, I wondered, would someone represent me as
said things I had never said or as having failed to say t
had said?

The answer crystallized when I put the question to a wri
I felt had misrepresented my work: "Why do you need to ma
ers wrong for you to be right?" Her response: "It's an argu
Aha, I thought, that explains it. When you're having an ar

omeone, your goal is not to listen and understand. Instead, se every tactic you can think of—including distorting what pponent just said—in order to win the argument.

t only the level of attention *You Just Don't Understand* ed but, even more, the subject of women and men, trig- the tendency to polarize. This tendency to stage a fight on sion or in print was posited on the conviction that opposi- eads to truth. Sometimes it does. But the trouble is, some- it doesn't. I was asked at the start of more than one talk or print interview, "What is the most controversial thing your book?" Opposition does not lead to truth when the controversial thing is not the most important.

e conviction that opposition leads to truth can tempt ly members of the press but just about anyone seeking act an audience to frame discussions as a fight between ncilable opposites. Even the Smithsonian Institution, to ate its 150th anniversary, sponsored a series of talks billed ates. They invited me to take part in one titled "The Battle Sexes." The organizer preempted my objection: "I know on't be happy with this title, but we want to get people sted." This is one of many assumptions I question in this Is it necessary to frame an interchange as a battle to get interested? And even if doing so succeeds in capturing on, does it risk dampening interest in the long run, as audi- weary of the din and begin to hunger for more substance?

ought-Provoking Just Provocative?

spring of 1995, Horizons Theatre in Arlington, Virginia, ced two one-act plays I had written about family relation- The director, wanting to contribute to the reconciliation en Blacks and Jews, mounted my plays in repertory with ne-act plays by an African American playwright, Caleen te Jennings. We had both written plays about three sisters plored the ethnic identities of our families (Jewish for me, n-American for her) and the relationship between those ies and the American context in which we grew up. To erest in the plays and to explore the parallels between her and mine, the theater planned a public dialogue between gs and me, to be held before the plays opened.

production got under way, I attended the audition of for my plays. After the auditions ended, just before eve- headed home, the theater's public relations volunteer uted copies of the flyer announcing the public dialogue e had readied for distribution. I was horrified. The flyer nced that Caleen and I would discuss "how past traumas understanding and conflict between Blacks and Jews " The flyer was trying to grab by the throat the issue e wished to address indirectly. Yes, we were concerned onflicts between Blacks and Jews, but neither of us is an ity on that conflict, and we had no intention of expound- it. We hoped to do our part to ameliorate the conflict using on commonalities. Our plays had many resonances en them. We wanted to talk about our work and let the nces speak for themselves.

Fortunately, we were able to stop the flyers before they were distributed and devise new ones that promised something we could deliver: "a discussion of heritage, identity, and complex family relationships in African-American and Jewish-American culture as represented in their plays." Jennings noticed that the original flyer said the evening would be "provocative" and changed it to "thought-provoking." What a world of difference is implied in that small change: how much better to make people think, rather than simply to "provoke" them—as often as not, to anger.

It is easy to understand why conflict is so often highlighted: Writers of headlines or promotional copy want to catch attention and attract an audience. They are usually under time pressure, which lures them to established, conventionalized ways of expressing ideas in the absence of leisure to think up entirely new ones. The promise of controversy seems an easy and natural way to rouse interest. But serious consequences are often unintended: Stirring up animosities to get a rise out of people, though easy and "provocative," can open old wounds or create new ones that are hard to heal. This is one of many dangers inherent in the argument culture.

For the Sake of Argument

In the argument culture, criticism, attack, or opposition are the predominant if not the only ways of responding to people or ideas. I use the phrase "culture of critique" to capture this aspect. "Critique" in this sense is not a general term for analysis or interpretation but rather a synonym for criticism.

It is the *automatic* nature of this response that I am calling attention to—and calling into question. Sometimes passionate opposition, strong verbal attack, are appropriate and called for. No one knows this better than those who have lived under repressive regimes that forbid public opposition. The Yugoslavian-born poet Charles Simic is one. "There are moments in life," he writes, "when true invective is called for, when it becomes an absolute necessity, out of a deep sense of justice, to denounce, mock, vituperate, lash out, in the strongest possible language." I applaud and endorse this view. There are times when it is necessary and right to fight—to defend your country or yourself, to argue for right against wrong or against offensive or dangerous ideas or actions.

What I question is the ubiquity, the knee-jerk nature, of approaching almost any issue, problem, or public person in an adversarial way. One of the dangers of the habitual use of adversarial rhetoric is a kind of verbal inflation—a rhetorical boy who cried wolf: The legitimate, necessary denunciation is muted, even lost, in the general cacophony of oppositional shouting. What I question is using opposition to accomplish *every* goal, even those that do not require fighting but might also (or better) be accomplished by other means, such as exploring, expanding, discussing, investigating, and the exchanging of ideas suggested by the word "dialogue." I am questioning the assumption that *everything* is a matter of polarized opposites, the proverbial "two sides to every question" that we think embodies open-mindedness and expansive thinking.

In a word, the type of opposition I am questioning is what I call "agonism." I use this term, which derives from the Greek word for "contest," *agonia,* to mean an automatic warlike stance—not the literal opposition of fighting against an attacker or the unavoidable opposition that arises organically in response to conflicting ideas or actions. An agonistic response, to me, is a kind of programmed contentiousness—a prepatterned, unthinking use of fighting to accomplish goals that do not necessarily require it.

How Useful Are Fights?

Noticing that public discourse so often takes the form of heated arguments—of having a fight—made me ask how useful it is in our personal lives to settle differences by arguing. Given what I know about having arguments in private life, I had to conclude that it is, in many cases, not very useful.

In close relationships it is possible to find ways of arguing that result in better understanding and solving problems. But with most arguments, little is resolved, worked out, or achieved when two people get angrier and less rational by the minute. When you're having an argument with someone, you're usually not trying to understand what the other person is saying, or what in their experience leads them to say it. Instead, you're readying your response: listening for weaknesses in logic to leap on, points you can distort to make the other person look bad and yourself look good. Sometimes you know, on some back burner of your mind, that you're doing this—that there's a kernel of truth in what your adversary is saying and a bit of unfair twisting in what you're saying. Sometimes you do this because you're angry, but sometimes it's just the temptation to take aim at a point made along the way because it's an easy target.

Here's an example of how this happened in an argument between a couple who had been married for over fifty years. The husband wanted to join an HMO by signing over their Medicare benefits to save money. The wife objected because it would mean she could no longer see the doctor she knew and trusted. In arguing her point of view, she said, "I like Dr. B. He knows me, he's interested in me. He calls me by my first name." The husband parried the last point: "I don't like that. He's much younger than we are. He shouldn't be calling us by first name." But the form of address Dr. B. uses was irrelevant. The wife was trying to communicate that she felt comfortable with the doctor she knew, that she had a relationship with him. His calling her by first name was just one of a list of details she was marshaling to explain her comfort with him. Picking on this one detail did not change her view—and did not address her concern. It was just a way to win the argument.

We all are guilty, at times, of seizing on irrelevant details, distorting someone else's position the better to oppose it, when we're arguing with those we're closest to. But we are rarely dependent on these fights as sources of information. The same tactics are common when public discourse is carried out on the model of personal fights. And the results are dangerous when listeners are looking to these interchanges to get needed information or practical results.

Fights have winners and losers. If you're fighting to win, the temptation is great to deny facts that support your opponent's views and to filter what you know, saying only what supports your side. In the extreme form, it encourages people to misrepresent or even to lie. We accept this risk because we believe we c when someone is lying. The problem is, we can't.

Paul Ekman, a psychologist at the University of Calif San Francisco, studies lying. He set up experiments in individuals were videotaped talking about their emc actions, or beliefs—some truthfully, some not. He has s these videotapes to thousands of people, asking them to id the liars and also to say how sure they were about their ments. His findings are chilling: Most people performe much better than chance, and those who did the worst ha as much confidence in their judgments as the few who really able to detect lies. Intrigued by the implications c research in various walks of life, Dr. Ekman repeated this iment with groups of people whose jobs require them tc out lies: judges, lawyers, police, psychotherapists, and en ees of the CIA, FBI, and ATF (Bureau of Alcohol, Tobacc Firearms). They were no better at detecting who was telli truth than the rest of us. The only group that did signifi better were members of the U.S. Secret Service. This fi gives some comfort when it comes to the Secret Service b much when it comes to every other facet of public life.

Two Sides to Every Question

Our determination to pursue truth by setting up a fight be two sides leads us to believe that every issue has two side more, no less: If both sides are given a forum to confron other, all the relevant information will emerge, and the be will be made for each side. But opposition does not lead t when an issue is not composed of two opposing sides b crystal of many sides. Often the truth is in the complex m not the oversimplified extremes.

We love using the word "debate" as a way of repres issues: the abortion debate, the health care debate, the af tive action debate—even "the great backpacking vs. car ca debate." The ubiquity of this word in itself shows our ten to conceptualize issues in a way that predisposes public c sion to be polarized, framed as two opposing sides that giv other no ground. There are many problems with this appro you begin with the assumption that there *must* be an "other you may end up scouring the margins of science or the f of lunacy to find it. As a result, proven facts, such as wh know about how the earth and its inhabitants evolved, are a par with claims that are known to have no basis in fact as creationism.

The conviction that there are two sides to every sto prompt writers or producers to dig up an "other side," so who state outright falsehoods are given a platform in publ course. This accounts, in part, for the bizarre phenome Holocaust denial. Deniers, as Emory University professo orah Lipstadt shows, have been successful in gaining tele airtime and campus newspaper coverage by masquerad "the other side" in a "debate."

Appearance in print or on television has a way of le legitimacy, so baseless claims take on a mantle of poss Lipstadt shows how Holocaust deniers dispute establishe of history, and then reasonable spokespersons use their isputed as a basis for questioning known facts. The .obert Mitchum, for example, interviewed in *Esquire,* ed doubt about the Holocaust. When the interviewer bout the slaughter of six million Jews, Mitchum replied, t know. People dispute that." Continual reference to "the de" results in a pervasive conviction that everything has side—with the result that people begin to doubt the ce of any facts at all.

Expense of Time and Spirit

t's book meticulously exposes the methods used by to falsify the overwhelming historic evidence that the ust occurred. That a scholar had to invest years of her ional life writing a book unraveling efforts to deny ing that was about as well known and well documented historical fact has ever been—while those who person- perienced and witnessed it are still alive—is testament her way that the argument culture limits our knowledge han expanding it. Talent and effort were wasted when uals who have been unfairly attacked must spend years creative lives defending themselves rather than advanc- ir work. The entire society loses their creative efforts. what happened with scientist Robert Gallo.

Gallo is the American virologist who codiscovered the virus. He is also the one who developed the technique lying T-cells, which made that discovery possible. And work was seminal in developing the test to detect the irus in blood, the first and for a long time the only means of stemming the tide of death from AIDS. But in 1989, ecame the object of a four-year investigation into allega- at he had stolen the AIDS virus from Luc Montagnier of teur Institute in Paris, who had independently identified DS virus. Simultaneous investigations by the National es of Health, the office of Michigan Congressman John , and the National Academy of Sciences barreled ahead ter Gallo and Montagnier settled the dispute to their satisfaction. In 1993 the investigations concluded that ad done nothing wrong. Nothing. But this exoneration be considered a happy ending. Never mind the personal g of Gallo, who was reviled when he should have been d as a hero. Never mind that, in his words, "These were t painful years and horrible years of my life." The dread- conscionable result of the fruitless investigations is that ad to spend four years fighting the accusations instead ing AIDS.

investigations, according to journalist Nicholas Wade, arked by an article about Gallo written in the currently spirit of demonography: not to praise the person it fea- it to bury him—to show his weaknesses, his villainous ie implication that Gallo has stolen the AIDS virus was to fill a requirement of the discourse: In demonography, must find negative sides of their subjects to display for who enjoy seeing heroes transformed into villains. The on led to investigations, and the investigations became a aut that acquired a life of its own, fed by the enthusiasm ck on public figures that is the culture of critique.

Metaphors: We Are What We Speak

Perhaps one reason suspicions of Robert Gallo were so zealously investigated is that the scenario of an ambitious scientist ready to do anything to defeat a rival appeals to our sense of story; it is the kind of narrative we are ready to believe. Culture, in a sense, is an environment of narratives that we hear repeatedly until they seem to make self-evident sense in explaining human behavior. Thinking of human interactions as battles is a metaphorical frame through which we learn to regard the world and the people in it.

All language uses metaphors to express ideas; some metaphoric words and expressions are novel, made up for the occasion, but more are calcified in the language. They are simply the way we think it is natural to express ideas. We don't think of them as metaphors. Someone who says, "Be careful: You aren't a cat, you don't have nine lives," is explicitly comparing you to a cat, because the cat is named in words. But what if someone says, "Don't pussyfoot around; get to the point"? There is no explicit comparison to a cat, but the comparison is there nonetheless, implied in the word "pussyfoot." This expression probably developed as a reference to the movement of a cat cautiously circling a suspicious object. I doubt that individuals using the word "pussyfoot" think consciously of cats. More often than not, we use expressions without thinking about their metaphoric implications. But that doesn't mean those implications are not influencing us.

At a meeting, a general discussion became so animated that a participant who wanted to comment prefaced his remark by saying, "I'd like to leap into the fray." Another participant called out, "Or share your thoughts." Everyone laughed. By suggesting a different phrasing, she called attention to what would probably have otherwise gone unnoticed: "Leap into the fray" characterized the lively discussion as a metaphorical battle.

Americans talk about almost everything as if it were a war. A book about the history of linguistics is called *The Linguistics Wars.* A magazine article about claims that science is not completely objective is titled "The Science Wars." One about breast cancer detection is "The Mammogram War"; about competition among caterers, "Party Wars"—and on and on in a potentially endless list. Politics, of course, is a prime candidate. One of innumerable possible examples, the headline of a story reporting that the Democratic National Convention nominated Bill Clinton to run for a second term declares, "DEMOCRATS SEND CLINTON INTO BATTLE FOR A 2ND TERM." But medicine is as frequent a candidate, as we talk about battling and conquering disease.

Headlines are intentionally devised to attract attention, but we all use military or attack imagery in everyday expressions without thinking about it: "Take a shot at it," "I don't want to be shot down," "He went off half cocked," "That's half the battle." Why does it matter that our public discourse is filled with military metaphors? Aren't they just words? Why not talk about something that matters—like actions?

Because words matter. When we think we are using language, language is using us. As linguist Dwight Bolinger put it (employing a military metaphor), language is like a loaded gun: It can be fired intentionally, but it can wound or kill just as surely when fired accidentally. The terms in which we talk about something shape the way we think about it—and even what we see.

The power of words to shape perception has been proven by researchers in controlled experiments. Psychologist Elizabeth Loftus and John Palmer, for example, found that the terms in which people are asked to recall something affect what they recall. The researchers showed subjects a film of two cars colliding, then asked how fast the cars were going; one week later, they asked whether there had been any broken glass. Some subjects were asked, "About how fast were the cars going when they smashed into each other?" Those who read the question with the verb "smashed" estimated that the cars were going faster. They were also more likely to "remember" having seen broken glass. (There wasn't any.)

This is how language works. It invisibly molds our way of thinking about people, actions, and the world around us. Military metaphors train us to think about—and see—everything in terms of fighting, conflict, and war. This perspective then limits our imaginations when we consider what we can do about situations we would like to understand or change.

Even in science, common metaphors that are taken for granted influence how researchers think about natural phenomena. Evelyn Fox Keller describes a case in which acceptance of a metaphor led scientists to see something that was not there. A mathematical biologist, Keller outlines the fascinating behavior of cellular slime mold. This unique mold can take two completely different forms: It can exist as single-cell organisms, or the separate cells can come together to form multicellular aggregates. The puzzle facing scientists was: What triggers aggregation? In other words, what makes the single cells join together? Scientist focused their investigations by asking what entity issued the order to start aggregating. They first called this bosslike entity a "founder cell," and later a "pacemaker cell," even though no one had seen any evidence for the existence of such a cell. Proceeding nonetheless from the assumption that such a cell must exist, they ignored evidence to the contrary: For example, when the center of the aggregate is removed, other centers form.

Scientists studying slime mold did not examine the interrelationship between the cells and their environment, nor the interrelationship between the functional systems within each cell, because they were busy looking for the pacemaker cell, which, as eventually became evident, did not exist. Instead, under conditions of nutritional deprivation, each individual cell begins to feel the urge to merge with others to form the conglomerate. It is a reaction of the cells to their environment, not to the orders of a boss. Keller recounts this tale to illustrate her insight that we tend to view nature through our understanding of human relations as hierarchical. In her words, "We risk imposing on nature the very stories we like to hear." In other words, the conceptual metaphor of hierarchical governance made scientists "see" something—a pacemaker cell—that wasn't there.

Among the stories many Americans most like to hear are war stories. According to historian Michael Sherry, the American war movie developed during World War II a been with us ever since. He shows that movies not exp about war were also war movies at heart, such as western their good guy–bad guy battles settled with guns. *High* for example, which became a model for later westerns, allegory of the Second World War: The happy ending on the pacifist taking up arms. We can also see this sto in contemporary adventure films: Think of *Star Wars,* w stirring finale in which Han Solo, having professed no est in or taste for battle, returns at the last moment to d the enemy and save the day. And precisely the same th found in a contemporary low-budget independent film, *Blade,* in which a peace-loving retarded man becomes at the end by murdering the man who has been tormenti family he has come to love.

Put up Your Dukes

If war provides the metaphors through which we view the and each other, we come to view others—and ourselv warriors in battle. Almost any human encounter can be as a fight between two opponents. Looking at it this way particular aspects of the event into focus and obscures ot

Framing interactions as fights affects not only the p pants but also the viewers. At a performance, the audie well as the performers, can be transformed. This effe noted by a reviewer in *The New York Times,* commentin musical event:

> **Showdown at Lincoln Center.** Jazz's ideological war o last several years led to a pitched battle in August betw John Lincoln Collier, the writer, and Wynton Mars the trumpeter, in a debate at Lincoln Center. Mr. Mars demolished Mr. Collier, point after point after point, what made the debate unpleasant was the crowd's bl lust; humiliation, not elucidation, was the desired end.

Military imagery pervades this account: the difference o ions between Collier and Marsalis was an "ideologica and the "debate" was a "pitched battle" in which M "demolished" Collier (not his arguments, but him). W commentator regrets, however, is that the audience got sv in the mood instigated by the way the debate was carri "the crowd's blood lust" for Collier's defeat.

This is one of the most dangerous aspects of regardin lectual interchange as a fight. It contributes to an atmosp animosity that spreads like a fever. In a society that includ ple who express their anger by shooting, the result of de ing those with whom we disagree can be truly tragic.

But do audiences necessarily harbor within thems "blood lust," or is it stirred in them by the performanc are offered? Another arts event was set up as a debate b a playwright and a theater director. In this case, the phor through which the debate was viewed was not v boxing—a sport that is in itself, like a debate, a metap battle that pitches one side against the other in an all-ou to win. A headline describing the event set the frame: "

ORNER . . . ," followed by the subhead "A Black Play- and White Critic Duke It Out." The story then reports:

face-off between August Wilson, the most successful k playwright in the American theater, and Robert stein, longtime drama critic for The New Republic artistic director of the American Repertory Theatre Cambridge, Mass. These two heavyweights had been ing in print since last June. . . .

Entering from opposite sides of the stage, the two shook hands and came out fighting—or at least ring.

, the article explains, had given a speech in which he d Black performers taking "white" roles in color-blind ; Brustein had written a column disagreeing; and both d up with further responses to each other.

ording to the article, "The drama of the Wilson-Brustein ntation lies in their mutual intransigence." No one would n that audiences crave drama. But is intransigence the ppealing source of drama? I happened to hear this debate ast on the radio. The line that triggered the loudest cheers e audience was the final question put to the two men by derator, Anna Deavere Smith: "What did you each learn e other in this debate?" The loud applause was evidence audience did not crave intransigence. They wanted to other kind of drama: the drama of change—change that from genuinely listening to someone with a different f view, not the transitory drama of two intransigent posi- stalemate.

encourage the staging of more dramas of change and f intransigence, we need new metaphors to supplement mplement the pervasive war and boxing match metaphors n which we take it for granted issues and events are best about and viewed.

d Splatters

ndness for the fight scenario leads us to frame many x human interactions as a battle between two sides. This apes the way we understand what happened and how rd the participants. One unfortunate result is that fights mess in which everyone is muddied. The person attacked deemed just as guilty as the attacker.

injustice of this is clear if you think back to childhood. f us still harbor anger as we recall a time (or many times) g or playmate started a fight—but both of us got blamed. s occur in a stream, each a response to what came before. you punctuate them can change their meaning just as n change the meaning of a sentence by punctuating it in ce or another.

a parent despairing of trying to sort out which child a fight, people often respond to those involved in a pub- ute as if both were equally guilty. When champion figure Nancy Kerrigan was struck on the knee shortly before 4 Olympics in Norway and the then-husband of another on skater, Tonya Harding, implicated his wife in plan- e attack, the event was characterized as a fight between two skaters that obscured their differing roles. As both skaters headed for the Olympic competition, their potential meeting was described as a "long-anticipated figure-skating shootout." Two years later, the event was referred to not as "the attack on Nancy Kerrigan" but as "the rivalry surrounding Tonya Harding and Nancy Kerrigan."

By a similar process, the Senate Judiciary Committee hearings to consider the nomination of Clarence Thomas for Supreme Court justice at which Anita Hill was called to testify are regularly referred to as the "Hill-Thomas hearings," obscuring the very different roles played by Hill and Thomas. Although testimony by Anita Hill was the occasion for reopening the hearings, they were still the Clarence Thomas confirmation hearings: Their purpose was to evaluate Thomas's candidacy. Framing these hearings as a two-sides dispute between Hill and Thomas allowed the senators to focus their investigation on cross-examining Hill rather than seeking other sorts of evidence, for example by consulting experts on sexual harassment to ascertain whether Hill's account seemed plausible.

Slash-and-Burn Thinking

Approaching situations like warriors in battle leads to the assumption that intellectual inquiry, too, is a game of attack, counterattack, and self-defense. In this spirit, critical thinking is synonymous with criticizing. In many classrooms, students are encouraged to read someone's life work, then rip it to shreds. Though criticism is one form of critical thinking—and an essential one—so are integrating ideas from disparate fields and examining the context out of which ideas grew. Opposition does not lead to the whole truth when we ask only "What's wrong with this?" and never "What can we use from this in building a new theory, a new understanding?"

There are many ways that unrelenting criticism is destructive in itself. In innumerable small dramas mirroring what happened to Robert Gallo (but on a much more modest scale), our most creative thinkers can waste time and effort responding to critics motivated less by a genuine concern about weaknesses in their work than by a desire to find something to attack. All of society loses when creative people are discouraged from their pursuits by unfair criticism. (This is particularly likely to happen since, as Kay Redfield Jamison shows in her book *Touched with Fire,* many of those who are unusually creative are also unusually sensitive; their sensitivity often drives their creativity.)

If the criticism is unwarranted, many will say, you are free to argue against it, to defend yourself. But there are problems with this, too. Not only does self-defense take time and draw off energy that would better be spent on new creative work, but any move to defend yourself makes you appear, well, defensive. For example, when an author wrote a letter to the editor protesting a review he considered unfair, the reviewer (who is typically given the last word) turned the very fact that the author defended himself into a weapon with which to attack again. The reviewer's response began, "I haven't much time to waste on the kind of writer who squanders his talent drafting angry letters to reviewers."

The argument culture limits the information we get rather than broadening it in another way. When a certain kind of interaction is the norm, those who feel comfortable with that type of interaction are drawn to participate, and those who do not feel comfortable with it recoil and go elsewhere. If public discourse included a broad range of types, we would be making room for individuals with different temperaments to take part and contribute their perspectives and insights. But when debate, opposition, and fights overwhelmingly predominate, those who enjoy verbal sparring are likely to take part—by calling in to talk shows, writing letters to the editor or articles, becoming journalists—and those who cannot comfortably take part in oppositional discourse, or do not wish to, are likely to opt out.

This winnowing process is easy to see in apprenticeship programs such as acting school, law school, and graduate school. A woman who was identified in her university drama program as showing exceptional promise was encouraged to go to New York to study acting. Full of enthusiasm, she was accepted by a famous acting school where the teaching method entailed the teacher screaming at students, goading and insulting them as a way to bring out the best in them. This worked well with many of the students but not with her. Rather than rising to the occasion when attacked, she cringed, becoming less able to draw on her talent, not more. After a year, she dropped out. It could be that she simply didn't have what it took—but this will never be known, because the adversarial style of teaching did not allow her to show what talent she had.

Polarizing Complexity: Nature or Nurture?

Few issues come with two neat, and neatly opposed, sides. Again, I have seen this in the domain of gender. One common polarization is an opposition between two sources of differences between women and men: "culture," or "nurture," on one hand and "biology," or "nature," on the other.

Shortly after the publication of *You Just Don't Understand,* I was asked by a journalist what question I most often encountered about women's and men's conversational styles. I told her, "Whether the differences I describe are biological or cultural." The journalist laughed. Puzzled, I asked why this made her laugh. She explained that she had always been so certain that any significant differences are cultural rather than biological in origin that the question struck her as absurd. So I should not have been surprised when I read, in the article she wrote, that the two questions I am most frequently asked are "Why do women nag?" and "Why won't men ask for directions?" Her ideological certainty that the question I am most frequently asked was absurd led her to ignore my answer and get a fact wrong in her report of my experience.

Some people are convinced that any significant differences between men and women are entirely or overwhelmingly due to cultural influences—the way we treat girls and boys, and men's dominance of women in society. Others are convinced that any significant differences are entirely or overwhelmingly due to biology: the physical facts of female and male bodies, hormones, and reproductive functions. Many problems are caused b ing the question as a dichotomy: Are behaviors that pat sex biological or cultural? This polarization encourages t one side to demonize those who take the other view, whic in turn to misrepresenting the work of those who are assi the opposing camp. Finally, and most devastatingly, it pre from exploring the interaction of biological and cultural fa factors that must, and can only, be understood togetl posing the question as either/or, we reinforce a false assu that biological and cultural factors are separable and precl investigations that would help us understand their interr ship. When a problem is posed in a way that polarizes, tl tion is often obscured before the search is under way.

Who's up? Who's Down?

Related to polarization is another aspect of the argume ture: our obsession with ratings and rankings. Magazin the 10, 50, or 100 best of everything: restaurants, mutua hospitals, even judges. Newsmagazines tell us Who's up, down, as in *Newsweek*'s "Conventional Wisdom Watc *Time*'s "Winners and Losers." Rankings and ratings taurants, products, schools, and people against each o a single scale, obscuring the myriad differences amon Maybe a small Thai restaurant in one neighborhood can' be compared to a pricey French one in another, any mc judges with a vast range of abilities and beliefs can be co on a single scale. And timing can skew results: Ohio Sta versity protested to *Time* magazine when its football te ranked at the bottom of a scale because only 29 percen team graduated. The year before it would have ranked the top six with 72 percent.

After a political debate, analysts comment not on w candidates said but on the question "Who won?" After th dent delivers an important speech, such as the State of th Address, expert commentators are asked to give it a grac ranking, grading establishes a competition. The bigges lem with asking what grade the president's speech dese who won and who lost a campaign debate, is what is nc and is therefore not answered: What was said, and wh significance of this for the country?

An Ethic of Aggression

In an argument culture aggressive tactics are valued f own sake. For example, a woman called in to a talk s which I was a guest to say, "When I'm in a place wher is smoking, and there's a no-smoking sign, instead of to him 'You aren't allowed to smoke in here. Put th I say, 'I'm awfully sorry, but I have asthma, so your s makes it hard for me to breathe. Would you mind terri smoking?' Whenever I say this, the man is extremely po solicitous, and he puts his cigarette out, and I say, 'Ol you, thank you!' as if he's done a wonderful thing for m do I do that?"

I think this woman expected me to say that she need iveness training to learn to confront smokers in a more ag er. Instead, I told her that there was nothing wrong with yle of getting the man to stop smoking. She gave him a saving way of doing what she asked, one that allowed him l chivalrous rather than chastised. This is kind to him, but also kind to herself, since it is more likely to lead to the she desires. If she tried to alter his behavior by remind-im of the rules, he might well rebel: "Who made you the cer? Mind your own business!" Indeed, who gives any of authority to set others straight when we think they're ing rules?

other caller disagreed with me, saying the first caller's was "self-abasing" and there was no reason for her to use I persisted: There is nothing necessarily destructive about ntional self-effacement. Human relations depend on the ment to use such verbal conventions. I believe the mistake aller was making—a mistake many of us make—was to se *ritual* self-effacement with the literal kind. All human ons require us to find ways to get what we want from oth-ithout seeming to dominate them. Allowing others to feel are doing what you want for a reason less humiliating to fulfills this need.

inking of yourself as the wronged party who is victimized awbreaking boor makes it harder to see the value of this od. But suppose you are the person addicted to smoking ights up (knowingly or not) in a no-smoking zone. Would ke strangers to yell at you to stop smoking, or would you be allowed to save face by being asked politely to stop er to help them out? Or imagine yourself having broken a advertently (which is not to imply rules are broken only stake; it is only to say that sometimes they are). Would you ome stranger to swoop down on you and begin berating r would you rather be asked politely to comply?

this example shows, conflicts can sometimes be resolved ut confrontational tactics, but current conventional wis-often devalues less confrontational tactics even if they well, favoring more aggressive strategies even if they get vorable results. It's as if we value a fight for its own sake, r its effectiveness in resolving disputes.

is ethic shows up in many contexts. In a review of a con-us book, for example, a reviewer wrote, "Always provoca-ometimes infuriating, this collection reminds us that the se of art is not to confirm and coddle but to provoke and nt." This false dichotomy encapsulates the belief that are not provoking and confronting, then you are con-ng and coddling—as if there weren't myriad other ways stion and learn. What about exploring, exposing, delv-alyzing, understanding, moving, connecting, integrating, nating . . . or any of innumerable verbs that capture other s of what art can do?

e Broader Picture

ncreasingly adversarial spirit of our contemporary lives lamentally related to a phenomenon that has been much ked upon in recent years: the breakdown of a sense of com-y. In this spirit, distinguished journalist and author Orville points out that in his day journalists routinely based their g on a sense of connection to their subjects—and that this sense of connection is missing from much that is written by journalists today. Quite the contrary, a spirit of demonography often prevails that has just the opposite effect: Far from encouraging us to feel connected to the subjects, it encourages us to feel critical, superior—and, as a result, distanced. The cumulative effect is that citizens feel more and more cut off from the people in public life they read about.

The argument culture dovetails with a general disconnection and breakdown of community in another way as well. Community norms and pressures exercise a restraint on the expression of hostility and destruction. Many cultures have rituals to channel and contain aggressive impulses, especially those of adolescent males. In just this spirit, at the 1996 Republican National Convention, both Colin Powell and Bob Dole talked about growing up in small communities where everyone knew who they were. This meant that many people would look out for them, but also that if they did something wrong, it would get back to their parents. Many Americans grew up in ethnic neighborhoods that worked the same way. If a young man stole something, committed vandalism, or broke a rule or law, it would be reported to his relatives, who would punish him or tell him how his actions were shaming the family. American culture today often lacks these brakes.

Community is a blend of connections and authority, and we are losing both. As Robert Bly shows in his book by that title, we now have a *Sibling Society:* Citizens are like squabbling siblings with no authority figures who can command enough respect to contain and channel their aggressive impulses. It is as if every day is a day with a substitute teacher who cannot control the class and maintain order.

The argument culture is both a product of and a contributor to this alienation, separating people, disconnecting them from each other and from those who are or might have been their leaders.

What Other Way Is There?

Philosopher John Dewey said, on his ninetieth birthday, "Democracy begins in conversation." I fear that it gets derailed in polarized debate.

In conversation we form the interpersonal ties that bind individuals together in personal relationships; in public discourse, we form similar ties on a larger scale, binding individuals into a community. In conversation, we exchange the many types of information we need to live our lives as members of a community. In public discourse, we exchange the information that citizens in a democracy need in order to decide how to vote. If public discourse provides entertainment first and foremost—and if entertainment is first and foremost watching fights—then citizens do not get the information they need to make meaningful use of their right to vote.

Of course it is the responsibility of intellectuals to explore potential weaknesses in others' arguments, and of journalists to represent serious opposition when it exists. But when opposition becomes the overwhelming avenue of inquiry—a formula that *requires* another side to be found or a criticism to be voiced; when the lust for opposition privileges extreme views and obscures complexity; when our eagerness to find weaknesses blinds us to strengths; when the atmosphere of animosity precludes respect and poisons our relations with one another; then the argument culture is doing more damage than good.

I offer this book not as a formal assault in the argument culture. That would be in the spirit of attack that I am questioning. It is an attempt to examine the argument culture—our use of attack, opposition, and debate in public discourse—to ask, What are its limits as well as its strengths? How has it served us well, but also how has it failed us? How is it related to culture and gender? What other options do we have?

I do not believe we should put aside the argument model of public discourse entirely, but we need to rethink whether this is the *only* way, or *always* the best way, to carry out our affairs. A step toward broadening our repertoires would be to pioneer reform by experimenting with metaphors other than sports and war, and with formats other than debate for framing the exchange of ideas. The change might be as simple as introducing a plural form. Instead of asking "What's the other side?" we might ask instead, "What are the other sides?" Instead of insisting on hearing "both sides," we might insist on hearing "all sides."

Another option is to expand our notion of "debate" to include more dialogue. This does not mean there can be no negativity, criticism, or disagreement. It simply means we can be more creative in our ways of managing all of these, which are inevitable and useful. In dialogue, each statement that one person makes is qualified by a statement made by someone else, until the series of statements and qualifications moves everyone closer to a fuller truth. Dialogue does not preclude negativity. Even saying "I agree" makes sense only against the background assumption that you might disagree. In dialogue, there is opposition, yes, but no head-on collision. Smashing heads does not open minds.

There are times when we need to disagree, criticize, oppose, and attack—to hold debates and view issues as polarized battles. Even cooperation, after all, is not the absence of conflict but a means of managing conflict. My goal is not a make-nice false veneer of agreement or a dangerous ignoring of true opposition. I'm questioning the *automatic* use of adversarial formats—the assumption that it's *always* best to address problems and issues by fighting over them. I'm hoping for a broader repertoire of ways to talk to each other and address issues vital to us.

Notes

Note: Sources referred to by short form are cited in full in the References.

[Numbers indicate page numbers of original document. Ed]

7. "*culture of critique*": I first introduced this term in an op-ed essay, "The Triumph of the Yell," *The New York Times,* Jan. 14, 1994, p. A29.
7. "*There are moments*": Charles Simic, "In Praise of Invective," *Harper's,* Aug. 1997, pp. 24, 26–27; the quote is from p. 26. The article is excerpted from *Orphan Factory* (Ann Arbor: University of Michigan Press, 1997). I am grateful to Amitai Etizioni for calling this article to my attention.
8. Both the term "agonism" and the phrase "programmed contentiousness" come from Walter Ong, *Fighting for Life.*
10. "*the great backpacking vs. car camping debate*": Steven Hendrix, "Hatchback vs. Backpack," *The Washington Po*[illegible] *Weekend,* Mar. 1, 1996, p. 6.
11. *creationism:* See, for example, Jessica Mathews, "Creatior Makes a Comeback," *The Washington Post,* Apr. 8, 1996, p
11. "*People dispute that*": Lipstadt, *Denying the Holocaust,* p. Lipstadt cites *Esquire,* Feb. 1983, for the interview with Mi
12. *Gallo had to spend:* See Nicholas Wade, "Method and Madness: The Vindication of Robert Gallo," *The New Yor Times Magazine,* Dec. 26, 1993, p. 12, and Elaine Richm "The Once and Future King," *The Sciences,* Nov.–Dec. 1996, pp. 12–15. The investigations of Gallo were among series of overly zealous investigations of suspected scien misconduct—all of which ended in the exoneration of the accused, but not before they had caused immense persona anguish and professional setbacks. Others similarly victi were Gallo's colleague Mike Popovic, immunologist The Imanishi-Kari, and her coauthor (not accused of wrongdc but harmed as a result of his defense of her), Nobel Prize winner David Baltimore. On Popovic, see Malcolm Glad "Science Friction," *The Washington Post Magazine,* Dec. 1992, pp. 18–21, 49–51. On Imanishi-Kari and Baltimore *The New Yorker,* May 27, 1996, pp. 94–98ff.
14. *potentially endless list:* Randy Allen Harris, *The Linguist Wars* (New York: Oxford University Press, 1993); "The S Wars," *Newsweek,* Apr. 21, 1997, p. 54; "The Mammogra War," *Newsweek,* Feb. 24, 1997, p. 54; "Party Wars," *New* June 2, 1997, cover. The subhead of the latter reads, "In t battle to feed New York's elite, the top caterers are taking their white gloves and sharpening their knives."
14. "DEMOCRATS SEND CLINTON": *The New York Times,* Aug. 1996, p. A1.
15. "*We risk imposing*": Keller, *Reflections on Gender and Science,* p. 157. Another such case is explained by paleontologist Stephen Jay Gould in his book *Wonderfu Life* about the Burgess shale—a spectacular deposit of 5 million-year-old fossils. In 1909, the first scientist to stu these fossils missed the significance of the find, becaus he "shoehorned every last Burgess animal into a moderi group, viewing the fauna collectively as a set of primiti ancestral versions of later, improved forms" (p. 24). Yea later, observers looked at the Burgess shale fossils with fresh eye and saw a very different reality: a panoply of forms, far more diverse and numerous than what exists The early scientists missed what was right before their because, Gould shows, they proceeded from a metaphor understanding of evolution as a linear march of progres the ancient and primitive to the modern and complex, w humans the inevitable, most complex apex. Accepting t metaphor of "the cone of increasing diversity" prevente early scientists from seeing what was really there.
16. "*Showdown at Lincoln Center*": Peter Watrous, "The Yea the Arts: Pop & Jazz/1994," *The New York Times,* Dec. 2 1994, sec. 2, p. 36.
17. "*the face-off between*": Jack Kroll, "And in This Corner . *Newsweek,* Feb. 10, 1997, p. 65.
18. *a fight between two skaters:* Though Harding was demon somewhat more as an unfeminine, boorish "Wicked Witc the West" (George Vecsey, "Let's Begin the Legal Olymp *The New York Times,* Feb. 13, 1994, sec. 8, p. 1.), Kerriga also demonized as cold and aloof, an "ice princess."

"*long-anticipated figure-skating shootout*": Jere Longman, "Kerrigan Glides Through Compulsory Interviews," *The New York Times,* Feb. 13, 1994, sec. 8, p. 9.

"*the rivalry surrounding*": Paul Farhi, "For NBC, Games Not Just for Guys; Network Tailors Its Coverage to Entice Women to Watch," *The Washington Post,* July 26, 1996, p. A1.

"*I haven't time": The Washington Post Book World,* June 16, 1996, p. 14.

even judges: Washingtonian, June 1996, ranked judges.

Ohio State University protested: Letter to the editor by Malcolm S. Baroway, Executive Director, University Communications, *Time,* Oct. 3, 1994, p. 14.

Overlaid on the talk show example is the gender issue: The woman who called wished she had the courage to stand up to a man and saw her habitual way of speaking as evidence of her insecurity. This interpretation is suggested by our assumptions about women and men. Many people, researchers included, start from the assumption that women are insecure, so ways they speak are scrutinized for evidence of insecurity. The result is often a failure to understand or appreciate women's styles on their own terms, so women are misinterpreted as defective men.

"*Always provocative, sometimes infuriating*": Jill Nelson, "Fighting Words," review of Ishmael Reed, *Airing Dirty Laundry, The New York Times Book Review,* Feb. 13, 1994, p. 28.

In this spirit: John Krich, "To Teach Is Glorious: A Conversation with the New Dean of Cal's Journalism School," Orville Schell, *Express,* Aug. 23, 1996, pp. 1, 14–16, 18, 20–22. The remark is from p. 15.

Many cultures have rituals: See Schlegel and Barry, *Adolescence.*

"*Democracy begins in conversation": Dialogue on John Dewey,* Corliss Lamont, ed. (New York: Horizon Press, 1959), p. 88. Thanks to Pete Becker for this reference.

In dialogue, there is: This insight comes from Walter Ong, who writes, "There is opposition here but no head-on collision, which stops dialogue. (Of course, sometimes dialogue has to be stopped, but that is another story.)" (*Fighting for Life,* p. 32).

References

Gould, Stephen Jay. *Wonderful Life: The Burgess Shale and the Nature of History* (New York: W. W. Norton, 1989).

Keller, Evelyn Fox. *Reflections on Gender and Science* (New Haven: Yale University Press, 1985).

Krich, John. "To Teach Is Glorious: A Conversation with the New Dean of Cal's Journalism School, Orville Schell." *Express,* Aug. 23, 1996, pp. 1, 14–16, 18, 20–22.

Lipstadt, Deborah. *Denying the Holocaust: The Growing Assault on Truth and Memory* (New York: Free Press, 1993).

Ong, Walter J. *Fighting for Life: Contest, Sexuality, and Consciousness* (Ithaca, N.Y.: Cornell University Press, 1981).

Schlegel, Alice, and Herbert Barry III. *Adolescence: An Anthropological Inquiry* (New York: Free Press, 1991).

Deborah Tannen is best known as the author of *You Just Don't Understand: Women and Men in Conversation,* which was on *The New York Times* bestseller list for nearly four years, including eight months as number one, and has been translated into twenty-four languages. Her book, *Talking from 9 to 5: Women and Men in the Workplace: Language, Sex, and Power,* was a *New York Times* Business bestseller. She has written for and been featured in *The New York Times, Newsweek, Time, USA Today, People,* and *The Washington Post.* Her many national television and radio appearances include *20/20, 48 Hours,* CBS *News,* ABC *World News Tonight,* and *Good Morning America.* She is one of only three University Professors at Georgetown University in Washington, D.C., where she is on the Linguistics Department faculty. *The Argument Culture* is her sixteenth book.

Deborah Tannen has also published short stories, essays, and poems. Her first play, *An Act of Devotion,* is included in *Best Short Plays 1993–1994.* It was produced, together with her play *Sisters,* by Horizons Theatre in Arlington, VA.

Expletive Deleted

Things not going too well this holiday . . .?

LAURA SPINNEY

"Fiddlesticks!" exclaimed Father Christmas as he overshot the chimney and landed in a cabbage patch. He could have said fiddle-de-dee, foo, fudge or any of a dozen or so decorous corruptions of the f-word. Santa has to avoid bad language because of the children, but for the rest of us the choice of words we can use to vent our frustration when things go wrong is nothing short of dazzling.

Swearing "recruits our expressive faculties to the fullest", writes Harvard psychologist Steven Pinker in his new book, *The Stuff of Thought.* Yet despite being a showcase for creativity, swear words are taboo in virtually all societies, even though their subject matter—usually sex or excretion—describes activities fundamental to human existence. So why are we such potty-mouths, and what gives certain words the power to shock?

One theory is that cussing is the form of language that comes closest to a physical act of aggression. When you swear at someone, you are forcing an unpleasant thought on them and, lacking earlids, they are helpless to repel this assault. "It's a substitute for physical violence," says Timothy Jay, a psychologist at the Massachusetts College of Liberal Arts in North Adams. "From an evolutionary point of view, it's an advantage for us to be able to say 'fuck you' from across the street," while not having to worry about getting instantly punched or kicked by the disgruntled recipient.

The idea that swearing packs an emotional punch is supported by neurobiological investigations that show it to have a powerful effect on the brain's emotional centre, the limbic system (see "Mind Your Language"). Most of us are able to restrain ourselves from launching these linguistic assaults–at least some of the time—but studies of people who lack this restraint are revealing.

Individuals with Tourette's syndrome have characteristic tics such as blinks and throat clearing, and between 10 and 20 per cent also exhibit involuntary swearing, otherwise known as coprolalia. Diana Van Lancker Sidtis, a neurolinguist and speech pathologist at New York University, says that coprolalia can be regarded as a kind of vocal limbic tic. People with Tourette's have damage to a part of the brain called the basal ganglia—clusters of neurons buried deep in the front half of the brain that are known to inhibit inappropriate behaviour. Without the basal ganglia to keep it in check, the limbic system is free to produce uncontrollable swearing, she says.

As Pinker sees it, the basal ganglia are responsible fo ging certain thoughts as taboo. When the "don't-go-there" is no longer applied, as with Tourette's, taboo thoughts can sert themselves and the urge to cuss becomes overwhel There is even one recorded case of a man with Tourette's was deaf from birth and expressed his coprolalia throug language. In 2000, doctors at London's National Hospit Neurology and Neurosurgery reported that his swearin randomly interspersed within his signed speech, just as i other people with coprolalia. What's more, rather than fli the finger or making other obscene gestures that hearing p deploy, he used the recognised signs for rude words (*Mov Disorders,* vol 15, p 318).

Tourette's aside, many people fear that bad language is increase. Most studies of the subject have found that men more than women. But a new survey by Mike Thelwall University of Wolverhampton in the UK now suggests that, a young British users of the social networking website My strong swear words are used by males and females about equ and a lot. "Where once the only swear words young people might have been furtively scribbled on the walls of publ lets, now they type them casually onto a computer screen, Thelwall. "And there, they never run out of space."

Don't Wear It Out

Over the past three decades Jay has recorded 10,000 p swearing spontaneously in public. Though it is diffic assess overall levels of bad language, he thinks that w and possibly children are swearing more than they used t that profanity has become common in various situations it was once rare, especially recreational ones. Jay believ widespread use of expletives reflects another important tion of swearing: to promote social bonding. Whether sw is perceived as aggressive or as a social entrée depends context, he notes. "In the locker room, the guy who d swear is the weirdo."

Jay's survey reveals that "fuck" and "shit" between account for about half of all swearing in the United Sta 2006, a contestant on the UK's Big Brother TV show us f-word 88 times in 20 minutes (all were bleeped out), l undits to lament that modern society was in danger of g it out. Their concern is misplaced, says Jay. He believes uber swear words retain their power because their usage tantly changing as they are adopted by new kinds of users we create new domains in which to express them.

guist Tony McEnery at the University of Lancaster in the thor of *Swearing in English,* says that the sheer versatil- he f-word should guarantee its enduring appeal. Usually express a strong negative emotion, it can also be used ely or ironically, as in "fucking marvellous", or to give sis, as in "abso-fucking-lutely", a construction whose ity places it in a linguistic category all its own.

long as we have institutions like the mass media and the ment that forbid us to say these things in public, they're to retain their power," Jay says. Yet the taboo nature of ves also means that many of us are afraid to explore the icon, which is why lay and others turned to people with alia to plumb the depths of foul language.

urette's unleashes the most socially inappropriate words guage," says Jay. It is thanks to this work that we know guages as far apart as Japanese and Danish have swear denoting faeces, the female genitals and incestuous sex- ations. It has also turned up some surprising items in the ity canon, such as the Italian rognoso (scabby) and the n verfaulte Knochen (rotten bones).

poring over this rich library of filth, researchers have ble to get a handle on just what makes a good swear It is not just its sound, says McEnery: after all, "shot", and "spit" are not considered obscene, whereas "shit" sides, the German and French equivalents sound quite nt and still pack a very satisfactory punch. It cannot just ut semantic content either, because the use of words ng faeces or sexual matters in a medical context remains able. "Something about the pairing of certain mean- nd sounds has a potent effect on people's emotions," says.

ear words also go in and out of fashion in line with the they breach. "Damn' was the undisputed king before arrived on the scene," says McEnery, but lost its piquancy fear of burning in hell faded. "Poxy", "leprous", "canker" her disease related words went the same way as hygiene ved. From the 19th century on, English-speakers have vented their frustration by reference to two different of taboo: the sexual and the scatological.

ay the f-word reigns supreme, but there is still room for tion. So, what will be the next big thing in swearing? experts decline to predict any winners. "Paedophile" to be an especially offensive thing to call someone today, IcEnery, and therefore a good candidate, but there is no ce it is gaining ground as a swear word. "Something is g with that word," he says. Pinker says the word "cancer", not yet obscene, is acquiring taboo characteristics; note is often referred to as "The Big C".

Mind Your Language

Bad language is intrinsically different from other language. The strongest evidence for this comes from instances of stroke patients whose brain damage has left them unable to speak but who retain the ability to swear. A particularly sad case was the 19th-century French poet Charles Baudelaire, who suffered a stroke at the age of 45. According to cognitive neuroscientist Sebastian Dieguez of the Swiss Federal Institute of Technology in Lausanne, who studied Baudelaire's case this year, the only vaguely meaningful sound the great poet uttered from then on was Cre nom!, short for Sacre nom de Dieu! (something like "goddamn"), an expletive that so offended the nuns who were looking after him that they banished him from their hospital and called in a priest to perform an exorcism (*Frontiers of Neurology and Neuroscience,* vol 22, p 121).

Baudelaire's stroke damaged the left hemisphere of his brain, a feature common to all foul-mouthed but otherwise speechless stroke patients. This has prompted neurologists to speculate that swear words are stored in the brain's right hemisphere. In fact, they suspect that all formulaic expressions, including other taboo words, prayers and song lyrics, reside in the right, while propositional language–in which words are combined according to grammatical rules–is stored in the left.

That's not all, though. Unlike most language, which is produced and processed in the cortex, the most recently evolved outer layer of the human brain, swearing involves the more ancient emotional network, the limbic system. Brain scans reveal that when people hear expletives, a structure that forms part of this system, known as the amygdala, is activated almost instantly. Intriguingly, when you stimulate the limbic system of a macaque monkey, it produces emotional vocalisations, a finding that has led Diana Van Lancker Sidtis at New York University to argue that these angry grunts and shrieks share neurological underpinnings with human profanity. "An emotional impulse can structure a vocalisation with a large amount of energy and intensity, and in humans that is used communicatively," she says. While monkeys appear to shriek, humans channel that energy through words.

Jay has road-tested a few contenders of his own. He once muttered "Expletive!" on a golf course, and got some strange looks. You can't impose swear words on a language, he notes, they arise organically. So if you're tempted to cry "Basting hell!" when you ruin the festive turkey, fine. Just don't expect it to catch on.

Laura Spinney is a writer based in London and Paris, who can swear imaginatively in two languages

I Can't Even Open My Mouth

Separating Messages from Metamessages in Family Ta

DEBORAH TANNEN

"Do you really need another piece of cake?" Donna asks George.

"You bet I do," he replies, with that edge to his voice that implies, "If I wasn't sure I needed it before, I am darned sure now."

Donna feels hamstrung. She knows that George is going to say later that he wished he hadn't had that second piece of cake.

"Why are you always watching what I eat?" George asks.

"I was just watching out for you," Donna replies. "I only say it because I love you."

Elizabeth, in her late twenties, is happy to be making Thanksgiving dinner for her extended family in her own home. Her mother, who is visiting, is helping out in the kitchen. As Elizabeth prepares the stuffing for the turkey, her mother remarks, "Oh, you put onions in the stuffing?"

Feeling suddenly as if she were sixteen years old again, Elizabeth turns on her mother and says, "*I'm* making the stuffing, Mom. Why do you have to criticize everything I do?"

"I didn't criticize," her mother replies. "I just asked a question. What's got into you? I can't even open my mouth."

The allure of family—which is, at heart, the allure of love—is to have someone who knows you so well that you don't have to explain yourself. It is the promise of someone who cares enough about you to protect you against the world of strangers who do not wish you well. Yet, by an odd and cruel twist, it is the family itself that often causes pain. Those we love are looking at us so close-up that they see all our blemishes—see them as if through a magnifying glass. Family members have innumerable opportunities to witness our faults and feel they have a right to point them out. Often their intention is to help us improve. They feel, as Donna did, "I only say it because I love you."

Family members also have a long shared history, so everything we say in a conversation today echoes with meanings from the past. If you have a tendency to be late, your parent, sibling, or spouse may say, "We have to leave at eight"—and then add, "It's really important. Don't be late. Please start your shower at seven, not seven-thirty!" These extra injunctions are demeaning and interfering, but they are based on experience. At the same time, having experienced negative judgments in the past, we develop a sixth sense to sniff out criticism in almost anything a loved one says—even an innocent question ingredients in the stuffing. That's why Elizabeth's mothe up feeling as if she can't even open her mouth—and Eli ends up feeling criticized.

When we are children our family constitutes the world. we grow up, family members—not only our spouses b our grown-up children and adult sisters and brothers—ke larger-than-life aura. We overreact to their judgments bec feels as if they were handed down by the Supreme Court a unassailable assessments of our value as human beings. W tle because these judgments seem unjust; or because we s kernel of truth we would rather not face; or because we fe if someone who knows us so well judges us harshly w really be guilty, so we risk losing not only that person' but everyone else's, too. Along with this heavy load of in tions comes a dark resentment that a loved one is judgin all—and has such power to wound.

"I still fight with my father," a man who had reached position in journalism said to me. "He's been dead twen years." I asked for an example. "He'd tell me that I had to my hair and dress better, that I'd learn when I grew u appearance is important." When he said this I noticed t hair was uncombed, and the tails of his faded shirt were ing out from the waist of his pants. He went on, "I told h ignore that. And now sometimes when I'm going some important, I'll look in the mirror and think—I'll say to my mind, 'See? I *am* a success and it didn't matter.'"

This man's "fights" with his father are about approv matter what age we've reached, no matter whether our p are alive or dead, whether we were close to them or not are times when theirs are the eyes through which we vie selves, theirs the standards against which we measure our when we wonder whether we have measured up. The cri of parents carries extra weight, even when children are a

I Care, Therefore I Criticize

Some family members feel they have not only a right obligation to tell you when they think you're doing som wrong. A woman from Thailand recalls that when she her late teens and early twenties, her mother frequent with her in which she tried to set her daughter straight. "At nd of each lecture," the woman says, "my mother would ys tell me, 'I have to complain about you because I am your er and I love you. Nobody else will talk to you the way I do use they don't care."

sometimes seems that family members operate under the "I care, therefore I criticize." To the one who is being told things differently, what comes through loudest and clearest criticism. But the one offering suggestions and judgments ually focused on the caring. A mother, for example, was ssing concern about her daughter's boyfriend: He didn't a serious job, he didn't seem to want one, and she didn't he was a good prospect for marriage. The daughter protested her mother disapproved of everyone she dated. Her mother nded indignantly, "Would you rather I didn't care?"

s family members we wonder why our parents, children, ngs, and spouses are so critical of us. But as family mem- we also feel frustrated because comments we make in the of caring are taken as criticizing.

oth sentiments are explained by the double meaning of giv- dvice: a loving sign of caring, a hurtful sign of criticizing. mpossible to say which is right; both meanings are there. ng out the ambiguous meanings of caring and criticizing is cult because language works on two levels: the message and netamessage. Separating these levels—and being aware of —is crucial to improving communication in the family.

e Intimate Critic: ıen Metamessages Hurt

use those closest to us have front-row seats to view our s, we quickly react—sometimes overreact—to any hint iticism. The result can be downright comic, as in Phyllis man's novel *Who's Afraid of Virginia Ham?* One scene, a ersation between the narrator and her adult daughter, Lily, s how criticism can be the metronome providing the beat e family theme song. The dialogue goes like this:

Am I too critical of people?

ıer: What people? Me?

Mamma, don't be so self-centered.

ıer: Lily, don't be so critical.

I knew it. You do think I'm critical. Mamma, why do you ways have to find something wrong with me?

mother then protests that it was Lily who asked if she was ritical, and now she's criticizing her mother for answering. responds, "I can't follow this. Sometimes you're impos- hard to talk to."

turns out that Lily is upset because her boyfriend, Brian, er she is too critical of him. She made a great effort to stop izing, but now she's having a hard time keeping her resolve. ave her a sexy outfit for her birthday—it's expensive and tiful—but the generous gift made her angry because she it as criticism of the way she usually dresses.

In this brief exchange Richman captures the layers of meaning that can make the most well-intentioned comment or action a source of conflict and hurt among family members. Key to understanding why Lily finds the conversation so hard to follow—and her mother so hard to talk to—is separating messages from metamessages. The *message* is the meaning of the words and sentences spoken, what anyone with a dictionary and a grammar book could figure out. Two people in a conversation usually agree on what the message is. The *metamessage* is meaning that is not said—at least not in so many words—but that we glean from every aspect of context: the way something is said, who is saying it, or the fact that it is said at all.

Because they do not reside in the words themselves, metamessages are hard to deal with. Yet they are often the source of both comfort and hurt. The message (as I've said) is the word meaning while the metamessage is the heart meaning—the meaning that we react to most strongly, that triggers emotion.

When Lily asked her mother if she was too critical of people, the message was a question about Lily's own personality. But her mother responded to what she perceived as the metamessage: that Lily was feeling critical of *her.* This was probably based on experience: Her daughter had been critical of her in the past. If Lily had responded to the message alone, she would have answered, "No, not you. I was thinking of Brian." But she, too, is reacting to a metamessage—that her mother had made herself the point of a comment that was not about her mother at all. Perhaps Lily's resentment was also triggered because her mother still looms so large in her life.

The mixing up of message and metamessage also explains Lily's confused response to the gift of sexy clothing from her boyfriend. The message is the gift. But what made Lily angry was what she thought the gift implied: that Brian finds the way she usually dresses not sexy enough—and unattractive. This implication is the metamessage, and it is what made Lily critical of the gift, of Brian, and of herself. Metamessages speak louder than messages, so this is what Lily reacted to most strongly.

It's impossible to know whether Brian intended this metamessage. It's possible that he wishes Lily would dress differently; it's also possible that he likes the way she dresses just fine but simply thought this particular outfit would look good on her. That's what makes metamessages so difficult to pinpoint and talk about: They're implicit, not explicit.

When we talk about messages, we are talking about the meanings of words. But when we talk about metamessages, we are talking about relationships. And when family members react to each other's comments, it's metamessages they are usually responding to. Richman's dialogue is funny because it shows how we all get confused between messages and metamessages when we talk to those we are close to. But when it happens in the context of a relationship we care about, our reactions often lead to hurt rather than to humor.

In all the conversations that follow, both in this chapter and throughout the book, a key to improving relationships within the family is distinguishing the message from the metamessage, and being clear about which one you are reacting to. One way you can do this is *metacommunicating*—talking about communication.

"What's Wrong with French Bread?" Try Metacommunicating

The movie *Divorce American Style* begins with Debbie Reynolds and Dick Van Dyke preparing for dinner guests—and arguing. She lodges a complaint: that all he does is criticize. He protests that he doesn't. She says she can't discuss it right then because she has to take the French bread out of the oven. He asks, "French bread?"

A simple question, right? Not even a question, just an observation. But on hearing it Debbie Reynolds turns on him, hands on hips, ready for battle: "What's wrong with French bread?" she asks, her voice full of challenge.

"Nothing," he says, all innocence. "It's just that I really like those little dinner rolls you usually make." This is like the bell that sets in motion a boxing match, which is stopped by another bell—the one at the front door announcing their guests have arrived.

Did he criticize or didn't he? On the message level, no. He simply asked a question to confirm what type of bread she was preparing. But on the metamessage level, yes. If he were satisfied with her choice of bread, he would not comment, except perhaps to compliment. Still, you might ask, So what? So what if he prefers the dinner rolls she usually makes to French bread? Why is it such a big deal? The big deal is explained by her original complaint: She feels that he is *always* criticizing—always telling her to do things differently than she chose to do them.

The big deal, in a larger sense, is a paradox of family: We depend on those closest to us to see our best side, and often they do. But because they are so close, they also see our worst side. You want the one you love to be an intimate ally who reassures you that you're doing things right, but sometimes you find instead an intimate critic who implies, time and again, that you're doing things wrong. It's the cumulative effect of minor, innocent suggestions that creates major problems. You will never work things out if you continue to talk about the message—about French bread versus dinner rolls—rather than the metamessage—the implication that your partner is dissatisfied with everything you do. (*Divorce American Style* was made in 1967; that it still rings true today is evidence of how common—and how recalcitrant—such conversational quagmires are.)

One way to approach a dilemma like this is to *metacommunicate*—to talk about ways of talking. He might *say* that he feels he can't open his mouth to make a suggestion or comment because she takes everything as criticism. She might *say* that she feels he's always dissatisfied with what she does, rather than turn on him in a challenging way. Once they both understand this dynamic, they will come up with their own ideas about how to address it. For example, he might decide to preface his question with a disclaimer: "I'm not criticizing the French bread." Or maybe he *does* want to make a request—a direct one—that she please make dinner rolls because he likes them. They might also set a limit on how many actions of hers he can question in a day. The important thing is to talk about the metamessage she is reacting to: that having too many of her actions questioned makes her feel that her partner in life has changed into an in-house inspection agent, on the lookout for wrong moves.

Living with the Recycling Polic

"This is recyclable," Helen exclaims, brandishing a small cylinder that was once at the center of a roll of toilet p There she stops, as if the damning evidence is sufficient tc her case.

"I know it's recyclable," says Samuel. "You don't have t me." He approves of recycling and generally practices it, i quite as enthusiastically (he would say obsessively) as H But this time he slipped: In a moment of haste he tosse cardboard toilet paper tube into the wastebasket. Now H has found it and wants to know why it was there. "You can through the garbage looking for things I threw away," Sa protests. "Our relationship is more important than a toilet p carcass."

"I'm not talking about our relationship," Helen protests. talking about recycling."

Helen was right: She *was* talking about recycling. But Sa was right, too. If you feel like you're living with the recy police—or the diet police, or the neatness police—som who assumes the role of judge of your actions and repea finds you guilty—it takes the joy out of living together. S times it even makes you wish, for a fleeting moment, tha lived alone, in peace. In that sense, Samuel was talking a the relationship.

Helen was focusing on the message: the benefits of recyc Samuel was focusing on the metamessage: the implicatic perceives that Helen is enforcing rules and telling him he b one. Perhaps, too, he is reacting to the metamessage of r superiority in Helen's being the more fervent recycler. Bec messages lie in words, Helen's position is more obviously d sible. But it's metamessages that have clout, because the emotions, and emotions are the currency of relationships.

In understanding Samuel's reaction, it's also crucial to in mind that the meaning of Helen's remark resides no in the conversation of the moment but in the resonance the conversations on the subject they've had in their together—as well as the conversations Samuel had before especially while growing up in his own family. Furthermore her *repeatedly* remarking on what he does or does not re that gives Samuel the impression that living with Helen is living with the recycling police.

Give Me Connection, Give Me Control

There is another dimension to this argument—another aspe communication that complicates everything we say to each but that is especially powerful in families. That is our simul ous but conflicting desires for connection and for control.

In her view Helen is simply calling her husband's atte to a small oversight in their mutual pursuit of a moral good expression of their connection. Their shared policy on cling reflects their shared life: his trash is her trash. But Sa feels that by installing herself as the judge of his actions is placing herself one-up. In protest he accuses, "You're t to control me."

oth connection and control are at the heart of family. There relationship as close—and none as deeply hierarchical—e relationship between parent and child, or between older younger sibling. To understand what goes on when famıembers talk to each other, you have to understand how orces of connection and control reflect both closeness and ırchy in a family.

Ie's like family," my mother says of someone she likes. ɛrlying this remark is the assumption that *family* connotes ›ness, being connected to each other. We all seek connec- It makes us feel safe; it makes us feel loved. But being means you care about what those you are close to think. tever you do has an impact on them, so you have to take needs and preferences into account. This gives them power ntrol your actions, limiting your independence and making feel hemmed in.

ırents and older siblings have power over children and ger siblings as a result of their age and their roles in the y. At the same time, *ways of talking create power.* Younger ıgs or children can make life wonderful or miserable for siblings or parents by what they say—or refuse to say. ɛ family members increase their chances of getting their by frequently speaking up, or by speaking more loudly and forcefully. Some increase their influence by holding their ıes, so others become more and more concerned about ing them over.

)on't tell me what to do. Don't try to control me" are fret protests within families. It is automatic for many of us to in terms of power relations and to see others' incursions ur freedom as control maneuvers. We are less likely to of them as connection maneuvers, but they often are that, At every moment we're struggling not only for control but for love, approval, and involvement. What's tough is that *ame* actions and comments can be either control maneuor connection maneuvers—or, as in most cases, both at .

ntrol Maneuver Connection Maneuver?

ı't start eating yet," Louis says to Claudia as he walks out ɛ kitchen. "I'll be right there."

ımished, Claudia eyes the pizza before her. The aroma of to sauce and melted cheese is so sweet, her mouth thinks as taken a bite. But Louis, always slow-moving, does not ı, and the pizza is cooling. Claudia feels a bit like their dog in when she was being trained: "Wait!" the instructor told in, as the hungry dog poised pitifully beside her bowl of After pausing long enough to be convinced Muffin would forever, the trainer would say, "Okay!" Only then would in fall into the food.

'as Louis intentionally taking his time in order to prove he make Claudia wait no matter how hungry she was? Or ıe just eager for them to sit down to dinner together? In words, when he said, "Don't start eating yet," was it a control maneuver, to make her adjust to his pace and timing, or a connection maneuver, to preserve their evening ritual of sharing food? The answer is, it was both. Eating together is one of the most evocative rituals that bond individuals as a family. At the same time, the requirement that they sit down to dinner together gave Louis the power to make Claudia wait. So the need for connection entailed control, and controlling each other is in itself a kind of connection.

Control and connection are intertwined, often conflicting forces that thread through everything said in a family. These dual forces explain the double meaning of caring and criticizing. Giving advice, suggesting changes, and making observations are signs of caring when looked at through the lens of connection. But looked at through the lens of control, they are put-downs, interfering with our desire to manage our own lives and actions, telling us to do things differently than we choose to do them. That's why caring and criticizing are tied up like a knot.

The drives toward connection and toward control are the forces that underlie our reactions to metamessages. So the second step in improving communication in the family—after distinguishing between message and metamessage—is understanding the double meaning of control and connection. Once these multiple layers are sorted out and brought into focus, talking about ways of talking—metacommunicating—can help solve family problems rather than making them worse.

Small Spark, Big Explosion

Given the intricacies of messages and metamessages, and of connection and control, the tiniest suggestion or correction can spark an explosion fueled by the stored energy of a history of criticism. One day, for example, Vivian was washing dishes. She tried to fix the drain cup in an open position so it would catch debris and still allow water to drain, but it kept falling into the closed position. With a mental shrug of her shoulders, she decided to leave it, since she didn't have many dishes to wash and the amount of water that would fill the sink wouldn't be that great. But a moment later her husband, Mel, happened by and glanced at the sink. "You should keep the drain open," he said, "so the water can drain."

This sounds innocent enough in the telling. Vivian could have said, "I tried, but it kept slipping in, so I figured it didn't matter that much." Or she could have said, "It's irritating to feel that you're looking over my shoulder all the time, telling me to do things differently from the way I'm doing them." This was, in fact, what she was feeling—and why she experienced, in reaction to Mel's suggestion, a small eruption of anger that she had to expend effort to suppress.

Vivian was surprised at what she did say. She made up a reason and implied she had acted on purpose: "I figured it would be easier to clean the strainer if I let it drain all at once." This thought *had* occurred to her when she decided not to struggle any longer to balance the drain cup in an open position, though it wasn't true that she did it on purpose for that reason. But by justifying her actions, Vivian gave Mel the opening to argue for his method, which he did.

"The whole sink gets dirty if you let it fill up with water," Mel said. Vivian decided to let it drop and remained silent. Had she spoken up, the result would probably have been an argument.

Throughout this interchange Vivian and Mel focused on the message: When you wash the dishes, should the drain cup be open or closed? Just laying out the dilemma in these terms shows how ridiculous it is to argue about. Wars are being fought; people are dying; accident or illness could throw this family into turmoil at any moment. The position of the drain cup in the sink is not a major factor in their lives. But the conversation wasn't really about the message—the drain cup—at least not for Vivian.

Mel probably thought he was just making a suggestion about the drain cup, and in the immediate context he was. But messages always bring metamessages in tow: In the context of the history of their relationship, Mel's comment was not so much about a drain cup as it was about Vivian's ability to do things right and Mel's role as judge of her actions.

This was clear to Vivian, which is why she bristled at his comment, but it was less clear to Mel. Our field of vision is different depending on whether we're criticizing or being criticized. The critic tends to focus on the message: "I just made a suggestion. Why are you so touchy?" The one who feels criticized, however, is responding to the metamessage, which is harder to explain. If Vivian had complained, "You're always telling me how to do things," Mel would surely have felt, and might well have said, "I can't even open my mouth."

At the same time, connection and control are in play. Mel's assumption that he and Vivian are on the same team makes him feel comfortable giving her pointers. Furthermore, if a problem develops with the sink's drainage, he's the one who will have to fix it. Their lives are intertwined; that's where the connection lies. But if Vivian feels she can't even wash dishes without Mel telling her to do it differently, then it seems to her that he is trying to control her. It's as if she has a boss to answer to in her own kitchen.

Vivian might explain her reaction in terms of metamessages. Understanding and respecting her perspective, Mel might decide to limit his suggestions and corrections. Or Vivian might decide that she is overinterpreting the metamessage and make an effort to focus more on the message, taking some of Mel's suggestions and ignoring others. Once they both understand the metamessages as well as the messages they are communicating and reacting to, they can metacommunicate: talk about each other's ways of talking and how they might talk differently to avoid hurt and recriminations.

"Wouldn't You Rather Have Salmon?"

Irene and David are looking over their menus in a restaurant. David says he will order a steak. Irene says, "Did you notice they also have salmon?"

This question exasperates David; he protests, "Will please stop criticizing what I eat?"

Irene feels unfairly accused: "I didn't criticize. I just poi out something on the menu I thought you might like."

The question "Did you notice they also have salmon not, on the message level, a criticism. It could easily be frie and helpful, calling attention to a menu item her husband n have missed. But, again, conversations between spouses between any two people who have a history—are always of an ongoing relationship. David knows that Irene think eats too much red meat, too much dessert, and, generally sp ing, too much.

Against the background of this aspect of their rela ship, any indication that Irene is noticing what he is eati a reminder to David that she disapproves of his eating ha That's why the question "Do you really want to have dess will be heard as "You shouldn't have dessert," and the obs tion "That's a big piece of cake" will communicate "That p of cake is too big," regardless of how they're intended. impression of disapproval comes not from the message- words spoken—but from the metamessage, which grows o their shared history.

It's possible that Irene really was not feeling disapp when she pointed out the salmon on the menu, but it's also sible that she was and preferred not to admit it. Asking a c tion is a handy way of expressing disapproval without see to. But to the extent that the disapproval comes through, indirect means of communicating can make for more a ments, and more hurt feelings on both sides. Irene sees D overreacting to an innocent, even helpful, remark, and he her hounding him about what he eats and then denying ing done so. Suppose he had announced he was going to salmon. Would she have said, "Did you notice they also steak?" Not likely. It is reasonable, in this context, to inte any alternative suggestion to an announced decision as dis faction with that decision.

Though Irene and David's argument has much in com with the previous examples, the salmon versus steak sion is weightier than French bread versus dinner rolls, cling, or drain cups. Irene feels that David's health—m even his life—is at stake. He has high cholesterol, an father died young of a heart attack. Irene has good re to want David to eat less red meat. She loves him, an health and life are irrevocably intertwined with hers. is another paradox of family: A blessing of being clo knowing that someone cares about you: cares what yo and what happens to you. But caring also means interfe and disapproval.

In other words, here again is the paradox of connectio control. From the perspective of control, Irene is judging interfering; from the perspective of connection, she is si recognizing that her life and David's are intertwined. potent brew is family: Just knowing that someone has the c ness to care and the right to pass judgment—and that you so much about that judgment—creates resentment that ca into anger.

ving Literal Meaning: w Not to Resolve Arguments

Irene protested, "I didn't criticize," she was crying literal ing: taking refuge in the message level of talk, ducking the nessage. All of us do that when we want to avoid a fight but et our point across. In many cases this defense is sincere, h it does not justify ignoring or denying the metamessage one else may have perceived. If the person we're talking to es it wasn't "just a suggestion," keeping the conversation ed on the message can result in interchanges that sound tape loop playing over and over. Let's look more closely actual conversation in which this happened—one that was by the people who had it.

ting at the dining room table, Evelyn is filling out an ation. Because Joel is the one who has access to a copy ine at work, the last step of the process will rest on his ders. Evelyn explains, "Okay, so you'll have to attach the d check here, after you make the Xerox copy. Okay?" Joel the papers, but Evelyn goes on: "Okay just—Please get ut tomorrow. I'm counting on you, hon. I'm counting on ove."

el reacts with annoyance: "Oh, for Pete's sake."

elyn is miffed in turn: "What do you mean by that?"

el turns her words back on her: "What do *you* mean by

e question "What do you mean by that?" is a challenge. communication runs smoothly, the meanings of words lf-evident, or at least we assume they are. (We may dis- later that we misinterpreted them.) Although "What do ean?" might be an innocent request for clarification, add- y that" usually signals not so much that you didn't under- what the other person meant but that you understood—all ell—the *implication* of the words, and you didn't like it.

elyn cries literal meaning. She sticks to the message: "Oh, , I just mean I'm *counting* on you."

el calls attention to the metamessage: "Yes, but you say it ay that suggests I can't be counted on."

elyn protests, accurately, "I never said that."

t Joel points to evidence of the metamessage: "I'm talking your *tone*."

uspect Joel was using *tone* as a catchall way of describ- e metamessage level of talk. Moreover, it probably wasn't he way Evelyn spoke—her tone—that he was reacting to e fact that Evelyn said it at all. If she really felt she could on him, she would just hand over the task. "I'm counting i" is what people say to reinforce the importance of doing hing when they believe extra reinforcement is needed. the shared history of the relationship adds meaning to etamessage as well. Joel has reason to believe that Evelyn he can't count on him.

er in the same conversation, Joel takes a turn crying literal ng. He unplugs the radio from the wall in the kitchen and it into the dining room so they can listen to the news. He on the table and turns it on.

"Why aren't you using the plug?" Evelyn asks. "Why waste the batteries?" This sparks a heated discussion about the relative importance of saving batteries. Evelyn then suggests, "Well, we could plug it in right here," and offers Joel the wire.

Joel shoots her a look.

Evelyn protests, "Why are you giving me a dirty look?"

And Joel cries literal meaning: "I'm not!" After all, you can't prove a facial expression; it's not in the message.

"You are!" Evelyn insists, reacting to the metamessage: "Just because I'm handing this to you to plug in."

I have no doubt that Joel did look at Evelyn with annoyance or worse, but not because she handed him a plug—that would be literal meaning, too. He was surely reacting to the metamessage of being corrected, of her judging his actions. For her part, Evelyn probably felt Joel was irrationally refusing to plug in the radio when an electrical outlet was staring them in the face.

How to sort through this jumble of messages and metamessages? The message level is a draw. Some people prefer the convenience of letting the radio run on batteries when it's moved from its normal perch to a temporary one. Others find it obviously reasonable to plug the radio in when there's an outlet handy, to save batteries. Convenience or frugality, take your pick. We all do. But when you live with someone else—caution! It may seem natural to suggest that others do things the way you would do them, but that is taking account only of the message. Giving the metamessage its due, the expense in spirit and goodwill is more costly than batteries. Being corrected all the time is wearying. And it's even more frustrating when you try to talk about what you believe they implied and they cry literal meaning—denying having "said" what you know they communicated.

Consider, too, the role of connection and control. Telling someone what to do is a control maneuver. But it is also a connection maneuver: Your lives are intertwined, and anything one person does has an impact on the other. In the earlier example, when Evelyn said, "I'm counting on you," I suspect some readers sympathized with Joel and others with Evelyn, depending on their own experience with people they've lived with. Does it affect your reaction to learn that Joel forgot to mail the application? Evelyn had good reason, based on years of living with Joel, to have doubts about whether he would remember to do what he said he would do.

Given this shared history, it might have been more constructive for Evelyn to admit that she did not feel she could completely count on Joel, rather than cry literal meaning and deny the metamessage of her words. Taking into account Joel's forgetfulness—or maybe his being overburdened at work—they could devise a plan: Joel might write himself a reminder and place it strategically in his briefcase. Or Evelyn might consider mailing the form herself, even though that would mean a trip to make copies. Whatever they decide, they stand a better chance of avoiding arguments—and getting the application mailed on time—if they acknowledge their metamessages and the reasons motivating them.

Who Burned the Popcorn?

Living together means coordinating so many tasks, it's inevitable that family members will have different ideas of how to perform those tasks. In addition, everyone makes mistakes; sometimes the dish breaks, you forget to mail the application, the drain cup falls into the closed position. At work, lines of responsibility and authority are clear (at least in principle). But in a family—especially when adults are trying to share responsibilities and authority—there are fewer and fewer domains that belong solely to one person. As couples share responsibility for more and more tasks, they also develop unique and firm opinions about how those tasks should be done—and a belief in their right to express their opinions.

Even the most mundane activity, such as making popcorn (unless you buy the microwave type or an electric popper), can spark conflict. First, it takes a little doing, and people have their own ideas of how to do it best. Second, popcorn is often made in the evening, when everyone's tired. Add to that the paradox of connection and control—wanting the person you love to approve of what you do, yet having someone right there to witness and judge mistakes—and you have a potful of kernels sizzling in oil, ready to pop right out of the pot.

More than one couple have told me of arguments about how to make popcorn. One such argument broke out between another couple who were taping their conversations. Since their words were recorded, we have a rare opportunity to listen in on a conversation very much like innumerable ones that vanish into air in homes all around the country. And we have the chance to think about how it could have been handled differently.

The seed of trouble is planted when Molly is in the kitchen and Kevin is watching their four-year-old son, Benny. Kevin calls out, "Molly! Mol! Let's switch. You take care of him. I'll do whatever you're doing."

"I'm making popcorn," Molly calls back. "You always burn it."

Molly's reply is, first and foremost, a sign of resistance. She doesn't want to switch jobs with Kevin. Maybe she's had enough of a four-year-old's company and is looking forward to being on her own in the kitchen. Maybe she is enjoying making popcorn. And maybe her reason is truly the one she gives: She doesn't want Kevin to make the popcorn because he always burns it. Whatever her motivation, Molly resists the switch Kevin proposes by impugning his ability to make popcorn. And this comes across as a call to arms.

Kevin protests, "No I don't! I never burn it. I make it perfect." He joins Molly in the kitchen and peers over her shoulder. "You making popcorn? In the big pot?" (Remember this line; it will become important later.)

"Yes," Molly says, "but you're going to ruin it."

"No I won't," Kevin says. "I'll get it just right." With that they make the switch. Kevin becomes the popcorn chef, Molly the caretaker. But she is not a happy caretaker.

Seeing a way she can be both caretaker and popcorn chef, Molly asks Benny, "You want to help Mommy make popcorn? Let's not let Daddy do it. Come on."

Hearing this, Kevin insists, "I know how to make popc
Then he ups the ante: "I can make popcorn better than you
After that the argument heats up faster than the popcorn. "I
every kernel!" Kevin says.

"No you won't," says Molly.

"I will too! It's never burned!" Kevin defends himself
he adds, "It always burns when you do it!"

"Don't make excuses!"

"There's a trick to it," he says.

And she says, "I know the trick!"

"No you don't," he retorts, "'cause you always burn it

"I do not!" she says. "What are you, crazy?"

It is possible that Kevin is right—that Molly, not he,
one who always burns the popcorn. It is also possible that
is right—that he always burns the popcorn, that she doesn'
that he has turned the accusation back onto her as a self-de
strategy. Move 1: I am not guilty. Move 2: You are guilty.

In any case, Kevin continues as popcorn chef. After a
Molly returns to the kitchen. "Just heat it!" she tells
"Heat it! No, I don't want you—"

"It's going, it's going," Kevin assures her. "Hear it?"

Molly is not reassured, because she does not like wh
hears. "It's too slow," she says. "It's all soaking in. Yo
that little—"

"It's not soaking in," Kevin insists. "It's fine."

"It's just a few kernels," Molly disagrees.

But Kevin is adamant: "All the popcorn is being popp

Acting on her mounting unease about the sounds c
from the popping corn, Molly makes another suggestio
reminds Kevin, "You gotta take the trash outside."

But Kevin isn't buying. "I can't," he says. "I'm doi
popcorn." And he declines Molly's offer to watch it wh
takes out the trash.

In the end Molly gets to say, "See, what'd I tell you
Kevin doesn't see the burned popcorn as a reason to admi
Remember his earlier question, "In the big pot?" Now h
tests, "Well, I never *use* this pot, I use the other pot."

Molly comes back, "It's not the pot! It's you!"

"It's the pot," Kevin persists. "It doesn't heat up prop
it did, then it would get hot." But pots can't really be at
those who choose pots can. So Kevin accuses, "You shoul
let me do it from the start."

"You *did* it from the start!" Molly says.

"No, I didn't," says Kevin. "You chose this pan. I wo
chosen a different pan." So it's the pot's fault, and Molly'
for choosing the pot.

This interchange is almost funny, especially for th
us—most of us, I'd bet—who have found ourselves in s
clashes.

How could Kevin and Molly have avoided this argu
Things might have turned out better if they had talked
their motivations: Is either one of them eager to get a bri
pite from caring for Benny? If so, is there another way th
accomplish that goal? (Perhaps they could set Benny u
a task he enjoys on his own.) With this motivation out
open, Molly might have declined to switch places when

›sed it, saying something like, "I'm making popcorn. I'm ·ing making it. I'd rather not switch." The justification y used, "You always burn it," may have seemed to her a r tactic because it claims her right to keep making popcorn e basis of the family good rather than her own preference. he metamessage of incompetence can come across as pro- ive, in addition to being hurtful.

s understandable that Kevin would be offended to have his orn-making skills impugned, but he would have done bet- avoid the temptation to counterattack by insisting he does ter, that it's Molly who burns it. He could have prevented rgument rather than escalate it if he had metacommuni- : "You can make the popcorn if you want," he might have "but you don't have to say I can't do it." For both Molly Kevin—as for any two people negotiating who's going to hat—metacommunicating is a way to avoid the flying met- sages of incompetence.

Know a Thing or Two"

of the most hurtful metamessages, and one of the frequent, that family talk entails is the implication of npetence—even (if not especially) when children grow up. that we're adults we feel we should be entitled to make our decisions, lead our own lives, imperfect though they may ut we still want to feel that our parents are proud of us, hey believe in our competence. That's the metamessage we for. Indeed, it's because we want their approval so much ve find the opposite metamessage—that they don't trust ompetence—so distressing.

artin and Gail knew that Gail's mother tended to be criti- f whatever they did, so they put off letting her see their home until the purchase was final. Once the deal was d they showed her, with pride, the home they had chosen the previous owner's furniture was still in it. They were he would be impressed by the house they were now able to d, as well as its spotless condition. But she managed to find thing to criticize—even if it was invisible: "They may've ou it's in move-in condition," she said with authority, "but w a thing or two, and when they take those pictures off the there will be holes!" Even though they were familiar with endency to find fault, Gail and Martin were flummoxed.

e aspect of the house Gail's mother found to criticize rofoundly insignificant: Every home has pictures on the every picture taken down leaves holes, and holes are eas- ackled in and painted over. It seems that Gail's mother eally reaching to find *something* about their new home ticize. From the perspective of control, it would be easy nclude that Gail's mother was trying to take the role of t in order to put them down, or even to spoil the joy of momentous purchase. But consider the perspective of con- on. Pointing out a problem that her children might not have ed shows that she can still be of use, even though they are n and have found this wonderful house without her help. vas being protective, watching out for them, making sure e pulled the wool over their eyes.

Because control and connection are inextricably intertwined, protection implies incompetence. If Gail and Martin need her mother's guidance, they are incapable of taking care of themselves. Though Gail's mother may well have been reacting to—and trying to overcome—the metamessage that they don't need her anymore, the metamessage they heard is that she can't approve wholeheartedly of anything they do.

"She Knew What Was Right"

In addition to concern about their children's choice of home, parents often have strong opinions about adult children's partners, jobs, and—especially—how they treat their own children. Raising children is something at which parents self-evidently have more experience, but metamessages of criticism in this area, though particularly common, are also particularly hurtful, because young parents want so much to be good parents.

A woman of seventy still recalls the pain she felt when her children were small and her mother-in-law regarded her as an incompetent parent. It started in the first week of her first child's life. Her mother-in-law had come to help—and didn't want to go home. Finally, her father-in-law told his wife it was time to leave the young couple on their own. Unconvinced, she said outright—in front of her son and his wife—"I can't trust them with the baby."

Usually signs of distrust are more subtle. For example, during a dinner conversation among three sisters and their mother, the sisters were discussing what the toddlers like to eat. When one said that her two-year-old liked fish, their mother cautioned, "Watch the bones." How easy it would be to take offense (though there was no indication this woman did): "You think I'm such an incompetent mother that I'm going to let my child swallow fish bones?" Yet the grandmother's comment was her way of making a contribution to the conversation—one that exercises her lifelong responsibility of protecting children.

It is easy to scoff at the mother-in-law who did not want to leave her son and his wife alone with their own baby. But consider the predicament of parents who become grandparents and see (or believe they see) their beloved grandchildren treated in ways they feel are hurtful. One woman told me that she loves being a grandmother—but the hardest part is having to bite her tongue when her daughter-in-law treats her child in a way the grandmother feels is misguided, unfair, or even harmful. "You see your children doing things you think aren't right," she commented, "but at least they're adults; they'll suffer the consequences. But a child is so defenseless."

In some cases grandparents really do know best. My parents recall with lingering guilt a time they refused to take a grandparent's advice—and later wished they had. When their first child, my sister Naomi, was born, my parents, like many of their generation, relied on expert advice for guidance in what was best for their child. At the time, the experts counseled that, once bedtime comes, a child who cries should not be picked up. After all, the reasoning went, that would simply encourage the baby to cry rather than go to sleep.

One night when she was about a year old, Naomi was crying after being put to sleep in her crib. My mother's mother, who lived with my parents, wanted to go in and pick her up, but my parents wouldn't let her. "It tore us apart to hear her cry," my father recalls, "but we wanted to do what was best for her." It later turned out that Naomi was crying because she was sick. My parents cringe when they tell this story. "My mother pleaded with us to pick her up," my mother says. "She knew what was right."

I'm Grown Up Now

Often a parent's criticism is hurtful—or makes us angry—even when we know it is right, maybe especially if we sense it is right. That comes clear in the following example.

Two couples were having dinner together. One husband, Barry, was telling about how he had finally—at the age of forty-five—learned to ignore his mother's criticism. His mother, he said, had commented that he is too invested in wanting the latest computer gizmo, the most up-to-date laptop, regardless of whether he needs it. At that point his wife interrupted. "It's true, you are," she said—and laughed. He laughed, too: "I know it's true." Then he went back to his story and continued, unfazed, about how in the past he would have been hurt by his mother's comment and would have tried to justify himself to her, but this time he just let it pass. How easily Barry acknowledged the validity of his mother's criticism—when it was his wife making it. Yet acknowledging that the criticism was valid didn't change his view of his mother's comment one whit: He still thought she was wrong to criticize him.

When we grow up we feel we should be free from our parents' judgment (even though we still want their approval). Ironically, there is often extra urgency in parents' tendency to judge children's behavior when children are adults, because parents have a lot riding on how their children turn out. If the results are good, everything they did as parents gets a seal of approval. My father, for example, recalls that as a young married man he visited an older cousin, a woman he did not know well. After a short time the cousin remarked, "Your mother did a good job." Apparently, my father had favorably impressed her, but instead of complimenting him, she credited his mother.

By the same token, if their adult children have problems—if they seem irresponsible or make wrong decisions—parents feel their life's work of child rearing has been a failure, and those around them feel that way, too. This gives extra intensity to parents' desire to set their children straight. But it also can blind them to the impact of their corrections and suggestions, just as those in power often underestimate the power they wield.

When adult children move into their own homes, the lid is lifted off the pressure cooker of family interaction, though the pot may still be simmering on the range. If they move far away—as more and more do—visits turn into intense interactions during which the pressure cooker lid is clicked back in place and the steam builds up once again. Many adult children feel like they're kids again when they stay with their parents. And parents often feel the same way: that their adult children are acting lik
Visits become immersion courses in return-to-family.

Parents with children living at home have the ul
power—asking their children to move out. But v
adult children have a new power of their own: The
threaten not to return, or to stay somewhere else. M
ret was thrilled that her daughter Amanda, who li
Oregon, would be coming home for a visit to the
farm in Minnesota. It had been nearly a year since
garet had seen her grandchildren, and she was ea
get reacquainted with them. But near the end of the
there was a flare-up. Margaret questioned whether A
da's children should be allowed to run outside bar
Margaret thought it was dangerous; Amanda thought
harmless. And Amanda unsheathed her sword: "Thi
working," she said. "Next time I won't stay at the
I'll find somewhere else to stay." Because Margaret
connection—time with her daughter and grandchild
the ability to dole out that connection gives her dau
power that used to be in Margaret's hands.

The Paradox of Family

When I was a child I walked to elementary school along
Island Avenue in Brooklyn, praying that if a war came
home with my family when it happened. During my chil
in the 1950s my teachers periodically surprised the class b
ing out, "Take cover!" At that cry we all ducked under our
and curled up in the way we had been taught: elbows and
tucked in, heads down, hands clasped over our necks. W
possibility of a nuclear attack made vivid by these exerc
walked to school in dread—not of war but of the possibili
it might strike when I was away from my family.

But there is another side to family, the one I have been e
ing in this chapter. My nephew Joshua Marx, at thirteen, p
out this paradox: "If you live with someone for too long
notice things about them," he said. "That's the reason you
like your parents, your brother. There's a kid I know wh
about his friend, 'Wouldn't it be cool if we were brothers
I said, 'Then you'd hate him.' "

We look to communication as a way through the minefi
this paradox. And often talking helps. But communication
is a minefield because of the complex workings of messag
metamessage. Distinguishing messages from metames
and taking into account the underlying needs for connectic
control, provides a basis for metacommunicating. With
insights as foundation, we can delve further into the intri
of family talk. Given our shared and individual histories
in relationships, and the enormous promise of love, under
ing, and listening that family holds out, it's worth the str
to continue juggling—and talking.

ticle 11

hakespeare in the Bush

JRA BOHANNAN

ust before I left Oxford for the Tiv in West Africa, conversa-tion turned to the season at Stratford. "You Americans," said a friend, "often have difficulty with Shakespeare. He was, all, a very English poet, and one can easily misinterpret the rsal by misunderstanding the particular."

rotested that human nature is pretty much the same the whole over; at least the general plot and motivation of the greater dies would always be clear—everywhere—although some s of custom might have to be explained and difficulties of ation might produce other slight changes. To end an argument ould not conclude, my friend gave me a copy of *Hamlet* to in the African bush: it would, he hoped, lift my mind above imitive surroundings, and possibly I might, by prolonged ation, achieve the grace of correct interpretation.

was my second field trip to that African tribe, and I thought lf ready to live in one of its remote sections—an area difficult ss even on foot. I eventually settled on the hillock of a very ledgeable old man, the head of a homestead of some hun-and forty people, all of whom were either his close relatives ir wives and children. Like the other elders of the vicinity, d man spent most of his time performing ceremonies sel-seen these days in the more accessible parts of the tribe. I elighted. Soon there would be three months of enforced iso-and leisure, between the harvest that takes place just before sing of the swamps and the clearing of new farms when the goes down. Then, I thought, they would have even more to perform ceremonies and explain them to me.

vas quite mistaken. Most of the ceremonies demanded the nce of elders from several homesteads. As the swamps rose, d men found it too difficult to walk from one homestead to ext, and the ceremonies gradually ceased. As the swamps ven higher, all activities but one came to an end. The women ed beer from maize and millet. Men, women, and children their hillocks and drank it.

ople began to drink at dawn. By midmorning the whole stead was singing, dancing, and drumming. When it rained, e had to sit inside their huts: there they drank and sang or they and told stories. In any case, by noon or before, I either had to he party or retire to my own hut and my books. "One does not ss serious matters when there is beer. Come, drink with us." I lacked their capacity for the thick native beer, I spent more nore time with *Hamlet.* Before the end of the second month, descended on me. I was quite sure that *Hamlet* had only one ole interpretation, and that one universally obvious.

Early every morning, in the hope of having some serious talk before the beer party, I used to call on the old man at his reception hut—a circle of posts supporting a thatched roof above a low mud wall to keep out wind and rain. One day I crawled through the low doorway and found most of the men of the homestead sitting huddled in their ragged cloths on stools, low plank beds, and reclining chairs, warming themselves against the chill of the rain around a smoky fire. In the center were three pots of beer. The party had started.

The old man greeted me cordially. "Sit down and drink." I accepted a large calabash full of beer, poured some into a small drinking gourd, and tossed it down. Then I poured some more into the same gourd for the man second in seniority to my host before I handed my calabash over to a young man for further dis-tribution. Important people shouldn't ladle beer themselves.

"It is better like this," the old man said, looking at me approv-ingly and plucking at the thatch that had caught in my hair. "You should sit and drink with us more often. Your servants tell me that when you are not with us, you sit inside your hut looking at a paper."

The old man was acquainted with four kinds of "papers": tax receipts, bride price receipts, court fee receipts, and letters. The messenger who brought him letters from the chief used them mainly as a badge of office, for he always knew what was in them and told the old man. Personal letters for the few who had relatives in the government or mission stations were kept until someone went to a large market where there was a letter writer and reader. Since my arrival, letters were brought to me to be read. A few men also brought me bride price receipts, privately, with requests to change the figures to a higher sum. I found moral arguments were of no avail, since in-laws are fair game, and the technical hazards of for-gery difficult to explain to an illiterate people. I did not wish them to think me silly enough to look at any such papers for days on end, and I hastily explained that my "paper" was one of the "things of long ago" of my country.

"Ah," said the old man. "Tell us."

I protested that I was not a storyteller. Story telling is a skilled art among them; their standards are high, and the audiences critical—and vocal in their criticism. I protested in vain. This morn-ing they wanted to hear a story while they drank. They threatened to tell me no more stories until I told them one of mine. Finally, the old man promised that no one would criticize my style "for we know you are struggling with our language." "But," put in one of the elders, "you must explain what we do not understand, as we do when we tell you our stories." Realizing that here was my chance to prove *Hamlet* universally intelligible, I agreed.

The old man handed me some more beer to help me on with my storytelling. Men filled their long wooden pipes and knocked coals from the fire to place in the pipe bowls; then, puffing contentedly, they sat back to listen. I began in the proper style, "Not yesterday, not yesterday, but long ago, a thing occurred. One night three men were keeping watch outside the homestead of the great chief, when suddenly they saw the former chief approach them."

"Why was he no longer their chief?"

"He was dead," I explained. "That is why they were troubled and afraid when they saw him."

"Impossible," began one of the elders, handing his pipe on to his neighbor, who interrupted, "Of course it wasn't the dead chief. It was an omen sent by a witch. Go on."

Slightly shaken, I continued. "One of these three was a man who knew things"—the closest translation for scholar, but unfortunately it also meant witch. The second elder looked triumphantly at the first. "So he spoke to the dead chief saying, 'Tell us what we must do so you may rest in your grave,' but the dead chief did not answer. He vanished, and they could see him no more. Then the man who knew things—his name was Horatio—said this event was the affair of the dead chief's son, Hamlet."

There was a general shaking of heads round the circle. "Had the dead chief no living brothers? Or was this son the chief?"

"No," I replied. "That is, he had one living brother who became the chief when the elder brother died."

The old men muttered: such omens were matters for chiefs and elders, not for youngsters; no good could come of going behind a chief's back; clearly Horatio was not a man who knew things.

"Yes, he was," I insisted, shooing a chicken away from my beer. "In our country the son is next to the father. The dead chief's younger brother had become the great chief. He had also married his elder brother's widow only about a month after the funeral."

"He did well," the old man beamed and announced to the others, "I told you that if we knew more about Europeans, we would find they really were very like us. In our country also," he added to me, "the younger brother marries the elder brother's widow and becomes the father of his children. Now, if your uncle, who married your widowed mother, is your father's full brother, then he will be a real father to you. Did Hamlet's father and uncle have one mother?"

His question barely penetrated my mind; I was too upset and thrown too far off balance by having one of the most important elements of *Hamlet* knocked straight out of the picture. Rather uncertainly I said that I thought they had the same mother, but I wasn't sure—the story didn't say. The old man told me severely that these genealogical details made all the difference and that when I got home I must ask the elders about it. He shouted out the door to one of his younger wives to bring his goatskin bag.

Determined to save what I could of the mother motif, I took a deep breath and began again. "The son, Hamlet, was very sad because his mother had married again so quickly. There was no need for her to do so, and it is our custom for a widow not to go to her next husband until she has mourned for two years."

"Two years is too long," objected the wife, who had appeared with the old man's battered goatskin bag. "Who will hoe your farms for you while you have no husband?"

"Hamlet," I retorted without thinking, "was old enough to hoe his mother's farms himself. There was no need for her to remarry." No one looked convinced. I gave up. "His mother and the great chief told Hamlet not to be sad, for the great chief himself would be a father to Hamlet. Furthermore, Hamlet would be the next therefore he must stay to learn the things of a chief. Hamlet to remain, and all the rest went off to drink beer."

While I paused, perplexed at how to render Hamlet's dis soliloquy to an audience convinced that Claudius and Gertru behaved in the best possible manner, one of the younger men me who had married the other wives of the dead chief.

"He had no other wives," I told him.

"But a chief must have many wives! How else can he beer and prepare food for all his guests?"

I said firmly that in our country even chiefs had only one that they had servants to do their work, and that they paid from tax money.

It was better, they returned, for a chief to have many and sons who would help him hoe his farms and fee people; then everyone loved the chief who gave much and nothing—taxes were a bad thing.

I agreed with the last comment, but for the rest fell ba their favorite way of fobbing off my questions: "That is th it is done, so that is how we do it."

I decided to skip the soliloquy. Even if Claudius wa thought quite right to marry his brother's widow, there ren the poison motif, and I knew they would disapprove of cide. More hopefully I resumed, "That night Hamlet kept with the three who had seen his dead father. The dead chief appeared, and although the others were afraid, Hamlet fol his dead father off to one side. When they were alone, Ha dead father spoke."

"Omens can't talk!" The old man was emphatic.

"Hamlet's dead father wasn't an omen. Seeing him migh been an omen, but he was not." My audience looked as con as I sounded. "It *was* Hamlet's dead father. It was a thing w a 'ghost.'" I had to use the English word, for unlike ma the neighboring tribes, these people didn't believe in the su after death of any individuating part of the personality.

"What is a 'ghost?' An omen?"

"No, a 'ghost' is someone who is dead but who walks arou can talk, and people can hear him and see him but not touch hir

They objected. "One can touch zombis."

"No, no! It was not a dead body the witches had anima sacrifice and eat. No one else made Hamlet's dead father He did it himself."

"Dead men can't walk," protested my audience as one m

I was quite willing to compromise. "A 'ghost' is the man's shadow."

But again they objected. "Dead men cast no shadows."

"They do in my country," I snapped.

The old man quelled the babble of disbelief that immediately and told me with that insincere, but cour agreement one extends to the fancies of the young, ignoran superstitious, "No doubt in your country the dead can also without being zombis." From the depths of his bag he pro a withered fragment of kola nut, bit off one end to show it w poisoned, and handed me the rest as a peace offering.

"Anyhow," I resumed, "Hamlet's dead father said that hi brother, the one who became chief, had poisoned him. He w Hamlet to avenge him. Hamlet believed this in his heart, for not like his father's brother." I took another swallow of bee the country of the great chief, living in the same homestead.

very large one, was an important elder who was often with ef to advise and help him. His name was Polonius. Hamlet urting his daughter, but her father and her brother . . . [I cast about for some tribal analogy] warned her not to let Hamlet er when she was alone on her farm, for he would be a great nd so could not marry her."

ny not?" asked the wife, who had settled down on the edge old man's chair. He frowned at her for asking stupid ques- nd growled, "They lived in the same homestead."

at was not the reason," I informed them. "Polonius was a er who lived in the homestead because he helped the chief, cause he was a relative."

en why couldn't Hamlet marry her?"

could have," I explained, "but Polonius didn't think he After all, Hamlet was a man of great importance who ought ry a chief's daughter, for in his country a man could have ne wife. Polonius was afraid that if Hamlet made love to his er, then no one else would give a high price for her."

at might be true," remarked one of the shrewder elders, "but 's son would give his mistress's father enough presents and age to more than make up the difference. Polonius sounds fool to me."

any people think he was," I agreed. "Meanwhile Polonius s son Laertes off to Paris to learn the things of that country, vas the homestead of a very great chief indeed. Because he raid that Laertes might waste a lot of money on beer and n and gambling, or get into trouble by fighting, he sent one servants to Paris secretly, to spy out what Laertes was doing. ay Hamlet came upon Polonius's daughter Ophelia. He ed so oddly he frightened her. Indeed"—I was fumbling for to express the dubious quality of Hamlet's madness—"the nd many others had also noticed that when Hamlet talked uld understand the words but not what they meant. Many thought that he had become mad." My audience suddenly e much more attentive. "The great chief wanted to know was wrong with Hamlet, so he sent for two of Hamlet's ates [school friends would have taken long explanation] to Hamlet and find out what troubled his heart. Hamlet, that they had been bribed by the chief to betray him, told nothing. Polonius, however, insisted that Hamlet was mad se he had been forbidden to see Ophelia, whom he loved."

hy," inquired a bewildered voice, "should anyone bewitch t on that account?"

ewitch him?"

s, only witchcraft can make anyone mad, unless, of course, es the beings that lurk in the forest."

topped being a storyteller, took out my notebook and ded to be told more about these two causes of madness. while they spoke and I jotted notes, I tried to calculate the of this new factor on the plot. Hamlet had not been exposed beings that lurk in the forests. Only his relatives in the ine could bewitch him. Barring relatives not mentioned by speare, it had to be Claudius who was attempting to harm nd, of course, it was.

the moment I staved off questions by saying that the great also refused to believe that Hamlet was mad for the love helia and nothing else. "He was sure that something much mportant was troubling Hamlet's heart."

"Now Hamlet's age mates," I continued, "had brought with them a famous storyteller. Hamlet decided to have this man tell the chief and all his homestead a story about a man who had poisoned his brother because he desired his brother's wife and wished to be chief himself. Hamlet was sure the great chief could not hear the story without making a sign if he was indeed guilty, and then he would discover whether his dead father had told him the truth."

The old man interrupted, with deep cunning, "Why should a father lie to his son?" he asked.

I hedged: "Hamlet wasn't sure that it really was his dead father." It was impossible to say anything, in that language, about devil-inspired visions.

"You mean," he said, "it actually was an omen, and he knew witches sometimes send false ones. Hamlet was a fool not to go to one skilled in reading omens and divining the truth in the first place. A man-who-sees-the-truth could have told him how his father died, if he really had been poisoned, and if there was witchcraft in it; then Hamlet could have called the elders to settle the matter."

The shrewd elder ventured to disagree. "Because his father's brother was a great chief, one-who-sees-the-truth might therefore have been afraid to tell it. I think it was for that reason that a friend of Hamlet's father—a witch and an elder—sent an omen so his friend's son would know. Was the omen true?"

"Yes," I said, abandoning ghosts and the devil; a witch-sent omen it would have to be. "It was true, for when the storyteller was telling his tale before all the homestead, the great chief rose in fear. Afraid that Hamlet knew his secret he planned to have him killed."

The stage set of the next bit presented some difficulties of translation. I began cautiously. "The great chief told Hamlet's mother to find out from her son what he knew. But because a woman's children are always first in her heart, he had the important elder Polonius hide behind a cloth that hung against the wall of Hamlet's mother's sleeping hut. Hamlet started to scold his mother for what she had done."

There was a shocked murmur from everyone. A man should never scold his mother.

"She called out in fear, and Polonius moved behind the cloth. Shouting, 'A rat!' Hamlet took his machete and slashed through the cloth." I paused for dramatic effect. "He had killed Polonius!"

The old men looked at each other in supreme disgust. "That Polonius truly was a fool and a man who knew nothing! What child would not know enough to shout, 'It's me!' " With a pang, I remembered that these people are ardent hunters, always armed with bow, arrow, and machete; at the first rustle in the grass an arrow is aimed and ready, and the hunter shouts "Game!" If no human voice answers immediately, the arrow speeds on its way. Like a good hunter Hamlet had shouted, "A rat!"

I rushed in to save Polonius's reputation. "Polonius did speak. Hamlet heard him. But he thought it was the chief and wished to kill him earlier that evening. . . ." I broke down, unable to describe to these pagans, who had no belief in individual afterlife, the difference between dying at one's prayers and dying "unhousell'd, disappointed, unaneled."

This time I had shocked my audience seriously. "For a man to raise his hand against his father's brother and the one who has become his father—that is a terrible thing. The elders ought to let such a man be bewitched."

I nibbled at my kola nut in some perplexity, then pointed out that after all the man had killed Hamlet's father.

"No," pronounced the old man, speaking less to me than to the young men sitting behind the elders. "If your father's brother has killed your father, you must appeal to your father's age mates; *they* may avenge him. No man may use violence against his senior relatives." Another thought struck him. "But if his father's brother had indeed been wicked enough to bewitch Hamlet and make him mad that would be a good story indeed, for it would be his fault that Hamlet, being mad, no longer had any sense and thus was ready to kill his father's brother."

There was a murmur of applause. *Hamlet* was again a good story to them, but it no longer seemed quite the same story to me. As I thought over the coming complications of plot and motive, I lost courage and decided to skim over dangerous ground quickly.

"The great chief," I went on, "was not sorry that Hamlet had killed Polonius. It gave him a reason to send Hamlet away, with his two treacherous mates, with letters to a chief of a far country, saying that Hamlet should be killed. But Hamlet changed the writing on their papers, so that the chief killed his age mates instead." I encountered a reproachful glare from one of the men whom I had told undetectable forgery was not merely immoral but beyond human skill. I looked the other way.

"Before Hamlet could return, Laertes came back for his father's funeral. The great chief told him Hamlet had killed Polonius. Laertes swore to kill Hamlet because of this, and because his sister Ophelia, hearing her father had been killed by the man she loved, went mad and drowned in the river."

"Have you already forgotten what we told you?" The old man was reproachful. "One cannot take vengeance on a madman; Hamlet killed Polonius in his madness. As for the girl, she not only went mad, she was drowned. Only witches can make people drown. Water itself can't hurt anything. It is merely something one drinks and bathes in."

I began to get cross. "If you don't like the story, I'll stop."

The old man made soothing noises and himself poured me some more beer. "You tell the story well, and we are listening. But it is clear that the elders of your country have never told you what the story really means. No, don't interrupt! We believe you when you say your marriage customs are different, or your clothes and weapons. But people are the same everywhere; therefore, there are always witches and it is we, the elders, who know how witches work. We told you it was the great chief who wished to kill Hamlet, and now your own words have proved us right. Who were Ophelia's male relatives?"

"There were only her father and her brother." *Hamlet* was clearly out of my hands.

"There must have been many more; this also you must ask of your elders when you get back to your country. From what you tell us, since Polonius was dead, it must have been Laertes who killed Ophelia, although I do not see the reason for it."

We had emptied one pot of beer, and the old men argu point with slightly tipsy interest. Finally one of them dem of me, "What did the servant of Polonius say on his return?

With difficulty I recollected Reynaldo and his missi don't think he did return before Polonius was killed."

"Listen," said the elder, "and I will tell you how it was an your story will go, then you may tell me if I am right. Po knew his son would get into trouble, and so he did. He had fines to pay for fighting, and debts from gambling. But he ha two ways of getting money quickly. One was to marry off his at once, but it is difficult to find a man who will marry a w desired by the son of a chief. For if the chief's heir commits ad with your wife, what can you do? Only a fool calls a case ag man who will someday be his judge. Therefore Laertes had t the second way: he killed his sister by witchcraft, drowning he could secretly sell her body to the witches."

I raised an objection. "They found her body and b it. Indeed Laertes jumped into the grave to see his sister more—so, you see, the body was truly there. Hamlet, wh just come back, jumped in after him."

"What did I tell you?" The elder appealed to the o "Laertes was up to no good with his sister's body. Hamle vented him, because the chief's heir, like a chief, does not any other man to grow rich and powerful. Laertes would be because he would have killed his sister without benefit to hi In our country he would try to kill Hamlet for that reason. not what happened?"

"More or less," I admitted. "When the great chief found H was still alive, he encouraged Laertes to try to kill Hamle arranged a fight with machetes between them. In the figh the young men were wounded to death. Hamlet's mother the poisoned beer that the chief meant for Hamlet in case h the fight. When he saw his mother die of poison, Hamlet, managed to kill his father's brother with his machete."

"You see, I was right!" exclaimed the elder.

"That was a very good story," added the old man, "an told it with very few mistakes. There was just one more at the very end. The poison Hamlet's mother drank was ously meant for the survivor of the fight, whichever it w Laertes had won, the great chief would have poisoned hi no one would know that he arranged Hamlet's death. The he need not fear Laertes' witchcraft; it takes a strong he kill one's only sister by witchcraft.

"Sometime," concluded the old man, gathering his ragge about him, "you must tell us some more stories of your co We, who are elders, will instruct you in their true meani that when you return to your own land your elders will se you have not been sitting in the bush, but among those who things and who have taught you wisdom."

LAURA BOHANNAN is a former professor of anthropology University of Illinois, at Chicago.

t a Loss for Words

Native-American language Salish–Pend d'Oreille n the brink of disappearing. re than half the world's 6,000 languages will be gone the end of the century.

AH GREY THOMASON

ohn Peter Paul, a rugged, dignified man, was extremely ill during the summer of 2000. He was ninety-one years old and suffering from stomach cancer. Still, every week isted on wheeling himself into the *Ussnétx*^{w} (Longhouse) Flathead reservation in northwestern Montana. There, he ther elders of the Salish and Pend d'Oreille tribes would r in meetings I had set up to expand and fine-tune the dic-y of their language and the collection of texts that we had working on together for many years.

one occasion in midsummer, when John's illness reached is point, he refused to go to the hospital because he didn't to miss our scheduled meeting the next day. As a result, he be rushed to the hospital in desperate condition the next ing. His fierce dedication to the task of documenting and rving his language almost cost him his life.

her elders I work with share his dedication to their language e culture it expresses. Some are Pend d'Oreilles, like John; st are Bitterroot Salish (also called Flatheads). Although re different tribes, they share the same language—which ed, logically enough, Salish–Pend d'Oreille—albeit with dialect differences.

t like so many indigenous languages on every populated ent, Salish–Pend d'Oreille is on the point of vanishing. than thirty fluent native speakers remain, and nearly them are elderly. The great majority of the roughly Salish and Pend d'Oreille tribal members do not speak ancestral language at all.

e fluent Salish–Pend d'Oreille speakers who work with port that the only opportunities they have to "talk Indian" the tribes' Culture Committee's weekly elders' meetings the fall through the spring, and in their weekly language ns with me during the summer. John Peter Paul, who died 1 at the age of ninety-two, was married to his wife Agnes Jim Paul, a Bitterroot Salish, for seventy-two years; they the last married couple who spoke their language regu-at home. Their oldest daughter, Josephine Quequesah, is a fluent and highly skilled speaker of the language, but some of her younger siblings have a more passive level of fluency.

What happened to bring Salish–Pend d'Oreille to this precarious position? The obvious answer—the absolute necessity for most Americans to speak English in order to survive economically, together with the appeal of mainstream American culture to most younger tribal members—tells only part of the story. Another factor is the boarding schools that many Native children were forced to attend, starting in the nineteenth century. Those schools implemented the United States government's policy of assimilating Indians by replacing their native cultures, including their languages, with Anglo culture and English. (The policy had close parallels in Canada and Australia.)

The assimilation policies that took place on the Flathead reservation—and elsewhere—were often brutal. Some teachers and principals beat children for speaking their language anywhere on the school grounds.

Louis Adams, a Bitterroot Salish elder in his late seventies, recounts what happened to him in the first grade, in a public school on the reservation. He and his friend Peter Pierre were talking Indian in the hallway of the school; a teacher heard them and broke her yardstick over Peter's head, then hit Louis with the biggest of the broken pieces. Next she took them to the principal, who said that if they spoke Indian again, he'd whip them with his belt. Louis complained to his father about the treatment and was told that he should do what the teachers wanted in school, but go on talking Salish outside of school. "Don't throw away your language," his father told him. Louis didn't, but many of his peers did.

The policy encouraged tribal members to suppress their own language. Harriet Whitworth, a Bitterroot Salish woman now in her late eighties, who—like all the remaining fluent speakers of Salish–Pend d'Oreille—has native-speaker fluency in both English and Salish, once told me she raised her five children to speak only English: "I didn't want my kids to go through what I went through." I asked whether she'd do things differently if she had known then that her language was in grave danger of vanishing forever: "Yes," she told me. "But it's too late now."

The circumstances that brought Salish–Pend d'Oreille to the brink of extinction differ from the stories of other communities only in the details. All dwindling languages fight against time in the face of increasing pressures to speak a dominant language. English, Spanish, French, Portuguese, Arabic, Russian, Mandarin, Quechua (before the Inca Empire was destroyed by invading Spaniards), and other expanding languages have all been spoken by powerful outsiders who imposed their own order and language on subjugated, or at least less powerful, peoples. Two obvious questions arise here: Just how widespread is the phenomenon of language loss? And, more fundamentally, so what?

Before answering those questions, let me clarify that when linguists talk about language death, we are not referring to languages like Latin. Latin certainly qualifies as a dead language, but it did not die by losing all its speakers to another language; instead, it evolved into a sizable group of descendants, the modern Romance languages, almost all of which still thrive. The vanishing languages that I'm talking about leave no descendants.

Estimates of the number of threatened languages vary. About 6,000 languages are spoken in the world today. Pessimists like the linguist Michael Krauss of the University of Alaska Fairbanks predict that 90 percent of them will be dead by the end of this century; optimists predict the demise of only about 60 percent by then. Either way, we are looking at a future of catastrophic language loss.

There are, of course, quite a few languages that are certainly not going to vanish in the foreseeable future: all the languages listed above except Quechua are safe, for instance. Millions of people speak those languages, many of which are official in one or more nations. In fact, among the 200 or so nations in the world, English ranks as the most popular official tongue, cited in fifty-two countries (not counting the United States, which stands nearly alone in having no official language). French follows, official in twenty-nine countries; Arabic and Spanish are tied, each with twenty-four; and Portuguese has eight countries that recognize it as official. Do the math. The count for those five languages totals 137 nations—a great majority of the world's countries.

One might assume that other languages with at least a million speakers should also be safe, but that's not necessarily so. Quechua, with several million speakers and official-language status in Bolivia and Peru, is steadily losing ground to Spanish, which is also official in both countries. If that is so, consider the plight of "smaller" languages, those with only 100 to 10,000 speakers—nearly half the languages in the world. Only the most isolated can be considered stable in their communities. But geographic and social isolation is itself vanishing fast, in every part of the world.

Does losing a language matter so much? Some people favor moving toward one world language, or at least toward a drastic reduction in the cacophony of thousands. One recurrent argument, voiced loudly by proponents of the "English Only" and "Official English" movements in the U.S., is that reducing the number of languages will promote understanding and therefore national (and, ultimately, world) peace. It's to take this argument seriously in a country that fought b Revolution and a Civil War in which both sides spoke En and in an era when Sunni and Shiite Iraqis, all speake Arabic, are killing each other by the hundreds almost dail

In addition to the profound loss to the community, language that dies without being thoroughly documente analyzed robs us of potential insights into human ling capabilities, and reduces our chances of arriving at a co hensive understanding of the workings of the human That may sound grandiose—after all, even if upwar 60 percent of the world's languages vanish during this tury, we'll still have a couple of thousand left, and bes scholars have other tools for figuring out how the mind w But there's a lot to the old notions that language is makes us human and that its structures open a windo the mind.

The variation in human languages is not infinite. The fa any human baby can learn any human language with equa is evidence of a fundamental similarity in all our langu Nevertheless, the amount of variation is immense, an understanding of the range and details of such variation ca challenge our theories about the nature of human languag

Even with the growing popularity of Chinese, Japanes Arabic, most foreign-language study in the West involves fa European languages. English, French, Spanish, German, It Russian, and Portuguese all belong to just one of the w hundreds of language families, the Indo-European family.

As a result, they share numerous structures in their mar, sound systems, and ways of organizing their vocabu Studying an unrelated language is an eye-opener: it's not matter of memorizing a lot of new words and learning h fit relatively familiar pronunciations and grammatical pa into new configurations. Languages outside the Indo-Eur family are different in ways you can't imagine until you e ence them.

Salish–Pend d'Oreille surprises me every summer. It inc sounds that are rarely heard in Indo-European languages: produced with a glottal catch, sounds produced with the ai ing noisily past the sides of the tongue (lateral fricatives), s pronounced far back in the pharynx (pharyngeal conson The alphabet used to spell the language therefore contai ters that look very different from English letters, as the fo ing examples illustrate. The language has no detectable on the number of consonants that can occur in a row, s there are marvelous words like *Ta qesm'l'm'él'čstmstx*^{w} (" play with it!"), with eight consonants in a row at the en *sx*^{w}*čšt'sqá* ("someone whose job it is to take care of livest with seven consonants at the beginning. It has words as lo your tongue, for instance *q*^{w}*o qɬ-č-tax̣*^{w}*l-m-nt-sút-m-nt-m* would come up to me"). The short word, *q*^{w}*o,* means "me long word has a root, *tax̣*^{w}*l* "start," preceded by two pr and followed by six suffixes, some of them repeated. Wo Indo-European languages don't have anything approachin exuberant deployment of prefixes and suffixes.

Salish makes subtle distinctions that would require more verbiage if expressed in an Indo-European language.

tés and *čłpntém* mean "s/he hunted it," for instance, but the ending in–*és* indicates that the hunter is the most promi- character in the narrative, whereas the verb ending in–*ém* ates that some character other than the hunter—maybe the ed creature—is more prominent than the hunter in this con- It's not that this distinction can't be expressed in English y other Indo-European language; of course it can. But not sily, and such specificity certainly isn't obligatory in West- anguages, as it is in Salish–Pend d'Oreille. Storytellers used this grammatical distinction to signal a subtle shift ention from one character to another.

ıt like other aspects of Salish–Pend d'Oreille culture, some e most "exotic" features of the language are fading: the last e speakers all speak English much more often than they Salish–Pend d'Oreille. To give one example of the effect as on sound systems, only about three or four of the elders k with pronounce clear pharyngeal consonants.

nd in some semantic domains, most strikingly in the area of ip categories and terminology, the much simpler English m has replaced much of the elaborate native Salish–Pend eille system. In my most recent session with the elders, summer of 2007, I wanted to find out how many of the inship terms are recognized by the current generation of s. The kinship terms were compiled in 1976 with the help group of elders who are all now deceased.

t first the current group of elders said that they had never ed the old words; but the more they talked about their ded families, the more words they remembered. Dolly bigler mentioned her father's brother: she always called er *smamá?,* but "after my dad died, everything changed— he was my *łwéstn*" ("aunt or uncle after the death of the ecting relative"). Josephine Quequesah remembered a , *smé?eł,* that meant either uncle or nephew, and then Louis ght of another reciprocal kin term: "Yeah, like my *t'ot'ó* used l me *her t'ot'ó* ("great-grandparent or great-grandchild"). olly also commented that people who come from big fami- ke hers got used to all the complicated terms, like *łqáqce?* man's older brother"), *q'e?éw's* ("middle brother"), and *e?* ("woman's younger brother"). But many words were ly beyond their memories, unrecognized. Like other com- ystems of kin terms around the world, Salish–Pend d'Oreille insights into the possible range of categories for human rela- hips. But the old system teeters on the brink of oblivion, and me is true of intricate kinship systems all over the world.

Within the next twenty or thirty years, there will be no speakers left who learned Salish–Pend d'Oreille as a first language, spoke it regularly in their younger years, and revisited it throughout their lives. There are twenty-two other languages in the Salishan family, and they await the same sad fate. When there are no longer any Salishan speakers who remember how their grandparents and great-grandparents spoke, the old kin terms will vanish, along with the other cultural and historical riches encoded in the ancestral languages.

Language death, much too much language death, seems inevitable in this and future decades. But the picture is not completely dark. Many communities whose languages are threatened, including the Salish–Pend d'Oreille tribes, have begun vigorous efforts to document and revitalize their languages, so that today's and tomorrow's children will be able to learn them. In a few spectacular recent cases, notably Maori in New Zealand and Hawaiian in the United States, heritage languages have been restored to the community's children. And in perhaps the most dramatic historical case, Modern Hebrew emerged as the native language of a new nation's children after 2,000 years of near-death.

Even when efforts to save heritage languages fail, that doesn't mean the effort has been wasted. If fluent native speakers help document a dying language, with a full grammatical description, a dictionary, and a collection of narratives, the possibility of revival will always be there. The revived version won't match the earlier version, but it can still serve its community. It can allow traditional practices and values to be expressed without the disruptions of translation, making the past more accessible. It can contribute its unique data to the scientific understanding of the universal human capacity for language.

Ultimately, though, if a community loses its language as its main vehicle of communication, both the community and its individual members lose an irreplaceable part of their identity. And at the same time, a part of our common world that their language uniquely illuminated goes dark.

Sarah Grey Thomason has worked with the Salish–Pend d'Oreille Culture Committee since 1981, compiling a dictionary and text collection in collaboration with tribal elders. Thomason, who is currently co-authoring a textbook on endangered languages for Cambridge University Press, is the William J. Gedney Collegiate Professor of Linguistics at the University of Michigan and is a former president of the Society for the Study of the Indigenous Languages of the Americas.

UNIT 3

The Organization of Society and Culture

Unit Selections

Key Points to Consider

- Which of the traditional Inuit (Eskimo) practices that are important for their survival in the circumstances they live in, do you find contrary to the values professed by the society you live in?
- What can contemporary hunter-collector societies tell us about the quality of life in the prehistoric past?
- What is the "Inuit paradox" and what can we learn from it about modern-day eating practices?
- What impact does women's economic independence have upon gender relationships, child rearing, and the overall violence in Zapotec society?
- What is the significance of "the gift" in traditional Hopi society?
- Are American Indian mascots, logos, and nicknames demeaning and racist or is there much ado about very little regarding this issue?
- How much of the relationship between poverty and health is a function of the relative disparities of socioeconomic status rather than simply the material circumstances of being poor?

Student Website

www.mhcls.com

Internet References

Patterns of Subsistence

http://anthro.palomar.edu/subsistence/default.htm

Smithsonian Institution Website

http://www.si.edu

Sociology Guy's Anthropology Links

http://www.trinity.edu/~mkearl/anthro.html

nan beings do not interact with one another or think their world in random fashion. They engage in struc-and recurrent physical and mental activities. In this sec-uch patterns of behavior and thought—referred to here organization of society and culture—may be seen in a er of different contexts, from the hunting tactics of the q Eskimos of the Arctic (see "Understanding Eskimo ce") to the value the Hopi place on the gift as a symbol of relations built on kinship and altruism (as discussed in That Bind").

special importance are the ways in which people make g—in other words, the production, distribution, and con-ion of goods and services. It is only by knowing the basic tence systems that we can hope to gain insight into other of social and cultural phenomena, for they are all inex-y bound together. Noting the various aspects of a socio-l system in harmonious balance, however, does not imply hropological seal of approval. To understand infanticide of the newborn) in the manner that it is practiced among peoples is neither to condone nor condemn it. The adaptive is that have been in existence for a great length of time, s many of the patterns of hunters and gatherers, probably heir existence to their contributions to long-term human l (see "The Inuit Paradox").

hropologists, however, are not content with the data d from individual experience. On the contrary, personal otions must become the basis for sound anthropologi-ory. Otherwise, they remain meaningless, isolated relics ure in the manner of museum pieces. Thus, in "Playing at Halftime," we come to understand some of the negative consequences of American Indian mascots, logos, and nick-names in school-related events and, in "Sick of Poverty," Robert Sapolsky tells us that the subjective state of *feeling* poor may be just as important in predicting ill health as is the objective case of *being* poor when it comes to predicting ill health.

© McGraw-Hill Companies, Inc./Gerald Wofford, photographer

In other words, while the articles in this unit are to some extent descriptive, they also serve to challenge both the academic and commonsense notions about why people behave and think the way they do. They remind us that assumptions are never really safe. As long as anthropologists are kept on their toes, the field as a whole will be better.

The Inuit Paradox

How can people who gorge on fat and rarely see a vegetable be healthier than we are?

Patricia Gadsby

Patricia Cochran, an Inupiat from Northwestern Alaska, is talking about the native foods of her childhood: “We pretty much had a subsistence way of life. Our food supply was right outside our front door. We did our hunting and foraging on the Seward Peninsula and along the Bering Sea.”

“Our meat was seal and walrus, marine mammals that live in cold water and have lots of fat. We used seal oil for our cooking and as a dipping sauce for food. We had moose, caribou, and reindeer. We hunted ducks, geese, and little land birds like quail, called ptarmigan. We caught crab and lots of fish—salmon, whitefish, tomcod, pike, and char. Our fish were cooked, dried, smoked, or frozen. We ate frozen raw whitefish, sliced thin. The elders liked stinkfish, fish buried in seal bags or cans in the tundra and left to ferment. And fermented seal flipper, they liked that too.”

Cochran's family also received shipments of whale meat from kin living farther north, near Barrow. Beluga was one she liked; raw muktuk, which is whale skin with its underlying blubber, she definitely did not. “To me it has a chew-on-a-tire consistency,” she says, “but to many people it's a mainstay.” In the short subarctic summers, the family searched for roots and greens and, best of all from a child's point of view, wild blueberries, crowberries, or salmonberries, which her aunts would mix with whipped fat to make a special treat called *akutuq*—in colloquial English, Eskimo ice cream.

Now Cochran directs the Alaska Native Science Commission, which promotes research on native cultures and the health and environmental issues that affect them. She sits at her keyboard in Anchorage, a bustling city offering fare from Taco Bell to French cuisine. But at home Cochran keeps a freezer filled with fish, seal, walrus, reindeer, and whale meat, sent by her family up north, and she and her husband fish and go berry picking—“sometimes a challenge in Anchorage,” she adds, laughing. “I eat fifty-fifty,” she explains, half traditional, half regular American.

No one, not even residents of the northernmost villages on Earth, eats an entirely traditional northern diet anymore. Even the groups we came to know as Eskimo—which include the Inupiat and the Yupiks of Alaska, the Canadian Inuit and Inuvialuit, Inuit Greenlanders, and the Siberian Yupiks—have pr
seen more changes in their diet in a lifetime than their anc
did over thousands of years. The closer people live to tow
the more access they have to stores and cash-paying jo
more likely they are to have westernized their eating. An
westernization, at least on the North American continent,
processed foods and cheap carbohydrates—Crisco, Tang,
cookies, chips, pizza, fries. “The young and urbanized,
Harriet Kuhnlein, director of the Centre for Indigenou
ples' Nutrition and Environment at McGill University in
treal, “are increasingly into fast food.” So much so that
diabetes, obesity, and other diseases of Western civilizati
becoming causes for concern there too.

Today, when diet books top the best-seller list and n
seems sure of what to eat to stay healthy, it's surpris
learn how well the Eskimo did on a high-protein, hi
diet. Shaped by glacial temperatures, stark landscape
protracted winters, the traditional Eskimo diet had little
way of plant food, no agricultural or dairy products, ar
unusually low in carbohydrates. Mostly people subsis
what they hunted and fished. Inland dwellers took adv
of caribou feeding on tundra mosses, lichens, and pla
tough for humans to stomach (though predigested veget
the animals' paunches became dinner as well). Coastal
exploited the sea. The main nutritional challenge was av
starvation in late winter if primary meat sources beca
scarce or lean.

These foods hardly make up the “balanced” diet n
us grew up with, and they look nothing like the mix of
fruits, vegetables, meat, eggs, and dairy we're accusto
seeing in conventional food pyramid diagrams. How cou
a diet possibly be adequate? How did people get along c
else but fat and animal protein?

The diet of the Far North shows that the are no essential foods—only essential nutrients.

at the diet of the Far North illustrates, says Harold Draper, hemist and expert in Eskimo nutrition, is that there are no ial foods—only essential nutrients. And humans can get nutrients from diverse and eye-opening sources.

e might, for instance, imagine gross vitamin deficien- ising from a diet with scarcely any fruits and vegetables. furnishes vitamin A, vital for eyes and bones? We derive of ours from colorful plant foods, constructing it from nted plant precursors called carotenoids (as in carrots). tamin A, which is oil soluble, is also plentiful in the oils l-water fishes and sea mammals, as well as in the animals' where fat is processed. These dietary staples also pro- itamin D, another oil-soluble vitamin needed for bones. of us living in temperate and tropical climates, on the hand, usually make vitamin D indirectly by exposing skin ng sun—hardly an option in the Arctic winter—and by ming fortified cow's milk, to which the indigenous north- oups had little access until recent decades and often don't e all that well.

for vitamin C, the source in the Eskimo diet was long a y. Most animals can synthesize their own vitamin C, or ic acid, in their livers, but humans are among the excep- along with other primates and oddballs like guinea pigs ts. If we don't ingest enough of it, we fall apart from , a gruesome connective-tissue disease. In the United today we can get ample supplies from orange juice, citrus and fresh vegetables. But vitamin C oxidizes with time; enough from a ship's provisions was tricky for early nd 19th-century voyagers to the polar regions. Scurvy— ain, rotting gums, leaky blood vessels, physical and men- eneration—plagued European and U.S. expeditions even 20th century. However, Arctic peoples living on fresh fish at were free of the disease.

ressed, the explorer Vilhjalmur Stefansson adopted an -style diet for five years during the two Arctic expedi- e led between 1908 and 1918. "The thing to do is to ur antiscorbutics where you are," he wrote. "Pick them ou go." In 1928, to convince skeptics, he and a young ue spent a year on an Americanized version of the diet medical supervision at Bellevue Hospital in New York he pair ate steaks, chops, organ meats like brain and liver, , fish, and fat with gusto. "If you have some fresh meat in et every day and don't overcook it," Stefansson declared hantly, "there will be enough C from that source alone to t scurvy."

act, all it takes to ward off scurvy is a daily dose of ligrams, says Karen Fediuk, a consulting dietitian and graduate student of Harriet Kuhnlein's who did her mas- esis on vitamin C. (That's far less than the U.S. recom- d daily allowance of 75 to 90 milligrams—75 for women, men.) Native foods easily supply those 10 milligrams vy prevention, especially when organ meats—preferably re on the menu. For a study published with Kuhnlein , Fediuk compared the vitamin C content of 100-gram unce) samples of foods eaten by Inuit women living in adian Arctic: Raw caribou liver supplied almost 24 mil- , seal brain close to 15 milligrams, and raw kelp more than 28 milligrams. Still higher levels were found in whale skin and muktuk.

As you might guess from its antiscorbutic role, vitamin C is crucial for the synthesis of connective tissue, including the matrix of skin. "Wherever collagen's made, you can expect vitamin C," says Kuhnlein. Thick skinned, chewy, and collagen rich, raw muktuk can serve up an impressive 36 milligrams in a 100-gram piece, according to Fediuk's analyses. "Weight for weight, it's as good as orange juice," she says. Traditional Inuit practices like freezing meat and fish and frequently eating them raw, she notes, conserve vitamin C, which is easily cooked off and lost in food processing.

Hunter-gatherer diets like those eaten by these northern groups and other traditional diets based on nomadic herding or subsistence farming are among the older approaches to human eating. Some of these eating plans might seem strange to us—diets centered around milk, meat, and blood among the East African pastoralists, enthusiastic tuber eating by the Quechua living in the High Andes, the staple use of the mongongo nut in the southern African !Kung—but all proved resourceful adaptations to particular eco-niches. No people, though, may have been forced to push the nutritional envelope further than those living at Earth's frozen extremes. The unusual makeup of the far-northern diet led Loren Cordain, a professor of evolutionary nutrition at Colorado State University at Fort Collins, to make an intriguing observation.

Four years ago, Cordain reviewed the macronutrient content (protein, carbohydrates, fat) in the diets of 229 hunter-gatherer groups listed in a series of journal articles collectively known as the Ethnographic Atlas. These are some of the oldest surviving human diets. In general, hunter-gatherers tend to eat more animal protein than we do in our standard Western diet, with its reliance on agriculture and carbohydrates derived from grains and starchy plants. Lowest of all in carbohydrate, and highest in combined fat and protein, are the diets of peoples living in the Far North, where they make up for fewer plant foods with extra fish. What's equally striking, though, says Cordain, is that these meat-and-fish diets also exhibit a natural "protein ceiling." Protein accounts for no more than 35 to 40 percent of their total calories, which suggests to him that's all the protein humans can comfortably handle.

Wild-animal fats are different from other fats. Farm animals typically have lots of highly saturated fat.

This ceiling, Cordain thinks, could be imposed by the way we process protein for energy. The simplest, fastest way to make energy is to convert carbohydrates into glucose, our body's primary fuel. But if the body is out of carbs, it can burn fat, or if necessary, break down protein. The name given to the convoluted business of making glucose from protein is gluconeogenesis. It takes place in the liver, uses a dizzying slew of enzymes, and creates nitrogen waste that has to be converted into urea and disposed of through the kidneys. On a truly traditional diet, says Draper, recalling his studies in the 1970s, Arctic people had plenty of protein but little carbohydrate, so they often relied on gluconeogenesis. Not only did they have bigger livers to handle the additional work but their urine volumes were also typically larger to get rid of the extra urea. Nonetheless, there appears to be a limit on how much protein the human liver can safely cope with: Too much overwhelms the liver's waste-disposal system, leading to protein poisoning—nausea, diarrhea, wasting, and death.

Whatever the metabolic reason for this syndrome, says John Speth, an archaeologist at the University of Michigan's Museum of Anthropology, plenty of evidence shows that hunters through the ages avoided protein excesses, discarding fat-depleted animals even when food was scarce. Early pioneers and trappers in North America encountered what looks like a similar affliction, sometimes referred to as rabbit starvation because rabbit meat is notoriously lean. Forced to subsist on fat-deficient meat, the men would gorge themselves, yet wither away. Protein can't be the sole source of energy for humans, concludes Cordain. Anyone eating a meaty diet that is low in carbohydrates must have fat as well.

Stefansson had arrived at this conclusion, too, while living among the Copper Eskimo. He recalled how he and his Eskimo companions had become quite ill after weeks of eating "caribou so skinny that there was no appreciable fat behind the eyes or in the marrow." Later he agreed to repeat the miserable experience at Bellevue Hospital, for science's sake, and for a while ate nothing but defatted meat. "The symptoms brought on at Bellevue by an incomplete meat diet [lean without fat] were exactly the same as in the Arctic . . . diarrhea and a feeling of general baffling discomfort," he wrote. He was restored with a fat fix but "had lost considerable weight." For the remainder of his year on meat, Stefansson tucked into his rations of chops and steaks with fat intact. "A normal meat diet is not a high-protein diet," he pronounced. "We were really getting three-quarters of our calories from fat." (Fat is more than twice as calorie dense as protein or carbohydrate, but even so, that's a lot of lard. A typical U.S diet provides about 35 percent of its calories from fat.)

Stefansson dropped 10 pounds on his meat-and-fat regimen and remarked on its "slenderizing" aspect, so perhaps it's no surprise he's been co-opted as a posthumous poster boy for Atkins-type diets. No discussion about diet these days can avoid Atkins. Even some researchers interviewed for this article couldn't resist referring to the Inuit way of eating as the "original Atkins." "Superficially, at a macronutrient level, the two diets certainly look similar," allows Samuel Klein, a nutrition researcher at Washington University in St. Louis, who's attempting to study how Atkins stacks up against conventional weight-loss diets. Like the Inuit diet, Atkins is low in carbohydrates and very high in fat. But numerous researchers, including Klein, point out that there are profound differences between the two diets, beginning with the type of meat and fat eaten.

Fats have been demonized in the United States, say Dewailly, a professor of preventive medicine at University in Quebec. But all fats are not created This lies at the heart of a paradox—the Inuit paradox, will. In the Nunavik villages in northern Quebec, adults o get almost half their calories from native foods, says De and they don't die of heart attacks at nearly the same ra other Canadians or Americans. Their cardiac death rate is half of ours, he says. As someone who looks for links be diet and cardiovascular health, he's intrigued by that re risk. Because the traditional Inuit diet is "so restricted," h it's easier to study than the famously heart-healthy M ranean diet, with its cornucopia of vegetables, fruits, herbs, spices, olive oil, and red wine.

A key difference in the typical Nunavik Inuit's diet more than 50 percent of the calories in Inuit native foods from fats. Much more important, the fats come from animals.

Wild-animal fats are different from both farm-anim and processed fats, says Dewailly. Farm animals, coo and stuffed with agricultural grains (carbohydrates) ty have lots of solid, highly saturated fat. Much of our pro food is also riddled with solid fats, or so-called trans fat as the reengineered vegetable oils and shortenings cac baked goods and snacks. "A lot of the packaged food on market shelves contains them. So do commercial french Dewailly adds.

Trans fats are polyunsaturated vegetable oils tricked make them more solid at room temperature. Manufactu this by hydrogenating the oils—adding extra hydrogen to their molecular structures—which "twists" their Dewailly makes twisting sound less like a chemical trans tion than a perversion, an act of public-health sabotage: man-made fats are dangerous, even worse for the hea saturated fats." They not only lower high-density lipo cholesterol (HDL, the "good" cholesterol) but they als low-density lipoprotein cholesterol (LDL, the "bad" terol) and triglycerides, he says. In the process, trans fats stage for heart attacks because they lead to the increase buildup in artery walls.

Wild animals that range freely and eat what nature in says Dewailly, have fat that is far more healthful. Less fat is saturated, and more of it is in the monounsaturate (like olive oil). What's more, cold-water fishes and sea mals are particularly rich in polyunsaturated fats called n acids or omega-3 fatty acids. These fats appear to ben heart and vascular system. But the polyunsaturated fats Americans' diets are the omega-6 fatty acids supplied etable oils. By contrast, whale blubber consists of 70 monounsaturated fat and close to 30 percent omega-3 Dewailly.

Dieting is the price we pay for too little exercise and too much mass-produced food.

mega-3s evidently help raise HDL cholesterol, lower trig-ides, and are known for anticlotting effects. (Ethnographers remarked on an Eskimo propensity for nosebleeds.) These acids are believed to protect the heart from life-threatening thmias that can lead to sudden cardiac death. And like a ral aspirin," adds Dewailly, omega-3 polyunsaturated fats put a damper on runaway inflammatory processes, which a part in atherosclerosis, arthritis, diabetes, and other so-l diseases of civilization.

ou can be sure, however, that Atkins devotees aren't rou-eating seal and whale blubber. Besides the acquired taste em, their commerce is extremely restricted in the United s by the Marine Mammal Protection Act, says Bruce b, a nutritional biochemist in the department of human gy and nutritional sciences at the University of Guelph tario.

n heartland America it's probable they're not eating in skimo-like way," says Gary Foster, clinical director of Veight and Eating Disorders Program at the Pennsylvania ol of Medicine. Foster, who describes himself as open-ed about Atkins, says he'd nonetheless worry if people he diet as a green light to eat all the butter and bacon—ated fats—they want. Just before rumors surfaced that rt Atkins had heart and weight problems when he died, s officials themselves were stressing saturated fat should unt for no more than 20 percent of dieters' calories. This s to be a clear retreat from the diet's original don't-count-lories approach to bacon and butter and its happy exhorta-to "plow into those prime ribs." Furthermore, 20 percent ories from saturated fats is *double* what most nutritionists e. Before plowing into those prime ribs, readers of a recent n of the *Dr. Atkins' New Diet Revolution* are urged to take a-3 pills to help protect their hearts. "If you watch care-" says Holub wryly, "you'll see many popular U.S. diets quietly added omega-3 pills, in the form of fish oil or flax-apsules, as supplements."

eedless to say, the subsistence diets of the Far North are dieting." Dieting is the price we pay for too little exercise o much mass-produced food. Northern diets were a way in places too cold for agriculture, where food, whether d, fished, or foraged, could not be taken for granted. They about keeping weight on.

is is not to say that people in the Far North were fat: Sub-ce living requires exercise—hard physical work. Indeed, g the good reasons for native people to maintain their old f eating, as far as it's possible today, is that it provides a hedge against obesity, type 2 diabetes, and heart disease. Unfortunately, no place on Earth is immune to the spreading taint of growth and development. The very well-being of the northern food chain is coming under threat from global warming, land development, and industrial pollutants in the marine environment. "I'm a pragmatist," says Cochran, whose organization is involved in pollution monitoring and disseminating food-safety information to native villages. "Global warming we don't have control over. But we can, for example, do cleanups of military sites in Alaska or of communication cables leaching lead into fish-spawning areas. We can help communities make informed food choices. A young woman of childbearing age may choose not to eat certain organ meats that concentrate contaminants. As individuals, we do have options. And eating our salmon and our seal is still a heck of a better option than pulling something processed that's full of additives off a store shelf."

Not often in our industrial society do we hear someone speak so familiarly about "our" food animals. We don't talk of "our pig" and "our beef." We've lost that creature feeling, that sense of kinship with food sources. "You're taught to think in boxes," says Cochran. "In our culture the connectivity between humans, animals, plants, the land they live on, and the air they share is ingrained in us from birth.

"You truthfully can't separate the way we get our food from the way we live," she says. "How we get our food is intrinsic to our culture. It's how we pass on our values and knowledge to the young. When you go out with your aunts and uncles to hunt or to gather, you learn to smell the air, watch the wind, understand the way the ice moves, know the land. You get to know where to pick which plant and what animal to take."

"It's part, too, of your development as a person. You share food with your community. You show respect to your elders by offering them the first catch. You give thanks to the animal that gave up its life for your sustenance. So you get all the physical activity of harvesting your own food, all the social activity of sharing and preparing it, and all the spiritual aspects as well," says Cochran. "You certainly don't get all that, do you, when you buy prepackaged food from a store."

"That's why some of us here in Anchorage are working to protect what's ours, so that others can continue to live back home in the villages," she adds. "Because if we don't take care of our food, it won't be there for us in the future. And if we lose our foods, we lose who we are." The word Inupiat means "the real people." "That's who we are," says Cochran.

Ties That Bind

Hopi gift culture and its first encounter with the United States.

PETER M. WHITELEY

In 1852, shortly after the United States had nominally annexed Hopi country, in northern Arizona, the Hopi people arranged for a diplomatic packet to reach President Millard Fillmore at the White House. Part message and part magical gift, the packet was delivered by a delegation of five prominent men from another Pueblo tribe, the Tewas of Tesuque Pueblo in New Mexico, who wanted to gain legal protection from Anglo and Hispanic settlers who were encroaching on their lands. The delegation traveled for nearly three months, on horseback, steamboat, and train, from Santa Fe to Washington, D.C., more than 2,600 miles away. The five men spoke fluent Spanish, the dominant European language of the region at the time—which made them ideally suited to convey the gift packet and its message to the president.

At the time, no U.S. government official had visited the Hopi (and few would do so before the 1890s). Their "unique diplomatic pacquet," in the words of the nineteenth-century ethnologist Henry Rowe Schoolcraft, offered "friendship and intercommunication . . . opening, symbolically, a road from the Moqui [Hopi] country to Washington." The packet was in two parts. The first part comprised two *pahos,* or prayer-sticks, at either end of a long cotton cord, dyed for part of its length. Separating the dyed from the undyed part of the cord were six varicolored feathers, knotted into a bunch. The *pahos* "represent the Moqui [Hopi] people and the President [respectively]," Schoolcraft wrote; "the cord is the road which separates them; the [bunch of feathers] tied to the cord is the meeting point."

As well as encoding a message, the *pahos* were an offering of a kind that Hopi deities such as Taawa, the Sun god, traditionally like to receive. By giving the president *pahos* worthy of the Sun, the Hopi signaled their expectation that he would reciprocate. Just as the Sun, on receiving the appropriate offerings, would send rain clouds for sustaining life and growth, so, too, the president would send protection for Hopi lives and lands—in this instance, protection from assaults by neighboring tribes such as the Navajo.

The second part of the packet comprised a cornstalk cigarette filled with tobacco ("to be smoked by the president") and a small cornhusk package that enclosed honey-soaked cornmeal. According to the Tesuque delegation, the honey-meal package was "a charm to call down rain from heaven." When the president smoked the cigarette, he would exhale clouds of smoke, which would sympathetically attract the clouds of the sky. Then, when he chewed the cornmeal and spat the wild honey on ground that needed rain, the Tesuque statement concluded, "the Moquis assure him that rain] will come."

In sum, the packet was three things at once: message, o and gift of magical power. In conveying those elements, th sought to open diplomatic relations with the U.S.

But their intent appears to have been lost on their recipien often happens when two cultures make contact, deep misunde ings can arise: What does a gift mean? What, if anything, d gift giver expect in return? Do the giver and the recipient both the same value to the gift? In twenty-five years of ethnographi work with the Hopi, it has been my goal to learn something history and culture. Recently I turned my attention to certain tant events, such as the Millard Fillmore episode, that mig light on how Hopi society changed as the U.S. developed. context Hopi gift giving and the ways it functions as a pillar social organization have been central to my studies. One le my work shines through: When nations exchange gifts, all t ties would do best to keep in mind the old adage, "It's the t that counts."

Given the differences between Hopi and Western tra and culture, perhaps it is not surprising that the Ho of "gift" is only loosely equivalent to the Western 1852 the Hopi people were still little affected by outside p tions, and Hopi land use spread across much of northern A and even into southern Utah. At that time, the Hopi lifesty traditional, based on farming, foraging, and some pasto Even today, important elements of the subsistence econom sist, though wage labor and small business provide supple income.

The Hopi typically divide their work according to gende done by men (such as farming and harvesting of crops) is perce a gift to the women; work done by women (such as gardening, ing of piñion nuts, grasses, wild fruits, berries, and the like) is pe as a gift to the men. Women also own and manage the distribu their household's goods and crops. In fact, Hopi women contr of the material economic life, whereas Hopi men largely con ritual and spiritual aspects.

The Hopi take part in an elaborate cycle of religious cerer to which a range of specialized offices and privileges is at But individuals gain those distinctive social positions not t ial wealth but rather through gender and kinship relations, are ordered in a matrilineal manner. In fact, clan heads and of religious societies are typically worse off materially than erage member of the clan. Hopi leaders are supposed to be ially poor, and a wealthy individual is often criticized as *i,* un-Hopi, for failing to share. Wealth and status among the is thus phrased in ritual terms: a poor person is one without onial prerogatives, not one without money. So averse are the to material accumulation that in May 2004, for the second they voted against casino gambling, despite substantial pov- n the reservation.

es such a primacy of value placed on ceremonial roles n the evanescent nature of the gift given to President ore? In what world of meaning did the packet represent great ? Indeed, what's in a gift?

A nthropologists have been making hay of that last question ever since 1925, when the French anthropologist Marcel Mauss published his groundbreaking *Essai sur le Don* ated into English as "The Gift"). Mauss convincingly argued small-scale societies (10,000 or fewer persons) gifts are "total facts." What he meant is that, in gift- or barter-based social ıs, divisions of social life into discrete domains—such as ny, politics, law, or religion—are meaningless; each sphere enetrates and overlaps the others.

in strict barter, an exchange in Hopi culture that begins king a gift to someone does not involve money, but it does e reciprocity. Thus goods, services, or knowledge "given" to ividual or a group are answered with something of equiva- alue. "Gifts" develop an interconnectedness between Hopi luals in a way that outright purchases cannot. Furthermore, pi offer gifts in a much broader range of circumstances than in Western cultures do, and the value of those gifts extends religious realm, tying individuals and groups to each other the realm of the spirits.

bably the key to understanding a gift-based system such as the Hopi is to recognize that such systems are built on kinship. ip"—the godzilla that has driven multitudes of college stu- creaming from anthropology 101—is, in this regard at least, tforward. It means simply that the great majority of human activity is framed in terms of reciprocal family ties. Where all al relationships are cast within the "kinship idiom" there are nbers of the society who are not kin to me, nor I to them.

ship terms encode behavioral expectations as well as famil- . As anthropologists never tire of saying, such terms are ily social, not biological: obviously if I call fifteen women r," as the average Hopi can do, I do not assume that each physically gave birth to me. But my "mothers" all have nd duties in relation to me. And, reciprocally, I have duties hts with respect to them: in fact, their duties are my rights, duties are their rights in the relationship. That is what reci- is all about. You give me food, I plant your cornfield, to give e example. But, in a kinship society, such a basic structure ual expectations forms the foundation for an entire appara- courtesy and manners, deference and respect, familiarity or e. Those expectations are concretely expressed by gifts— neous and planned, routine and special, trivial and grand. re thus communications in a language of social belonging.

So averse are the Hopi to material accumulation that in May 2004 they voted against casino gambling.

So-called gift economies entail a certain kind of sociality, or sense of what it means to belong to a community. In such an economy, one gives a gift to mark social relations built on kinship and altruism, but without the expectation of direct repayment. According to some arguments, gifts are also given to foster a sense of community, as well as sustainable interrelations with the local environment. In fact, in some respects the giver still "owns" some part of the gift, and it is the intangible connection between the two parties, mediated by the gift, that forms the basis of interpersonal relationships.

In contrast, in exchange economies, commodities dominate social interchange. Competitive markets, governed by the profit motive, connect buyer and seller, and social relations are characterized by individualism. A gift, once given, belongs entirely to the recipient; only when the item given has sentimental value does it keep the bond between giver and recipient alive.

That is not to say the Hopi did not engage in the more impersonal, "Western" forms of material exchange. In the Hopi language, as in English, several words describe how an item is transferred from one person to another: *maqa* ("to give"); *hùuya* ("to barter or trade"); and *tu'i* ("to buy"). Those words all antedate the arrival of Europeans—and anthropological classifications. Barter and purchase, as well as gifts, have all long been present in Hopi life. Furthermore, gift exchange in the West can also function as it does among the Hopi, as part of kinship obligations or ordinary social life.

What is distinctive about Hopi custom is the fact that the gift economy is responsible for the great majority of exchanges. Furthermore, there is no such thing as a free gift. The strong interpersonal bonds created by a gift make giving almost de rigueur at ceremonial events. Gifts, particularly gifts of food or utensils, are transmitted during ceremonies of personal milestones (at a birth or a marriage), as well as at public gatherings.

For example, at the annual so-called basket dances, girls and women distribute a variety of objects they have collected for the occasion. The dances illustrate the Hopi lack of acquisitiveness. The women form a semicircle and dance and sing; after each song two girls fling gifts into the crowd of men assembled outside the circle. Among the gifts are valuable baskets and buckskins, though inexpensive utensils and manufactured items are also popular. Each man zealously grabs for the flying objects, and if two men happen to catch the same item, both wrestle with the object, often until it has been totally destroyed.

Although gift giving has been a pillar of Hopi society, trade has also flourished in Hopi towns since prehistory, with a network that extended from the Great Plains to the Pacific Coast, and from the Great Basin, centered on present-day Nevada and Utah, to the Valley of Mexico. Manufactured goods, raw materials, and gems drove the trade, supplemented by exotic items such as parrots. The Hopis were producers as well, manufacturing large quantities of cotton cloth and ceramics for the trade. To this day, interhousehold trade and barter, especially for items of traditional manufacture for ceremonial use (such as basketry, bows, cloth, moccasins, pottery, and rattles), remain vigorous.

For hundreds of years, at least, the Hopi traded with the Rio Grande Pueblos to acquire turquoise, *heishi* (shell necklaces), and buckskins; one long string of *heishi,* for instance, was worth two Hopi woven cotton mantas. Similarly, songs, dances, and other ritual elements were often exchanged for an agreed-upon equivalent.

The high value the Hopi placed on the items they acquired by trade correlate, in many respects, with the value Europeans placed on them. Silver, for instance, had high value among both Westerners and Native Americans as money and as jewelry. *Siiva,* the Hopi word both for "money" and for "silver jewelry" was borrowed directly from the English word "silver" Paper money itself was often treated the way traditional resources were: older Hopi men bundled it and stored it in trunks, stacked by denomination.

It was not until the 1890s, however, that silver jewelry began to be produced by the Hopi. A man named Sikyatala learned silversmithing from a Zuni man, and his craftsmanship quickly made silver jewelry into treasured adornments. Those among the Hopi who cared for it too much, though, were criticized for vanity; one nickname, Siisiva ("[wearing] a lot of silver"), characterized a fop.

Some jewels, such as turquoise, traditionally had a sacred value, beyond adornment. Even today, flakes of turquoise are occasionally offered to the spirits in religious ceremonies. Turquoise and shell necklaces appear in many ritual settings, frequently adorning the costumes of *katsinas* (ceremonial figures) and performers in the social dances.

How much the Hopi value turquoise becomes apparent toward the close of a ritual enactment known as the Clown Ceremony. The "clowns"—more than mere entertainers—represent unbridled human impulses. Warrior *katsinas* arrive to punish the clowns for licentious behavior and teach them good Hopi behavior: modest and quiet in conduct, careful and decorous in speech, abstemious and sharing about food, and unselfish about other things. The clowns fail miserably (and hilariously) at their lessons. Eventually the warrior chief presents an ultimatum: stop flaunting chaos or die. The clown chief then offers him a turquoise necklace as a "mortgage" on the clowns' lives. The warrior chief accepts, the downs receive a lesser punishment, and community life goes on—not with perfection, but with a human mixture of the virtuous and the flawed.

In Hopi tradition, the first clan among the Hopi, and the one that supplied the *kikmongwi,* or village chief, was Bear. When other clans arrived, their leaders approached the *kikmongwi* to request entry into the village. He asked what they had to contribute, such as a beneficial ceremony. So challenged, each clan performed its ceremony, and if successful, say, in producing rain, its members were invited to live in the village, assigned an area for housing, and granted agricultural lands to work in the valley below. In return, the clan agreed to perform its ceremony, as part of a cycle of ceremonies throughout the year, and to intermarry with the other clans of the community, a practice called exogamous marriage. In that way, the Snake clan brought the Snake Dance, the Badger clan introduced principal katsina ceremonies, and the Fire clan brought the Warriors' society to the Hopi village. The villages thus came to be made up of mutually interdependent clans.

One of the essential principles expressed here, and the ver nerstone of Hopi society and sociality, is the exchange of ally beneficial gifts—ceremonies for land, people in exog marriage—and the relationships reconfigured by those exchange the same model is extended to the supernatural world: the god be propitiated with offerings of ritual gifts, and thus reminded c dependence upon and obligations to mortal people.

The items sent to President Fillmore conform to the arch Hopi offering. Seeking to incorporate the president into the world, the appropriate strategy was to give him valuable presen sought something in return, and to make sure he understood wh meant. Addressing him with prayer-sticks the way they might a the Sun father, the delegation sought to engage him within the and kinship idiom. The instructions delivered with the packet- across a succession of translations—spoke clearly of the Hopi As with the turquoise mortgage of the *katsina* clowns, the idea c procity is central. If the president wants more of, say, rain-ma must give back: he must receive the gift and its political propos provide something in return.

Alas, the magico-religious sensibility of the Hopi view and the offer of serial reciprocity clashed with fest Destiny and the assimilationist ideology of Fill presidency. Historical records make it clear that he did not the cigarette, nor chew nor spit the honey-meal, and, so far know, he sent no formal reply. None of the objects has survi

What the five men of the Tesuque delegation received no perplexed them as much as the packet they delivered perplex president: Each man was given a Millard Fillmore peace a Western-style business suit, and a daguerreotype portr now lost, as well). They also got a tour of standard destinat Washington, including the Patent Office and the Smithsonia tution, where they were introduced to the "wonders of e ity," according to a contemporary newspaper account in the *National Intelligencer.* In their meeting with Fillmore they the president say he "hoped the Great Spirit would bless and them till they again returned to the bosom of their families."

Certainly Fillmore expressed the goodwill of the U.S. the Pueblos in general and to the Tesuque party in particular- in all probability, conveyed that sentiment to the Hopi. But t sonance between gift and exchange economies helps expla the Hopis did not achieve their goals. (The U.S. did not prot Hopi from intrusions by the Navajo or by anyone else.)

The Hopi sought to embrace the president in their own sp sociality and mutuality—to extend kinship to him. But in a system like the president's, where gifts are not total social fa political belongs in a separate domain from the religious or t nomic, and kinship is secondary. The gift of a jeweled sw instance, might have impressed Fillmore more, but for the H strictly symbolic value—as an item for display, but with no cal, religious, or social value—would not have ensured a r social connection built on mutual exchange. More, by Hopi ards, presenting such a gift might have seemed inhospitab materialistic, indeed, undiplomatic and even selfish. Thu understanding fail between nations.

laying Indian at Halftime

e Controversy over American Indian Mascots, gos, and Nicknames in School-Related Events

NEL D. PEWEWARDY

very school year, classroom teachers face the reality and challenge of educating diverse children in a multicultural society. Teaching multiculturally requires educators to examine sen- diverse topics and cultural issues. It means looking at histori- contemporary events from various perspectives, rather than a one. Teachers and administrators whose knowledge of history rrent events is monocultural in scope and who are unaware of wn prejudices are likely to hinder the academic success and al development of many students, however unintentional this (Bennett 1999). Multicultural teaching encourages students stigate the institutional racism, classism, and sexism that have different populations in discriminatory ways. Educators can onocultural classes and schools examine their own biases and ypes related to different cultural groups. Although one's ethnic s just one of a number of possible identity sources, ethnicity heart of the equity problem in American society. Therefore, ions about achieving educational excellence should address thnic groups that have been consistently cut off from equal to a quality education.

ucators have a professional responsibility to eliminate rac- all aspects of school life. Accordingly, educators should nore multicultural issues in school. Instead, these issues become teachable moments in which these concerns are nted and discussed. Accurate information can begin to dis- he myths that many students hold about others. Today, one ble moment is the controversy over using American Indian s, logos, and nicknames in school-related events. Support- such mascots claim they honor American Indian people, y institutional traditions, foster a shared identity, and fy the pleasures of sports and athletics. According to those pose them, however, the mascots give life to racial stereo- s well as revivify historical patterns of appropriation and sion. These results often foster discomfort and pain among an Indian people (Springwood and King 2001).

-Indian people may not be culturally aware that some an Indian symbols used by cheerleaders and cheering war chants, peace pipes, eagle feathers, war bonnets, and —are highly revered or even sacred in many American Indian tribal communities. Many mascots, logos, and nicknames represent stereotypical and racist images that relegate American Indian people to a colonial representation history. The exploitation of Indian mascots, logos, and nicknames in schools is, in reality, an issue of decolonization and educational equity.[1]

This article discusses the creation of stereotypical Indian mascots, how our society reinforces and accepts those stereotypes, how negative stereotypes have affected the relationship between American Indians and the rest of society, and it suggests solutions educators might use to eliminate these mascots from school-related events. In writing this article, I hope not to demean schools but to provide a rationale and approach by which ethnocentrism, elitism, sexism, and racism effectively can be eradicated in schools.

Countering the Assault of American Indian Mascots, Logos, and Nicknames

Using the word *countering*, which means to confront defensive or retaliatory attacks or arguments, to describe certain behaviors and thinking in our society is a strong indictment of the existing social fabric of the United States. Many educators in this country are serious players when it comes to countering racism, thereby protecting the mental health of school children today. However, many more teachers are unresponsive to or unaware of the issues of racism in schools today. Like these teachers, parents, educators, and liberals who deny being racists but remain silent when confronted with the issue also allow institutional racism to continue.

This issue has turned into a debate and torn schools and communities apart. Administrators spend months fending off angry alumni on both sides of the issue, calming students, and dealing with mainstream news media that oversimplify these issues. After it is all over, school districts often must spend additional time and energy healing the wounds and community ruptures left in the wake of efforts to counter institutional racism by eradicating American Indian mascots, logos, and nicknames in schools (Riede 2001).

Still "Playing Indian" in School

Many schools around the country "play Indian" by exhibiting American Indian mascots, logos, and nicknames at sporting events: school bands play so-called "Indian" fight songs (for example, "One-little-two-little- three-little Indians . . .") during both pregame and halftime entertainment; mascots dress in stereotypical cartoon character-like costumes and beat hand drums and/or carry foam tomahawks; and fans do the "tomahawk chop"[2] in unison. These all are inauthentic representations of American Indian cultures. Many school officials claim they are honoring American Indians and insist that the activities are not offensive. I argue otherwise and contend that these racist activities are forms of cultural violence in schools (Pewewardy 1999; 2001).

After studying this issue for fifteen years, I found that groups outside the American Indian community imposed most Indian mascots, logos, and nicknames on athletic teams. Even in the earliest U.S. government boarding schools, Indian children had no involvement in choosing their schools' mascots, logos, and nicknames. For example, the first recorded instance of an "Indian" nickname for a sports team was in 1894 at the Carlisle Indian School, an off-reservation U.S. government boarding school for American Indian students, located in Carlisle, Pennsylvania. Mainstream sports journalists praised the team's football performance in the early years of their program. From 1894 until 1917, the Carlisle football team defeated the major power football team of the day (Adams 1995). Subsequently, opposing college football teams and sports media nicknamed team members the Carlisle "Indians." Ironically, most American Indians have always opposed the use of "Indian" mascots, logos, and nicknames for sports teams. Yet, these traditions of doing so are enthusiastically supported by most European Americans (Muir 1999).

Although images of Indians in mainstream sports culture have become as American as apple pie and baseball, educators should be aware that American Indians never would have associated sacred practices with the hoopla of high school pep rallies and halftime entertainments.

How American Indian Mascots, Logos, and Nicknames Become Racist

The unfortunate portrayal of Indian mascots in sports today takes many forms. Some teams use generic Indian names—such as Indians, Braves, Warriors, or Chiefs—while others adopt specific tribal names—such as Seminoles, Comanches, or Apaches. Indian mascots exhibit either idealized or comical facial features and native dress, ranging from body-length feathered (usually turkey) headdresses to fake buckskin attire or skimpy loincloths. Some teams and supporters display counterfeit Indian paraphernalia, including foam tomahawks, feathers, face paints, drums, and pipes. They also use mock "Indian" behaviors, such as the tomahawk chop, dances, war (for example, at Florida State University), drum beatin whooping, and symbolic scalping. Many European Am rely on these manufactured images to anchor them to tl and verify a false account of a shared history. These "In however, exist only in the imagination: they provide serving historical connection that leaves actual American people untethered and rootless in or erased from the his accounts of European Americans (Spindel 2000).

Many school officials are all too familiar with the curre and educational battles toward eliminating Indian mascots and nicknames from school related events. The U.S. Co sion of Civil Rights (CCR), the highest official govern body of its kind, issued a strong statement in 2001 co ing their use and recommending that schools eliminate images and nicknames as sports symbols (U.S. Departr Justice 2001). Grassroots efforts of thousands of American parents nationwide prompted this decision among CCR bers. Moreover, the critical mass of American Indian educ organizations and professionals supported the CCR sta American Indian educators showed school officials that n images, symbols, and behaviors play a crucial role in di and warping American Indian children's cultural percept themselves, as well as non-Indian children's attitudes tow simplistic understanding of American Indian culture. Hol scriptwriters originally manufactured most of these stere Over time, they have evolved into contemporary racist that prevent millions of school-age students from unders American Indians' past and present experiences.

How Stereotypical Images Imp Young Children's Self-Esteem

Children begin to develop racial awareness at an early a haps as early as three or four years old. Clinical psych have established that negative stereotypes and derogatory engender and perpetuate undemocratic and unhealthy a in children, plaguing them for years to come. Many non children exposed to these Hollywood stereotypes at ear grow into adults who may unwittingly or unknowing criminate against American Indians. These children ha prevented from developing authentic, healthy attitude Indians. Moreover, Indian children who constantly se selves being stereotyped and their cultures belittled gr adults who feel and act inferior to other people. Thes and inauthentic behaviors mock Indian culture and caus Indian youngsters to have low self-esteem and feel sham their cultural identity. School environments should be where students unlearn negative stereotypes that such r represent and promote. However, athletic events where mascots are frequently used teach children the exact op

Perhaps some people at these sporting events do not l foul language being shouted out in the stands and seating associated with the usage of Indian mascots, logos, and nic The most obvious offenses are the terms *redskins* (lady re and *squaws*. According to one explanation, the word originated in early colonial times when European coloni

ies for Indians' red skins—thereby coining the term *redskin.* /ord *squaw* is a French corruption of the Iroquois word *otsis-* meaning female properties. Both words are almost always in a derogatory fashion in sporting events. Although these may be facing increasing social disdain, they certainly are)m dead. These words accentuate the differences in appear- culture, gender, nationality, or sexual orientation of people nderplay—if not to deny—the similarities between people.

ven this background, no one, especially those associated schools, should allow students to adopt a cartoon version ierican Indian cultures as a mascot or logo. Educators and nts need to be more educated about the negative effects ist Indian mascots and logos on American Indian people. students do not recognize that the Indian mascot issue is portant in the American Indian community as alcoholism, ince abuse, and poverty. Some people excuse their ambiv- e on the issue by saying there is "too much fuss over team s," "we're just having fun," "we're not harming anybody," hat's the point?" They miss the connection because they moved from the issues of American Indian education. It d to take American Indians seriously or to empathize with when they are always portrayed as speaking in old, bro- toic Indian clichés, such as "many moons ago"; dressed Halloween or Thanksgiving costumes; or acting crazy "bunch of wild Indians." These make-believe Indians are)ited from changing over time to be like real people. On ic fields and in gymnasiums, they are denied the dignity of ribal histories, the validity of their major contributions to rn American society, and the distinctiveness of their mul- l identities.

1998, Children Now initiated a study of children's per- ns of race and class in the media, focusing on images of ican Indians presented in national news and entertain- The Children Now study revealed similar results to the)tions survey conducted by the League of Women Voters '5: most children in America view American Indians far ed from their own way of life.[3] Not only do these stud- ve to be conducted and their results disseminated, but the nceptions and stereotypes about American Indian people, bombard the child from outside of the classroom, need counteracted.

king Racism Visible chool-Related Events

e years of cultural diversity teacher training and integration of ultural education lesson plans into the school curricula, chil- ill play "cowboys and Indians" at some schools. Most teach- doubtedly, have seen (or perhaps even supported) children g around in turkey feathers and cardboard headbands, carry- nemade bows and arrows, patting a hand against their mouth lling "woo-woo-woo," or raising their hands over their shoul- d saying "how." The perpetuation of these invented Indian ors reflects the influence of peer socialization, schooling, and ream movies. They mock American Indian cultural practices, n actual human beings, and treat American Indian people as nans incapable of verbal communication. This manufactured image of the Indian as something wild and inferior implies white superiority, a value judgment made namely by Hollywood script-writers (Rollins and O'Connor 1998).

Another popular character born of the racist images of American Indian people is the clown. Traditional clown societies of many tribes (for example, Apaches, Pueblos) attempt to make their people laugh during celebrations and ceremonies. On the other hand, the contemporary clown, born of American popular culture, is more like the jester or the fool, the inferior one responsible for making his superiors laugh. The use of clowns has always been a major way to assert dominance over a particular person or a certain group of people. During ballgames, the exaggerated images of Indians become clown-like, serving to manipulate and keep in place negative images during school-related events.

However, I hypothesize that the use of American Indian mascots in sporting events was influenced by the philosophical views of the Enlightenment and the developing Romantic movement. During those periods, American Indians were seen either as amusing exotics or as Noble Savages, excellent types for representing ideas in literature, in film, or on the stage. But the reality was that these figures were never more than white characters with cliché comic or noble personalities, thinly disguised in red skins and feathered costumes. American Indian people were never considered real human beings whose existence might be dramatically interesting (Jones 1988).

Defensive Tactics and Attributes

Who should decide what is demeaning and racist? Clearly, the affected party determines what is offensive. Unaffected members of society should not dictate how the affected party should feel. Moreover, efforts to retire Indian mascots, logos, and nicknames should not be met with ugly alumni and student backlashes that label grassroots complainants as troublemakers, activist, militant, gadflies, or practitioners of politically correctness. Therefore, educators who advocate and affirm cultural diversity must be ready for a challenge. Only a concerted effort to debunk Hollywood's mythology can alter the distorted image of the American Indian people for the better.

Educators should examine the biases and stereotypes their students hold. These stereotypes, caused by ignorance, hard times, and folk wisdom socialization, can be countered by accurate and culturally responsive information. Education can become a tool for liberation from bigotry—rather than a facilitator of racism (Corntassel n.d.).

Large School Districts and Organizations as Trailblazers

Hope for change can be found in two large school districts in the United States. Both Dallas Public Schools and Los Angeles Public Schools have already eliminated Indian mascots from their school districts as the result of active parent and education advocacy groups working [together] with school officials. The states of Wisconsin and Minnesota also have recommended that publicly funded schools eliminate the use of Indian mascots, logos, and nicknames deemed offensive to American Indians.

Professional organizations dedicated to the unique problems of American Indians must take forthright positions on this issue as well. As a teacher educator, I show future teachers why Indian mascots are one cause of low self-esteem among American Indian children in schools. Throughout my practical experience working in K–8 schools, I have learned that self-esteem fuels academic performance. Educators must realize that this issue is detrimental to the academic achievement of all students. As such, negative Indian mascots, logos, and nicknames are harmful to both Indian and non-Indian students. American Indian students endure the psychological damage and dehumanizing effects of seeing caricatures of themselves embodied in school mascots, logos, and nicknames. It is no coincidence that American Indians have the highest suicide, school dropout, and unemployment rates of any ethnic group in the U.S. (Rider 1999). To illustrate my point, I refer to the mental health organizations that have rushed to support the elimination of negative Indian mascots used in schools (for example, the American Indian Mental Health Association of Minnesota in 1992 and the Society of Indian Psychologists of the Americas in 1999). They drafted statements condemning the presence of ethnic images as psychologically destructive to the minds of American Indian children. Other professional organizations that have passed resolutions in support of eliminating negative Indian mascots used in school-related activities and events include the National Indian Education Association, United Indian Nations of Oklahoma, Governors' Interstate Indian Council, Great Lakes Inter Tribal Council, National Congress of American Indians, National Association for the Advancement of Colored People, and National College Athletic Association.

Although such resolutions exist today, political and cultural leaders in many states (such as Oklahoma) have hundreds of Indian mascots and logos in use in school-related events but remain unconcerned with this national issue. They are uneducated about the issues or have little educational leadership to initiate transformational change toward truly honoring American Indians. Consequently, there is a critical need for experts to monitor more carefully these destructive influences in our shared physical, mental, social, and spiritual environments. Educators, parents, and community leaders must build coalitions to preserve the reality of our shared history. Educators must develop educational materials, artistic productions, economic structures, fashions, and concepts that counteract these damaging stereotypes.

What Must Be Done

The recognition of embedded racism in the English language is an important first step. Consciousness of the influence of language on our perceptions can help negate much of that influence. But it is not enough to simply be aware of the effects of racist language in conditioning attitudes. Although society may not be able to change the entire language, educators can help students change their use of many unkind words. Educators should not use degrading and dehumanizing words and should make a conscious effort to use terminology that reflects a progressive, rather than distorting, perspective. Most important, educators should provide students with opportunities to increase thei[r cul]tural awareness by exploring racism in language and also s[hould] teach terminology that is culturally responsive and does no[t per]petuate negative human values and experiences.

To correct these negative stereotypes, concerned indi[vidu]als or groups should consult the local school Title IX I[ndian] Education Program coordinator, curriculum specialist, cu[ltural] resource librarian, university professor, or the National I[ndian] Education Association to assist in the elimination of ne[gative] ethnic images and materials from the academic curriculu[m and] school-related events. Some complainants of Indian m[ascots] and logos have also filed complaints with the U.S. Depar[tment] of Education, Office of Civil Rights. Every public schoo[l dis]trict is required to have a complaint procedure adopted b[y the] school board for residents to use.

One of the finest award-winning reference books on this [topic] is *American Indian Stereotypes in the World of Children* by A[rlene] Hirschfelder, Paulette Fairbanks Molin, and Yvonne Wakim ([...] Robert Eurich also maintains a comprehensive website on Am[erican] Indian sports teams mascots at http://earnestman.tripod.com/f[...] .retrospective.htm. This website tracks all schools that have [...] names as well as those schools that have been changed to [...] Indian mascots.[4]

Every school year, American Indian students, parents, edu[cators,] and other allies must continue the hard work to educate our [...] people and us about how Indian mascots are used in school-[related] events. We must find every opportunity to celebrate ourselves[, chal]lenging the fear that causes us to hesitate in taking control of o[ur] ethnic images. We must work together and have faith that our s[...] will be successful, regardless of the opposition.

Conclusion

The ongoing use of Indian mascots in school-sponsored [...] is an issue of educational equity. Therefore, my profes[sional] challenge is to educators. As long as such mascots remain [in] the arena of school activities, both Indian and non-India[n chil]dren are learning to tolerate racism in schools. By tolerati[ng the] use of demeaning stereotypes in our public schools, we [...] desensitize entire generations of children (Milner 1991, 6[...] a result, schools reinforce the stereotypical negative imag[es pro]jected in the broader mainstream American cultural imagi[nation.] Sport teams with Indian mascots, logos, and nicknames [teach] them that it is acceptable to demean a race or group of [people] through American sports culture. Educators must turn t[...] of these mascots, logos, and nicknames into powerful [teach]ing moments that could help counter the fabricated imag[es and] manufactured pictures of Indians that most school-age c[hildren] have ingrained in their psyche by one hundred years o[f] media. Finally, I challenge administrators and policyma[kers to] provide the intellectual school leadership that truly em[braces] multicultural education, helping to eliminate the cultur[al vio]lence associated with and triggered by the use of Am[erican] Indian mascots in school-related events.

As a former kindergarten teacher and principal, I have found respect and admiration for teachers and adminis[trators.] The work they do is honorable, although rarely cherish[ed] ame time, I recognize that many teachers and administra-ave not been given the time or support to help them teach : most culturally responsive way. I hope this explanation of educators should not ignore Indian mascots is a tool both ers and administrators can use to help children think criti- about multicultural issues in another school year.

tes

Many of the contemporary Indian mascots, logos, and nicknames of today originated at the turn of the twenty-first century. However, crude stereotyping of these ethnic characters became more and more obvious as the first half of the century progressed, even surviving the social reconstruction of the Civil Rights Era.

The tomahawk chop is a social phenomenon created by those ports fans who perceive the need for a supportive physical isplay of action to cheer on the favored athletic team. It is the extension of a single arm out in front on an individual—winging the hand and forearm in an up and down motion. The ct of the tomahawk chop usually takes place in large crowds n sport stadiums accompanied by a so-called Indian war chant. The tomahawk perpetuates the negative stereotype of the Noble Savage that falsely represents American Indians, and it certainly s not reflective of modern America.

See Children Now: Native American children's perceptions of ace and class in the media. . . .

ee Robert Eurich's website dedicated to educating individuals bout Indian mascots. . . .

ferences

s, D. W. 1995. *Education for extinction: American Indians and e boarding school experience, 1875–1928.* Lawrence, KS: niversity Press of Kansas.

tt, C. I. 1999. *Comprehensive multicultural education: Theory nd practice.* Boston: Allyn and Bacon.

Corntassel, J. J. n.d. *Let's teach respect, not racism: Ethnic mascots demean American Indians.* . . .

Hirschfelder, A., P. Fairbanks Molin, and Y. Wakim. 1999. *American Indian stereotypes in the world of children: A reader and bibliography.* Lanham, MA: Scarecrow Press.

Jones, E. H. *Native Americans as shown on the stage, 1753–1916.* Metuchen, NJ: The Scarecrow Press.

Miner, B. 1991. The Danger of Harmless School Mascots. In *Rethinking Columbus: A special issue of Rethinking Schools:* 67.

Muir, S. P. 1999. Native Americans as Sports Mascots. *Social Education* 63 (1): 56–57.

Pewewardy, C. 1999. From enemy to mascot: The deculturation of Indian mascots in sport culture. *Canadian Journal of Native Education* 23 (2): 176–89.

———. 2001. Educators and mascots: Challenging contradictions. In *Team spirits: The Native American mascots controversy.* Eds. C. R. King and C. F. Springwood. Lincoln, NE: University of Nebraska Press, 257–78.

Rider, D. P. 1999. *Stereotypes/Discrimination/Identity.* . . .

Riede, P. 2001. More Than a Mascot. *The School Administrator* 58(8): 27–33.

Rollins, P. C., and J. E. O'Connor. 1998. *Hollywood's Indian: The portrayal of the Native American in film.* Lexington, KY: University Press of Kentucky.

Spindel, C. *Dancing at halftime: Sports and the controversy over American Indian mascots.* New York: New York University Press.

Springwood, C. F., and C. R. King. Playing Indian: Why Native American Mascots Must End. *The Chronicle of Higher Education: The Chronicle Review,* November 19, 2001.

U. S. Department of Justice. Racism Report by *U.S. Department of Justice.* . . .

Cornel D. Pewewardy is an associate professor in the Department of Teaching and Leadership at the University of Kansas in Lawrence.

Sick of Poverty

New studies suggest that the stress of being poor has a staggeringly harmful influence on health.

ROBERT SAPOLSKY

Rudolph Virchow, the 19th-century German neuroscientist, physician and political activist, came of age with two dramatic events—a typhoid outbreak in 1847 and the failed revolutions of 1848. Out of those experiences came two insights for him: first, that the spread of disease has much to do with appalling living conditions, and second, that those in power have enormous means to subjugate the powerless. As Virchow summarized in his famous epigram, "Physicians are the natural attorneys of the poor."

Physicians (and biomedical scientists) are advocates of the underprivileged because poverty and poor health tend to go hand in hand. Poverty means bad or insufficient food, unhealthy living conditions and endless other factors that lead to illness. Yet it is not merely that poor people tend to be unhealthy while everyone else is well. When you examine socioeconomic status (SES), a composite measure that includes income, occupation, education and housing conditions, it becomes clear that, starting with the wealthiest stratum of society, every step downward in SES correlates with poorer health.

This "SES gradient" has been documented throughout Westernized societies for problems that include respiratory and cardiovascular diseases, ulcers, rheumatoid disorders, psychiatric diseases and a number of cancers. It is not a subtle statistical phenomenon. When you compare the highest versus the lowest rungs of the SES ladder, the risk of some diseases varies 10-fold. Some countries exhibit a five- to 10-year difference in life expectancy across the SES spectrum. Of the Western nations, the U.S. has the steepest gradient; for example, one study showed that the poorest white males in America die about a decade earlier than the richest.

So what causes this correlation between SES and health? Lower SES may give rise to poorer health, but conversely, poorer health could also give rise to lower SES. After all, chronic illness can compromise one's education and work productivity, in addition to generating enormous expenses.

Nevertheless, the bulk of the facts suggests that the arrow goes from economic status to health—that SES at some point in life predicts health measures later on. Among the many demonstrations of this point is a remarkable study of elderly American nuns. All had taken their vows as young adults and had spent many years thereafter sharing diet, health care and ho thereby controlling for those lifestyle factors. Yet in the age, patterns of disease, incidence of dementia and long were still significantly predicted by their SES status from they became nuns, at least half a century before.

Inadequate Explanations

So, to use a marvelous phrase common to this field, how SES get "under the skin" and influence health? The answer seem most obvious, it turns out, do not hold much water such explanation, for instance, posits that for the poor, care may be less easily accessible and of lower quality possibility is plausible when one considers that for many poor in America, the family physician does not exist, and cal care consists solely of trips to the emergency room.

But that explanation soon falls by the wayside, for re made clearest in the famed Whitehall studies by Mich Marmot of University College London over the past decades. Marmot and his colleagues have documented an of dramatic SES gradients in a conveniently stratified p tion, namely, the members of the British civil service (ra from blue-collar workers to high-powered executives). messengers and porters, for example, have far higher mo rates from chronic heart disease than administrators and p sionals do. Lack of access to medical attention cannot e the phenomenon, because the U.K., unlike the U.S., ha versal health care. Similar SES gradients also occur in countries with socialized medicine, including the healt Edens of Scandinavia, and the differences remain sign even after researchers factor in how much the subjects ac use the medical services.

Another telling finding is that SES gradients exist for di for which health care access is irrelevant. No amount of cal checkups, blood tests and scans will change the likelih someone getting type 1 (juvenile-onset) diabetes or rheu arthritis, yet both conditions are more common among the

The next "obvious" explanation centers on unhealthy life As you descend the SES ladder in Westernized societies, are more likely to smoke, to drink excessively, to be obese, a violent or polluted or densely populated neighborhood. ɔeople are also less likely to have access to clean water, y food and health clubs, not to mention adequate heat in the · and air-conditioning in the summer. Thus, it seems self-ıt that lower SES gets under the skin by increasing risks and ısing protective factors. As mordantly stated by Robert G. of the University of British Columbia, "Drinking sewage ɔably unwise, even for Bill Gates."

ıat is surprising, though, is how little of the SES gradient risk and protective factors explain. In the Whitehall stud-ontrolling for factors such as smoking and level of exercise nted for only about a third of the gradient. This same point is by studies comparing health and wealth among, rather than , nations. It is reasonable to assume that the wealthier a coun-ɛ more financial resources its citizens have to buy protection ʻoid risk. If so, health should improve incrementally as one ; up the wealth gradient among nations, as well as among the ıs within individual nations. But it does not. Instead, among ɛalthiest quarter of countries on earth, there is no relation ɛn a country's wealth and the health of its people.

us, health care access, health care utilization, and exposure and protective factors explain the SES/health gradient far ell than one might have guessed. One must therefore con-vhether most of the gradient arises from a different set of lerations: the psychosocial consequences of SES.

ychosocial Stress

y, the body is in homeostatic balance, a state in which the neasures of human function—heart rate, blood pressure, sugar levels and so on—are in their optimal ranges. A ɔr is anything that threatens to disrupt homeostasis. For ɔrganisms, a stressor is an acute physical challenge—for ɔle, the need for an injured gazelle to sprint for its life a hungry predator to chase down a meal. The body is ɔly adapted to dealing with short-term physical challenges neostasis. Stores of energy, including the sugar glucose, eased, and cardiovascular tone increases to facilitate the ry of fuel to exercising muscle throughout the body. Diges-rowth, tissue repair, reproduction and other physiological sses not needed to survive the crisis are suppressed. The ıe system steps up to thwart opportunistic pathogens. ry and the senses transiently sharpen.

ɩ cognitively and socially sophisticated species, such as ımates, routinely inhabit a different realm of stress. For ɔst stressors concern interactions with our own species, w physically disrupt homeostasis. Instead these psycho-stressors involve the anticipation (accurate or otherwise) impending challenge. And the striking characteristic of sychological and social stress is its chronicity. For most ıals, a stressor lasts only a few minutes. In contrast, we ıs can worry chronically over a 30-year mortgage.

fortunately, our body's response, though adaptive for an physical stressor, is pathogenic for prolonged psycho-stress. Chronic increase in cardiovascular tone brings induced hypertension. The constant mobilization of · increases the risk or severity of diseases such as type 2 onset) diabetes. The prolonged inhibition of digestion, growth, tissue repair and reproduction increases the risks of various gastrointestinal disorders, impaired growth in children, failure to ovulate in females and erectile dysfunction in males. A too-extended immune stress response ultimately suppresses immunity and impairs disease defenses. And chronic activation of the stress response impairs cognition, as well as the health, functioning and even survival of some types of neurons.

An extensive biomedical literature has established that individuals are more likely to activate a stress response and are more at risk for a stress-sensitive disease if they (a) feel as if they have minimal control over stressors, (b) feel as if they have no predictive information about the duration and intensity of the stressor, (c) have few outlets for the frustration caused by the stressor, (d) interpret the stressor as evidence of circumstances worsening, and (e) lack social support—for the duress caused by the stressors.

Psychosocial stressors are not evenly distributed across society. Just as the poor have a disproportionate share of physical stressors (hunger, manual labor, chronic sleep deprivation with a second job, the bad mattress that can't be replaced), they have a disproportionate share of psychosocial ones. Numbing assembly-line work and an occupational lifetime spent taking orders erode workers' sense of control. Unreliable cars that may not start in the morning and paychecks that may not last the month inflict unpredictability. Poverty rarely allows stress-relieving options such as health club memberships, costly but relaxing hobbies, or sabbaticals for rethinking one's priorities. And despite the heartwarming stereotype of the "poor but loving community," the working poor typically have less social support than the middle and upper classes, thanks to the extra jobs, the long commutes on public transit, and other burdens. Marmot has shown that regardless of SES, the less autonomy one has at work, the worse one's cardiovascular health. Furthermore, low control in the workplace accounts for about half the SES gradient in cardiovascular disease in his Whitehall population.

Feeling Poor

Three lines of research provide more support for the influence of psychological stress on SES-related health gradients. Over the past decade Nancy E. Adler of the University of California, San Francisco, has explored the difference between objective and subjective SES and the relation of each to health. Test subjects were shown a simple diagram of a ladder with 10 rungs and then asked, "In society, where on this ladder would you rank yourself in terms of how well you're doing?" The very openness of the question allowed the person to define the comparison group that felt most emotionally salient.

As Adler has shown, a person's subjective assessment of his or her SES takes into account the usual objective measures (education, income, occupation and residence) as well as measures of life satisfaction and of anxiety about the future. Adler's provocative finding is that subjective SES is at least as good as objective SES at predicting patterns of cardiovascular function, measures of metabolism, incidences of obesity and levels of stress hormones—suggesting that the subjective feelings may help explain the objective results.

This same point emerges from comparisons of the SES/health gradient among nations. A relatively poor person in the U.S. may objectively have more financial resources to purchase health care and protective factors than a relatively wealthy person in a less developed country yet, on average, will still have a shorter life expectancy. For example, as Stephen Bezruchka of the University of Washington emphasizes, people in Greece on average earn half the income of Americans yet have a longer life expectancy. Once the minimal resources are available to sustain a basic level of health through adequate food and housing, absolute levels of income are of remarkably little importance to health. Although Adler's work suggests that the objective state of being poor adversely affects health, at the core of that result is the subjective state of feeling poor.

Being Made to Feel Poor

Another body of research arguing that psychosocial factors mediate most of the SES/health gradient comes from Richard Wilkinson of the University of Nottingham in England. Over the past 15 years he and his colleagues have reported that the extent of income inequality in a community is even more predictive than SES for an array of health measures. In other words, absolute levels of income aside, greater disparities in income between the poorest and the wealthiest in a community predict worse average health. (David H. Abbott of the Wisconsin National Primate Research Center and I, along with our colleagues, found a roughly equivalent phenomenon in animals: among many nonhuman primate species, less egalitarian social structures correlate with higher resting levels of a key stress hormone—an index for worse health—among socially subordinate animals.)

Wilkinson's subtle and critical finding has generated considerable controversy. One dispute concerns its generality. His original work suggested that income inequality was relevant to health in many European and North American countries and communities. It has become clear, however, that this relation holds only in the developed country with the greatest of income inequalities, namely, the U.S.

Whether considered at the level of cities or states, income inequality predicts mortality rates across nearly all ages in the U.S. Why, though, is this relation not observed in, say, Canada or Denmark? One possibility is that these countries have too little income variability to tease out the correlation.

Some critics have questioned whether the linkage between income inequality and worse health is merely a mathematical quirk. The relation between SES and health follows an asymptotic curve: dropping from the uppermost rung of society's ladder to the next-to-top step reduces life expectancy and other measures much less drastically than plunging from the next-to-bottom rung to the lowest level. Because a community with high levels of income inequality will have a relatively high number of individuals at the very bottom, where health prospects are so dismal, the community's average life expectancy will inevitably be lower than that of an egalitarian community, for reasons that have nothing to do with psychosocial factors. Wilkinson has shown, however, that decreased income inequality predicts better health for both the poor and the wealthy. This strongly indicates that the association between illnes inequality is more than just a mathematical artifact.

Wilkinson and others in the field have long argued that th unequal income in a community is, the more psychosocial there will be for the poor. Higher income inequality intens community's hierarchy and makes social support less ava truly symmetrical, reciprocal, affiliative support exists only a equals. Moreover, having your nose rubbed in your poverty is to lessen your sense of control in life, to aggravate the frustr of poverty and to intensify the sense of life worsening.

If Adler's work demonstrates the adverse health effe feeling poor, Wilkinson's income inequality work sugges the surest way to feel poor is to be made to feel poor—to b lessly made aware of the haves when you are a have-not. our global village, we are constantly made aware of the m and celebrities whose resources dwarf ours.

John W. Lynch and George A. Kaplan of the Univers Michigan at Ann Arbor have recently proposed another wa people are made to feel poor. Their "neomaterialist" inter tion of the income inequality phenomenon—which is reasonable and, ultimately, deeply depressing—runs as fo Spending money on public goods (better public transit, uni health care and so on) is a way to improve the quality for the average person. But by definition, the bigger the i inequality in a society, the greater the financial distance be the average and the wealthy. The bigger this distance, th the wealthy have to gain from expenditures on the public Instead they would benefit more from keeping their tax to spend on their private good—a better chauffeur, a gatec munity, bottled water, private schools, private health insu So the more unequal the income is in a community, the incentive the wealthy will have to oppose public expen benefiting the health of the community. And within the U. more income inequality there is, the more power will be portionately in the hands of the wealthy to oppose such expenditures. According to health economist Evans, this sc ultimately leads to "private affluence and public squalor."

This "secession of the wealthy" can worsen the SES/heal dient in two ways: by aggravating the conditions in low-i communities (which account for at least part of the increased risks for the poor) and by adding to the psychosocial stress social and psychological stressors are entwined with feeling and even more so with feeling poor while being confronte the wealthy, they will be even more stressful when the weal striving to decrease the goods and services available to the p

Social Capital

A third branch of support for psychosocial explanations for t tion between income inequality and health comes from th of Ichiro Kawachi of Harvard University, based on the con "social capital." Although it is still being refined as a measure capital refers to the broad levels of trust and efficacy in a com Do people generally trust one another and help one another c people feel an incentive to take care of commonly held resour example, to clean up graffiti in public parks)? And do people f organizations—such as unions or tenant associations—actually an impact? Most studies of social capital employ two simple sures, namely, how many organizations people belong to and people answer a question such as, "Do you think most people d try to take advantage of you if they got a chance?"

/hat Kawachi and others have shown is that at the levels of s, provinces, cities and neighborhoods, low social capital icts bad health, bad self-reported health and high mortality . Using a complex statistical technique called path analysis, achi has demonstrated that (once one controls for the effects solute income) the strongest route from income inequality oor health is through the social capital measures—to wit, degrees of income inequality come with low levels of trust support, which increases stress and harms health.

'one of this is surprising. As a culture, America has neglected cial safety nets while making it easier for the most successful atop the pyramids of inequality. Moreover, we have chosen rgo the social capital that comes from small, stable commus in exchange for unprecedented opportunities for mobility anonymity. As a result, all measures of social epidemiology vorsening in the U.S. Of Westernized nations, America has reatest income inequality (40 percent of the wealth is cond by 1 percent of the population) and the greatest discrep- between expenditures on health care (number one in the d) and life expectancy (as of 2003, number 29).

he importance of psychosocial factors in explaining the /health gradient generates a critical conclusion: when it es to health, there is far more to poverty than simply not ng enough money. (As Evans once stated, "Most graduate ents have had the experience of having very little money, not of poverty. They are very different things.") The psyocial school has occasionally been accused of promulgatan anti-progressive message: don't bother with universal h care, affordable medicines and other salutary measures use there will still be a robust SES/health gradient after all eforms. But the lesson of this research is not to abandon societal change. It is that so much more is needed.

erview/Status and Health

Researchers have long known that people with low socioeconomic status [SES] have dramatically higher disease risks and shorter life spans than do people in the wealthier strata of society. The conventional explanations—that the poor have less access to health care and a greater incidence of harmful lifestyles such as smoking and obesity—cannot account for the huge discrepancy in health outcomes.

New studies indicate that the psychosocial stresses associated with poverty may increase the risks of many illnesses. The chronic stress induced by living in a poor, violent neighborhood, for example, could increase one's susceptibility to cardiovascular disease, depression and diabetes.

Other studies have shown a correlation between income inequality and poor health in the U.S. Some researchers believe that the poor feel poorer, and hence suffer greater stress, in communities with wide gaps between the highest and lowest incomes.

The Good and Bad Effects of Stress

The human body is superb at responding to the acute stress of a physical challenge, such as chasing down prey or escaping a predator. The circulatory, nervous and immune systems are mobilized while the digestive and reproductive processes are suppressed. If the stress becomes chronic, though, the continual repetition of these responses can cause major damage.

Effects of Acute Stress

Brain Increased alertness and less perception of pain

Thymus Gland and Other Immune Tissues Immune system readied for possible injury

Circulatory System Heart beats faster, and blood vessels constrict to bring more oxygen to muscles

Adrenal Glands Secrete hormones that mobilize energy supplies

Reproductive Organs Reproductive functions are temporarily suppressed

Effects of Chronic Stress

Brain Impaired memory and increased risk of depression

Thymus Gland and Other Immune Tissues Deteriorated immune response

Circulatory System Elevated blood pressure and higher risk of cardiovascular disease

Adrenal Glands High hormone levels slow recovery from acute stress

Reproductive Organs Higher risks of infertility and miscarriage

More to Explore

Mind the Gap: Hierarchies, Health and Human Evolution. Richard Wilkinson. Weidenfeld and Nicolson, 2000.

The Health of Nations: Why Inequality Is Harmful to Your Health. Ichiro Kawachi and Bruce P. Kennedy. New Press, 2002.

The Status Syndrome. Michael Marmot. Henry Holt and Company, 2004.

Why Zebras Don't Get Ulcers: A Guide to Stress, Stress-Related Diseases and Coping. Robert Sapolsky. Third edition. Henry Holt and Company, 2004.

Robert Sapolsky is professor of biological sciences, neurology and neurological sciences at Stanford University and a research associate at the National Museums of Kenya. In his laboratory work, he focuses on how stress can damage the brain and on gene therapy for the nervous system. In addition, he studies populations of wild baboons in East Africa, trying to determine the relation between the social rank of a baboon and its health. His latest book is *Monkeyluv and Other Essays on Our Lives as Animals* [Scribner, 2005].

UNIT 4

Other Families, Other Ways

Unit Selections

Key Points to Consider

- If the incest taboo has to do with biological reasons, then how come it varies according to different cultures?
- Why do you think "fraternal polyandry" is socially acceptable in Tibet but not in our society?
- How have dietary changes affected birth rates and women's health?
- What are the pros and cons of arranged marriages versus love marriages?
- Does the stability of Japanese marriages necessarily imply compatibility and contentment?

Student Website

www.mhcls.com

Internet References

Arranged Marriages
http://women3rdworld.miningco.com/cs/arrangedmarriage/

Kinship and Social Organization
http://www.umanitoba.ca/anthropology

Sex and Marriage
http://anthro.palomar.edu/marriage/default.htm

Wedding Traditions and Customs
http://worldweddingtraditions.com/

ecause most people in small-scale societies of the past spent whole lives within a local area, it is understandable that their ary interactions—economic, religious, and otherwise—were their relatives. It also makes sense that, through marriage oms, they strengthened those kinship relationships that clearly ed their mutual rights and obligations. Indeed, the resulting y structure may be surprisingly flexible and adaptive, as wited in the essays "When Brothers Share a Wife" by Melvyn stein, and "Arranging a Marriage in India" by Serena Nanda.

or these reasons, anthropologists have looked upon famnd kinship as the key mechanisms for transmitting culture one generation to the next. Social changes may have been to take place throughout the world, but as social horizons widened, family relationships and community alliances ncreasingly based upon new principles. Even as birth rates increased, kinship networks have diminished in size and gth. As people have increasingly become involved with rs as co-workers in a market economy, our associations nd more and more upon factors such as personal aptis, educational backgrounds, and job opportunities. Yet the y still exists. Except for some rather unusual exceptions, amily is small, but still functions in its age-old nurturing and ctive role, even under conditions where there is little affec(see "Who Needs Love! by Nicholas Kristof) or under cons of extreme poverty and a high infant mortality rate (see th without Weeping" by Nancy Scheper-Hughes). Beyond mmediate family, the situation is in a state of flux. Certain c groups, especially those in poverty, still have a need for roader network and in some ways seem to be reformulating e ties.

We do not know where the changes described in this section will lead us and which ones will ultimately prevail. One thing is certain: anthropologists will be there to document the trends, for the discipline of anthropology has had to change as well. One important feature of the essays in this section is the growing interest of anthropologists in the study of complex societies where old theoretical perspectives are inadequate.

The current trends, however, do not necessarily depict the decline of the kinship unit. The large family network is still the best guarantee of individual survival and well-being in an urban setting.

When Brothers Share a Wife

Among Tibetans, the Good Life Relegates Many Women to Spinsterhood

MELVYN C. GOLDSTEIN

Eager to reach home, Dorje drives his yaks hard over the 17,000-foot mountain pass, stopping only once to rest. He and his two older brothers, Pema and Sonam, are jointly marrying a woman from the next village in a few weeks, and he has to help with the preparations.

Dorje, Pema, and Sonam are Tibetans living in Limi, a 200-square-mile area in the northwest corner of Nepal, across the border from Tibet. The form of marriage they are about to enter—fraternal polyandry in anthropological parlance—is one of the world's rarest forms of marriage but is not uncommon in Tibetan society, where it has been practiced from time immemorial. For many Tibetan social strata, it traditionally represented the ideal form of marriage and family.

The mechanics of fraternal polyandry are simple. Two, three, four, or more brothers jointly take a wife, who leaves her home to come and live with them. Traditionally, marriage was arranged by parents, with children, particularly females, having little or no say. This is changing somewhat nowadays, but it is still unusual for children to marry without their parents' consent. Marriage ceremonies vary by income and region and range from all the brothers sitting together as grooms to only the eldest one formally doing so. The age of the brothers plays an important role in determining this: very young brothers almost never participate in actual marriage ceremonies, although they typically join the marriage when they reach their mid-teens.

The eldest brother is normally dominant in terms of authority, that is, in managing the household, but all the brothers share the work and participate as sexual partners. Tibetan males and females do not find the sexual aspect of sharing a spouse the least bit unusual, repulsive, or scandalous, and the norm is for the wife to treat all the brothers the same.

Offspring are treated similarly. There is no attempt to link children biologically to particular brothers, and a brother shows no favoritism toward his child even if he knows he is the real father because, for example, his other brothers were away at the time the wife became pregnant. The children, in turn, consider all of the brothers as their fathers and treat them equally, even if they also know who is their real father. In some regions children use the term "father" for the eldest brother and "father's brother" for the others, while in other areas they call a brothers by one term, modifying this by the use of "elder "younger."

Unlike our own society, where monogamy is the only fc marriage permitted, Tibetan society allows a variety of ma types, including monogamy, fraternal polyandry, and poly Fraternal polyandry and monogamy are the most common of marriage, while polygyny typically occurs in cases whe first wife is barren. The widespread practice of fraternal pc dry, therefore, is not the outcome of a law requiring broth marry jointly. There is choice, and in fact, divorce traditic was relatively simple in Tibetan society. If a brother in a androus marriage became dissatisfied and wanted to sep he simply left the main house and set up his own house In such cases, all the children stayed in the main hous with the remaining brother(s), even if the departing brothe known to be the real father of one or more of the children

The Tibetans' own explanation for choosing fraternal andry is materialistic. For example, when I asked Dorje he decided to marry with his two brothers rather than tal own wife, he thought for a moment, then said it prevente division of his family's farm (and animals) and thus facil all of them achieving a higher standard of living. And w later asked Dorje's bride whether it wasn't difficult for h cope with three brothers as husbands, she laughed and ec the rationale of avoiding fragmentation of the family and adding that she expected to be better off economically, sinc would have three husbands working for her and her childr

Exotic as it may seem to Westerners, Tibetan fra polyandry is thus in many ways analogous to the way p geniture functioned in nineteenth-century England. P geniture dictated that the eldest son inherited the family e while younger sons had to leave home and seek their employment—for example, in the military or the clergy mogeniture maintained family estates intact over genera by permitting only one heir per generation. Fraternal poly also accomplishes this but does so by keeping all the brc together with just one wife so that there is only one *set* of per generation.

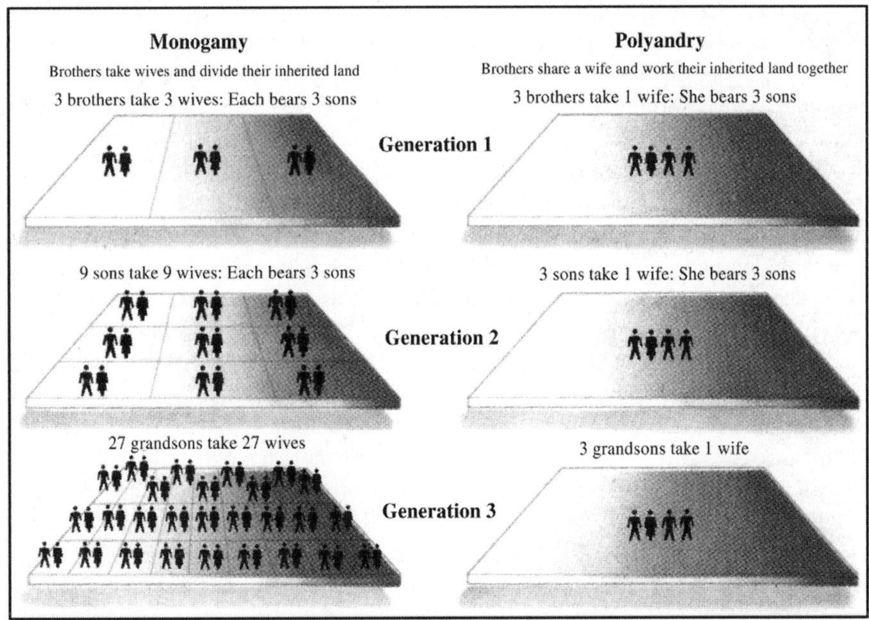
Monogamy
Brothers take wives and divide their inherited land
3 brothers take 3 wives: Each bears 3 sons
Polyandry
Brothers share a wife and work their inherited land together
3 brothers take 1 wife: She bears 3 sons
Generation 1
9 sons take 9 wives: Each bears 3 sons
3 sons take 1 wife: She bears 3 sons
Generation 2
27 grandsons take 27 wives
3 grandsons take 1 wife
Generation 3

Joe LeMonnier

Planning in Tibet An economic rationale for fraternal polyandry is outlined in the diagram, which emphasizes only the male ıg in each generation. If every wife is assumed to bear three sons, a family splitting up into monogamous households would multiply and fragment the family land. In this case, a rule of inheritance, such as primogeniture, could retain the family land out only at the cost of creating many landless male offspring. In contrast, the family practicing fraternal polyandry maintains a ratio of persons to land.

le Tibetans believe that in this way fraternal polyan- luces the risk of family fission, monogamous marriages brothers need not necessarily precipitate the division of ıily estate: brothers could continue to live together, and nily land could continue to be worked jointly. When I Tibetans about this, however, they invariably responded ch joint families are unstable because each wife is pri- oriented to her own children and interested in their suc- d well-being over that of the children of the other wives. mple, if the youngest brother's wife had three sons while est brother's wife had only one daughter, the wife of the st brother might begin to demand more resources for her n since, as males, they represent the future of the family. he children from different wives in the same generation npeting sets of heirs, and this makes such families inher- nstable. Tibetans perceive that conflict will spread from ves to their husbands and consider this likely to cause fission. Consequently, it is almost never done.

ough Tibetans see an economic advantage to fraternal dry, they do not value the sharing of a wife as an end in On the contrary, they articulate a number of problems ıt in the practice. For example, because authority is cus- ly exercised by the eldest brother, his younger male sib- ave to subordinate themselves with little hope of changing atus within the family. When these younger brothers are sive and individualistic, tensions and difficulties often lespite there being only one set of heirs.

ddition, tension and conflict may arise in polyandrous s because of sexual favoritism. The bride normally sleeps with the eldest brother, and the two have the responsibility to see to it that the other males have opportunities for sexual access. Since the Tibetan subsistence economy requires males to travel a lot, the temporary absence of one or more brothers facilitates this, but there are also other rotation practices. The cultural ideal unambiguously calls for the wife to show equal affection and sexuality to each of the brothers (and vice versa), but deviations from this ideal occur, especially when there is a sizable difference in age between the partners in the marriage.

Dorje's family represents just such a potential situation. He is fifteen years old and his two older brothers are twenty-five and twenty-two years old. The new bride is twenty-three years old, eight years Dorje's senior. Sometimes such a bride finds the youngest husband immature and adolescent and does not treat him with equal affection; alternatively, she may find his youth attractive and lavish special attention on him. Apart from that consideration, when a younger male like Dorje grows up, he may consider his wife "ancient" and prefer the company of a woman his own age or younger. Consequently, although men and women do not find the idea of sharing a bride or bridegroom repulsive, individual likes and dislikes can cause familial discord.

Two reasons have commonly been offered for the perpetuation of fraternal polyandry in Tibet: that Tibetans practice female infanticide and therefore have to marry polyandrously, owing to a shortage of females; and that Tibet, lying at extremely high altitudes, is so barren and bleak that Tibetans would starve without resort to this mechanism. A Jesuit who lived in Tibet during the eighteenth century articulated this second view: "One reason for this most odious custom is the sterility of the soil, and the small amount of land that can be cultivated owing to the lack of water. The crops may suffice if the brothers all live together, but if they form separate families they would be reduced to beggary."

Both explanations are wrong, however. Not only has there never been institutionalized female infanticide in Tibet, but Tibetan society gives females considerable rights, including inheriting the family estate in the absence of brothers. In such cases, the woman takes a bridegroom who comes to live in her family and adopts her family's name and identity. Moreover, there is no demographic evidence of a shortage of females. In Limi, for example, there were (in 1974) sixty females and fifty-three males in the fifteen- to thirty-five-year age category, and many adult females were unmarried.

The second reason is also incorrect. The climate in Tibet is extremely harsh, and ecological factors do play a major role perpetuating polyandry, but polyandry is not a means of preventing starvation. It is characteristic, not of the poorest segments of the society, but rather of the peasant landowning families.

In the old society, the landless poor could not realistically aspire to prosperity, but they did not fear starvation. There was a persistent labor shortage throughout Tibet, and very poor families with little or no land and few animals could subsist through agricultural labor, tenant farming, craft occupations such as carpentry, or by working as servants. Although the per person family income could increase somewhat if brothers married polyandrously and pooled their wages, in the absence of inheritable land, the advantage of fraternal polyandry was not generally sufficient to prevent them from setting up their own households. A more skilled or energetic younger brother could do as well or better alone, since he would completely control his income and would not have to share it with his siblings. Consequently, while there was and is some polyandry among the poor, it is much less frequent and more prone to result in divorce and family fission.

An alternative reason for the persistence of fraternal polyandry is that it reduces population growth (and thereby reduces the pressure on resources) by relegating some females to lifetime spinsterhood. Fraternal polyandrous marriages in Limi (in 1974) averaged 2.35 men per woman, and not surprisingly, 31 percent of the females of child-bearing age (twenty to forty-nine) were unmarried. These spinsters either continued to live at home, set up their own households, or worked as servants for other families. They could also become Buddhist nuns. Being unmarried is not synonymous with exclusion from the reproductive pool. Discreet extramarital relationships are tolerated, and actually half of the adult unmarried women in Limi had one or more children. They raised these children as single mothers, working for wages or weaving cloth and blankets for sale. As a group, however, the unmarried woman had far fewer off-spring than the married women, averaging only 0.7 children per woman, compared with 3.3 for married women, whether polyandrous, monogamous, or polygynous. While polyandry helps regulate population, this function of polyandry is not consciously perceived by Tibetans and is not the reason they consistently choose it.

If neither a shortage of females nor the fear of sta perpetuates fraternal polyandry, what motivates brothe ticularly younger brothers, to opt for this system of ma From the perspective of the younger brother in a land-h family, the main incentive is the attainment or maintena the good life. With polyandry, he can expect a more secu higher standard of living, with access not only to this fa land and animals but also to its inherited collection of c jewelry, rugs, saddles, and horses. In addition, he will ence less work pressure and much greater security beca responsibility does not fall on one "father." For Tibetan ers, the question is whether to trade off the greater person dom inherent in monogamy for the real or potential eco security, affluence, and social prestige associated with li larger, labor-rich polyandrous family.

A brother thinking of separating from his polyandrou riage and taking his own wife would face various disadva Although in the majority of Tibetan regions all brothers th ically have rights to their family's estate, in reality Tibet reluctant to divide their land into small fragments. Gene younger brother who insists on leaving the family will only a small plot of land, if that. Because of its pow wealth, the rest of the family usually can block any atte the younger brother to increase his share of land through tion. Moreover, a younger brother may not even get a hou cannot expect to receive much above the minimum in te movable possessions, such as furniture, pots, and pans. brother contemplating going it on his own must plan on a ing economic security and the good life not through inhe but through his own work.

The obvious solution for younger brothers—creatin fields from virgin land—is generally not a feasible optior Tibetan populations live at high altitudes (above 12,00 where arable land is extremely scarce. For example, in l village, agriculture ranges only from about 12,900 feet, th est point in the area, to 13,300 feet. Above that altitude, ear and snow destroy the staple barley crop. Furthermore, b of the low rainfall caused by the Himalayan rain shadow areas in Tibet and northern Nepal that are within the appr altitude range for agriculture have no reliable sources of tion. In the end, although there is plenty of unused land areas, most of it is either too high or too arid.

Even where unused land capable of being farmed clearing the land and building the substantial terraces sary for irrigation constitute a great undertaking. Each p to be completely dug out to a depth of two to two and ha so that the large rocks and boulders can be removed. A a man might be able to bring a few new fields under c tion in the first years after separating from his brothers, could not expect to acquire substantial amounts of arab this way.

In addition, because of the limited farmland, the Tibeta sistence economy characteristically includes a strong em on animal husbandry. Tibetan farmers regularly maintain yaks, goats, and sheep, grazing them in the areas too h agriculture. These herds produce wool, milk, cheese, meat, and skins. To obtain these resources, however, she

accompany the animals on a daily basis. When first set-
ıp a monogamous household, a younger brother like Dorje
d find it difficult to both farm and manage animals.

traditional Tibetan society, there was an even more criti-
actor that operated to perpetuate fraternal polyandry—a
of hereditary servitude somewhat analogous to serfdom in
pe. Peasants were tied to large estates held by aristocrats,
ısteries, and the Lhasa government. They were allowed the
f some farmland to produce their own subsistence but were
ıred to provide taxes in kind and corvée (free labor) to their
. The corvée was a substantial hardship, since a peasant
ehold was in many cases required to furnish the lord with
aborer daily for most of the year and more on specific occa-
such as the harvest. This enforced labor, along with the
of new land and ecological pressure to pursue both agri-
re and animal husbandry, made polyandrous families par-
ırly beneficial. The polyandrous family allowed an internal
ion of adult labor, maximizing economic advantage. For
ıple, while the wife worked the family fields, one brother could perform the lord's corvée, another could look after the animals, and a third could engage in trade.

Although social scientists often discount other people's explanations of why they do things, in the case of Tibetan fraternal polyandry, such explanations are very close to the truth. The custom, however, is very sensitive to changes in its political and economic milieu and, not surprisingly, is in decline in most Tibetan areas. Made less important by the elimination of the traditional serf-based economy, it is disparaged by the dominant non-Tibetan leaders of India, China, and Nepal. New opportunities for economic and social mobility in these countries, such as the tourist trade and government employment, are also eroding the rationale for polyandry, and so it may vanish within the next generation.

Melvyn C. Goldstein, now a professor of anthropology at Case Western Reserve University in Cleveland, has been interested in the Tibetan practice of fraternal polyandry (several brothers marrying one wife) since he was a graduate student in the 1960s.

Death without Weeping

Has poverty ravaged mother love in the shantytowns of Brazil?

Nancy Scheper-Hughes

I have seen death without weeping,
The destiny of the Northeast is death,
Cattle they kill,
To the people they do something worse
—*Anonymous Brazilian singer (1965)*

"Why do the church bells ring so often?" I asked Nailza de Arruda soon after I moved into a corner of her tiny mud-walled hut near the top of the shantytown called the Alto do Cruzeiro (Crucifix Hill). I was then a Peace Corps volunteer and community development/health worker. It was the dry and blazing hot summer of 1965, the months following the military coup in Brazil, and save for the rusty, clanging bells of N. S. das Dores Church, an eerie quiet had settled over the market town that I call Bom Jesus da Mata. Beneath the quiet, however, there was chaos and panic. "It's nothing," replied Nailza, "just another little angel gone to heaven."

Nailza had sent more than her share of little angels to heaven, and sometimes at night I could hear her engaged in a muffled but passionate discourse with one of them, two-year-old Joana. Joana's photograph, taken as she lay propped up in her tiny cardboard coffin, her eyes open, hung on a wall next to one of Nailza and Ze Antonio taken on the day they eloped.

Nailza could barely remember the other infants and babies who came and went in close succession. Most had died unnamed and were hastily baptized in their coffins. Few lived more than a month or two. Only Joana, properly baptized in church at the close of her first year and placed under the protection of a powerful saint, Joan of Arc, had been expected to live. And Nailza had dangerously allowed herself to love the little girl.

In addressing the dead child, Nailza's voice would range from tearful imploring to angry recrimination: "Why did you leave me? Was your patron saint so greedy that she could not allow me one child on this earth?" Ze Antonio advised me to ignore Nailza's odd behavior, which he understood as a kind of madness that, like the birth and death of children, came and went. Indeed, the premature birth of a stillborn son some months later "cured" Nailza of her "inappropriate" grief, and the day came when she removed Joana's photo and carefully packed it away.

More than fifteen years elapsed before I returned to th do Cruzeiro, and it was anthropology that provided the v of my return. Since 1982 I have returned several times in to pursue a problem that first attracted my attention in the My involvement with the people of the Alto do Cruzeir spans a quarter of a century and three generations of par in a community where mothers and daughters are often taneously pregnant.

The Alto do Cruzeiro is one of three shantytowns surr ing the large market town of Bom Jesus in the sugar plan zone of Pernambuco in Northeast Brazil, one of the many of neglect that have emerged in the shadow of the now tar economic miracle of Brazil. For the women and children Alto do Cruzeiro the only miracle is that some of them managed to stay alive at all.

The Northeast is a region of vast proportions (approxir twice the size of Texas) and of equally vast social and de mental problems. The nine states that make up the region a poorest in the country and are representative of the Third within a dynamic and rapidly industrializing nation. D waves of migrations from the interior to the teeming sh towns of coastal cities, the majority still live in rural are farms and ranches, sugar plantations and mills.

Life expectancy in the Northeast is only forty years, la because of the appallingly high rate of infant and child m ity. Approximately one million children in Brazil under th of five die each year. The children of the Northeast, espe those born in shantytowns on the periphery of urban life, a very high risk of death. In these areas, children are born w the traditional protection of breast-feeding, subsistence ga stable marriages, and multiple adult caretakers that exists interior. In the hillside shantytowns that spring up aroun ies or, in this case, interior market towns, marriages are b single parenting is the norm, and women are frequently f into the shadow economy of domestic work in the hom the rich or into unprotected and oftentimes "scab" wage on the surrounding sugar plantations, where they clear la planting and weed for a pittance, sometimes less than a a day. The women of the Alto may not bring their babies them into the homes of the wealthy, where the often-sick i onsidered sources of contamination, and they cannot carry ttle ones to the riverbanks where they wash clothes because ver is heavily infested with schistosomes and other deadly ites. Nor can they carry their young children to the planta- , which are often several miles away. At wages of a dollar , the women of the Alto cannot hire baby sitters. Older ren who are not in school will sometimes serve as some- indifferent caretakers. But any child not in school is also cted to find wage work. In most cases, babies are simply home alone, the door securely fastened. And so many also one and unattended.

om Jesus da Mata, centrally located in the plantation of Pernambuco, is within commuting distance of sev- sugar plantations and mills. Consequently, Bom Jesus een a magnet for rural workers forced off their small istence plots by large landowners wanting to use every able piece of land for sugar cultivation. Initially, the migrants to Bom Jesus were squatters who were given approval by the mayor to put up temporary straw huts ach of the three hills overlooking the town. The Alto ruzeiro is the oldest, the largest, and the poorest of hantytowns. Over the past three decades many of the nal migrants have become permanent residents, and the itive and temporary straw huts have been replaced by l homes (usually of two rooms) made of wattle and daub, times covered with plaster. The more affluent residents ricks and tiles. In most Alto homes, dangerous kerosene s have been replaced by light bulbs. The once tattered garb, often fashioned from used sugar sacking, has like- been replaced by store-bought clothes, often castoffs a wealthy *patrão* (boss). The trappings are modern, but unger, sickness, and death that they conceal are tradi- l, deeply rooted in a history of feudalism, exploitation, nstitutionalized dependency.

y research agenda never wavered. The questions I addressed rystalized during a veritable "die-off" of Alto babies during ere drought in 1965. The food and water shortages and the cal and economic chaos occasioned by the military coup reflected in the handwritten entries of births and deaths in usty, yellowed pages of the ledger books kept at the public ry office in Bom Jesus. More than 350 babies died in the during 1965 alone—this from a shantytown population of more than 5,000. But that wasn't what surprised me. There reasons enough for the deaths in the miserable conditions antytown life. What puzzled me was the seeming indif- ce of Alto women to the death of their infants, and their ngness to attribute to their own tiny offspring an aversion that made their death seem wholly natural, indeed all but pated.

though I found that it was possible, and hardly difficult, to e infants and toddlers from death by diarrhea and dehydra- vith a simple sugar, salt, and water solution (even bottled -Cola worked fine), it was more difficult to enlist a mother lf in the rescue of a child she perceived as ill-fated for life ter off dead, or to convince her to take back into her threat- and besieged home a baby she had already come to think an angel rather than as a son or daughter.

I learned that the high expectancy of death, and the ability to face child death with stoicism and equanimity, produced patterns of nurturing that differentiated between those infants thought of as thrivers and survivors and those thought of as born already "wanting to die." The survivors were nurtured, while stigmatized, doomed infants were left to die, as mothers say, *a mingua,* "of neglect." Mothers stepped back and allowed nature to take its course. This pattern, which I call mortal selective neglect, is called passive infanticide by anthropologist Marvin Harris. The Alto situation, although culturally specific in the form that it takes, is not unique to Third World shantytown communities and may have its correlates in our own impoverished urban communities in some cases of "failure to thrive" infants.

I use as an example the story of Zezinho, the thirteen-month-old toddler of one of my neighbors, Lourdes. I became involved with Zezinho when I was called in to help Lourdes in the delivery of another child, this one a fair and robust little tyke with a lusty cry. I noted that while Lourdes showed great interest in the newborn, she totally ignored Zezinho who, wasted and severely malnourished, was curled up in a fetal position on a piece of urine- and feces-soaked cardboard placed under his mother's hammock. Eyes open and vacant, mouth slack, the little boy seemed doomed.

When I carried Zezinho up to the community day-care center at the top of the hill, the Alto women who took turns caring for one another's children (in order to free themselves for part-time work in the cane fields or washing clothes) laughed at my efforts to save Ze, agreeing with Lourdes that here was a baby without a ghost of a chance. Leave him alone, they cautioned. It makes no sense to fight with death. But I did do battle with Ze, and after several weeks of force-feeding (malnourished babies lose their interest in food), Ze began to succumb to my ministrations. He acquired some flesh across his taut chest bones, learned to sit up, and even tried to smile. When he seemed well enough, I returned him to Lourdes in her miserable scrap-material lean-to, but not without guilt about what I had done. I wondered whether returning Ze was at all fair to Lourdes and to his little brother. But I was busy and washed my hands of the matter. And Lourdes did seem more interested in Ze now that he was looking more human.

When I returned in 1982, there was Lourdes among the women who formed my sample of Alto mothers—still struggling to put together some semblance of life for a now grown Ze and her five other surviving children. Much was made of my reunion with Ze in 1982, and everyone enjoyed retelling the story of Ze's rescue and of how his mother had given him up for dead. Ze would laugh the loudest when told how I had had to force-feed him like a fiesta turkey. There was no hint of guilt on the part of Lourdes and no resentment on the part of Ze. In fact, when questioned in private as to who was the best friend he ever had in life, Ze took a long drag on his cigarette and answered without a trace of irony, "Why my mother, of course." "But of course," I replied.

Part of learning how to mother in the Alto do Cruzeiro is learning when to let go of a child who shows that it "wants" to die or that it has no "knack" or no "taste" for life. Another part is learning when it is safe to let oneself love a child. Frequent child death remains a powerful shaper of maternal thinking and practice. In the absence of firm expectation that a child will survive, mother love as we conceptualize it (whether in popular terms or in the psychobiological notion of maternal bonding) is attenuated and delayed with consequences for infant survival. In an environment already precarious to young life, the emotional detachment of mothers toward some of their babies contributes even further to the spiral of high mortality—high fertility in a kind of macabre lock-step dance of death.

The average woman of the Alto experiences 9.5 pregnancies, 3.5 child deaths, and 1.5 stillbirths. Seventy percent of all child deaths in the Alto occur in the first six months of life, and 82 percent by the end of the first year. Of all deaths in the community each year, about 45 percent are of children under the age of five.

Women of the Alto distinguish between child deaths understood as natural (caused by diarrhea and communicable diseases) and those resulting from sorcery, the evil eye, or other magical or supernatural afflictions. They also recognize a large category of infant deaths seen as fated and inevitable. These hopeless cases are classified by mothers under the folk terminology "child sickness" or "child attack." Women say that there are at least fourteen different types of hopeless child sickness, but most can be subsumed under two categories—chronic and acute. The chronic cases refer to infants who are born small and wasted. They are deathly pale, mothers say, as well as weak and passive. They demonstrate no vital force, no liveliness. They do not suck vigorously; they hardly cry. Such babies can be this way at birth or they can be born sound but soon show no resistance, no "fight" against the common crises of infancy: diarrhea, respiratory infections, tropical fevers.

The acute cases are those doomed infants who die suddenly and violently. They are taken by stealth overnight, often following convulsions that bring on head banging, shaking, grimacing, and shrieking. Women say it is horrible to look at such a baby. If the infant begins to foam at the mouth or gnash its teeth or go rigid with its eyes turned back inside its head, there is absolutely no hope. The infant is "put aside"—left alone—often on the floor in a back room, and allowed to die. These symptoms (which accompany high fevers, dehydration, third-stage malnutrition, and encephalitis) are equated by Alto women with madness, epilepsy, and worst of all, rabies, which is greatly feared and highly stigmatized.

Most of the infants presented to me as suffering from chronic child sickness were tiny, wasted famine victims, while those labeled as victims of acute child attack seemed to be infants suffering from the deliriums of high fever or the convulsions that can accompany electrolyte imbalance in dehydrated babies.

Local midwives and traditional healers, praying women, as they are called, advise Alto women on when to allow a baby to die. One midwife explained: "If I can see that a baby was born unfortuitously, I tell the mother that she need not wash the infant or give it a cleansing tea. I tell her just to dust the infant with baby powder and wait for it to die." Allowing nature to take its course is not seen as sinful by these often very devout Catholic women. Rather, it is understood as cooperating with God's plan.

Often I have been asked how consciously women of the behave in this regard. I would have to say that consciousn always shifting between allowed and disallowed levels of a ness. For example, I was awakened early one morning in by two neighborhood children who had been sent to fetc to a hastily organized wake for a two-month-old infant w mother I had unsuccessfully urged to breast-feed. The i was being sustained on sugar water, which the mother ref to as *soro* (serum), using a medical term for the infant's s tion regime in light of his chronic diarrhea. I had cautione mother that an infant could not live on *soro* forever.

The two girls urged me to console the young moth telling her that it was "too bad" that her infant was so that Jesus had to take him. They were coaching me in p Alto etiquette. I agreed, of course, but asked, "And what d think?" Xoxa, the eleven-year-old, looked down at her flip-flops and blurted out, "Oh, Dona Nanci, that baby neve enough to eat, but you must never say that!" And so the of hungry babies remains one of the best kept secrets of Bom Jesus da Mata.

Most victims are waked quickly and with a minimum o emony. No tears are shed, and the neighborhood children f tiny procession, carrying the baby to the town graveyard w it will join a multitude of others. Although a few fresh fl may be scattered over the tiny grave, no stone or wooden will mark the place, and the same spot will be reused wit few months' time. The mother will never visit the grave, w soon becomes an anonymous one.

What, then, can be said of these women? What emo what sentiments motivate them? How are they able to do in fact, must be done? What does mother love mean in this i pitable context? Are grief, mourning, and melancholia pr although deeply repressed? If so, where shall we look for t And if not, how are we to understand the moral vision moral sensibilities that guide their actions?

I have been criticized more than once for presenti unflattering portrait of poor Brazilian women, women wh after all, themselves the victims of severe social and institu neglect. I have described these women as allowing some o children to die, as if this were an unnatural and inhuma rather than, as I would assert, the way any one of us mig reasonably and rationally, under similarly desperate condi Perhaps I have not emphasized enough the real pathogens environment of high risk: poverty, deprivation, sexism, ch hunger, and economic exploitation. If mother love is, as psychologists and some feminists believe, a seemingly n and universal maternal script, what does it mean to wom whom scarcity, loss, sickness, and deprivation have mad love frantic and robbed them of their grief, seeming to tur hearts to stone?

Throughout much of human history—as in a great d the impoverished Third World today—women have had t birth and to nurture children under ecological condition social arrangements hostile to child survival, as well as t own well-being. Under circumstances of high childhood tality, patterns of selective neglect and passive infanticid be seen as active survival strategies.

ey also seem to be fairly common practices historically cross cultures. In societies characterized by high childhood lity and by a correspondingly high (replacement) fertility, al practices of infant and child care tend to be organized rily around survival goals. But what this means is a prag- recognition that not all of one's children can be expected e. The nervousness about child survival in areas of north- Brazil, northern India, or Bangladesh, where a 30 percent percent mortality rate in the first years of life is common, ead to forms of delayed attachment and a casual or benign ct that serves to weed out the worst bets so as to enhance fe chances of healthier siblings, including those yet to be Practices similar to those that I am describing have been ded for parts of Africa, India, and Central America.

fe in the Alto do Cruzeiro resembles nothing so much as a field or an emergency room in an overcrowded inner-city c hospital. Consequently, mortality is guided by a kind of boat ethics," the morality of triage. The seemingly stud- ndifference toward the suffering of some of their infants, eyed in such sayings as "little critters have no feelings," is rstandable in light of these women's obligation to carry on their reproductive and nurturing lives.

their slowness to anthropomorphize and personalize their ts, everything is mobilized so as to prevent maternal over- nment and, therefore, grief at death. The bereaved mother d not to cry, that her tears will dampen the wings of her angel so that she cannot fly up to her heavenly home. Grief death of an angel is not only inappropriate, it is a symptom adness and of a profound lack of faith.

fant death becomes routine in an environment in which is anticipated and bets are hedged. While the routinization ath in the context of shantytown life is not hard to under- , and quite possible to empathize with, its routinization in ormal institutions of public life in Bom Jesus is not as easy cept uncritically. Here the social production of indifference on a different, even a malevolent, cast.

a society where triplicates of every form are required for ost banal events (registering a car, for example), the reg- on of infant and child death is informal, incomplete, and . It requires no documentation, takes less than five minutes, lemands no witnesses other than office clerks. No ques- are asked concerning the circumstances of the death, and use of death is left blank, unquestioned and unexamined. ighbor, grandmother, older sibling, or common-law hus- may register the death. Since most infants die at home, is no question of a medical record.

om the registry office, the parent proceeds to the town hall, the mayor will give him or her a voucher for a free baby . The full-time municipal coffinmaker cannot tell you y how many baby coffins are dispatched each week. It , he says, with the seasons. There are more needed during ought months and during the big festivals of Carnaval and tmas and São Joao's Day because people are too busy, he ses, to take their babies to the clinic. Record keeping is y.

milarly, there is a failure on the part of city-employed doc- vorking at two free clinics to recognize the malnutrition of babies who are weighed, measured, and immunized without comment and as if they were not, in fact, anemic, stunted, fussy, and irritated starvation babies. At best the mothers are told to pick up free vitamins or a health "tonic" at the municipal chambers. At worst, clinic personnel will give tranquilizers and sleeping pills to quiet the hungry cries of "sick-to-death" Alto babies.

The church, too, contributes to the routinization of, and indifference toward, child death. Traditionally, the local Catholic church taught patience and resignation to domestic tragedies that were said to reveal the imponderable workings of God's will. If an infant died suddenly, it was because a particular saint had claimed the child. The infant would be an angel in the service of his or her heavenly patron. It would be wrong, a sign of a lack of faith, to weep for a child with such good fortune. The infant funeral was, in the past, an event celebrated with joy. Today, however, under the new regime of "liberation theology," the bells of N. S. das Dores parish church no longer peal for the death of Alto babies, and no priest accompanies the procession of angels to the cemetery where their bodies are disposed of casually and without ceremony. Children bury children in Bom Jesus da Mata. In this most Catholic of communities, the coffin is handed to the disabled and irritable municipal gravedigger, who often chides the children for one reason or another. It may be that the coffin is larger than expected and the gravedigger can find no appropriate space. The children do not wait for the gravedigger to complete his task. No prayers are recited and no sign of the cross made as the tiny coffin goes into its shallow grave.

When I asked the local priest, Padre Marcos, about the lack of church ceremony surrounding infant and childhood death today in Bom Jesus, he replied; "In the old days, child death was richly celebrated. But those were the baroque customs of a conservative church that wallowed in death and misery. The new church is a church of hope and joy. We no longer celebrate the death of child angels. We try to tell mothers that Jesus doesn't want all the dead babies they send him." Similarly, the new church has changed its baptismal customs, now often refusing to baptize dying babies brought to the back door of a church or rectory. The mothers are scolded by the church attendants and told to go home and take care of their sick babies. Baptism, they are told, is for the living; it is not to be confused with the sacrament of extreme unction, which is the anointing of the dying. And so it appears to the women of the Alto that even the church has turned away from them, denying the traditional comfort of folk Catholicism.

The contemporary Catholic church is caught in the clutches of a double bind. The new theology of liberation imagines a kingdom of God on earth based on justice and equality, a world without hunger, sickness, or childhood mortality. At the same time, the church has not changed its official position on sexuality and reproduction, including its sanctions against birth control, abortion, and sterilization. The padre of Bom Jesus da Mata recognizes this contradiction intuitively, although he shies away from discussions on the topic, saying that he prefers to leave questions of family planning to the discretion and the "good consciences" of his impoverished parishioners. But this, of course, sidesteps the extent to which those good consciences have been shaped by traditional church teachings in Bom Jesus, especially by his recent predecessors. Hence, we can begin to see that the seeming indifference of Alto mothers toward the death of some of their infants is but a pale reflection of the official indifference of church and state to the plight of poor women and children.

Nonetheless, the women of Bom Jesus are survivors. One woman, Biu, told me her life history, returning again and again to the themes of child death, her first husband's suicide, abandonment by her father and later by her second husband, and all the other losses and disappointments she had suffered in her long forty-five years. She concluded with great force, reflecting on the days of Carnaval '88 that were fast approaching:

> No, Dona Nanci, I won't cry, and I won't waste my life thinking about it from morning to night. . . . Can I argue with God for the state that I'm in? No! And so I'll dance and I'll jump and I'll play Carnaval! And yes, I'll laugh and people will wonder at a *pobre* like me who can have such a good time.

And no one did blame Biu for dancing in the streets ing the four days of Carnaval—not even on Ash Wedne the day following Carnaval '88 when we all assembled riedly to assist in the burial of Mercea, Biu's beloved *ca* her last-born daughter who had died at home of pneum during the festivities. The rest of the family barely had to change out of their costumes. Severino, the child's and godfather, sprinkled holy water over the little angel he prayed: "Mercea, I don't know whether you were c taken, or thrown out of this world. But look down at us your heavenly home with tenderness, with pity, and mercy." So be it.

Nancy Scheper-Hughes is a professor in the Department of A pology at the University of California, Berkeley. She has written *Without Weeping: Violence of Everyday Life in Brazil* (1992).

---

rranging a Marriage in India

ENA NANDA

Sister and doctor brother-in-law invite correspondence from North Indian professionals only, for a beautiful, talented, sophisticated, intelligent sister, 5'3", slim, M.A. in textile design, father a senior civil officer. Would prefer immigrant doctors, between 26–29 years. Reply with full details and returnable photo. A well-settled uncle invites matrimonial correspondence from slim, fair, educated South Indian girl, for his nephew, 25 years, smart, M.B.A., green card holder, 5'6". Full particulars with returnable photo appreciated.

—*Matrimonial Advertisements,*
India Abroad

n India, almost all marriages are arranged. Even among the educated middle classes in modern, urban ndia, marriage is as much a concern of the families s of the individuals. So customary is the practice of ged marriage that there is a special name for a mar- which is not arranged: It is called a "love match."

my first field trip to India, I met many young men vomen whose parents were in the process of "get- hem married." In many cases, the bride and groom d not meet each other before the marriage. At most might meet for a brief conversation, and this meet- ould take place only after their parents had decided he match was suitable. Parents do not compel their en to marry a person who either marriage partner objectionable. But only after one match is refused nother be sought.

a young American woman in India for the first time, d this custom of arranged marriage oppressive. How any intelligent young person agree to such a mar- without great reluctance? It was contrary to every- I believed about the importance of romantic love as ly basis of a happy marriage. It also clashed with my gly held notions that the choice of such an intimate ermanent relationship could be made only by the duals involved. Had anyone tried to arrange my mar- I would have been defiant and rebellious!

At the first opportunity, I began, with more curiosity than tact, to question the young people I met on how they felt about this practice. Sita, one of my young informants, was a college graduate with a degree in political science. She had been waiting for over a year while her parents were arranging a match for her. I found it difficult to accept the docile manner in which this well-educated young woman awaited the outcome of a process that would result in her spending the rest of her life with a man she hardly knew, a virtual stranger, picked out by her parents.

"How can you go along with this?" I asked her, in frustration and distress. "Don't you care who you marry?"

"Of course I care," she answered." This is why I must let my parents choose a boy for me. My marriage is too important to be arranged by such an inexperienced person as myself. In such matters, it is better to have my parents' guidance."

I had learned that young men and women in India do not date and have very little social life involving members of the opposite sex. Although I could not disagree with Sita's reasoning, I continued to pursue the subject.

Young men and women do not date and have very little social life involving members of the opposite sex.

"But how can you marry the first man you have ever met? Not only have you missed the fun of meeting a lot of different people, but you have not given yourself the chance to know who is the right man for you."

"Meeting with a lot of different people doesn't sound like any fun at all," Sita answered. "One hears that in America the girls are spending all their time worrying about whether they will meet a man and get married. Here we have the chance to enjoy our life and let our parents do this work and worrying for us."

She had me there. The high anxiety of the competition to "be popular" with the opposite sex certainly was the most prominent feature of life as an American teenager in the late fifties. The endless worrying about the rules that governed our behavior and about our popularity ratings sapped both our self-esteem and our enjoyment of adolescence. I reflected that absence of this competition in India most certainly may have contributed to the self-confidence and natural charm of so many of the young women I met.

And yet, the idea of marrying a perfect stranger, whom one did not know and did not "love," so offended my American ideas of individualism and romanticism, that I persisted with my objections.

"I still can't imagine it," I said. "How can you agree to marry a man you hardly know?"

"But of course he will be known. My parents would never arrange a marriage for me without knowing all about the boy's family background. Naturally we will not rely only on what the family tells us. We will check the particulars out ourselves. No one will want their daughter to marry into a family that is not good. All these things we will know beforehand."

Impatiently, I responded, "Sita, I don't mean know the family, I mean, know the man. How can you marry someone you don't know personally and don't love? How can you think of spending your life with someone you may not even like?"

"If he is a good man, why should I not like him?" she said. "With you people, you know the boy so well before you marry, where will be the fun to get married? There will be no mystery and no romance. Here we have the whole of our married life to get to know and love our husband. This way is better, is it not?"

Her response made further sense, and I began to have second thoughts on the matter. Indeed, during months of meeting many intelligent young Indian people, both male and female, who had the same ideas as Sita, I saw arranged marriages in a different light. I also saw the importance of the family in Indian life and realized that a couple who took their marriage into their own hands was taking a big risk, particularly if their families were irreconcilably opposed to the match. In a country where every important resource in life—a job, a house, a social circle—is gained through family connections, it seemed foolhardy to cut oneself off from a supportive social network and depend solely on one person for happiness and success.

Six years later I returned to India to again do fieldwork, this time among the middle class in Bombay, a modern, sophisticated city. From the experience of my earlier visit, I decided to include a study of arranged marriages in my project. By this time I had met many Indian couples whose marriages had been arranged and who seemed very happy. Particularly in contrast to the fate of many of my married friends in the United States who were already in the process of divorce, the positive aspects of arranged riages appeared to me to outweigh the negatives. In I thought I might even participate in arranging a mar myself. I had been fairly successful in the United S in "fixing up" many of my friends, and I was conf that my matchmaking skills could be easily applied t new situation, once I learned the basic rules. "After a thought, "how complicated can it be? People want p much the same things in a marriage whether it is in or America."

An opportunity presented itself almost immediate friend from my previous Indian trip was in the pro of arranging for the marriage of her eldest son. In there is a perceived shortage of "good boys," and my friend's family was eminently respectable and th himself personable, well educated, and nice looking, sure that by the end of my year's fieldwork, we w have found a match.

The basic rule seems to be that a family's reputati most important. It is understood that matches wou arranged only within the same caste and general s class, although some crossing of subcastes is permis if the class positions of the bride's and groom's fam are similar. Although dowry is now prohibited by la India, extensive gift exchanges took place with every riage. Even when the boy's family do not "make dema every girl's family nevertheless feels the obligation to the traditional gifts, to the girl, to the boy, and to the b family. Particularly when the couple would be livi the joint family—that is, with the boy's parents an married brothers and their families, as well as with un ried siblings—which is still very common even amon urban, upper-middle class in India, the girls' paren anxious to establish smooth relations between their fa and that of the boy. Offering the proper gifts, even not called "dowry," is often an important factor in encing the relationship between the bride's and gro families and perhaps, also, the treatment of the bri her new home.

In a society where divorce is still a scan and where, in fact, the divorce rate is exceedingly low, an arranged marriage is the beginning of a lifetime relationshi not just between the bride and groom bu between their families as well.

In a society where divorce is still a scandal and w in fact, the divorce rate is exceedingly low, an arra marriage is the beginning of a lifetime relationship no between the bride and groom but between their fa

today, almost all marriages in India are arranged. It is believed that parents are much more effective at deciding whom their hters should marry.

ell. Thus, while a girl's looks are important, her char- is even more so, for she is being judged as a pro-tive daughter-in-law as much as a prospective bride. re she would be living in a joint family, as was the with my friend, the girls's ability to get along harmo-sly in a family is perhaps the single most important ity in assessing her suitability.

y friend is a highly esteemed wife, mother, and hter-in-law. She is religious, soft-spoken, modest, deferential. She rarely gossips and never quarrels, two ities highly desirable in a woman. A family that has eputation for gossip and conflict among its women-will not find it easy to get good wives for their sons. nts will not want to send their daughter to a house in h there is conflict.

y friend's family were originally from North India. had lived in Bombay, where her husband owned a ness, for forty years. The family had delayed in seek- match for their eldest son because he had been an Force pilot for several years, stationed in such remote s that it had seemed fruitless to try to find a girl who d be willing to accompany him. In their social class, litary career, despite its economic security, has little prestige and is considered a drawback in finding a suitable bride. Many families would not allow their daughters to marry a man in an occupation so potentially dangerous and which requires so much moving around.

The son had recently left the military and joined his father's business. Since he was a college graduate, modern, and well traveled, from such a good family, and, I thought, quite handsome, it seemed to me that he, or rather his family, was in a position to pick and choose. I said as much to my friend.

While she agreed that there were many advantages on their side, she also said, "We must keep in mind that my son is both short and dark; these are drawbacks in finding the right match." While the boy's height had not escaped my notice, "dark" seemed to me inaccurate; I would have called him "wheat" colored perhaps, and in any case, I did not realize that color would be a consideration. I discovered, however, that while a boy's skin color is a less important consideration than a girl's, it is still a factor.

An important source of contacts in trying to arrange her son's marriage was my friend's social club in Bombay. Many of the women had daughters of the right age, and some had already expressed an interest in my friend's son.

I was most enthusiastic about the possibilities of one particular family who had five daughters, all of whom were pretty, demure, and well educated. Their mother had told my friend, "You can have your pick for your son, whichever one of my daughters appeals to you most."

I saw a match in sight. "Surely," I said to my friend, "we will find one there. Let's go visit and make our choice." But my friend held back; she did not seem to share my enthusiasm, for reasons I could not then fathom.

When I kept pressing for an explanation of her reluctance, she admitted, "See, Serena, here is the problem. The family has so many daughters, how will they be able to provide nicely for any of them? We are not making any demands, but still, with so many daughters to marry off, one wonders whether she will even be able to make a proper wedding. Since this is our eldest son, it's best if we marry him to a girl who is the only daughter, then the wedding will truly be a gala affair." I argued that surely the quality of the girls themselves made up for any deficiency in the elaborateness of the wedding. My friend admitted this point but still seemed reluctant to proceed.

"Is there something else," I asked her, "some factor I have missed?" "Well," she finally said, "there is one other thing. They have one daughter already married and living in Bombay. The mother is always complaining to me that the girl's in-laws don't let her visit her own family often enough. So it makes me wonder, will she be that kind of mother who always wants her daughter at her own home? This will prevent the girl from adjusting to our house. It is not a good thing." And so, this family of five daughters was dropped as a possibility.

Somewhat disappointed, I nevertheless respected my friend's reasoning and geared up for the next prospect. This was also the daughter of a woman in my friend's social club. There was clear interest in this family and I could see why. The family's reputation was excellent; in fact, they came from a subcaste slightly higher than my friend's own. The girl, who was an only daughter, was pretty and well educated and had a brother studying in the United States. Yet, after expressing an interest to me in this family, all talk of them suddenly died down and the search began elsewhere.

"What happened to that girl as a prospect?" I asked one day. "You never mention her any more. She is so pretty and so educated, what did you find wrong?"

"She is too educated. We've decided against it. My husband's father saw the girl on the bus the other day and thought her forward. A girl who 'roams about' the city by herself is not the girl for our family." My disappointment this time was even greater, as I thought the son would have liked the girl very much. But then I thought, my friend is right, a girl who is going to live in a joint family cannot be too independent or she will make life miserable for everyone. I also learned that if the family of the girl even a slightly higher social status than the family of boy, the bride may think herself too good for them, this too will cause problems. Later my friend admitte me that this had been an important factor in her deci not to pursue the match.

The next candidate was the daughter of a client of friend's husband. When the client learned that the fa was looking for a match for their son, he said, "Loo further, we have a daughter." This man then invited friends to dinner to see the girl. He had already seen son at the office and decided that "he liked the boy." W went together for tea, rather than dinner—it was less commitment—and while we were there, the girl's mc showed us around the house. The girl was studying fo exams and was briefly introduced to us.

After we left, I was anxious to hear my friend's o ion. While her husband liked the family very much was impressed with his client's business accomplishm and reputation, the wife didn't like the girl's looks. " is short, no doubt, which is an important plus point, she is also fat and wears glasses." My friend obvio thought she could do better for her son and asked her band to make his excuses to his client by saying that had decided to postpone the boy's marriage indefinit

By this time almost six months had passed and I becoming impatient. What I had thought would be an matter to arrange was turning out to be quite complic I began to believe that between my friend's desire for a who was modest enough to fit into her joint family attractive and educated enough to be an acceptable ner for her son, she would not find anyone suitable. friend laughed at my impatience: "Don't be so much hurry," she said. "You Americans want everything dor quickly. You get married quickly and then just as qui get divorced. Here we take marriage more seriously must take all the factors into account. It is not enoug us to learn by our mistakes. This is too serious a busi If a mistake is made we have not only ruined the li our son or daughter, but we have spoiled the reputatic our family as well. And that will make it much harde their brothers and sisters to get married. So we must be careful."

If a mistake is made we have not only ruined the life of our son or daughter, bu we have spoiled the reputation of our fan as well.

What she said was true and I promised myself t more patient, though it was not easy. I had really h

ppendix
urther Reflections on Arranged Marriage. . .

is essay was written from the point of view of a family eking a daughter-in-law. Arranged marriage looks somenat different from the point of view of the bride and her mily. Arranged marriage continues to be preferred, even nong the more educated, Westernized sections of the dian population. Many young women from these famis still go along, more or less willingly, with the practice, d also with the specific choices of their families. Young omen do get excited about the prospects of their marriage, t there is also ambivalence and increasing uncertainty, as e bride contemplates leaving the comfort and familiarity her own home, where as a "temporary guest" she had en been indulged, to live among strangers. Even in the st situation she will now come under the close scrutiny of r husband's family. How she dresses, how she behaves, w she gets along with others, where she goes, how she ends her time, her domestic abilities—all of this and much re—will be observed and commented on by a whole new t of relations. Her interaction with her family of birth will monitored and curtailed considerably. Not only will she ave their home, but with increasing geographic mobil-, she may also live very far from them, perhaps even on other continent. Too much expression of her fondness for r own family, or her desire to visit them, may be interpeted as an inability to adjust to her new family, and may come a source of conflict. In an arranged marriage the rden of adjustment is clearly heavier for a woman than for nan. And that is in the best of situations.

In less happy circumstances, the bride may be a tart of resentment and hostility from her husband's family, particularly her mother-in-law or her husband's unmarried sisters, for whom she is now a source of competition for the affection, loyalty, and economic resources of their son or brother. If she is psychologically, or even physically abused, her options are limited, as returning to her parents' home, or divorce, are still very stigmatized. For most Indians, marriage and motherhood are still considered the only suitable roles for a woman, even for those who have careers, and few women can comfortably contemplate remaining unmarried. Most families still consider "marrying off" their daughters as a compelling religious duty and social necessity. This increases a bride's sense of obligation to make the marriage a success, at whatever cost to her own personal happiness.

The vulnerability of a new bride may also be intensified by the issue of dowry, which although illegal, has become a more pressing issue in the consumer conscious society of contemporary urban India. In many cases, where a groom's family is not satisfied with the amount of dowry a bride brings to her marriage, the young bride will be constantly harassed to get her parents to give more. In extreme cases, the bride may even be murdered, and the murder disguised as an accident or suicide. This also offers the husband's family an opportunity to arrange another match for him, thus bringing in another dowry. This phenomena, called dowry death, calls attention not just to the "evils of dowry" but also to larger issues of the powerlessness of women as well.

Serena Nanda
March 1998

xpected that the match would be made before my n India was up. But it was not to be. When I left India iend seemed no further along in finding a suitable for her son than when I had arrived.

o years later, I returned to India and still my friend ot found a girl for her son. By this time, he was close ty, and I think she was a little worried. Since she knew friends all over India, and I was going to be there for , she asked me to "help her in this work" and keep an t for someone suitable. I was flattered that my judgwas respected, but knowing now how complicated the s was, I had lost my earlier confidence as a match-. Nevertheless, I promised that I would try.

vas almost at the end of my year's stay in India met a family with a marriageable daughter whom I ight be a good possibility for my friend's son. The father was related to a good friend of mine and by dence came from the same village as my friend's nd. This new family had a successful business in ium-sized city in central India and were from the same sub-caste as my friend. The daughter was pretty and chic; in fact, she had studied fashion design in college. Her parents would not allow her to go off by herself to any of the major cities in India where she could make a career, but they had compromised with her wish to work by allowing her to run a small dress-making boutique from their home. In spite of her desire to have a career, the daughter was both modest and home-loving and had had a traditional, sheltered upbringing. She had only one other sister, already married, and a brother who was in his father's business.

I mentioned the possibility of a match with my friend's son. The girl's parents were most interested. Although their daughter was not eager to marry just yet, the idea of living in Bombay—a sophisticated, extremely fashion-conscious city where she could continue her education in clothing design—was a great inducement. I gave the girl's father my friend's address and suggested that when they went to Bombay on some business or whatever, they look up the boy's family.

Returning to Bombay on my way to New York, I told my friend of this newly discovered possibility. She seemed to feel there was potential but, in spite of my urging, would not make any moves herself. She rather preferred to wait for the girl's family to call upon them. I hoped something would come of this introduction, though by now I had learned to rein in my optimism.

A year later I received a letter from my friend. The family had indeed come to visit Bombay, and their daughter and my friend's daughter, who were near in age, had become very good friends. During that year, the two girls had frequently visited each other. I thought things lc promising.

Last week I received an invitation to a wedding friend's son and the girl were getting married. Since found the match, my presence was particularly requ at the wedding. I was thrilled. Success at last! As pared to leave for India, I began thinking, "Now friend's younger son, who do I know who has a nic for him. . .?"

Edited by **Philip R. DeVita.**

'ho Needs Love!

Japan, Many Couples Don't

HOLAS D. KRISTOF

uri Uemura sat on the straw tatami mat of her living room and chatted cheerfully about her 40-year marriage to a man whom, she mused, she never particu- ked.

ere was never any love between me and my husband," d blithely, recalling how he used to beat her. "But, well, vived."

2-year-old midwife, her face as weathered as an old base- d etched with a thousand seams, Mrs. Uemura said that sband had never told her that he liked her, never compli- l her on a meal, never told her "thank you," never held nd, never given her a present, never shown her affection way. He never calls her by her name, but summons her e equivalent of a grunt or a "Hey, you."

en with animals, the males cooperate to bring the females ood," Mrs. Uemura said sadly, noting the contrast to her arriage. "When I see that, it brings tears to my eyes."

hort, the Uemuras have a marriage that is as durable as it is y, one couple's tribute to the Japanese sanctity of family. divorce rate in Japan is at a record high but still less than at of the United States, and Japan arguably has one of ongest family structures in the industrialized world. As ited States and Europe fret about the disintegration of the nal family, most Japanese families remain as solid as the ed table on which Mrs. Uemura rested her tea.

es not seem that Japanese families ve because husbands and wives love other more than American couples, ather because they perhaps love each less.

udy published last year by the Population Council, an tional nonprofit group based in New York, suggested that litional two-parent household is on the wane not only rica but throughout most of the world. There was one ent exception: Japan.

In Japan, for example, only 1.1 percent of births are to unwed mothers—virtually unchanged from 25 years ago. In the United States, the figure is 30.1 percent and rising rapidly.

Yet if one comes to a little Japanese town like Omiya to learn the secrets of the Japanese family, the people are not as happy as the statistics.

"I haven't lived for myself," Mrs. Uemura said, with a touch of melancholy, "but for my kids, and for my family, and for society."

Mrs. Uemura's marriage does not seem exceptional in Japan, whether in the big cities or here in Omiya. The people of Omiya, a community of 5,700 nestled in the rain-drenched hills of the Kii Peninsula in Mie Prefecture, nearly 200 miles southwest of Tokyo, have spoken periodically to a reporter about various aspects of their daily lives. On this visit they talked about their families.

Survival Secrets, Often the Couples Expect Little

Osamums Torida furrowed his brow and looked perplexed when he was asked if he loved his wife of 33 years.

"Yeah, so-so, I guess," said Mr. Torida, a cattle farmer. "She's like air or water. You couldn't live without it, but most of the time, you're not conscious of its existence."

The secret to the survival of the marriage, Mr. Torida acknowledged, was not mutual passion.

"Sure, we had fights about our work," he explained as he stood beside his barn. "But we were preoccupied by work and our debts, so we had no time to fool around."

That is a common theme in Omiya. It does not seem that Japanese families survive because husbands and wives love each other more than American couples, but rather because they perhaps love each other less.

"I think love marriages are more fragile than arranged marriages," said Tomika Kusukawa, 49, who married her high-school sweetheart and now runs a car repair shop with him. "In love marriages, when something happens or if the couple falls out of love, they split up."

If there is a secret to the strength of the Japanese family it consists of three ingredients: low expectations, patience, and shame.

GETTING ALONG

Matchmaker, Matchmaker

How countries compare on an index of compatibility of spouses, based on answers to questions about politics, sex, social issues, religion and ethics, from a survey by the Dentsu Research Institute and Leisure Development Center in Japan. A score of 500 would indicate perfect compatibility.

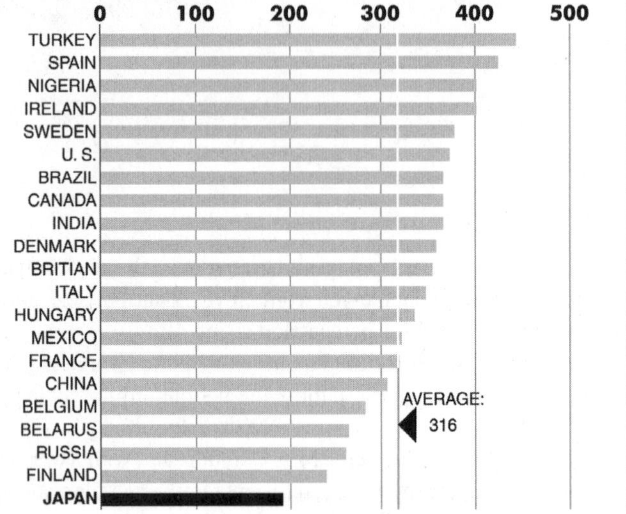

0 100 200 300 400 500

TURKEY
SPAIN
NIGERIA
IRELAND
SWEDEN
U. S.
BRAZIL
CANADA
INDIA
DENMARK
BRITIAN
ITALY
HUNGARY
MEXICO
FRANCE
CHINA
BELGIUM
BELARUS
RUSSIA
FINLAND
JAPAN

AVERAGE: 316

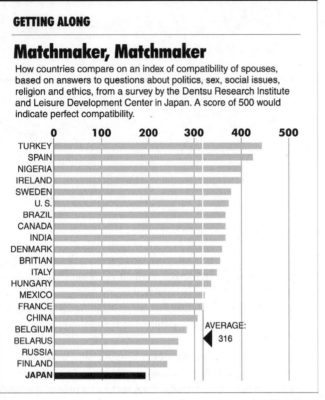

New York Times

The advantage of marriages based on low expectations is that they have built in shock absorbers. If the couple discover that they have nothing in common, that they do not even like each other, then that is not so much a reason for divorce as it is par for the course.

Even the discovery that one's spouse is having an affair is often not as traumatic in a Japanese marriage as it is in the West. A little sexual infidelity on the part of a man (though not on the part of his wife) was traditionally tolerated, so long as he did not become so besotted as to pay his mistress more than he could afford.

Tsuzuya Fukuyama, who runs a convenience store and will mark her 50th wedding anniversary this year, toasted her hands on an electric heater in the front of the store and declared that a woman would be wrong to get angry if her husband had an affair.

The durability of the Japanese family is particularly wondrous because couples are, by international standards, exceptionally incompatible.

"It's never just one side that's at fault," Mrs. Fukuyama said sternly. "Maybe the husband had an affair because his wife wasn't so hot herself. So she should look at her own faults."

Mrs. Fukuyama's daughter came to her a few years ago, suspecting that her husband was having an affair and asking what to do.

"I told her, 'Once you left this house, you can only come back if you divorce; if you're not prepared to get a divorce, then you'd better be patient,'" Mrs. Fukuyama recalled. "And was patient. And then she got pregnant and had a kid, an they're close again."

The word that Mrs. Fukuyama used for patience is "ga a term that comes up whenever marriage is discussed in It means toughing it out, enduring hardship, and many Ja regard gaman with pride as a national trait.

Many people complain that younger folks divorce b they do not have enough gaman, and the frequency with the term is used suggests a rather bleak understandi marriage.

"I didn't know my husband very well when we marrie afterward we used to get into bitter fights," said Yoshiko H aki, 56, a store owner. "But then we had children, and I g busy with the kids and with this shop. Time passed."

Now Mrs. Hirowaki has been married 34 years, and sh plains about young people who do not stick to their vows

"In the old days, wives had more gaman," she said. kids just don't have enough gaman."

The durability of the Japanese family is particularly drous because couples are, by international standards, tionally incompatible.

One survey asked married men and their wives in 37 tries how they felt about politics, sex, religion, ethics and issues. Japanese couples ranked dead last in compatib views, by a huge margin. Indeed, another survey found they were doing it over again, only about one-third of Ja would marry the same person.

A national survey found that 30 percent of fathers spend less than 15 minutes a day on weekends talking with or playi with their children.

Incompatibility might not matter so much, however, b Japanese husbands and wives spend very little time tal each other.

"I kind of feel there's nothing new to say to her," said M Ogita, an egg farmer, explaining his reticence.

In a small town like Omiya, couples usually have together, but in Japanese cities there are many "7-11 hus so called because they leave at 7 A.M. and return after 1

Masahiko Kondo now lives in Omiya, working in the ber of commerce, but he used to be a salesman in sev cities. He would leave for work each morning at 7, an four nights a week would go out for after-work drinking jongg sessions with buddies.

"I only saw my baby on Saturdays or Sundays," said Mr. a lanky good-natured man of 37. "But in fact, I really e that life. It didn't bother me that I never spent time with on weekdays."

Mr. Kondo's wife, Keiko, had her own life, spent w child and the wives of other workaholic husbands.

"We had birthday parties, but they were with the kids mothers," she remembers. "No fathers ever came."

national survey found that 30 percent of fathers spend less 15 minutes a day on weekdays talking with or playing with children. Among eighth graders, 51 percent reported that never spoke with their fathers on weekdays.

ditionally, many companies were reluctant romote employees who had divorced or had major problems at home.

s a result, the figures in Japan for single-parent households e deceptive. The father is often more a theoretical presence a homework-helping reality.

ill, younger people sometimes want to see the spouses in ght, and a result is a gradual change in focus of lives from to family. Two decades ago, nearly half of young people in surveys that they wanted their fathers to put priority on rather than family. Now only one-quarter say that.

cial Pressures

me Is Keeping Bonds in Place

ose who find themselves desperately unhappy, one source essure to keep plugging is shame.

f you divorce, you lose face in society," said Tatsumi Kinos- a tea farmer. "People say, 'His wife escaped.' So folks n married because they hate to be gossiped about."

ame is a powerful social sanction in Japan, and it is not matter of gossip. Traditionally, many companies were ant to promote employees who had divorced or who had problems at home.

you divorce, it weakens your position at work," said Akihiko a, 27, who works in a local government office. "Your bosses give you such good ratings, and it'll always be a negative "

e idea, Mr. Kanda noted, is that if an employee cannot ge his own life properly, he should not be entrusted with tant corporate matters.

ancial sanctions are also a major disincentive for divorce. nother gets the children in three-quarters of divorces, but mothers in Japan do not have careers and have few finan- esources. Fathers pay child support in only 15 percent of orces with children, partly because women often hesitate o court to demand payments and partly because men often pay even when the court orders it.

"The main reason for lack of divorce is that women can't support themselves," said Mizuko Kanda, a 51-year-old house-wife. "My friends complain about their husbands and say that they'd divorce if they could, but they can't afford to."

The result of these social and economic pressures is clear.

Even in Japan, there are about 24 divorces for every 100 marriages, but that compares with 32 in France, and 42 in England, and 55 in the United States.

The Outlook

Change Creeps in, Imperiling Family

But society is changing in Japan, and it is an open question whether these changes will undermine the traditional family as they have elsewhere around the globe.

The nuclear family has already largely replaced the extended family in Japan, and shame is eroding as a sanction. Haruko Okumura, for example, runs a kindergarten and speaks openly about her divorce.

"My Mom was uneasy about it, but I never had an inferiority complex about being divorced," said Mrs. Okumura, as dozens of children played in the next room. "And people accepted me easily."

Mrs. Okumura sees evidence of the changes in family patterns every day: fathers are playing more of a role in the kindergarten. At Christmas parties and sports contests, fathers have started to show up along with mothers. And Mrs. Okumura believes that divorce is on the upswing.

"If there's a weakening of the economic and social pressures to stay married," she said, "surely divorce rates will soar."

Already divorce rates are rising, approximately doubling over the last 25 years. But couples are very reluctant to divorce when they have children, and so single-parent households account for exactly the same proportion today as in 1965.

Shinsuke Kawaguchi, a young tea farmer, is one of the men for whom life is changing. Americans are not likely to be impressed by Mr. Kawaguchi's open-mindedness, but he is.

"I take good care of my wife," he said. "I may not say 'I love you,' but I do hold her hand. And I might say, after she makes dinner, 'This tastes good.'"

"Of course," Mr. Kawaguchi quickly added, "I wouldn't say that unless I'd just done something really bad."

Even Mrs. Uemura, the elderly woman whose husband used to beat her, said that her husband was treating her better.

"The other day, he tried to pour me a cup of tea," Mrs. Uemura recalled excitedly. "It was a big change. I told all my friends."

UNIT 5

Gender and Status

Unit Selections

Key Points to Consider

- What is a "berdache" and how does it highlight the ways in which different societies accommodate atypical individuals?
- How and why do perceptions of feminine beauty vary from culture to culture?
- What social forces have contributed to the increasing death rate of females in Asia?
- Why is there a rising number of dowry deaths in India?

Student Website

www.mhcls.com

Internet References

Bonobo Sex and Society

http://songweaver.com/info/bonobos.html

FGM Research

http://www.amnesty.org/ailib/intcam/femgen/fgm1.htm

OMIM Home Page-Online Mendelian Inheritance in Man

http://www.nslij-genetics.org/search_omim.html

Reflections on Sinai Bedouin Women

http://www.sherryart.com/women/bedouin.html

Women Watch

http://www.un.org/womenwatch/about/

feminist movement in the United States has had a significant impact upon the development of anthropology. Feminists rightly charged that anthropologists have tended to gloss over roles of women in studies of society and culture. In part this is because, until recent times, most anthropologists have been men. The result has been an undue emphasis on male activities as well as male perspectives in descriptions of particular societies.

These charges, however, have proven to be a firm corrective. In the last few years, anthropologists have begun to study women and, more particularly, the division of labor based on gender and its relation to biology, as well as, to social and political status. In addition, these changes in emphasis have been accompanied by an increase in the number of women in the field.

Feminist anthropologists have begun to attack critically some of the established anthropological beliefs. They have shown, for example, that field studies of nonhuman primates, which were often used to demonstrate the evolutionary basis of male dominance, distorted the actual evolutionary record by focusing primarily on baboons. (Male baboons are especially dominant and aggressive.) Other, less-quoted primate studies show how dominance and aggression are highly situational phenomena, sensitive to ecological variation. Feminist anthropologists have also shown that the subsistence contribution of women has likewise been ignored by anthropologists. A classic case is that of the !Kung, a hunting and gathering group in southern Africa, where women provide the bulk of the food supply, including most of the available protein, and who, not coincidentally, enjoy a more egalitarian relationship than usual with men. Thus, since political control is a matter of cultural

© Ian Coles

variation, male authority is not biologically predetermined. In fact, there are many cultures in which some men may play a more feminine or, at least, asexual role, as described in "The Berdache Tradition" and, as we see in "Where Fat Is a Mark of Beauty," gender relationships are deeply embedded in social experience.

Lest we think that gender issues are primarily academic, we need only consider the articles, ". . . but What If It's a Girl?" by Carla Power and "Rising Number of Dowry Deaths in India" by Amanda Hitchcock to realize that gender equality in this world is still a distant dream.

The Berdache Tradition

WALTER L. WILLIAMS

Because it is such a powerful force in the world today, the Western Judeo-Christian tradition is often accepted as the arbiter of "natural" behavior of humans. If Europeans and their descendant nations of North America accept something as normal, then anything different is seen as abnormal. Such a view ignores the great diversity of human existence.

This is the case of the study of gender. How many genders are there? To a modern Anglo-American, nothing might seem more definite than the answer that there are two: men and women. But not all societies around the world agree with Western culture's view that all humans are either women or men. The commonly accepted notion of "the opposite sex," based on anatomy, is itself an artifact of our society's rigid sex roles.

Among many cultures, there have existed different alternatives to "man" or "woman." An alternative role in many American Indian societies is referred to by anthropologists as *berdache*. . . . The role varied from one Native American culture to another, which is a reflection of the vast diversity of aboriginal New World societies. Small bands of hunter-gatherers existed in some areas, with advanced civilizations of farming peoples in other areas. With hundreds of different languages, economies, religions, and social patterns existing in North America alone, every generalization about a cultural tradition must acknowledge many exceptions.

This diversity is true for the berdache tradition as well, and must be kept in mind. My statements should be read as being specific to a particular culture, with generalizations being treated as loose patterns that might not apply to peoples even in nearby areas.

Briefly, a berdache can be defined as a morphological male who does not fill a society's standard man's role, who has a nonmasculine character. This type of person is often stereotyped as effeminate, but a more accurate characterization is androgyny. Such a person has a clearly recognized and accepted social status, often based on a secure place in the tribal mythology. Berdaches have special ceremonial roles in many Native American religions, and important economic roles in their families. They will do at least some women's work, and mix together much of the behavior, dress, and social roles of women and men. Berdaches gain social prestige by their spiritual, intellectual, or craftwork/artistic contributions, and by their reputation for hard work and generosity. They serve a mediating function between women and men, precisely because their character is seen as distinct from either sex. They are not seen as men, yet th not seen as women either. They occupy an alternative g role that is a mixture of diverse elements.

In their erotic behavior berdaches also generally (b always) take a nonmasculine role, either being asex becoming the passive partner in sex with men. In some cu the berdache might become a wife to a man. This male sexual behavior became the focus of an attack on berdac "sodomites" by the Europeans who, early on, came into c with them. From the first Spanish conquistadors to the W frontiersmen and the Christian missionaries and gover officials, Western culture has had a considerable imp the berdache tradition. In the last two decades, the most impact on the tradition is the adaptation of a modern W gay identity.

To Western eyes berdachism is a complex and puzzlin nomenon, mixing and redefining the very concepts of w considered male and female. In a culture with only tw ognized genders, such individuals are gender nonconf abnormal, deviant. But to American Indians, the institu another gender role means that berdaches are not dev indeed, they do conform to the requirements of a cus which their culture tells them they fit. Berdachism is a w society to recognize and assimilate some atypical indi without imposing a change on them or stigmatizing th deviant. This cultural institution confirms their legitima what they are.

Societies often bestow power upon that which do neatly fit into the usual. Since no cultural system can e everything, a common way that many cultures deal wit inconsistencies is to imbue them with negative power, as pollution, witchcraft, or sin. That which is not unders seen as a threat. But an alternative method of dealing wi things, or people, is to take them out of the realm of thr to sanctify them.[1] The berdaches' role as mediator is th just between women and men, but also between the physi the spiritual. American Indian cultures have taken what W culture calls negative, and made it a positive; they have s fully utilized the different skills and insights of a class of that Western culture has stigmatized and whose spiritual have been wasted.

Many Native Americans also understood that gende have to do with more than just biological sex. The s ɜrn view that one's sex is always a certainty, and that one's ɜr identity and sex role always conform to one's morpho- ıl sex is a view that dies hard. Western thought is typi- ɔy such dichotomies of groups perceived to be mutually sive: male and female, black and white, right and wrong, and evil. Clearly, the world is not so simple; such clear ons are not always realistic. Most American Indian world- generally are much more accepting of the ambiguities of acceptance of gender variation in the berdache tradition is ıl of many native cultures' approach to life in general.

'erall, these are generalizations based on those Native ican societies that had an accepted role for berdaches. Not ltures recognized such a respected status. Berdachism in ginal North America was most established among tribes in reas: first, the Prairie and western Great Lakes, the north- d central Great Plains, and the lower Mississippi Valley; d, Florida and the Caribbean; third, the Southwest, the Basin, and California; and fourth, scattered areas of the west, western Canada, and Alaska. For some reason it is ɔticeable in eastern North America, with the exception of ıthern rim. . . .

erican Indian Religions

: American religions offered an explanation for human ity by their creation stories. In some tribal religions, the Spiritual Being is conceived as neither male nor female a combination of both. Among the Kamia of the South- for example, the bearer of plant seeds and the introducer mia culture was a man-woman spirit named Warharmi.[2] episode of the Zuni creation story involves a battle en the kachina spirits of the agricultural Zunis and the hunter spirits. Every four years an elaborate ceremony emorates this myth. In the story a kachina spirit called *mana* was captured by the enemy spirits and transformed process. This transformed spirit became a mediator en the two sides, using his peacemaking skills to merge fering lifestyles of hunters and farmers. In the ceremony, atic reenactment of the myth, the part of the transformed *mana* spirit, is performed by a berdache.[3] The Zuni word rdache is *lhamana,* denoting its closeness to the spiritual tor who brought hunting and farming together.[4] The moral story is that the berdache was created by the deities for al purpose, and that this creation led to the improvement iety. The continual reenactment of this story provides a ation for the Zuni berdache in each generation.

ontrast to this, the lack of spiritual justification in a crea- yth could denote a lack of tolerance for gender varia- he Pimas, unlike most of their Southwestern neighbors, t respect a berdache status. *Wi-kovat,* their derogatory means "like a girl," but it does not signify a recognized role. Pima mythology reflects this lack of acceptance, lk tale that explains male androgyny as due to Papago raft. Knowing that the Papagos respected berdaches, the blamed such an occurrence on an alien influence.[5] While nas' condemnatory attitude is unusual, it does point out the importance of spiritual explanations for the acceptance of gender variance in a culture.

Other Native American creation stories stand in sharp contrast to the Pima explanation. A good example is the account of the Navajos, which presents women and men as equals. The Navajo origin tale is told as a story of five worlds. The first people were First Man and First Woman, who were created equally and at the same time. The first two worlds that they lived in were bleak and unhappy, so they escaped to the third world. In the third world lived two twins, Turquoise Boy and White Shell Girl, who were the first berdaches. In the Navajo language the world for berdache is *nadle,* which means "changing one" or "one who is transformed." It is applied to hermaphrodites—those who are born with the genitals of both male and female—and also to "those who pretend to be *nadle,*" who take on a social role that is distinct from either men or women.[6]

In the third world, First Man and First Woman began farming, with the help of the changing twins. One of the twins noticed some clay and, holding it in the palm of his/her hand, shaped it into the first pottery bowl. Then he/she formed a plate, a water dipper, and a pipe. The second twin observed some reeds and began to weave them, making the first basket. Together they shaped axes and grinding stones from rocks, and hoes from bone. All these new inventions made the people very happy.[7]

The message of this story is that humans are dependent for many good things on the inventiveness of *nadle.* Such individuals were present from the earliest eras of human existence, and their presence was never questioned. They were part of the natural order of the universe, with a special contribution to make.

Later on in the Navajo creation story, White Shell Girl entered the moon and became the Moon Bearer. Turquoise Boy, however, remained with the people. When First Man realized that Turquoise Boy could do all manner of women's work as well as women, all the men left the women and crossed a big river. The men hunted and planted crops. Turquoise Boy ground the corn, cooked the food, and weaved cloth for the men. Four years passed with the women and men separated, and the men were happy with the *nadle.* Later, however the women wanted to learn how to grind corn from the *nadle,* and both the men and women had decided that it was not good to continue living separately. So the women crossed the river and the people were reunited.[8]

They continued living happily in the third world, until one day a great flood began. The people ran to the highest mountaintop, but the water kept rising and they all feared they would be drowned. But just in time, the ever-inventive Turquoise Boy found a large reed. They climbed upward inside the tall hollow reed, and came out at the top into the fourth world. From there, White Shell Girl brought another reed, and they climbed again to the fifth world, which is the present world of the Navajos.[9]

These stories suggest that the very survival of humanity is dependent on the inventiveness of berdaches. With such a mythological belief system, it is no wonder that the Navajos held *nadle* in high regard. The concept of the *nadle* is well formulated in the creation story. As children were educated by these stories, and all Navajos believed in them, the high status accorded to gender variation was passed down from generation to generation. Such stories also provided instruction for *nadle* themselves to live by. A spiritual explanation guaranteed a special place for a person who was considered different but not deviant.

For American Indians, the important explanations of the world are spiritual ones. In their view, there is a deeper reality than the here-and-now. The real essence or wisdom occurs when one finally gives up trying to explain events in terms of "logic" and "reality." Many confusing aspects of existence can better be explained by actions of a multiplicity of spirits. Instead of a concept of a single god, there is an awareness of "that which we do not understand." In Lakota religion, for example, the term *Wakan Tanka* is often translated as "god." But a more proper translation, according to the medicine people who taught me, is "The Great Mystery."[10]

While rationality can explain much, there are limits to human capabilities of understanding. The English language is structured to account for cause and effect. For example, English speakers say, "It is raining," with the implication that there is a cause "it" that leads to rain. Many Indian languages, on the other hand, merely note what is most accurately translated as "raining" as an observable fact. Such an approach brings a freedom to stop worrying about causes of things, and merely to relax and accept that our human insights can go only so far. By not taking ourselves too seriously, or overinflating human importance, we can get beyond the logical world.

The emphasis of American Indian religions, then, is on the spiritual nature of all things. To understand the physical world, one must appreciate the underlying spiritual essence. Then one can begin to see that the physical is only a faint shadow, a partial reflection, of a supernatural and extrarational world. By the Indian view, everything that exists is spiritual. Every object—plants, rocks, water, air, the moon, animals, humans, the earth itself—has a spirit. The spirit of one thing (including a human) is not superior to the spirit of any other. Such a view promotes a sophisticated ecological awareness of the place that humans have in the larger environment. The function of religion is not to try to condemn or to change what exists, but to accept the realities of the world and to appreciate their contributions to life. Everything that exists has a purpose.[11]

One of the basic tenets of American Indian religion is the notion that everything in the universe is related. Nevertheless, things that exist are often seen as having a counterpart: sky and earth, plant and animal, water and fire. In all of these polarities, there exist mediators. The role of the mediator is to hold the polarities together, to keep the world from disintegrating. Polarities exist within human society also. The most important category within Indian society is gender. The notions of Woman and Man underlie much of social interaction and are comparable to the other major polarities. Women, with their nurtural qualities, are associated with the earth, while men are associated with the sky. Women gatherers and farmers deal with plants (of the earth), while men hunters deal with animals.

The mediator between the polarities of woman and man, in the American Indian religious explanation, is a being that combines the elements of both genders. This might be a combination in a physical sense, as in the case of hermaphrodites. Many Native American religions accept this phenomenon same way that they accept other variations from the norm more important is their acceptance of the idea that gende be combined in ways other than physical hermaphroditism physical aspects of a thing or a person, after all, are not r as important as its spirit. American Indians use the concep person's *spirit* in the way that other Americans use the conc a person's *character.* Consequently, physical hermaphro is not necessary for the idea of gender mixing. A person's acter, their spiritual essence, is the crucial thing.

The Berdache's Spirit

Individuals who are physically normal might have the sp the other sex, might range somewhere between the two or might have a spirit that is distinct from either women or Whatever category they fall into, they are seen as being dif from men. They are accepted spiritually as "Not Man." W ever option is chosen, Indian religions offer spiritual ex tions. Among the Arapahos of the Plains, berdaches are *haxu'xan* and are seen to be that way as a result of a supern gift from birds or animals. Arapaho mythology recounts the of Nih'a'ca, the first *haxu'xan.* He pretended to be a w and married the mountain lion, a symbol for masculinit myth, as recorded by ethnographer Alfred Kroeber about recounted that "These people had the natural desire to be women, and as they grew up gradually became women. gave up the desires of men. They were married to men. had miraculous power and could do supernatural thing instance, it was one of them that first made an intoxican rainwater."[12] Besides the theme of inventiveness, similar Navajo creation story, the berdache role is seen as a produ "natural desire." Berdaches "gradually became women," underscores the notion of woman as a social category than as a fixed biological entity. Physical biological sex important in gender classification than a person's desire– spirit.

They myths contain no prescriptions for trying to c berdaches who are acting out their desires of the heart many other cultures' myths, the Zuni origin myths simply tion the idea that gender can be transformed independe biological sex.[13] Indeed, myths warn of dire consequence interference with such a transformation is attempted. Alexander Maximilian of the German state of Wied, tra in the northern Plains in the 1830s, heard a myth about rior who once tried to force a berdache to avoid women's ing. The berdache resisted, and the warrior shot him w arrow. Immediately the berdache disappeared, and the w saw only a pile of stones with his arrow in them. Sinc the story concluded, no intelligent person would try to a berdache.[14] Making the point even more directly, a M myth told of an Indian who tried to force *mihdake* (berc to give up their distinctive dress and status, which led the to punish many people with death. After that, no Mandan fered with berdaches.[15]

With this kind of attitude, reinforced by myth and histo aboriginal view accepts human diversity. The creation s

Iohave of the Colorado River Valley speaks of a time when le were not sexually differentiated. From this perspective, easy to accept that certain individuals might combine eles of masculinity and femininity.[16] A respected Mohave , speaking in the 1930s, stated this viewpoint simply: n the very beginning of the world it was meant that there d be [berdaches], just as it was instituted that there should amans. They were intended for that purpose."[17]

is elder also explained that a child's tendencies to become a che are apparent early, by about age nine to twelve, before ild reaches puberty: "That is the time when young persons me initiated into the functions of their sex. . . . None but g people will become berdaches as a rule."[18] Many tribes a public ceremony that acknowledges the acceptance of che status. A Mohave shaman related the ceremony for ibe: "When the child was about ten years old his relatives d begin discussing his strange ways. Some of them disliked t the more intelligent began envisaging an initiation cery." The relatives prepare for the ceremony without letting oy know of it. It is meant to take him by surprise, to be an initiation and a test of his true inclinations. People from us settlements are invited to attend. The family wants the nunity to see it and become accustomed to accepting the s an *alyha.*

n the day of the ceremony, the shaman explained, the boy into a circle: "If the boy showed a willingness to remain ing in the circle, exposed to the public eye, it was almost n that he would go through with the ceremony. The singer, n behind the crowd, began singing the songs. As soon as ound reached the boy he began to dance as women do." If oy is unwilling to assume *alyha* status, he would refuse to . But if his character—his spirit—is *alyha,* "the song goes to his heart and he will dance with much intensity. He canelp it. After the fourth song he is proclaimed." After the cery, the boy is carefully bathed and receives a woman's skirt. then led back to the dance ground, dressed as an *alyha,* nnounces his new feminine name to the crowd. After that ould resent being called by his old male name.[19]

nong the Yuman tribes of the Southwest, the transformas marked by a social gathering, in which the berdache res a meal for the friends of the family.[20] Ethnographer Underhill, doing fieldwork among the Papago Indians in rly 1930s, wrote that berdaches were common among the go Indians, and were usually publicly acknowledged in ood. She recounted that a boy's parents would test him y noticed that he preferred female pursuits. The regular n, mentioned by many of Underhill's Papago informants, build a small brush enclosure. Inside the enclosure they d a man's bow and arrows, and also a woman's basket. appointed time the boy was brought to the enclosure as ults watched from outside. The boy was told to go inside rcle of brush. Once he was inside, the adults "set fire to the sure. They watched what he took with him as he ran out it was the basketry materials, they reconciled themselves being a berdache."[21]

hat is important to recognize in all of these practices is that sumption of a berdache role was not forced on the boy by others. While adults might have their suspicions, it was only when the child made the proper move that he was considered a berdache. By doing woman's dancing, preparing a meal, or taking the woman's basket he was making an important symbolic gesture. Indian children were not stupid, and they knew the implications of these ceremonies beforehand. A boy in the enclosure could have left without taking anything, or could have taken both the man's and the woman's tools. With the community standing by watching, he was well aware that his choice would mark his assumption of berdache status. Rather than being seen as an involuntary test of his reflexes, this ceremony may be interpreted as a definite statement by the child to take on the berdache role.

Indians do not see the assumption of berdache status, however, as a free will choice on the part of the boy. People felt that the boy was acting out his basic character. The Lakota shaman Lame Deer explained:

> They were not like other men, but the Great Spirit made them *winktes* and we accepted them as such. . . . We think that if a woman has two little ones growing inside her, if she is going to have twins, sometimes instead of giving birth to two babies they have formed up in her womb into just one, into a half-man/half-woman kind of being. . . . To us a man is what nature, or his dreams, make him. We accept him for what he wants to be. That's up to him.[22]

While most of the sources indicate that once a person becomes a berdache it is a lifelong status, directions from the spirits determine everything. In at least one documented case, concerning a nineteenth-century Klamath berdache named Lele'ks, he later had a supernatural experience that led him to leave the berdache role. At that time Lele'ks began dressing and acting like a man, then married women, and eventually became one of the most famous Klamath chiefs.[23] What is important is that both in assuming berdache status and in leaving it, supernatural dictate is the determining factor.

Dreams and Visions

Many tribes see the berdache role as signifying an individual's proclivities as a dreamer and a visionary. . . .

Among the northern Plains and related Great Lakes tribes, the idea of supernatural dictate through dreaming—the vision quest—had its highest development. The goal of the vision quest is to try to get beyond the rational world by sensory deprivation and fasting. By depriving one's body of nourishment, the brain could escape from logical thought and connect with the higher reality of the supernatural. The person doing the quest simply sits and waits for a vision. But a vision might not come easily; the person might have to wait for days.

The best way that I can describe the process is to refer to my own vision quest, which I experienced when I was living on a Lakota reservation in 1982. After a long series of prayers and blessings, the shaman who had prepared me for the ceremony took me out to an isolated area where a sweat lodge had been set up for my quest. As I walked to the spot, I worried that I might not be able to stand it. Would I be overcome by hunger?

Could I tolerate the thirst? What would I do if I had to go to the toilet? The shaman told me not to worry, that a whole group of holy people would be praying and singing for me while I was on my quest.

He had me remove my clothes, symbolizing my disconnection from the material would, and crawl into the sweat lodge. Before he left me I asked him, "What do I think about?" He said, "Do not think. Just pray for spiritual guidance." After a prayer he closed the flap tightly and I was left in total darkness. I still do not understand what happened to me during my vision quest, but during the day and a half that I was out there, I never once felt hungry or thirsty or the need to go to the toilet. What happened was an intensely personal experience that I cannot and do not wish to explain, a process of being that cannot be described in rational terms.

When the shaman came to get me at the end of my time, I actually resented having to end it. He did not need to ask if my vision quest was successful. He knew that it was even before seeing me, he explained, because he saw an eagle circling over me while I underwent the quest. He helped interpret the signs I had seen, then after more prayers and singing he led me back to the others. I felt relieved, cleansed, joyful, and serene. I had been through an experience that will be a part of my memories always.

If a vision quest could have such an effect on a person not even raised in Indian society, imagine its impact on a boy who from his earliest years had been waiting for the day when he could seek his vision. Gaining his spiritual power from his first vision, it would tell him what role to take in adult life. The vision might instruct him that he is going to be a great hunter, a craftsman, a warrior, or a shaman. Or it might tell him that he will be a berdache. Among the Lakotas, or Sioux, there are several symbols for various types of visions. A person becomes *wakan* (a sacred person) if she or he dreams of a bear, a wolf, thunder, a buffalo, a white buffalo calf, or Double Woman. Each dream results in a different gift, whether it is the power to cure illness or wounds, a promise of good hunting, or the exalted role of a *heyoka* (doing things backward).

A white buffalo calf is believed to be a berdache. If a person has a dream of the sacred Double Woman, this means that she or he will have the power to seduce men. Males who have a vision of Double Woman are presented with female tools. Taking such tools means that the male will become a berdache. The Lakota word *winkte* is composed of *win,* "woman," and *kte,* "would become."[24] A contemporary Lakota berdache explains, "To become a *winkte,* you have a medicine man put you up on the hill, to search for your vision. "You can become a *winkte* if you truly are by nature. You see a vision of the White Buffalo Calf Pipe. Sometimes it varies. A vision is like a scene in a movie."[25] Another way to become a *winkte* is to have a vision given by a *winkte* from the past.[26]. . .

By interpreting the result of the vision as being the work of a spirit, the vision quest frees the person from feeling responsible for his transformation. The person might even claim that the change was done against his will and without his control. Such a claim does not suggest a negative attitude about berdache status, because it is common for people to claim reluctance to fulfill their spiritual duty no matter what vision appears to t Becoming any kind of sacred person involves taking on va social responsibilities and burdens.[27]. . .

A story was told among the Lakotas in the 1880s of a who tried to resist following his vision from Double Wo But according to Lakota informants "few men succeed ir effort after having taken the strap in the dream." Having reb against the instructions given him by the Moon Being, he mitted suicide.[28] The moral of that story is that one shoul resist spiritual guidance, because it will lead only to grie another case, an Omaha young man told of being addr by a spirit as "daughter," whereupon he discovered that he unconsciously using feminine styles of speech. He tried t male speech patterns, but could not. As a result of this vi when he returned to his people he resolved himself to dres woman.[29] Such stories function to justify personal peculia as due to a fate over which the individual has no control.

Despite the usual pattern in Indian societies of using cule to enforce conformity, receiving instructions from a v inhibits others from trying to change the berdache. R explanation provides a way out. It also excuses the comm from worrying about the cause of that person's differenc the feeling that it is society's duty to try to change him.[30] N American religions, above all else, encourage a basic re for nature. If nature makes a person different, many In conclude, a mere human should not undertake to counte spiritual dictate. Someone who is "unusual" can be accon dated without being stigmatized as "abnormal." Berdachi thus not alien or threatening; it is a reflection of spiritual

Notes

1. Mary Douglas, *Purity and Danger* (Baltimore: Penguin, 19 p. 52. I am grateful to Theda Perdue for convincing me that Douglas's ideas apply to berdachism. For an application of Douglas's thesis to berdaches, see James Thayer, "The Ber of the Northern Plains: A Socioreligious Perspective," *Jour Anthropological Research 36* (1980): 292–93.
2. E. W. Gifford, "The Kamia of Imperial Valley," *Bureau of American Ethnology Bulletin 97* (1931): 12.
3. By using present tense verbs in this text, I am not implying such activities are necessarily continuing today. I sometime use the present tense in the "ethnographic present," unless I use the past tense when I am referring to something that has not continued. Past tense implies that all such practices have disappeared. In the absence of fieldwork to prove suc disappearance, I am not prepared to make that assumption, the historic changes in the berdache tradition.
4. Elsie Clews Parsons, "The Zuni La' Mana," *American Anthropologist* 18 (1916): 521; Matilda Coxe Stevenson, " Indians," *Bureau of American Ethnology Annual Report 23* (1903): 37; Franklin Cushing, "Zuni Creation Myths," *Bur of American Ethnology Annual Report 13* (1894): 401–3. W Roscoe clarified this origin story for me.
5. W. W. Hill, "Note on the Pima Berdache," *American Anthropologist 40* (1938): 339.
6. Aileen O'Bryan, "The Dine': Origin Myths of the Navaho Indians," *Bureau of American Ethnology Bulletin 163* (195

W. W. Hill, "The Status of the Hermaphrodite and Transvestite in Navaho Culture,"*American Anthropologist 37* (1935): 273.

Martha S. Link, *The Pollen Path: A Collection of Navajo Myths* (Stanford: Stanford University Press, 1956).

O'Bryan, "Dine'," pp. 5, 7, 9–10.

bid.

akota informants, July 1982. See also William Powers, *Oglala Religion* (Lincoln: University of Nebraska Press, 1977).

For this admittedly generalized overview of American Indian religious values, I am indebted to traditionalist informants of many tribes, but especially those of the Lakotas. For a discussion of native religions see Dennis Tedlock, *Finding the Center* (New York: Dial Press, 1972); Ruth Underhill, *Red Man's Religion* (Chicago: University of Chicago Press, 1965); and Elsi Clews Parsons, *Pueblo Indian Religion* (Chicago: University of Chicago Press, 1939).

Alfred Kroeber, "The Arapaho," *Bulletin of the American Museum of Natural History 18* (1902–7): 19.

Parsons, "Zuni La' Mana," p. 525.

Alexander Maximilian, *Travels in the interior of North America, 1832–1834,* vol. 22 of *Early Western Travels,* ed. Reuben Gold Thwaites, 32 vols. (Cleveland: A. H. Clark, 1906), pp. 283–84, 354. Maximilian was quoted in German in the early homosexual rights book by Ferdinand Karsch-Haack, *Das Gleichgeschlechtliche Leben der Naturvölker* (The same-sex life of nature peoples) (Munich: Verlag von Ernst Reinhardt, 1911; reprinted New York: Arno Press, 1975), pp. 314, 564.

Oscar Koch, *Der Indianishe Eros* (Berlin: Verlag Continent, 1925), p. 61.

George Devereux, "Institutionalized Homosexuality of the Mohave Indians," *Human Biology 9* (1937): 509.

bid., p. 501

bid.

bid., pp. 508–9.

20. C. Daryll Forde, "Ethnography of the Yuma Indians," *University of California Publications in American Archaeology and Ethnology 28* (1931): 157.

21. Ruth Underhill, *Social Organization of the Papago Indians* (New York: Columbia University Press, 1938), p. 186. This story is also mentioned in Ruth Underhill, ed., *The Autobiography of a Papago Woman* (Menasha, Wisc.: American Anthropological Association, 1936), p. 39.

22. John Fire and Richard Erdoes, *Lame Deer, Seeker of Visions* (New York: Simon and Schuster, 1972), pp. 117, 149.

23. Theodore Stern, *The Klamath Tribe: A People and Their Reservation* (Seattle: University of Washington Press, 1965), pp. 20, 24; Theodore Stern, "Some Sources of Variability in Klamath Mythology,"*Journal of American Folklore 69* (1956): 242ff; Leshe Spier, *Klamath Ethnography* (Berkeley: University of California Press, 1930), p. 52.

24. Clark Wissler, "Societies and Ceremonial Associations in the Oglala Division of the Teton Dakota," *Anthoropological Papers of the American Museum of Natural History 11,* pt. 1 (1916): 92; Powers, *Oglala Religion,* pp. 57–59.

25. Ronnie Loud Hawk, Lakota informant 4, July 1982.

26. Terry Calling Eagle, Lakota informant 5, July 1982.

27. James S. Thayer, "The Berdache of the Northern Plains: A Socioreligious Perspective," *Journal of Anthropological Research 36* (1980): 289.

28. Fletcher, "Elk Mystery," p. 281.

29. Alice Fletcher and Francis La Flesche, "The Omaha Tribe," *Bureau of American Ethnology Annual Report 27* (1905–6): 132.

30. Harriet Whitehead offers a valuable discussion of this element of the vision quest in "The Bow and the Burden Strap: A New Look at Institutionalized Homosexuality in Native North America," in *Sexual Meanings,* ed. Sherry Ortner and Harriet Whitehead (Cambridge: Cambridge University Press, 1981), pp. 99–102. See also Erikson, "Childhood," p. 329.

Where Fat Is a Mark of Beauty

In a rite of passage, some Nigerian girls spend months gaining weight and learning customs in a special room. "To be called a 'slim princess' is an abuse," says a defender of the practice.

ANN M. SIMMONS

Margaret Bassey Ene currently has one mission in life: gaining weight.

The Nigerian teenager has spent every day since early June in a "fattening room" specially set aside in her father's mud-and-thatch house. Most of her waking hours are spent eating bowl after bowl of rice, yams, plantains, beans and *gari,* a porridge-like mixture of dried cassava and water.

After three more months of starchy diet and forced inactivity, Margaret will be ready to reenter society bearing the traditional mark of female beauty among her Efik people: fat.

In contrast to many Western cultures where thin is in, many culture-conscious people in the Efik and other communities in Nigeria's southeastern Cross River state hail a woman's rotundity as a sign of good health, prosperity and allure.

The fattening room is at the center of a centuries-old rite of passage from maidenhood to womanhood. The months spent in pursuit of poundage are supplemented by daily visits from elderly matrons who impart tips on how to be a successful wife and mother. Nowadays, though, girls who are not yet marriage-bound do a tour in the rooms purely as a coming-of-age ceremony. And sometimes, nursing mothers return to the rooms to put on more weight.

"The fattening room is like a kind of school where the girl is taught about motherhood," said Sylvester Odey, director of the Cultural Center Board in Calabar, capital of Cross River state. "Your daily routine is to sleep, eat and grow fat."

Like many traditional African customs, the fattening room is facing relentless pressure from Western influences. Health campaigns linking excess fat to heart disease and other illnesses are changing the eating habits of many Nigerians, and urban dwellers are opting out of the time-consuming process.

Effiong Okon Etim, an Efik village chief in the district of Akpabuyo, said some families cannot afford to constantly feed a daughter for more than a few months. That compares with a stay of up to two years, as was common earlier this century, he said.

But the practice continues partly because "people r laugh at you because you didn't have money to allow your to pass through the rite of passage," Etim said. What's r many believe an unfattened girl will be sickly or unable to children.

Etim, 65, put his two daughters in a fattening room tog when they were 12 and 15 years old, but some girls unc the process as early as age 7, after undergoing the controve practice of genital excision.

Bigger Is Better, According to Custom

As for how fat is fat enough, there is no set standard. But the u ten rule is the bigger the better, said Mkoyo Edet, Etim's siste

"Beauty is in the weight," said Edet, a woman in her 50s spent three months in a fattening room when she was 7. " called a 'slim princess' is an abuse. The girl is fed cons whether she likes it or not."

In Margaret's family, there was never any question th would enter the fattening room.

"We inherited it from our forefathers; it is one of the ages we must continue," said Edet Essien Okon, 25, Marg stepfather and a language and linguistics graduate of the versity of Calabar. "It's a good thing to do; it's an initi rite."

His wife, Nkoyo Effiong, 27, agreed: "As a woman, I fee proper for me to put my daughter in there, so she can be educa

Effiong, a mother of five, spent four months in a fatt room at the age of 10.

Margaret, an attractive girl with a cheerful smile and hair p in fluffy bumps, needs only six months in the fattening because she was already naturally plump, her stepfather said

During the process, she is treated as a goddess, bu days are monotonous. To amuse herself, Margaret has or ment made out of a soda bottle with a hole in it, which she on her hand to play traditional tunes.

ll, the 16-year-old says she is enjoying the highly ritual- attening practice.

m very happy about this," she said, her belly already distended he waist of her loincloth. "I enjoy the food, except for *gari.*"

y in, day out, Margaret must sit cross-legged on a special inside the secluded fattening room. When it is time to eat, ts on the floor on a large, dried plantain leaf, which also s as her bed. She washes down the mounds of food with pots of water and takes traditional medicine made from s and herbs to ensure proper digestion.

part of the rite, Margaret's face is decorated with a white, ke chalk.

'ou have to prepare the child so that if a man sees her, she e attractive," Chief Etim said.

fts of palm leaf fiber, braided and dyed red, are hung d Margaret's neck and tied like bangles around her wrists nkles. They are adjusted as she grows.

pically, Margaret would receive body massages using the chalk powder mixed with heavy red palm oil. But the teen ıer parents believe the skin-softening, blood-stimulating ges might cause her to expand further than necessary.

argaret is barred from doing her usual chores or any other ous physical activities. And she is forbidden to receive rs, save for the half a dozen matrons who school Margaret etiquette of the Efik clan.

ey teach her such basics as how to sit, walk and talk in of her husband. And they impart wisdom about clean- ewing, child care and cooking—Efik women are known ghout Nigeria for their chicken pepper soup, pounded and other culinary creations.

hey advise me to keep calm and quiet, to eat the *gari,* and have many boyfriends so that I avoid unwanted pregnancy," aret said of her matron teachers. "They say that unless you assed through this, you will not be a full-grown woman."

nat little exercise Margaret gets comes in dance lessons. atrons teach her the traditional *ekombi,* which she will be ted to perform before an audience on the day she emerges seclusion—usually on the girl's wedding day, Etim said.

t Okon said his aim is to prepare his stepdaughter for ture, not to marry her off immediately. Efik girls receive education than girls in most parts of Nigeria, and Okon Margaret will return to school and embark on a career as nstress before getting married.

Weddings Also Steeped in Tradition

Once she does wed, Margaret will probably honor southeastern Nigeria's rich marriage tradition. It begins with a letter from the family of the groom to the family of the bride, explaining that "our son has seen a flower, a jewel, or something beautiful in your family, that we are interested in," said Josephine Effah-Chukwuma, program officer for women and children at the Constitutional Rights Project, a law-oriented nongovernmental organization based in the Nigerian commercial capital of Lagos.

If the girl and her family consent, a meeting is arranged. The groom and his relatives arrive with alcoholic beverages, soft drinks and native brews, and the bride's parents provide the food. The would-be bride's name is never uttered, and the couple are not allowed to speak, but if all goes well, a date is set for handing over the dowry. On that occasion, the bride's parents receive about $30 as a token of appreciation for their care of the young woman. "If you make the groom pay too much, it is like selling your daughter," Effah-Chukwuma said. Then, more drinks are served, and the engagement is official.

On the day of the wedding, the bride sits on a specially built wooden throne, covered by an extravagantly decorated canopy. Maidens surround her as relatives bestow gifts such as pots, pans, brooms, plates, glasses, table covers—everything she will need to start her new home. During the festivities, the bride changes clothes three times.

The high point is the performance of the *ekombi,* in which the bride twists and twirls, shielded by maidens and resisting the advances of her husband. It is his task to break through the ring and claim his bride.

Traditionalists are glad that some wedding customs are thriving despite the onslaught of modernity.

Traditional weddings are much more prevalent in southeastern Nigeria than so-called white weddings, introduced by colonialists and conducted in a church or registry office.

"In order to be considered married, you have to be married in the traditional way," said Maureen Okon, a woman of the Qua ethnic group who wed seven years ago but skipped the fattening room because she did not want to sacrifice the time. "Tradition identifies a people. It is important to keep up a culture. There is quite a bit of beauty in Efik and Qua marriages."

Article 23

. . . but What If It's a Girl?

Modern technology is helping parents in Asia indulge in a hideous practice—killing off their girl children. It's never been easier to identify a female foetus and abort it.

CARLA POWER

Grey hair pulled into a tidy bun, blood-orange sari crisp, Sangam Satyavathi marches into the hospital, her team scurrying after her. She is on a raid. As district health officer for Hyderabad, Dr. Satyavathi is on a "sting operation"—a surprise visit to a maternity hospital to check its ultrasound records. A nervous knot of doctors and nurses forms around her, under a portrait of the baby Krishna and an advertisement for a General Electric ultrasound machine. This features a pregnant belly and the slogan "We bring good things to life". Satyavathi and her team frown over ledgers and a pile of Form Fs, required whenever a pregnant woman has an ultrasound scan. Like all the other hospitals in Hyderabad District, this one has been ordered, as part of a local campaign against female foeticide, to present detailed records of any such procedures.

"No reports," says Satyavathi, frowning. "And no consent forms."

"Consent form we are not taking, madam," ventures a doctor.

More poring over ledgers. "You haven't submitted your forms on time."

"Next time, madam."

"Next time?" she asks. "Now we are going to seize the machine."

Dr. Satyavathi's men go to work. They shroud the ultrasound machine in a sheet, then wrap it in lashings of surgical gauze. They drip red molten wax on the knots. Satyavathi whips out a five-rupee coin and presses it to the wax, sealing the suspect machine with the design of the three-headed lion, symbol of the Indian government.

"You see," she says grimly. "The act is so powerful."

The Prenatal Diagnostic Techniques Act is powerful indeed, but rarely enforced. Passed after India realised that modern medical techniques such as ultrasound scans and amniocentesis were frequently being used to identify female foetuses—which are then aborted—the PNDT Act requires the registration of all ultrasound machines, and bans doctors from revealing the sex of the foetus to expectant parents. The 1994 law was an attempt to reverse India's rampant use of sex-selective abortion, and the lopsided sex ratio this has produced. India's 2001 c showed that there were 927 girls to every 1,000 boys, from 945:1,000 in 1991 and 962:1,000 in 1981. Until rec no doctors had been put in prison under the PNDT Act. Bu last month a doctor was jailed for three years after telli undercover investigator that her foetus was female, and hi that she could abort it. Arvind Kumar, Hyderabad distric lector and Satyavathi's boss, sees the law as the only pra tool for tackling India's female foeticide epidemic. Doctor practise sex-selective abortion, he says, "like any other c nals, should be treated like criminals".

It is uncertain how many such crimes have been comm A January study in the *Lancet* estimated that ten million f foeticides had occurred in India over the past two decades. the Indian Medical Association and anti-sex-selection act disputed the findings, saying the numbers were too high. the numbers may be a matter of debate, the general trend i the ratio of girls to boys in India has been dwindling ov past two decades. In 1991, not a single district in India child sex ratio of less than 800:1,000. By 2001, there we "What we're dealing with," says Sabu George, India's le activist, "is a genocide."

The prospects are even bleaker elsewhere in Asia. In Korea and China, official numbers suggest that there ar girls for every 1,000 boys. In the case of China, indepe experts put it even lower, at 826:1,000. Whichever is corre Chinese demographic picture is more unbalanced than b 1990, when the statistics showed 901 girls for every 1,000 Today, in parts of Hainan and Guangdong Provinces, the r 769:1,000. The Chinese scenario has already produced a g bachelors, which experts say will only get worse. A 2002 in *International Security* magazine estimated that by 2020 will be up to 33 million guang guan ("bare branches"), as young, unmarried men are known. Some demographers put the figure even higher, at 40 million.

The unwanted girl has a long history in Asia. The first ten record of female infanticide dates back to Japan's Toku period, between 1600 and 1868, when there were nine ıny boys born as girls. A British colonial official in India ded cases of female infanticide as long ago as the 1780s. ·al India today, there are dais, traditional birth attendants, still know how to get rid of unwanted baby girls. Classic ɔds include feeding the newborn rice or salt, or smothering ıby with a pillow.

recent decades, female infanticide has been eclipsed by rn methods of sex determination, including amniocentesis rasound scan, followed by abortion. Activists say female ·ide is merely the first assault on Indian women, and can- e seen as separate from the whole life cycle of anti-girl ices in India: girl-child neglect, early marriage, the dowry m, domestic violence and honour killings. "Being a girl," Sabu George, "is considered a congenital defect."

is tempting to dismiss Asia's female foeticide problem as duct of the sexism of "backward" societies. To be sure, the em stems from traditional belief systems favouring boys, ıe prevalence of sex selection is an unexpected side effect dernity. Female foeticide has been boosted by precisely the s that make China and India the great success stories of the hties: economic liberalisation, growing affluence, increased s to technology, and controlled population explosions.

ia's dearth of girls, say researchers, is partly a func- f official reproductive health policies. In the late 20th ry, both China and India embarked on population-control ammes. In China, from the 1950s to the 1970s, when the nment needed female workers, female infanticide dropped lowest levels the country had ever known, a 2004 study *Journal of Population Research* reported. After 1979, ver, when the infamous one-child policy was introduced, e infanticide and foeticide became more common. In , the muscular public health campaigns of the 1970s and drummed home the official line: happy families were ones. Abortion, legalised in 1970, "was pursued with an t patriotic zeal", recalls Dr. Puneet Bedi, a Delhi obstetri- nd anti-sex-selection activist. Tellingly, the Indian states id particularly well in curbing population growth—the b, Delhi and Haryana among them—are today those with ost skewed sex ratios. "A large part of the small-family is achieved by eliminating girls," says George. Pressured government to keep their families small, and by society duce boys, Indian women turned to modern technology to e that they got their treasured sons.

lia's new open markets have made it easier. Economic lib- ation in the early 1990s brought not just foreign cars and ıtsourcing boom, but the rise of what Bedi calls "medi- ıtrepreneurship". Easy credit and aggressive marketing reign companies made it possible for thousands of clin- buy ultrasound machines. "The ultrasound machine was ted like Coca-Cola," Bedi says. Between 1988 and 2003, was a 33-fold increase in the annual manufacture of ultra- equipment in India. Doctors advertised their possibili- idely. "Boy or girl?" asked adverts, before the PNDT Act ved them. A 2005 report by the Geneva Centre for the ɔcratic Control of Armed Forces noted that sex selection ecome "a booming business" not only in India, but also in and South Korea.

In India, the recent *Lancet* study found sex-selective abortion was far more prevalent among the urban middle classes than the illiterate poor: the more educated the mother, the less likely she was to give birth to a second child who was a girl. Though the practice has recently begun to spread to remote areas and to the south, it has been most widely practised in cities, particularly in the north. It is rare among Dalits and remote tribes and common among Sikhs and Jains, historically wealthy business communities. In Delhi, the leafiest suburbs have the worst sex ratios. Shailaja Chandra, a top-tier civil servant, says that preference for boys is common among the capital's elites.

"They want to keep property in the family," she says. "Because boys traditionally inherit the wealth, people want boys."

For many activists, India's female foeticide problem is entwined with the consumer society the country has become over the past 15 years. If one can order a BMW, goes the mindset, one can order a boy. Mira Shiva, a member of both the National Commission for Women and the National Commission on Population, sees the issue of female foeticide as just one example of the rise in violent crime against women, created by India's quicksilver modernisation. "We're going through a time of increasing consumerism and materialism, where our values are changing," she says. "Marketwise, things that are deemed not of value are expendable."

Other traditions have helped make girls seem expendable in Asia. Usually boys, not girls, carry on the family name. In Hinduism, it is the son who lights the funeral pyre when his parents die. In China and South Korea, ancestor-worship rituals are performed by sons and grandsons. In both China and India, boys are viewed as pension schemes, supporting their parents in old age.

If boys are a boon, girls are a liability. In India, the birth of a girl eventually entails a dowry, an increasingly expensive proposition. Where the grandmothers of today recall going to their husbands' homes with a pot or two and a few rupees, a modern dowry can cost hundreds of thousands of rupees. Girls are viewed as both an economic drain and a hassle. The protection of their virginity—central to family honour—creates further stress for parents. Boy-preference is so ingrained in the Indian family system that many women don't feel they have done their wifely duty until they produce a son. "They want to bend their heads, like sheep being slaughtered," observes Dr. Soubhagya Bhat, an obstetrician-gynaecologist in Belgaum, Karnataka. "The only way they feel their life is fulfilled is if they produce a son."

Governments are trying to change the conventional mindset. In 2003, India's national government launched a policy of paying homeless women money to help with their newborn babies: girls get double the rupees boys do. In Delhi, the Directorate of Family Welfare has recently come out with a clutch of "Respect the Girls" advertisements, with slogans such as: "If you kill daughters, you will keep searching for mothers, daughters and wives" and "Indira Gandhi and Mother Teresa: your daughter can be one of them!" They haven't worked. The latest statistics suggest that Delhi's sex ratio stands at roughly 814 girls to 1,000 boys. This is down from 845:1,000 in 2003.

If such trends continue, the future could be nightmarish. In their 2004 book *Bare Branches: The security implications of*

Asia's surplus male population, the political scientists Andrea den Boer and Valerie Hudson argue that the existence of all these millions of frustrated Asian bachelors will boost crime and lawlessness. They speculate that, to find an outlet for the continent's sex-starved males, Asian governments might even need to resort to fomenting wars. Indian activists also fear that the girl shortage will create a hyper-macho society.

Spiralling numbers of rapes and rates of violence will lead to the increasing sequestration of women. Men with money will be able to afford wives, who will quickly become a status symbol. "Powerful men would maintain zanankhanas [harems] to demonstrate their power and influence," writes the activist R. P. Ravindra. Poorer men, "finding no companions, might resort to any means to force a woman into a sexual/marital relationship".

In pockets of India, this has already begun. In Haryana and the Punjab, home to India's most unbalanced sex ratios, trafficking in women has skyrocketed. Men from these wealthy areas are purchasing wives from impoverished eastern states such as East Bengal and Bihar. This trend of "killing girls in the womb in western states is hurting girls in eastern states who hav vived in the womb", argues Kamal Kumar Pandey, a la with the Shakti Vahini network, an anti-trafficking NGO.

Rishi Kant, the network's founder, brandishes a r snapshot showing a bloody, decapitated corpse: a 12-yea bride wearing a yellow dress. The girl was murdered b man who bought her for 25,000 rupees, says Kant, becaus had refused to sleep with his brother. Tales of violence ag bought women, and of brothers sharing wives, are increas common in parts of northern India.

The spectre of millions of lawless bachelors seems a fa from the bureaucratic world-view of Arvind Kumar in Hyder If India's officials could just implement the PNDT Ac believes, the demographic tide could be reversed. He is 18 months into the campaign, and so he sounds cautious, b latest figures suggest that Hyderabad's sex ratio might be t back into balance. He tells of a letter he received recently a 13-year-old girl who was being belittled by her family fo being a son. Just hearing of his work, she had written, had her strength enough not to be ashamed of being a girl.

ising Number of Dowry eaths in India

ANDA HITCHCOCK

y 27: Young Housewife Burnt ve for Dowry

now: For nineteen-year-old Rinki the dream of a happily ed life was never to be. Barely a month after her marriage, as allegedly tortured and then set ablaze by her in-laws for y in Indiranagar in the small hours of Saturday. Daughter e Gyan Chand, a fish contractor who expired a year ago, was married to Anil on April 19 . . . However, soon after arriage, Balakram [Anil's father] demanded a colour telen instead of a black and white one and a motorcycle as When Rinki's mother failed to meet their demands, the ge housewife was subjected to severe physical torture, edly by her husband and mother-in-law . . . On Saturday ing she [her mother] was informed that Rinki was charred ath when a kerosene lamp accidentally fell on her and her es caught fire. However, prima-facie it appeared that the n was first attacked as her teeth were found broken. Injuvere also apparent on her wrist and chest.

ne 7: Woman Ends Life e to Dowry Harassment

ri: Dowry harassment claimed yet another life here recently. , daughter of Chandrashekhar Byadagi, married to Ajjappa ppa Kaginelle in Guttal village (Haveri taluk) had taken fe after being allegedly harassed by her husband Ajjappa, er-in-law Kotravva, sister-in-law Nagavva and father-iniddappa for more dowry, the police said. Police said that arassment compelled her to consume poison. . . . The Gutlice have arrested her husband and father-in-law.

ne 7: Body Found Floating

ri: The police said that a woman's body was found floatn a well at Tilawalli (Hanagal taluk) near here. . . . The sed has been identified as Akhilabanu Yadawad (26). The said that Akhilabanu was married to Abdul Razaksab wad five years ago. In spite of dowry being given, her husand his family tortured her to bring some more dowry. Her father, Abdulrope Pyati in his complaint, alleged that she was killed by them. Her husband and his two brothers have been arrested, the police added.

These three chilling reports from *The Times of India* are typical of the many accounts of dowry-related deaths that take place in the country every year. One cannot help but be struck by the offhand way in which a young woman's life and death is summed up, matter of factly, without any undue cause for alarm or probing of the causes. It is much as one would report a traffic accident or the death of a cancer patient—tragic certainly, but such things are to be expected.

The character of the articles points to the fact that the harassment, beating and in some cases murder of women over dowry is both common and commonly ignored or even tacitly condoned in official circles—by the police, the courts, politicians and media. These crimes are not isolated to particular groups, social strata, geographical regions or even religions. Moreover, they appear to be on the rise.

According to an article in *Time* magazine, deaths in India related to dowry demands have increase 15-fold since the mid-1980s from 400 a year to around 5,800 a year by the middle of the 1990s. Some commentators claim that the rising number simply indicates that more cases are being reported as a result of increased activity of women's organisations. Others, however, insist that the incidence of dowry-related deaths has increased.

An accurate picture is difficult to obtain, as statistics are varied and contradictory. In 1995, the National Crime Bureau of the Government of India reported about 6,000 dowry deaths every year. A more recent police report stated that dowry deaths had risen by 170 percent in the decade to 1997. All of these official figures are considered to be gross understatements of the real situation. Unofficial estimates cited in a 1999 article by Himendra Thakur "Are our sisters and daughters for sale?" put the number of deaths at 25,000 women a year, with many more left maimed and scarred as a result of attempts on their lives.

Some of the reasons for the under-reporting are obvious. As in other countries, women are reluctant to report threats and abuse to the police for fear of retaliation against themselves and their families. But in India there is an added disincentive. Any attempt to seek police involvement in disputes over dowry transactions may result in members of the woman's own family being subject to criminal proceedings and potentially imprisoned. Moreover, police action is unlikely to stop the demands for dowry payments.

The anti-dowry laws in India were enacted in 1961 but both parties to the dowry—the families of the husband and wife—are criminalised. The laws themselves have done nothing to halt dowry transactions and the violence that is often associated with them. Police and the courts are notorious for turning a blind eye to cases of violence against women and dowry associated deaths. It was not until 1983 that domestic violence became punishable by law.

Many of the victims are burnt to death—they are doused in kerosene and set light to. Routinely the in-laws claim that what happened was simply an accident. The kerosene stoves used in many poorer households are dangerous. When evidence of foul play is too obvious to ignore, the story changes to suicide—the wife, it is said, could not adjust to new family life and subsequently killed herself.

Research done in the late 1990s by Vimochana, a women's group in the southern city of Bangalore, revealed that many deaths are quickly written off by police. The police record of interview with the dying woman—often taken with her husband and relatives present—is often the sole consideration in determining whether an investigation should proceed or not. As Vimochana was able to demonstrate, what a victim will say in a state of shock and under threat from her husband's relatives will often change markedly in later interviews.

Of the 1,133 cases of "unnatural deaths" of women in Bangalore in 1997, only 157 were treated as murder while 546 were categorised as "suicides" and 430 as "accidents". But as Vimochana activist V. Gowramma explained: "We found that of 550 cases reported between January and September 1997, 71 percent were closed as 'kitchen/cooking accidents' and 'stove-bursts' after investigations under section 174 of the Code of Criminal Procedures." The fact that a large proportion of the victims were daughters-in-law was either ignored or treated as a coincidence by police.

Figures cited in *Frontline* indicate what can be expected in court, even in cases where murder charges are laid. In August 1998, there were 1,600 cases pending in the only special court in Bangalore dealing with allegations of violence against women. In the same year three new courts were set up to deal with the large backlog but cases were still expected to take six to seven years to complete. Prosecution rates are low. *Frontline* reported the results of one court: "Of the 730 cases pending in his court at the end of 1998, 58 resulted in acquittals and only 11 in convictions. At the end of June 1999, out of 381 cases pending, 51 resulted in acquittals and only eight in convictions."

Marriage as a Financial Transaction

Young married women are particularly vulnerable. By custom they go to live in the house of their husband's family following the wedding. The marriage is frequently arranged, often in response to advertisements in newspapers. Issues of status, caste and religion may come into the decision, but money is nevertheless central to the transactions between the fami the bride and groom.

The wife is often seen as a servant, or if she works, a of income, but has no special relationship with the me of her new household and therefore no base of support. 40 percent of women are married before the legal age Illiteracy among women is high, in some rural areas 63 percent. As a result they are isolated and often in no p to assert themselves.

Demands for dowry can go on for years. Religious ce nies and the birth of children often become the occasic further requests for money or goods. The inability of the family to comply with these demands often leads to the da in-law being treated as a pariah and subject to abuse. worst cases, wives are simply killed to make way for financial transaction—that is, another marriage.

A recent survey of 10,000 Indian women conducted by Health Ministry found that more than half of those interv considered violence to be a normal part of married lif most common cause being the failure to perform do duties up to the expectations of their husband's family.

The underlying causes for violence connected to dow undoubtedly complex. While the dowry has roots in trad Indian society, the reasons for prevalence of dowry-assc deaths have comparatively recent origins.

Traditionally a dowry entitled a woman to be a full m of the husband's family and allowed her to enter the r home with her own wealth. It was seen as a substitute for i tance, offering some security to the wife. But under the sures of cash economy introduced under British colonia the dowry like many of the structures of pre-capitalist Ind profoundly transformed.

Historian Veena Oldenburg in an essay entitled "I Murders in India: A Preliminary Examination of the His Evidence" commented that the old customs of dowry ha perverted "from a strongly spun safety net twist into a c noose". Under the burden of heavy land taxes, peasant fa were inevitably compelled to find cash where they could c their land. As a result the dowry increasingly came to be s a vital source of income for the husband's family.

Oldenburg explains: "The will to obtain large dowries the family of daughters-in-law, to demand more in cash, go other liquid assets, becomes vivid after leafing through pa official reports that dutifully record the effects of indebte foreclosures, barren plots and cattle dying for lack of f The voluntary aspects of dowry, its meaning as a mark o for the daughter, gradually evaporates. Dowry becomes dr payments on demand that accompany and follow the ma of a daughter."

What Oldenburg explains about the impact of money tions on dowry is underscored by the fact that dowry d wither away in India in the 20th century but took on new f Dowry and dowry-related violence is not confined to rural or to the poor, or even just to adherents of the Hindu rel Under the impact of capitalism, the old custom has been formed into a vital source of income for families desper meet pressing social needs.

number of studies have shown that the lower ranks of the le class are particularly prone. According to the Institute evelopment and Communication, "The quantum of dowry nge may still be greater among the middle classes, but rcent of dowry death and 80 percent of dowry harassment s in the middle and lower stratas." Statistics produced by chana in Bangalore show that 90 percent of the cases of y violence involve women from poorer families, who are le to meet dowry demands.

ere is a definite market in India for brides and grooms. papers are filled with pages of women seeking husbands nen advertising their eligibility and social prowess, usu- sing their caste as a bargaining chip. A "good" marriage en seen by the wife's family as a means to advance up the l ladder. But the catch is that there is a price to be paid in rm of a dowry. If for any reason that dowry arrangements ot be met then it is the young woman who suffers.

ne critic, Annuppa Caleekal, commented on the rising lev- f dowry, particularly during the last decade. "The price of dian groom astronomically increased and was based on his fications, profession and income. Doctors, charted accoun- and engineers even prior to graduation develop the divine to expect a 'fat' dowry as they become the most sought cream of the graduating and educated dowry league."

e other side of the dowry equation is that daughters are ably regarded as an unwelcome burden, compounding the dy oppressed position of women in Indian society. There high incidence of gender-based abortions—almost two n female babies a year. One article noted the particularly billboard advertisements in Bombay encouraging preg- women to spend 500 rupees on a gender test to "save" ential 50,000 rupees on dowry in the future. According to the UN Population Fund report for the year 2000, female infanticide has also increased dramatically over the past decade and infant mortality rates are 40 percent higher for girl babies than boys.

Critics of the dowry system point to the fact that the situation has worsened in the 1990s. As the Indian economy has been opened up for international investment, the gulf between rich and poor widened and so did the economic uncertainty facing the majority of people including the relatively well-off. It was a recipe for sharp tensions that have led to the worsening of a number of social problems.

One commentator Zenia Wadhwani noted: "At a time when India is enjoying unprecedented economic advances and boasts the world's fastest growing middle class, the country is also experiencing a dramatic escalation in reported dowry deaths and bride burnings. Hindu tradition has been transformed as a means to escaping poverty, augmenting one's wealth or acquiring the modern conveniences that are now advertised daily on television."

Domestic violence against women is certainly not isolated to India. The official rate of domestic violence is significantly lower than in the US, for example, where, according to UN statistics, a woman is battered somewhere in the country on average once every 15 seconds. In all countries this violence is bound up with a mixture of cultural backwardness that relegates women to an inferior status combined with the tensions produced by the pressures of growing economic uncertainty and want.

In India, however, where capitalism has fashioned out of the traditions of dowry a particularly naked nexus between marriage and money, and where the stresses of everyday life are being heightened by widening social polarisation, the violence takes correspondingly brutal and grotesque forms.

UNIT 6

Religion, Belief, and Ritual

Unit Selections

Key Points to Consider

- How can we best identify shamans and shamanic traditions apart from our own assumptions, stereotypes, desires, and expectations about them?
- How do beliefs about the supernatural contribute to a sense of personal security, individual responsibility, and social harmor
- What are the basic tenets of Islam? Do they really clash with Western values?
- How has voodoo become an important form of social control in rural Haiti?
- In what ways are magic rituals practical and rational?
- How did rituals and taboos get established in the first place?
- What role do rituals and taboos play in our modern industrial society?

Student Website

www.mhcls.com

Internet References

Anthropology Resources Page
http://www.usd.edu/anth/

Apologetics Index
http://www.apologeticsindex.org/site/index-c/

Magic and Religion
http://anthro.palomar.edu/religion/default.htm

Yahoo: Society and Culture: Death
http://dir.yahoo.com/Society_and_Culture/Death_and_Dying/

e anthropological interest in religion, belief, and ritual is not erned with the scientific validity of such phenomena but r with the way in which people relate various concepts of upernatural to their everyday lives. From this practical per-tive, some anthropologists have found that some traditional ual healing is just as helpful in the treatment of illness, as odern medicine; that voodoo is a form of social control (as he Secrets of Haiti's Living Dead"); and that the ritual and ual preparation for playing the game of baseball can be as important as spring training (see "Baseball Magic"). The ng of belief systems in these types of social contexts thus s to not only counter popular stereotypes, but also serves to ote a greater understanding of and appreciation for other points (see "Understanding Islam").

very society is composed of feeling, thinking, and acting an beings, who at one time or another, are either conforming altering the social order into which they were born. As ribed in "The Adaptive Value of Religious Ritual", religion ideological framework that gives special legitimacy and ty to human experience within any given socio-cultural sys- In this way, monogamy as a marriage form, or monarchy political form, ceases to be simply one of many alterna-ways in which a society can be organized, but becomes, for eliever, the only legitimate way. Religion considers certain an values and activities as sacred and inviolable. It is this ic function that helps explain the strong ideological attach-ts that some people have, regardless of the scientific merits eir points of view.

hile, under some conditions, religion may in fact be "the e of the masses," under other conditions such a belief sys-may be a rallying point for social and economic protest. A emporary example of the former might be the "Moonies" nbers of the Unification Church founded by Sun Myung n), while a good example of the latter is the role of the black ch in the American civil rights movement, along with the

© Mark Downey/Getty Images

prominence of religious figures such as Martin Luther King Jr. and Jesse Jackson. A word of caution must be set forth concerning attempts to understand belief systems of other cultures. At times,the prevailing attitude seems to be, "What I believe in is religion, and what you believe in is superstition." While anthropologists generally do not subscribe to this view, some tend to explain such behavior as incomprehensible and impractical without considering its full meaning and function within its cultural context. The articles in this unit should serve as a strong warning concerning the pitfalls of that approach.

Finally, it should be pointed out that mystical beliefs and rituals are not absent from the modern world. "Body Ritual among the Nacirema" reveals that even our daily routines have mystic overtones.

In summary, the writings in this unit show religion, belief, and ritual in relationship to practical human affairs.

Article 25

Shamanisms

Past and Present

DAVID KOZAK

For centuries, the exotic and romantic image and story line of the shaman as a religious virtuoso who takes magical, hallucinatory flights into the supernatural world, learning from or skirmishing with animal spirits and human ghosts, capturing and returning lost souls, and dwelling in a nether world of trance and ecstacy, has dominated both the scholarly and popular imaginations. The shaman has been perceived and represented as the prototypic, primordial religious practitioner who has direct contact with the supernatural, nonordinary realm of the phantasmic, a perception that has led to the widespread assumption that this is the central defining characteristic of this specialist. Along these lines, the shaman is viewed by some—in the past and in the present—as representative of a person who pursues an "authentic" religious experience and who consider shamanism as an "authentic" religious system when compared to various "inauthentic" institutionalized world religions. This often exotic and romantic image of shamans and shamanisms misrepresents or at least it misunderstands them. And importantly, if not ironically, to understand shamans and shamanisms we must look to ourselves and the stories we have told and continue to tell about them.

The study of shamans and shamanisms has been plagued with a number of conceptual problems. At root is the ethnographic-based difficulty in creating a satisfactory standardized definition. This is because, on the one hand, shamanisms are highly diverse, culturally and historically relative phenomena, encompassing a vast array of social behaviors and beliefs. On the other hand, it is possible to identify shared or perhaps core shamanic phenomena. Yet, to pin a tidy label and definition on what shamanism is, is to risk the social scientific sin of overly particularizing or generalizing a constellation of behaviors and beliefs. Another problem relates to how the shaman's psychological and phenomenological status has taken precedence in the literature. Central to this precedence is the interest in what is today called Altered States of Consciousness (ASC), the affective, inspirational, emotional, and ecstatic states experienced by many shamans. This emphasis is problematic because it largely ignores the very real problems of social history that place each shamanism in context and the individual culture history that drives the transformations that all individual shamanisms experience. While ASC is certainly important, it is debatable that it should be taken as an unproblematic feature of shamanisms. Finall related to the emphasis on ASC and shaman phenomen is that it has contributed to a line of self-help, self-actuali "New Age," neo-shamanism literature that often bears su ingly little resemblance to what the ethnographic record t of indigenous forms of shamanism.

In this essay I propose to work backwards in that I will with a general discussion of the difficulties with the c tion of scholarly and popular writings and perceptions o manisms in the present. I then move toward providing a working definition and general description of shamanism anthropologists and other scholars explain shamanism i lined prior to my offering three ethnographic (particula case studies. I trust that the case-study approach that focu cultural particulars will demonstrate the difficulties inher defining the generalities of this subject matter. Moreove selection of case studies is intended to juxtapose the so- "classical" Siberian shamanism with how colonialism, capitalization, and Christian missionization have differer affected Tohono O'odham and Putumayo shamanisms. essay is not intended to be comprehensive—a perhaps ir sible task. However, refer to Jane M. Atkinson and Jo Townsend for excellent literature reviews and discussions relevant issues.[1] Here I offer a more modest goal: to provi reader a basis for exploring and learning more about this important religious phenomenon.

The Stories We Tell

Shamans and shamanic traditions continue to captivate bo scholarly and popular consciousness. This captivation ha and continues to run the gamut of admiration to condemn acceptance to persecution, emulation to fear. While it may strange, shamans and shamanisms as we know them are i the rhetorical inventions of the Western intellectual and po cultural imaginations. Oftentimes the stories that outsid shamanic traditions tell about them are based less in emp reality than in the storyteller's own assumptions, stereot desires and expectations about what they themselves want the exotic "other." The inaccuracies in these stories have l do with cultural secrecy or of shamans intentionally misle

›pologists than with the author's failure to appropriately ›ent the phenomena. Perhaps such ill-informed storytell- innocuous enough, but it is frequently the case that such elling serves political, cultural, social, "racial," even per- ends, from the usurping of sacred cultural traditions for ›al needs at one end of a continuum to outright state-level ›al repression, domination, and oppression at the other Moreover, shamanism has served as a multivocal symbol ›cial, political, and religious purposes of the West. For ›ce, in the past, animistic religions were viewed by late ›enth-century social evolutionists (e.g., E.B. Tylor, Sir › Frazer) as occupying an inferior or impoverished level ›gious evolution and achievement, far behind the assumed ›iority of monotheism found in the "civilized" West. Juxta- › to this unfavorable view, shamanism is today frequently ›ed by people who are unhappy with institutionalized and ›rchal Christianity. In the United States, the "New Age," ›hamanism, and self-actualization movements make much ›f shamanic (tribal) symbolism and ideas, taken largely ›f context, in order to cobble together a personal religious › system and ritual practice that satisfies the individual's ›. Whether historically or contemporarily, shamanism is uncritically evoked as either impoverished as a pagan and ›ic religious expression or exalted as the solution to con- ›orary human ecological, existential, and personal crises.

›nthropologists early recognized the importance of shaman- › human religious history and cultures and have formulated ›us explanations and interpretations. The explanatory and ›retive stories that anthropologists tell include evolution- ›unctional, structural, psychological, Marxist, cultural, and ›cal-economic strategies. And while the emphasis of sha- ›stic research has been on the shaman as healer, as bridge ›een this and other worlds, as individual, as an evolutionary a more recent trend has emerged with an emphasis on the ›f the shaman and shamanisms as parts of larger politi- ›istorical, and economic contexts in the burgeoning global ›cal economy. Various anthropologists have rightly criti- the emphasis that had been placed on such things as the ›ctions made between the so-called "classical" shamans of ›ia and all others, the affective and hallucinatory states that ›ans experience, the abnormal personality traits supposedly ›ited by individual shamans, and so on. The emphasis has ›een on the universal characteristics shared by shamans and ›anistic systems. In response to the bulk of the literature, anthropologists have gone so far as to say that "shaman- is an invented and contentious category of disparate items, ›d out of context, artificially if artfully associated and all of ›amed up in the West with little basis in reality.[2]

›s indicated, anthropologists are not the only ones who find ›anisms of interest. In fact, the scholarly and the popu- ›nages merge with shamanism. Today there is a burgeon- ›opular, nonacademic and practitioner-based interest in ›ans, and particularly in their altered states of conscious- and ultimately in self-help and self-actualization as ›nded frequently in Jungian psychology. And while the self- ›lization approach is largely denigrated by anthropologists ›pportunistic, superficial, and self-serving in its treatment of shamanism, it was originally anthropologists who promoted, if indirectly, the current popularity. It is reasonable to say that the current popular and self-help interest of the neo-shamanism, New Age, and self-actualization movements stem from the publications of anthropologists Carlos Casteñada, Ake Hultkrantz, and Michael Harner, and the religious historian Mircea Eliade.[3] There is a distinct romanticizing and exoticizing of shamanism in their publications which appeals to a consumer group who feels that their lives as members of Western industrial societies are vacuous and that institutional forms of religion are inauthentic. In this literature, whether stated implicitly or not, shamanism offers what is believed to be an authentic method for establishing a relation between the individual and the natural and supernatural worlds.

The overarching rhetorical strategy used by the aforementioned authors is what I call the "shaman-as-hero" archetype, as the striving, seeking, brave, self-assured individual (the image is usually male). With not a little irony, this shaman-as-hero is transformed by such speculations and interpretations into the quintessential laissezfaire "self-made man," the rugged individualist-equivalent of the non-Western, "primitive" world. In other words, the shaman becomes imbued with the idealistic Western characteristics of hyper-individualism in order to better correspond to the lives of people who wish to use shamanism for their own psychic and spiritual needs, rather than for understanding the shaman on his or her own cultural terms. The shaman-as-hero archetype and hero rhetoric, as rugged individualist, thus become acceptable and appropriable. But in this process, the shaman becomes yet another commodity for consumer culture. Herein lies the crux of the storytelling quandary.

The shaman has been used to tell stories distinctly not of the shaman's making. Rather, the stories often tell as much if not more about the tellers of scholarly or popular culture stories. All such characterizations are deeply flawed as they neglect to account for the social context in which all shamans are a part. Shamanism is nothing, after all, if not a community-centered activity. What lacks in much of the literature on shamanisms is an appreciation for the social, political, historical, gendered, and economic contexts that shamans participate in. The struggles of shamans with other shamans, with other villagers, and with outside forces have significantly modified their cultures and religious practices. And the danger of representing the shaman as the rugged individual hero and archetype is that shamanism is trivilized, reduced to a caricature, and is literally eviscerated of its social meaning and context. This trivilization, of course, serves an important storytelling purpose: It affords outsiders easy access to the complex traditions of shamanism without forcing them to understand the intricacies of context or to become part of a community where shamanism is only a fraction of a much larger social and cultural whole. Importantly, it allows the storyteller's imagination to conjure and speculate freely; shamanism as aesthetics rather than science. But this is ideally not what the anthropological study of shamans and shamanisms is about. Rather, anthropologists wish to understand and perhaps partly explain some of the phenomena associated with this compelling and important social role and religious practice. Anthropological understanding is gained up close, through fieldwork observation and participation, through learning the language of the shaman's community, and distinctly not from a "safe" distance where insight derives from one's own imaginative flights of fancy or creative speculation.

Defining Shamanisms

Defining shamans and shamanisms is not an easy task. In fact, shamanism is truly many things to many people. For myself, I would prefer to avoid making categorical or definitional statements altogether. Yet it is reasonably possible to make a few general statements about shamans and shamanisms. Realize, however, that generalizations on this subject are tentative and any claim must be viewed and evaluated in the context of ethnographic data.

Let us begin by saying that a shaman is a ritualist who is able to divine, predict, and effect future outcomes, provide medical care, who is believed to have direct access to the supernatural, phantasmic realm, and who gains his or her powers and abilities by being tutored by spirits including deceased ancestors. Shamans are frequently skilled orators or singers. The social role of the shaman is often the only or one of only a few distinct social roles available in the culture. This general definition of the shaman shares characteristics with other ritualists known variously as medicine man, medium, spirit or faith healer, priest, oracle, witch doctor, among others.

Origins of Shamanism. For many anthropologists today the origins of shamanism is a moot question because it must remain largely conjectural reconstruction and is ultimately unprovable. Despite this, hypothesizing and research continue. Siberian and Arctic shamanism is considered by some to be the original source and prototypic form of shamanism in the world. The word "shaman" was originally derived from the Tungus (a central Siberian tribe) word *saman,* with the English word shaman being derived from the German noun *der schaman.* Others argue that Tungus shamanism was itself influenced by Buddhism. For this latter suggestion a linguistic affiliation has been explored with the Sanskrit word *sramana,* which translates as "one who practices austerities." Siberian origin also relates to the Bering Straights land bridge hypothesis which explains the peopling of the New World. This hypothesis is widely accepted by archaeologists and argues that the ancestors of today's Native Americans migrated from Northern Asia to North America, bringing their religious and shamanic practices with them. This diaspora hypothesis is based on linguistic and physiological data and partly on the similar, cross culturally shared shamanic practices which indicate a common heritage.[4]

Ancient rock art has produced some of the more intriguing sources of data and interpretation regarding the origins question. Several researchers suggest that some rock art styles are actually the renderings of the shaman's altered states of consciousness and of the shamanic cosmos dating to as long ago as 8,000 to 25,000 years. Rock art data suggesting paleolithic origins derive from Lascaux cave paintings in France, southern Africa, and the British Isles and are based on neurologically based entoptic phenomenon. Entoptic phenomena are those visual phenomena that people see while experiencing ous altered states of consciousness, visual phenomena th argued to follow distinctive pan-human patterns and for is claimed that these visual forms and patterns were then eled or painted on stone and were used as sacred mnemon didactic devices. Moreover, it is argued that shamanistic came to reside in the shaman's ability to control such a states and visions and the creation of sacred images.[5]

While it is not possible to know the absolute origins o manism, interesting research and hypothesizing contin be accomplished. The assumption that Siberian shamani prototypical and diffused outward, as with all origin the must be viewed with a healthy skepticism. The fact that cu change, adapting and culling beliefs and practices, in n patterns, it becomes impossible to pinpoint the genesis shamanic science and art.

Where Shamanisms Are Found. Shamans and sh isms are found throughout North and South America, Si parts of Asia, Polynesia, and Africa, virtually througho entire world. The ethnographic record reveals that shama are related to a variety of levels of social structure. Gat hunter, egalitarian populations like the San of southern A are the most likely to possess a shamanistic system. Yet, ralists like the Tungus of Siberia or the Somali of northe Africa and agriculturalists like the Pima of southern Ar also have shamanic traditions. Recent studies of highly fied, state-level systems of governing, as in Korea, have documented the presence of shamanistic systems. Ther much of where we find shamanisms depends on how sha are defined. Gatherer-hunter populations are largely egali with minor status differentiation who subsist on a diet ch terized by feast-and-famine food availability which rad fluctuates throughout the yearly cycle. The shaman's role often tenuous subsistence setting, for example, is that of m tor between his or her village and the environment where live and the spirit forces that control food and water availa The shaman divines to locate game animals and to dia and cure spirit sicknesses, soul loss, and sorcery malevo Spirit-caused sicknesses are frequently the result of human tention to or disrespect for the spirit and natural worlds.

Shamanic Cosmos. The cosmos is frequently, th not always, divided into a series of horizontally stacke ers, three or more. Humans occupy a middle earth leve is loosely demarcated by permeable boundaries by uppe lower spirit worlds. The upper and lower worlds are nonp cal in character and accessible only through spiritual m The various levels are linked and readily accessible to sha The spirit worlds are sources of power for human bene version of "balance" between these worlds is the desired and it is the shaman whose job it is to maintain this bal Imbalances are manifested in humans as illnesses, or in th of game animals, or in natural disasters. As in the human w so too in the spirit world, there is an emphasis on recipr with the spirits who inhabit the supernatural realm. A sha job is to keep the spirits happy or at least mollified and f ers healthy. The afterlife locality is conceived of as either proved version of the human community or an ill-defined . It is usually not a location of punishment or reward for a n's actions in life. The concept of sin seems to be absent. s, including human ghosts or ancestors, may be malevo- enevolent, both, or benign. In any case, spirits have a sig- nt impact on the human community.

aman's Training. Direct contact with spirits is a uni- feature of the shaman's practice. A shaman's contact spirits makes the power from the other nonearthly cos- ayers accessible to a larger community of people in the e earth level. A shaman is taught this power by a spirit(s) he teaching consists of learning songs, chants, speeches, techniques, and in the construction and use of shaman's such as a drum or other musical instruments, clothing, e, feathers, rattles, and crystals. A shaman ideally uses upernatural knowledge and power to aid his or her com- y members' health and well-being, although shamans are ble to use this power to harm other humans. Frequently, man has the ability for soul flight, or at the very least the an is capable of making nocturnal journeys as guided by tutelaries.

shaman may inherit his or her abilities or be selected by s to accept this important social responsibility. A person e approached by spirits as a child or at any time in one's r that matter. Often, the selection occurs during an acute ing period in a person's life such as psychological stress, cal illness, accident, or a "near death" experience. A person has the choice of accepting or rejecting a spirit's advances, e shaman role. If a person accepts a spirit's advances, the s) will tutor their pupil in the shamanic sciences during rnal dreams or in hallucinatory or trance-induced states. A an's training is a lifelong process and a shaman's abilities ffectiveness may wax and wane over a lifetime.

s of Consciousness. The literature is crowded with ssions of the shaman's altered state of consciousness, anic State of Consciousness (SSC), magic flight, trance, inatory, inspirational, and ecstatic abilities. Made famous ircea Eliade, the shaman's ecstacy has come largely to —as discussed above—much of what we think of as ssentially shamanic. Altered states of consciousness are induced with hallucinogenic plants, including fungi, th nonhallucinogenic alcoholic drinks, tobacco smoke, ventilation, meditation, and rhythmic drumming. It is not tered state per se that is important but rather the communi- that the altered state facilitates between spirit-animal and an or shaman and the lost soul that he or she searches for. entioned above, the altered state is also a time when the an is tutored by spirits.

amental Actions. Blowing, sucking, singing, massag- pitting, smudging, painting, chanting, touching, fanning, , and sprinkling water, ashes, and corn meal are all sac- tal actions used by shamans as taught to them by spirit ries. By sacramental I mean how a shaman uses his soul, ented by the soul(s) of his spirit helpers or tutelaries and tools (i.e., feathers, water, smoke, peyote, or other hallucinogens) to positively affect the soul of a patient and/or of an entire community. The sacramental act of blowing, for instance, may come in the form of singing songs to patients, reciting chants to spirits, or even of blowing cigarette smoke over a patient to illuminate embedded sickness or discover the location of sorcery objects. A sacrament's performative intent is to improve the living condition of a person or of a community through sacredly endowed actions: blessings made physically manifest for all to see. A shaman's sacramental actions are always for good; in comparison, sorcery could be classified as an antisacramental act.

Shamanic Discourses. The verbalizations of shamans provide a rich avenue for understanding shamanism. Songs, chants, narratives, and verbal explanations given by shamans are ways to examine the internal and cultural dimensions and perceptions held by practitioners themselves. This area of research is perhaps the most challenging for an anthropologist as it demands the researcher to possess a firm grasp of the shaman's own language.[6] Text transcription and translation become central in this work and interpretations and explanations of a single or a few key words may be the foundation for an entire study. A rich corpus of song and chant texts has revealed the art of various shamanisms, but also the meaning and centrality of shamanic discourses in the work of healing or divining.

Empirical Observations. Since the social evolutionist E.B. Tylor's time (late 1800s), some anthropologists have argued that religious beliefs and practices are ultimately based in people's systematic observations of the sentient world around them. Empirical observations of the physical world serve as a template for their ultimate conceptions of the soul, human body, the sacred, and the role of religious belief in human affairs. Furthermore, people are also astute observers of human-animal and human-plant interactions. As such, the empirical observations and experiments that people conduct in their natural world serve as the basis for their public and private religious lives.

Explaining Shamanisms

Anthropologists use various theoretical orientations to understand and explain the shamanism phenomenon. I will briefly discuss two general orientations: the psychological-physiological and the political-economic. This brief discussion lumps together general tendencies and the two theoretical categories could be divided in other ways.

Psychology and Physiology. The belief that shamans are mentally ill, who suffer from neuroses, psychoses, or schizophrenia, has roots in the eighteenth century. During that time shamanic practices competed, if indirectly, with the ascendancy of rationalist principles being developed with the scientific revolution. At the time, inspirationally or mythically based ways of knowing were being systematically discredited as irrational and as nonsense. The shaman as crazy person penetrated well into the twentieth century with anthropologists such as A.L. Kroeber, Ralph Linton, and A.F.C. Wallace. These anthropologists, using one or another psychoanalytic theory, concluded that the shaman and potential shamans suffer from a number of severe mental or physical complaints. Kroeber went so far as to say that so-called primitive cultures not only condoned but exalted psychotic behavior, that the shaman's claim to see and deal with spirits was nothing other than a delusional psychopathology. The mental illness theory of the shaman persisted until the 1960s when counter-arguments mounted against this unfortunate interpretation. By the late 1960s shaman's behaviors were considered psychologically normal. And as Jane M. Atkinson has pointed out, the change of attitude that occurred in the 1960s toward shamanic psychology and behavior was affected by changing notions of consciousness in general spurred on by hallucinogenic-modified consciousness in particular and the effectiveness of shamanism as psychotherapy in general.[7]

The continued interest in the psychic states of shamans, anthropologists, and other behavioralist researchers, wishing to ground their work on a scientific footing, developed their research around the concept of altered states of consciousness or shamanic states of consciousness. The emphasis of this research is on the phenomenological experience of the practitioner, the cross-culturally shared trance-state characteristics, and more recently an interest in the neurophysiological bases of ASC. Of note in this regard are studies related to the role of endorphins and other chemicals released in the brain during rituals. More recently is an interest in what Michael Winkelman calls "neurognostic structures" of the psyche. He argues that shamanism is a biologically based transpersonal mode of consciousness.[8] It is suggested that the capacity for shamanic behavior—that is, trance and vision flights—is a biologically based memory device of sorts, a shamanistic equivalent of a Chomskyan "deep structure" of linguistic ability or a Jungian "archetype" of collective consciousness, whereby shamanic behavior is a hard-wired and universal human characteristic and is evidenced in the similarities shared by shamans in vastly different cultures.

Politics, Economics, and History. Complementing the biological- and psychological-based explanations for shamanism is a recent interest in the political, historical, and economic factors related to shamans, cultures with shamanic systems, and how these relate to state-level and global capitalist structures of power and institutionalized religions. This interest area reflects a general trend in anthropology that emphasizes historical and political economic factors.

Foremost in this approach is an appreciation for how shamanisms have been affected by various state, economic, and institutionalized religious structures. Due to the impacts of colonialism and neo-colonialism, the historical and political economic approach takes for granted that much of what we know of as shamanism today is the result of contact and change initiated by institutions stemming from the West. The implication is that to understand shamanism we must also understand how the structures of power have been manifested at the local level. Thus, much of the published work stemming from this general orientation takes change as inevitable, that shamanic-oriented cultures have been victimized, and that the search for pristine and "authentic" versions of shamanisms is fallacious and naïve. In response to the psychological-physiological approaches, to understand shaman psychology, ASC, an actions, the researcher must be rigorous in defining the political, and economic context(s) in which individual sh isms are expressed. Thus, this general approach emphasi social rather than the individual, the historical rathe the immediate, the cultural rather than the psychologic the relations of power rather than altered states.[9]

The primary drawback to this general political ec orientation is that it may sacrifice the richness of loca interpretations and individualistic articulations for its em on structure, history, and power relations. Real people ar lost in a maze of political and economic and historic fact seemingly override the agency of individual actors.

In sum, the theories that anthropologists use to exp interpret shamanisms are of necessity incomplete. T because human experience is far more complex and ric our abstractions of it. Thus, our theories are ways to ass comprehension of a culturally rich realm of humanne each theory tends to privilege partial elements of that ric

Three Case Studies

Ethnographic description, the product of intensive fiel conducted by an anthropologist who lives for an extende with the people being studied, is crucial to the work of so tural anthropologists. The ethnographic method is perha superior way for understanding shamanisms and it also the potential for a critical appraisal and reevaluation of pa rytelling inaccuracies and excesses regarding the study manisms around the world. Because the fieldwork expe demands that the anthropologist live among and partici the subject's community life and have a familiarity wi host culture's language, the anthropological perspective out promise for a nuanced understanding and documenta be found in this religious-medicinal practice. It is also a able source for critiquing the frequently problematic cate analyses, and assumptions made by outside observers c manic phenomena. To illustrate this point and present a ment of the diversity of shamanisms found in the world and to demonstrate its range of applicability, I here offe case studies of shamanism in Northern Asia, North An and South America. The case studies reveal that shamanis a complex interweaving of cultural practices, gifted indi practitioners, political economic issues, and ASC. They how shamanisms change, how they are influenced by the tutionalized religions like Christianity, and by global capi and social change. Each case study demonstrates in its ow how the category of a generalized shamanism is a theo oversimplification at best and that shamanisms undergo c and modification to fit the needs of a people.

Siberian Shamanisms

Siberian shamanism is often referred to as the "classical" that used to exist. Mircea Eliade made Siberian sham famous and identified it by their exotic and mystical ritua costumes, hallucinations, trances, the mastering of spirit cosmic travels. Since Eliade's work, many shamanisms valuated and compared with it. As Caroline Humphrey[10] inted out, Eliade's characterization is seriously flawed as s social and historical context. Moreover, she criticizes 's representations for effectively crystallizing the current in the context-free view of shamanism as a mysterious rely inspirational phenomenon. In order to offer a context rian shamanism I draw extensively from the research of e Hamayon.[11]

cording to Hamayon there are two primary types of Siberian nism: hunting and pastoral. Each corresponds to distinct organizational forms, economic, and political characteris- berian "hunting shamanism" is present in tribal, noncen- d, forest-dwelling societies like the Chugchee. Hunting nism is characteristic of the form Eliade spoke of in his gs. "Pastoral shamanism" as found among the Tungus is terized by people who are patrilineal and patrilocal, who ticate livestock, and live in regions that border the forest ppe regions. A potential third type, what Hamayon calls heral shamanism," is only marginally identifiable as sha- n as it is related to state formation and how the traditional n's role and power were usurped by Lamaist Buddhist and through the decentralization and feminization of the n's role in Siberian shamanic societies. With state forma- nstitutional religion gains power and pushes traditional tional religious practices and beliefs to the margins of where women may become shamans as men become ist lamas. In many ways state or institutionalized religion timizes shamanism.

fundamental element of "hunting shamanism" is that of animal species are contacted directly by a shaman nakes compacts with them in order to supply humans good luck at hunting. The divinely inspired and expe- d shaman-spirit compacts assure food availability for n consumption. This compact is not conceived as one- in that while animal spirits supply humans with food h hunting successes, the other half of the compact is that is will eventually supply the spirits with human flesh ood. Such is the source and cause of much human sick- nd death. The task, however, is for the shaman to limit ount of human sickness and death while maximizing the nt of animal flesh available for human consumption. A n's success at this depends on another kind of compact: his ritual marriage to the daughter of the game spirit (an reindeer spirit).

exchanges and compacts established between spirit- ls and humans make them trading partners in an ongoing mic and social relationship. The relationship is a form of lized reciprocity where the exchanges are never equally ed and immediate in return. Rather, delayed and non- lent exchanges keep the relationship alive and in need tinual tinkering by the shaman and spirit(s). To balance eir reciprocity would mean an end to their relationship. a shaman's power resides in his ability to maintain this ocity. His authority in the human community, therefore, from his usefulness to his peers, in the shaman's ability ure a plentiful supply of game animals while minimizing ss and death.

The human-animal compacts—of food and marriage—serve as the model of social organization. The dualistic spirit-human relationship is replicated in human-animal relations and in the human kinship system of moieties or clan subdivisions. Here, too, in the human world of marriage alliances, society is predicated on compacts between moieties just as the shaman makes compacts with the animal-spirit world.

Reliance on the domestication of animals (pastoralism) presents a second type of Siberian shamanism and is related to alterations in inheritance patterns which are linked to changes in social organization which is in turn linked to a transformation in conceptions of the supernatural. With "pastoral shamanism," no longer does food flow directly from compacts made in the supernatural world but it instead derives from various locations in the observable environment where grazing and herding occur. For the Tungus, pasturage is associated with patrilineal descent groups (in this case, clan segments), and nearby mountains become the locations where ancestors reside after death. Patrilocal residence becomes important and land or pasture inheritance follows the male line. Sickness is no longer caused by animal spirits but is associated with transgressions of patrilineal kinship rules and by one's ancestral spirits. Pastoral shamans do not make compacts with spirit animals, nor do they ritually marry the daughter of the game spirit as food comes from other sources. Here the shaman's role changes in that it is entrusted with ensuring the fertility of both the domesticated animals and human villagers. Pastoralist shamans are related to tribal mythology where the shaman is synonymous with the tribal founder.

Here we see that even the classic Siberian shamanism takes several forms. Importantly, the forms are related to the mode of subsistence, social organization, residence patterns, and whether the shaman has intimate contact with animal spirits or deceased ancestor spirits who participate with the shaman in ongoing reciprocal exchanges.

Tohono O'odham Christian-Shamanism

The Tohono O'odham (formerly known as Papago) of southern Arizona and northern Sonora, Mexico, were gatherer-hunters and horticulturalists until the early part of the twentieth century.[12] This form of shamanism is comparable to the hunting shamanism of Siberia. Their subsistence strategy made the best of an existence in the heart of the Sonoran Desert where scarce and unpredictable rainfall made growing corn, beans, and squash very tenuous. Despite this, O'odham subsistence practices emphasized the importance of rain and crop production. In fact, O'odham ritual life—both individual and public—centered around moisture. The public ritual of the annual rain ceremony focused the community's religious sentiments on securing adequate moisture for plant, animal, and human consumption.

Village well-being was symbolized by sufficient rainfall, and the village shaman was in part responsible for securing it. Shamans worked together to sing for, divine, and encourage the rains to fall. They directed the annual rain festivities by overseeing the production of a mildly intoxicating wine brewed from the syrup of saguaro cactus fruits. During the rain dance ceremony, shamans from various villages gave speeches and sang songs to attract the rain clouds from the "rain houses" positioned at the cardinal directions. The proper execution of the ceremony secured the ultimate fertility of the natural and human worlds.

The other central role of O'odham shamans was to diagnose a series of sicknesses unique to the O'odham people. Until the middle of the twentieth century it was thought in O'odham cosmology and medical theory that there were approximately 50 "staying sicknesses" (only O'odham contract them) that were caused by the spirit protectors of various animal-persons (e.g., deer, badger, coyote), insect-persons (e.g., fly, butterfly), natural phenomena-persons (e.g., wind, lightning), humans (e.g., ghosts, prostitutes), plant-persons (e.g., peyote, jimson weed), reptile-persons (e.g., rattle snake, chuckwalla), and bird-persons (e.g., eagle, owl, swallow) species. Being sickened is the result of a human's impropriety or disrespect toward or transgression on the integrity of the spirit species. The person does not know the moment that sickness is contracted, but once symptoms emerge, the person consults a shaman for diagnosis. Once diagnosed, which can take a quick or a protracted form, the person is instructed to have the appropriate curing songs sung for them.

A shaman's ability to diagnose, and to cure, derives from spirit helpers who tutor the shaman during nighttime dreams. Thus spirits both cause sicknesses and provide the means for their cure. This tutoring takes the form of learning songs that are authored and sung by the spirit species to the shaman who memorizes them verbatim. The songs are densely meaningful, haiku-like poems that tell brief stories of experiences that the shaman has had with the spirit, present images of a landscape, or are statements about the quirkiness of the spirit itself.

This version of O'odham shamanism has been modified during the past three hundred years of contact with Spanish, then Mexican, and finally with American colonizers and Catholic missionaries. Catholicism has made significant inroads in O'odham religious culture since their early contact with the Jesuit priest Eusebio Kino in the late 1690s. Catholicism continues to be a strong element of O'odham identity. Another significant source of change came with the introduction of cattle into the U.S. Southwest regional economy. The external influences of Catholicism and cattle capitalism prompted changes in O'odham shamanism in several ways. First, shamans gained power from Christian deities as spirit tutelaries, primarily the saints, but Jesus and God also, just as they did from the traditional spirit-beings. As the O'odham adopted Catholic public rituals and theological beliefs, and as they began to adopt saints for village patrons and for individuals, people began to be sickened by these Christian spirits in a manner similar to that described above. Saint sickness became an illness diagnosed and treated by shamans.

Second, the O'odham also began, by the late 1880s, to be sickened by the instruments of frontier capitalism—cattle and horses (known collectively as devil sickness). O'odham readily adopted a cowboy lifestyle and are still cattle ranchers to this day. Here too O'odham shamans became charged with the responsibility of contending with the new contagions. Today, devil sickness is thought by some O'odham to be the most commonly diagnosed staying sickness.

Saint and devil sicknesses in the O'odham theory o ness and cure represent what I call Christian-shamanis only do shamans continue to use the traditional tools of t smoke, eagle and owl feathers, and crystals to augmer power in diagnostic sessions, but many shamans also use images, a Christian cross, and holy water. Perhaps more is the fact that the Christian deities (spirits) also come mans in the same manner as the traditional spirits—in d singing and tutoring their human pupils in the diagnosti ing art and science.

Christian-shamanism can be understood as a manife of significant political, religious, and economic chang affected this culture. For the O'odham, shamanism ha effectively used to attend to and ameliorate the change ceived in the three-hundred-year plus period of colonizati missionization. Some might conclude that the O'odha manic system as described has been "corrupted" or "po by the Christian influence. I do not think so, nor do I thi most O'odham think so either. In many ways, the O'odh merely using all that is available to them to make thei better and healthier.

Shamanism, Terror, and the Putumayo of Colombia

By the turn of the twentieth century, in the industrializing the demand for rubber expanded quickly. Far from the cr cities of London, Los Angeles, Chicago, and Paris, the mayo Indians of the sparsely populated lowland Ama jungles of southern Colombia were being forcibly incorp into the Industrial Revolution as rubber tree tappers. This poration was often violent and terrifying. To coerce wc of this recalcitrant labor force, the Putumayo Indians we jected to systematic torture, murder, and sexual abuses troubling period in Putumayo and Colombian social l continues to haunt and permeate the present in the form *aire* (evil wind)[13] and in the shamanistic beliefs and pr that heal it. Current shamanic practice can be partly unde as an attempt to ameliorate the unquiet souls of the vi tortured and murdered Putumayo Indians of the southern zon jungle.[14]

Michael Taussig argues in his provocative book *Sh ism, Colonialism, and the Wild Man* that contemporary y hallucinogenic drink) shamanism in southern Colombi effort to heal the tortured memories of the violently killec mayo Indians. Sorcery and evil air are the two sickness shamans currently treat. It is the latter that stems directl rubber tapping and Christianization. Currently, both India non-Indians of the region view the ancient ones, call Huitoto (ancestral Putumayo), as sorcerers, demonic, an Huitoto means "the people from below"— below the g and below in the jungles. They were the people conc during the Spanish conquest, people who were labele viewed by Europeans as evil, devil worshipping idolater Spanish times. The ideology of the Spanish was that the violent, sorcerers, cannibals, and thus fearsome. This logically charged characterization persisted until the ti r exploration and production. The image of the savage and of the wild, primordial jungles struck fear in the of the rubber plantation managers. The managers saw conspiracies and treachery everywhere. In their zeal to t rubber and labor, company managers hired and trained to carry out retribution stemming from their fears of the ge" Putumayo. Rumors of the atrocities committed by bber companies led to an investigation and the eventual ation of Sir Roger Casement's revealing report in 1912 substantiated the rumors' veracity.

e violent memories created in the colonial, and later the list, contexts revisioned the shamanism of the region. ess was now thought to be caused by the evil airs emanat- om below in the jungles, from the rotting evil ancestors es) buried beneath the ground. This miasmatic theory is uated by locals, native and nonnative alike.

this context, according to Taussig, Putumayo shamanism ve all else a healing of history, a healing of the excesses ristian ideology and capitalist extraction. It is as if the r set the stage for the latter. Hence, for the Putumayo, nism is the method through which people attend to the c memories embedded in the history of the region. It is as history-as-sorcery that today's Putumayo shamans strive e.

e three examples come nowhere near exhausting the pos- thnographic variation that continues to exist in the world Research into questions of history, global economy, and tation add to an already rich anthropological literature on aman's ASC, personality, and phenomenological char- stics. It is through a continued documentation of local ssions of shamanism, juxtaposed to macrolevel processes, ur understanding will be improved in this most dynamic of human spirituality.

nclusion

terest and study of shamanism has a long and often check- istory. Shamanism storytellings are varied and continue tightly bound to the defining culture's attitude toward nous peoples and their cultural practices. In the 1990s nisms have not only been tolerated but they have also xulted as the true, authentic religious expression worthy ulation. As discussed, this admiration has not always been eferred story. Yet, this admiration, while meant with the f intentions, must also be seen as potentially problematic, s yet another way people use shamanism in other than ntended contexts. And whether shamanisms are exalted igrated, both are equally stereotypic responses. It is my ion that shamans and shamanisms will continue to serve etorical needs of members of Western or other dominant ies. It appears that the need for people to tell stories about people remains strong. It also appears to matter not that ories are only loosely, at best, based in empirical reality. s I began this essay, it is important to remember that the s we tell about others may say more about ourselves than those of whom we supposedly tell the stories.

Notes

1. The combined reviews of Jane Monnig Atkinson, "Shamanisms Today," *Annual Review of Anthropology* 21:307–330, 1992, and Joan B. Townsend, "Shamanism," in Stephan Glazier, ed., *Anthropology of Religion: A Handbook* (Westport, CT: Greenwood Press, 1997), offer a wide-ranging and thorough overview of the subjects. One book by religious studies scholar Margaret Stutley, *Shamanism: An Introduction* (London: Routledge, 2003) provides general descriptive materials of shamanism throughout the world.
2. Perhaps most strident in this regard is Michael Taussig, who argues in "The Nervous System: Homesickness and Dada," *Stanford Humanities Review* 1(1):44–81, 1989, that shamanism is a "made-up," "artful reification of disparate practices" that are the creations of academic programs such as religious studies and anthropology. Much earlier, Clifford Geertz in "Religion as a Cultural System," in Michael Banton, ed., *Anthropological Approaches to the Study of Religion* (London: Tavistock, 1966), came to the same conclusion as Taussig. What Taussig and Geertz criticize are the overly large generalizations and characterizations that anthropologists and others have made of shamanisms, and, particularly for Taussig, how such characterizations reflect Western notions of religiosity. More recently, anthropologist Alice Kehoe takes up this critical stance in *Shamans and Religion: An Anthropological Exploration in Critical Thinking* (Prospect Heights, IL: Waveland Press, 2000).
3. Among the most influential of both anthropology and popular interest in shamanism are Eliade's *Shamanism: Archaic Techniques of Ecstacy* (Princeton, NJ: Princeton University Press, 1964); Casteñada's *The Teachings of Don Juan: A Yaqui Way of Knowledge* (New York: Ballantine Books, 1968); Harner's *Hallucinogens and Shamanism* (Oxford: Oxford University Press, 1973); and Hultkrantz's various articles on the subject: "An Ecological Approach to Religion," *Ethos* 31:131–150, 1966; "Spirit Lodge: A North American Shamanistic Seance," in Carl-Martin Edsman, ed., *Studies in Shamanism* (Stockholm: Almqvist and Wiksell, 1967); and "A Definition of Shamanism," *Temenos* 9:25–37, 1973. Of these works, it is perhaps the first two that have had the longest and most profound impact on shamanic studies in general and popular consciousness in particular.
4. Alice Kehoe in "Primal Gaia," in J. Clifton, ed., *The Invented Indian* (Somerset, NJ: Transaction Press, 1990); Michael Winkelman in "Shamans and Other 'Magico-Religious' Healers," *Ethos* 18(3):308–352, 1990; Ake Hultkrantz in "Ecological and Phenomenological Aspects of Shamanism, in L. Backman and A. Hultkrantz, eds. *Studies in Lapp Shamanism* (Stockholm: Almquivst and Wiksell, 1978); J.D. Lewis-Williams and T. Dowson in "The Signs of All Times," *Current Anthropology* 29(2):201–245, 1988; and Peter Furst in "The Roots and Continuities of Shamanism," in A. Brodzky, R. Daneswich, and N. Johnson, eds., *Stones, Bones, and Skin* (Toronto: Society for Art Publications, 1977), offer various perspectives of the paleolithic origins question. In general, origins are traced to the Siberian and Arctic shamanisms and are considered the "classic" form. Yet others such as Sergei Shirokogoroff in *Psychomental Complex of the Tungus* (London: Kegan Paul, Trench, Trubner and Company, 1935) and Mircea Eliade in *Shamanism: Archaic Techniques of Ecstacy* (Princeton, NJ: Princeton University Press, 1964), postulate that Buddhist Lamaism drastically modified Tungus shamanism. Thus, one version of origins suggests that shamanisms have a Tibetan source.
5. J.D. Lewis-Williams's name is synonymous with the work on entoptic phenomena. His works *Believing and Seeing* (New York: Academic Press, 1981) and "Cognitive and Optical

Illusions in San Rock Art," *Current Anthropology* 27:171–178, 1986 are exemplary in this regard. See also his collaboration with T.A. Dowson, "The Signs of All Times," 1988, and "On Vision and Power in the Neolithic," *Current Anthropology* 34:55–65, 1993.

6. *Piman Shamanism and Staying Sickness* by Donald Bahr, Juan Gregorio, David Lopez, and Albert Alvarez (Tucson: University of Arizona Press, 1974) stands out as one of the first and is still one of the finest discussions between a shaman, Gregorio, an anthropologist, Donald Bahr, and two native speaker-translators, Lopez and Alvarez. Bahr has also written on shamanic song texts in "A Grey and Fervent Shamanism," *Journal of the Society of the Americas,* 67:7–26, 1991. Other collaborative and innovative work has been completed by Larry Evers and Felipe Molina in *Yaqui Deer Songs* (Tucson: University of Arizona Press, 1987), Jane Monnig Atkinson's *Wana Shamanship* (Berkeley: University of California Press, 1989), Anna Siikala's "Two Types of Shamanizing and Categories of Shamanistic Songs," in L. Honko and V. Voigt, eds., *Akademiai Kiado* (Budapest, 1980), and in B. Walraven's *Muga: The Songs of Korean Shamanism* (Dordredt: ICG Printing, 1985). A general beautifully illustrated guide to Native American Indian shamanism is Norman Bancroft Hunt, *Shamanism in North America* (Buffalo, NY: Firefly Books, 2003).
7. For arguments against the mentally ill shaman stereotype, see Alfred Kroeber, *The Nature of Culture* (Chicago: University of Chicago Press, 1952); L.B. Boyer, "Shamans: To Set the Record Straight," *American Anthropologist* 71(2):307–309, 1969; D. Handelman, "Shamanizing on an Empty Stomach," *American Anthropologist* 70(2):353–356, 1968; and George Murdock, "Tenino Shamanism," *Ethnology* 4:165–171, 1965, among others.
8. The desire to empirically ground the study of shamanic consciousness has led to this interesting version of a biopsychological approach. For a general discussion of this hypothesis, see C. Laughlin, J. McManus, and E. d'Aquili, *Brain, Symbol and Experience: Toward a Neurophenomenology of Consciousness* (New York: Columbia University Press, 1992) and Michael Winkelman, "Trance States: A Theoretical Model and Cross-Cultural Analysis," *Ethos* 14(2):174–203, 1986, and "Altered States of Consciousness and Religious Behavior," in S. Glazier, ed., *Anthropology of Religion* (Westport, CT: Greenwood Press, 1997).
9. A few recent examples of this work include Michael Tau *Shamanism, Colonialism, and the Wild Man* (Chicago: University of Chicago Press, 1987); N. Thomas and C. Humphrey's edited volume *Shamanism, History, and the State* (Ann Arbor: University of Michigan Press, 1994); a Atkinson's book cited in Endnote 6.
10. Refer to C. Humphrey's "Shamanic Practices and the Sta Northern Asia," in Nicholas Thomas and Carolyn Humph eds., *Shamanism, History and the State* (Ann Arbor: Univ of Michigan Press, 1994).
11. This section on Siberian shamanism draws heavily from two works of R. Hamayon: *La Chasse à l'âme: Esquisse d'une Theorie du Chamanisme Siberien* (Société d'ethno Nanterre, 1990) and "Shamanism in Siberia," in N. Thom C. Humphrey, eds., *Shamanism, History, and the State* (A Arbor: University of Michigan Press, 1994). Her researc writing are exemplary for placing shamanism into a nuan format rather than reifying much of what is assumed to b about Siberian shamanism. See also Caroline Humphrey' "Shamanic Practices and the State in Northern Asia," in N Thomas and C. Humphrey, eds., *Shamanism, History, an State* (Ann Arbor: University of Michigan Press, 1994).
12. This section on Tohono O'odham shamanism is based on r own research in various communities on the Sells Reserva and on several published monographs. See Ruth Underhill classic, *Papago Indian Religion* (New York: Columbia Uni Press, 1946) and the collaborative work *Piman Shamanism and Staying Sickness* by Donald Bahr, Juan Gregorio, Davi Lopez, and Albert Alvarez (Tucson: University of Arizona 1974). For a detailed treatment of a single staying sickness my *Devil Sickness and Devil Songs: Tohono O'odham Poe* (Washington, DC: Smithsonian Institution Press, 1999).
13. Mal aire is a widespread "folk" illness found throughout of North and South America as well as in parts of Europe air sickness in the New World is thought by most observe be an import from the Old World.
14. This case study relies on the intriguing and ingenious wo M. Taussig, "History as Sorcery," *Representations* 7:87–1 1984, and *Shamanism, Colonialism, and the Wild Man* (Chicago: University of Chicago Press, 1987).

David Kozak Fort Lewis College.

he Adaptive Value of Religious Ritual

ıals promote group cohesion by requiring members to engage in behavior : is too costly to fake.

IARD SOSIS

as 15 years old the first time I went to Jerusalem's Old City ıd visited the 2,000-year-old remains of the Second Tem- e, known as the Western Wall. It may have foreshadowed ure life as an anthropologist, but on my first glimpse of the t stones I was more taken by the people standing at the f the structure than by the wall itself. Women stood in en sun, facing the Wall in solemn worship, wearing long- d shirts, head coverings and heavy skirts that scraped the d. Men in their thick beards, long black coats and fur hats emed oblivious to the summer heat as they swayed fer- and sang praises to God. I turned to a friend, "Why would e in their right mind dress for a New England winter only ıd the afternoon praying in the desert heat?" At the time I ıt there was no rational explanation and decided that my religious brethren might well be mad.

course, "strange" behavior is not unique to ultraorthodox Many religious acts appear peculiar to the outsider. Pious nts the world over physically differentiate themselves others: Moonies shave their heads, Jain monks of India contraptions on their heads and feet to avoid killing s, and clergy almost everywhere dress in outfits that uish them from the rest of society. Many peoples also e in some form of surgical alteration. Australian aborigi- rform a ritual operation on adolescent boys in which a or a stone is inserted into the penis through an incision in ethra. Jews and Muslims submit their sons to circumci- nd in some Muslim societies daughters are also subject umcision or other forms of genital mutilation. Groups erse as the Nuer of Sudan and the latmul of New Guinea their adolescents to undergo ritual scarification. Initia- remonies, otherwise known as rites of passage, are often Among Native Americans, Apache boys were forced to n icy water, Luiseno initiates were required to lie motion- hile being bitten by hordes of ants, and Tukuna girls had air plucked out.

w can we begin to understand such behavior? If human are rational creatures, then why do we spend so much energy and resources on acts that can be so painful or, at ry least, uncomfortable? Archaeologists tell us that our species has engaged in ritual behavior for at least 100,000 years, and every known culture practices some form of religion. It even survives covertly in those cultures where governments have attempted to eliminate spiritual practices. And, despite the unparalleled triumph of scientific rationalism in the 20th century, religion continued to flourish. In the United States a steady 40 percent of the population attended church regularly throughout the century. A belief in God (about 96 percent), the afterlife (about 72 percent), heaven (about 72 percent) and hell (about 58 percent) remained substantial and remarkably constant. Why do religious beliefs, practices and institutions continue to be an essential component of human social life?

Such questions have intrigued me for years. Initially my training in anthropology did not provide an answer. Indeed, my studies only increased my bewilderment. I received my training in a subfield known as human behavioral ecology, which studies the adaptive design of behavior with attention to its ecological setting. Behavioral ecologists assume that natural selection has shaped the human nervous system to respond successfully to varying ecological circumstances. All organisms must balance trade-offs: Time spent doing one thing prevents them from pursuing other activities that can enhance their survival or reproductive success. Animals that maximize the rate at which they acquire resources, such as food and mates, can maximize the number of descendants, which is exactly what the game of natural selection is all about.

Behavioral ecologists assume that natural selection has designed our decision-making mechanisms to optimize the rate at which human beings accrue resources under diverse ecological conditions—a basic prediction of *optimal foraging theory.* Optimality models offer predictions of the "perfectly adapted" behavioral response, given a set of environmental constraints. Of course, a perfect fit with the environment is almost never achieved because organisms rarely have perfect information and because environments are always changing. Nevertheless, this assumption has provided a powerful framework to analyze a variety of decisions, and most research (largely conducted among foraging populations) has shown that our species broadly conforms to these expectations.

If our species is designed to optimize the rate at which we extract energy from the environment, why would we engage in religious behavior that seems so counterproductive? Indeed, some religious practices, such as ritual sacrifices, are a conspicuous display of wasted resources. Anthropologists can explain why foragers regularly share their food with others in the group, but why would anyone share their food with a dead ancestor by burning it to ashes on an altar? A common response to this question is that people believe in the efficacy of the rituals and the tenets of the faith that give meaning to the ceremonies. But this response merely begs the question. We must really ask why natural selection has favored a psychology that believes in the supernatural and engages in the costly manifestations of those beliefs.

Ritual Sacrifice

Behavioral ecologists have only recently begun to consider the curiosities of religious activities, so at first I had to search other disciplines to understand these practices. The scholarly literature suggested that I wasn't the only one who believed that intense religious behavior was a sign of madness. Some of the greatest minds of the past two centuries, such as Marx and Freud, supported my thesis. And the early anthropological theorists also held that spiritual beliefs were indicative of a primitive and simple mind. In the 19th century, Edward B. Tylor, often noted as one of the founding fathers of anthropology, maintained that religion arose out of a misunderstanding among "primitives" that dreams are real. He argued that dreams about deceased ancestors might have led the primitives to believe that spirits can survive death.

Eventually the discipline of anthropology matured, and its practitioners moved beyond the equation that "primitive equals irrational." Instead, they began to seek functional explanations of religion. Most prominent among these early 20th-century theorists was the Polish-born anthropologist Bronislaw Malinowski. He argued that religion arose out of "the real tragedies of human life, out of the conflict between human plans and realities." Although religion may serve to allay our fears of death, and provide comfort from our incessant search for answers, Malinowski's thesis did not seem to explain the origin of rituals. Standing in the midday desert sun in several layers of black clothing seems more like a recipe for increasing anxiety than treating it. The classical anthropologists didn't have the right answers to my questions. I needed to look elsewhere.

Fortunately, a new generation of anthropologists has begun to provide some explanations. It turns out that the strangeness of religious practices and their inherent costs are actually the critical features that contribute to the success of religion as a universal cultural strategy and why natural selection has favored such behavior in the human lineage. To understand this unexpected benefit we need to recognize the adaptive problem that ritual behavior solves. William Irons, a behavioral ecologist at Northwestern University, has suggested that the universal dilemma is the promotion of cooperation within a community. Irons argues that the primary adaptive benefit of religion is its ability to facilitate cooperation within a group—while hunting, sharing defending against attacks and waging war—all critical ac in our evolutionary history. But, as Irons points out, alt everyone is better off if everybody cooperates, this ideal i very difficult to coordinate and achieve. The problem is individual is even better off if everyone else does the c ating, while he or she remains at home enjoying an aft siesta. Cooperation requires social mechanisms that p individuals from free riding on the efforts of others. Irons that religion is such a mechanism.

The key is that religious rituals are a form of communi which anthropologists have long maintained. They bor this insight from ethologists who observed that many s engage in patterned behavior, which they referred to as " Ethologists recognized that ritualistic behaviors served as of communication between members of the same specie often between members of different species. For examp males of many avian species engage in courtship rituals- as bowing, head wagging, wing waving and hopping (many other gestures)—to signal their amorous intents be prospective mate. And, of course, the vibration of a rattles tail is a powerful threat display to other species that er personal space.

Irons's insight is that religious activities signal comm to other members of the group. By engaging in the ritu member effectively says, "I identify with the group and I b in what the group stands for." Through its ability to signa mitment, religious behavior can overcome the problem riders and promote cooperation within the group. It d because trust lies at the heart of the problem: A membe assure everyone that he or she will participate in acq food or in defending the group. Of course, hunters an riors may make promises—"you have my word, I'll sh tomorrow"—but unless the trust is already established statements are not believable.

It turns out that there is a robust way to secure trust. biologist Amotz Zahavi observes that it is often in the bes est of an animal to send a dishonest signal—perhaps to f size, speed, strength, health or beauty. The only signal th be believed is one that is too costly to fake, which he refe as a "handicap." Zahavi argues that natural selection has f the evolution of handicaps. For example, when a spri antelope spots a predator it often *stots*—it jumps up and This extraordinary behavior puzzled biologists for years would an antelope waste precious energy that could be u escape the predator? And why would the animal make more visible to something that wants to eat it? The re that the springbok is displaying its quality to the predat ability to escape, effectively saying, "Don't bother chasi Look how strong my legs are, you won't be able to catc The only reason a predator believes the springbok is b the signal is too costly to fake. An antelope that is not enough to escape cannot imitate the signal because it strong enough to repeatedly jump to a certain height. a display can provide honest information if the signals costly to perform that lower quality organisms cannot by imitating the signal.

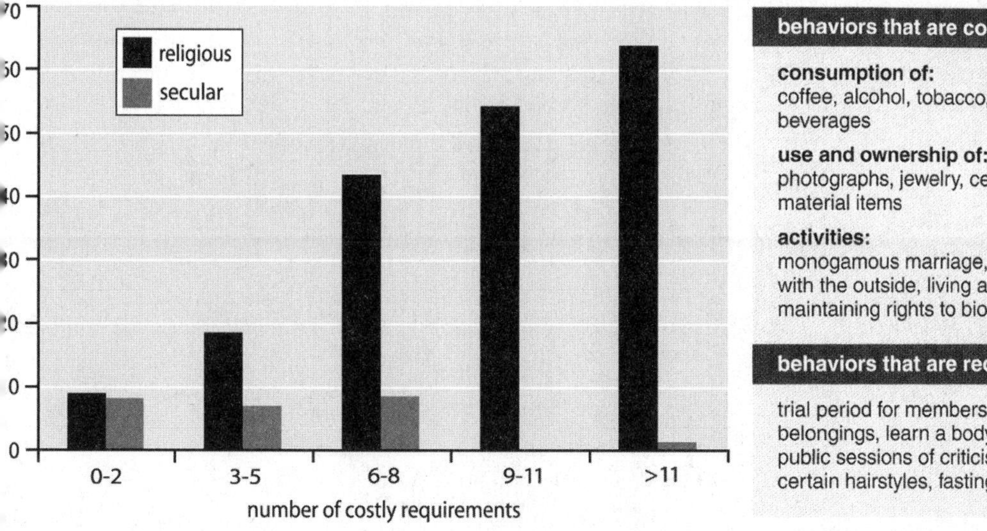

behaviors that are constrained

consumption of:
coffee, alcohol, tobacco, meat, other foods or beverages

use and ownership of:
photographs, jewelry, certain technology, other material items

activities:
monogamous marriage, gambling, communication with the outside, living as a nuclear family, maintaining rights to biological children

behaviors that are required

trial period for membership, surrender of material belongings, learn a body of knowledge, endure public sessions of criticism, certain clothing styles, certain hairstyles, fasting

nuch the same way, religious behavior is also a costly By donning several layers of clothing and standing out in dday sun, ultraorthodox Jewish men are signaling to oth- ley! Look, I'm a *haredi* Jew. If you are also a member of oup you can trust me because why else would I be dressed s? No one would do this *unless* they believed in the teach- f ultraorthodox Judaism and were fully committed to its and goals." The quality that these men are signaling is vel of commitment to a specific religious group.

ierence to a set of religious beliefs entails a host of ritual ions and expected behaviors. Although there may be al or psychological benefits associated with some rit- ictices, the significant time, energy and financial costs ed serve as effective deterrents for anyone who does not in the teachings of a particular religion. There is no ve for nonbelievers to join or remain in a religious group, e the costs of maintaining membership—such as praying imes a day, eating only kosher food, donating a certain your income to charity and so on—are simply too high. se who engage in the suite of ritual requirements imposed ligious group can be trusted to believe sincerely in the es of their respective religious communities. As a result eased levels of trust and commitment among group mem- eligious groups minimize costly monitoring mechanisms e otherwise necessary to overcome free-rider problems pically plague communal pursuits. Hence, the adaptive of ritual behavior is its ability to promote and maintain ation, a challenge that our ancestors presumably faced hout our evolutionary history.

efits of Membership

ediction of the "costly signaling theory of ritual" is that that impose the greatest demands on their members will ie highest levels of devotion and commitment. Only com- members will be willing to dress and behave in ways ffer from the rest of society. Groups that maintain more- tted members can also offer more because it's easier for attain their collective goals than groups whose members are less committed. This may explain a paradox in the religious marketplace: Churches that require the most of their adherents are experiencing rapid rates of growth. For example, the Church of Jesus Christ of Latter-day Saints (Mormons), Seventh-day Adventists and Jehovah's Witnesses, who respectively abstain from caffeine, meat and blood transfusions (among other things), have been growing at exceptional rates. In contrast, liberal Protestant denominations such as the Episcopalians, Methodists and Presbyterians have been steadily losing members.

Economist Lawrence Iannaccone, of George Mason University, has also noted that the most demanding groups also have the greatest number of committed members. He found that the more distinct a religious group was—how much the group's lifestyle differed from mainstream America—the higher its attendance rates at services. Sociologists Roger Finke and Rodney Stark, of Penn State and the University of Washington, respectively, have argued that when the Second Vatican Council in 1962 repealed many of the Catholic Church's prohibitions and reduced the level of strictness in the church, it initiated a decline in church attendance among American Catholics and reduced the enrollments in seminaries. Indeed, in the late 1950s almost 75 percent of American Catholics were attending Mass weekly, but since the Vatican's actions there has been a steady decline to the current rate of about 45 percent.

The costly signaling theory of ritual also predicts that greater commitment will translate into greater cooperation within groups. My colleague Eric Bressler, a graduate student at McMaster University, and I addressed this question by looking at data from the records of 19th-century communes. All communes face an inherent problem of promoting and sustaining cooperation because individuals can free ride on the efforts of others. Because cooperation is key to a commune's survival, we employed commune longevity as a measure of cooperation. Compared to their secular counterparts, the religious communes did indeed demand more of their members, including such behavior as celibacy, the surrender of all material possessions and vegetarianism. Communes that demanded more of their members survived longer, overcoming the fundamental challenges of cooperation. By placing greater demands on their

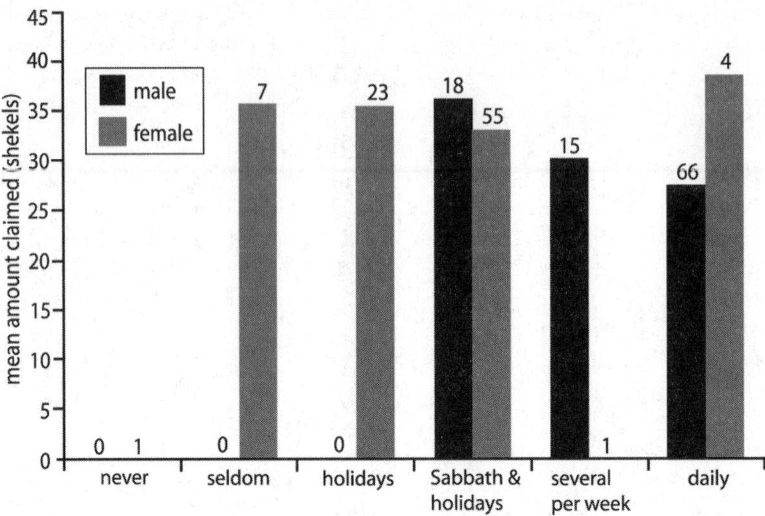

members, they were presumably able to elicit greater belief in and commitment toward the community's common ideology and goals.

I also wanted to evaluate the costly signaling theory of ritual within modern communal societies. The kibbutzim I had visited in Israel as a teenager provided an ideal opportunity to examine these hypotheses. For most of their 100-year history, these communal societies have lived by the dictum, "From each according to his abilities, to each according to his needs." The majority of the more than 270 kibbutzim are secular (and often ideologically antireligious); fewer than 20 are religiously oriented. Because of a massive economic failure—a collective debt of more than $4 billion—the kibbutzim are now moving in the direction of increased privatization and reduced communality. When news of the extraordinary debt surfaced in the late 1980s, it went largely unnoticed that the religious kibbutzim were financially stable. In the words of the Religious Kibbutz Movement Federation, "the economic position of the religious kibbutzim is sound, and they remain uninvolved in the economic crisis."

The success of the religious kibbutzim is especially remarkable given that many of their rituals inhibit economic productivity. For example, Jewish law does not permit Jews to milk cows on the Sabbath. Although rabbinic rulings now permit milking by kibbutz members to prevent the cows from suffering, in the early years none of this milk was used commercially. There are also significant constraints imposed by Jewish law on agricultural productivity. Fruits are not allowed to be eaten for the first few years of the tree's life, agricultural fields must lie fallow every seven years, and the corners of fields can never be harvested—they must be left for society's poor. Although these constraints appear detrimental to productivity, the costly signaling theory of ritual suggests that they may actually be the key to the economic success of the religious kibbutzim.

I decided to study this issue with economist Bradley Ruffle of Israel's Ben Gurion University. We developed a game to determine whether there were differences in how the members of secular and religious kibbutzim cooperated with each other. The game involves two members from the same kibbutz who remain anonymous to each other. Each member is told there are 100 shekels in an envelope to which both member access. Each participant decides how many shekels to wit and keep. If the sum of both requests exceeds 100 shekel members receive no money and the game is over. Howe the requests are less than or equal to 100 shekels, the remaining in the envelope is increased by 50 percent and d evenly among the participants. Each member also kee original amount he or she requested. The game is an exan a common-pool resource dilemma in which publicly acc goods are no longer available once they are consumed. Si goods are available to more than one person, the mainten the resources requires individual self-restraint; in other cooperation.

After we controlled for a number of variables, inc the age and size of the kibbutz and the amount of pri tion, we found not only that religious kibbutzniks were cooperative with each other than secular kibbutzniks, b male religious kibbutz members were also significantly cooperative than female members. Among secular kibbu we found no sex differences at all. This result is unde able if we appreciate the types of rituals and demands in on religious Jews. Although there are a variety of require that are imposed equally on males and females, such as ing kosher and refraining from work on the Sabbath, ma als are largely performed in public, whereas female ritu generally pursued privately. Indeed, none of the three requirements imposed exclusively on women—attendin ual bath, separating a portion of dough when baking bre lighting Shabbat and holiday candles—are publicly perf They are not rituals that signal commitment to a wider instead they appear to signal commitment to the family however, engage in highly visible rituals, most notably prayer, which they are expected to perform three times Among male religious kibbutz members, synagogue atte is positively correlated with cooperative behavior. Ther similar correlation among females. This is not surprisin that women are not required to attend services, and so the ence does not signal commitment to the group. Here the signaling theory of ritual provides a unique explanation c ıgs. We expect that further work will provide even more ht into the ability of ritual to promote trust, commitment ooperation.

'e know that many other species engage in ritual behav- hat appear to enhance trust and cooperation. For example, opologists John Watanabe of Dartmouth University and ara Smuts at the University of Michigan have shown that ings between male olive baboons serve to signal trust and nitment between former rivals. So why are human ritu- ften cloaked in mystery and the supernatural? Cognitive opologists Scott Atran of the University of Michigan and l Boyer at Washington University in St. Louis have pointed at the counterintuitive nature of supernatural concepts are easily remembered than mundane ideas, which facilitates cultural transmission. Belief in supernatural agents such ds, spirits and ghosts also appears to be critical to reli- s ability to promote long-term cooperation. In our study of century communes, Eric Bressler and I found that the strong ve relationship between the number of costly require- imposed on members and commune longevity only held igious communes, not secular ones. We were surprised by esult because secular groups such as militaries and frater- appear to successfully employ costly rituals to maintain ration. Cultural ecologist Roy Rappaport explained, how- that although religious and secular rituals can both pro- cooperation, religious rituals ironically generate greater and commitment because they sanctify unfalsifiable ıents that are beyond the possibility of examination. Since ıents containing supernatural elements, such as "Jesus is n of God," cannot be proved or disproved, believers verify "emotionally." In contrast to religious propositions, the z's guiding dictum, taken from Karl Marx, is not beyond on; it can be evaluated by living according to its direc- y distributing labor and resources appropriately. Indeed, economic situation on the kibbutzim has worsened, this nental proposition of kibbutz life has been challenged and disregarded by many who are pushing their communi- accept differential pay scales. The ability of religious to evoke emotional experiences that can be associated nduring supernatural concepts and symbols differentiates rom both animal and secular rituals and lies at the heart of fficiency in promoting and maintaining long-term group ration and commitment.

olutionary research on religious behavior is in its infancy, any questions remain to be addressed. The costly signal- eory of ritual appears to provide some answers, and, of , it has given me a better understanding of the questions I as a teenager. The real value of the costly signaling theory al will be determined by its ability to explain religious mena across societies. Most of us, including ultraorthodox Jews, are not living in communes. Nevertheless, contemporary religious congregations that demand much of their members are able to achieve a close-knit social community—an impressive accomplishment in today's individualistic world.

Religion has probably always served to enhance the union of its practitioners; unfortunately, there is also a dark side to this unity. If the intragroup solidarity that religion promotes is one of its significant adaptive benefits, then from its beginning religion has probably always played a role in intergroup conflicts. In other words, one of the benefits for individuals of intragroup solidarity is the ability of unified groups to defend and compete against other groups. This seems to be as true today as it ever was, and is nowhere more apparent than the region I visited as a 15-year-old boy—which is where I am as I write these words. As I conduct my fieldwork in the center of this war zone, I hope that by appreciating the depth of the religious need in the human psyche, and by understanding this powerful adaptation, we can learn how to promote cooperation rather than conflict.

References

Atran, S. 2002. *In Gods We Trust.* New York: Oxford University Press.

Iannaccone, L. 1992. Sacrifice and stigma: Reducing free-riding in cults, communes, and other collectives. *Journal of Political Economy* 100:271–291.

Iannaccone, L. 1994. Why strict churches are strong. *American Journal of Sociology* 99:1180–1211.

Irons, W. 2001. Religion as a hard-to-fake sign of commitment. In *Evolution and the Capacity for Commitment,* ed. R. Nesse, pp. 292–309. New York: Russell Sage Foundation.

Rappaport, R. 1999. *Ritual and Religion in the Making of Humanity.* Cambridge: Cambridge University Press.

Sosis, R. 2003. Why aren't we all Hutterites? Costly signaling theory and religious behavior. *Human Nature* 14:91–127.

Sosis, R., and C. Alcorta. 2003. Signaling, solidarity, and the sacred: The evolution of religious behavior. *Evolutionary Anthropology* 12:264–274.

Sosis, R., and E. Bressler. 2003. Cooperation and commune longevity: A test of the costly signaling theory of religion. *Cross-Cultural Research* 37:211–239.

Sosis, R., and B. Ruffle. 2003. Religious ritual and cooperation: Testing for a relationship on Israeli religious and secular kibbutzim. *Current Anthropology* 44:713–722.

Zahavi, A., and A. Zahavi. 1997. *The Handicap Principle.* New York: Oxford University Press.

Richard Sosis is an assistant professor of anthropology at the University of Connecticut. His research interests include the evolution of cooperation, utopian societies and the behavioral ecology of religion. Address: Department of Anthropology, U-2176, University of Connecticut, Storrs, CT 06269–2176. Internet: richard.sosis@uconn.edu

Article 27

Understanding Islam

KENNETH JOST

Is Islam Compatible with Western Values?

With more than 1 billion adherents, Islam is the world's second-largest religion after Christianity. Within its mainstream traditions, Islam teaches piety, virtue and tolerance. Ever since the Sept. 11, 2001, terrorist attacks in the United States, however, many Americans have associated Islam with the fundamentalist groups that preach violence against the West and regard "moderate" Muslims as heretics. Mainstream Muslims and religious scholars say Islam is wrongly blamed for the violence and intolerance of a few. But some critics say Muslims have not done enough to oppose terrorism and violence. They also contend that Islam's emphasis on a strong relationship between religion and the state is at odds with Western views of secularism and pluralism. Some Muslims are calling for a more progressive form of Islam. But radical Islamist views are attracting a growing number of young Muslims in the Islamic world and in Europe.

Overview

Aishah Azmi was dressed all in black, her face veiled by a *niqab* that revealed only her brown eyes through a narrow slit.

"Muslim women who wear the veil are not aliens," the 24-year-old suspended bilingual teaching assistant told reporters in Leeds, England, on Oct. 19. "Integration [of Muslims into British society] requires people like me to be in the workplace so that people can see that we are not to be feared or mistrusted."

But school officials defended their decision to suspend Azmi for refusing to remove her veil in class with a male teacher, saying it interfered with her ability to communicate with her students—most of them Muslims and, like Azmi, British Asians.

"The school and the local authority had to balance the rights of the children to receive the best quality education possible and Mrs. Azmi's desire to express her cultural beliefs," said local Education Minister Jim Dodds.

Although an employment tribunal rejected Azmi's discrimination and harassment claims, it said the school council had handled her complaint poorly and awarded her 1,100 British pounds—about $2,300.

Azmi's widely discussed case has become part of a wrenching debate in predominantly Christian England over relations with the country's growing Muslim population.

In September, a little more than a year after subwa bus bombings in London claimed 55 lives, a govern minister called on Muslim parents to do more to steer children away from violence and terrorism. Then, in Oct a leaked report being prepared by the interfaith advis the Church of England complained that what he calle government's policy of "privileged attention" toward lims had backfired and was creating increased "disaffe and separation."

The simmering controversy grew even hotter after Straw, leader of the House of Commons and former foreig retary under Prime Minister Tony Blair, called full-face ve visible statement of separation and difference" that pro separatism between Muslims and non-Muslims. Straw, constituency in northwestern England includes an esti 25 percent Muslim population aired the comments in a newspaper column.

Hamid Qureshi, chairman of the Lancashire Coun Mosques, called Straw's remarks "blatant Muslim-bashin

"Muslims feel they are on center stage, and everyb Muslim-bashing," says Anjum Anwar, the council's direc education. "They feel very sensitive."

Britain's estimated 1.5 million Muslims—comprising r Pakistani or Indian immigrants and their British-born child are only a tiny fraction of Islam's estimated 1.2 billion adh worldwide. But the tensions surfacing in the face-veil exemplify the increasingly strained relations between th dominantly Christian West and the Muslim world.

The world's two largest religions—Christianity has 2 billion adherents—have had a difficult relationship a since the time of the European Crusades against Musli ers, or caliphs, almost 1,000 years ago. Mutual suspici hostility have intensified since recent terrorist attacks a the world by militant Islamic groups and President Geo Bush proclaimed a worldwide "war on terror" in response Sept. 11, 2001, attacks in the United States.

Bush, who stumbled early on by referring to a "cr against terrorism, has tried many times since then to perceptions of any official hostility toward Islam or M generally. In Britain, Blair's government has carried on year-old policy of "multiculturalism" aimed at promoting sion among the country's various communities, Musl particular.

spite those efforts, widespread distrust of Islam and Mus- prevails on both sides of the Atlantic. In a recent poll in nited States, 45 percent of those surveyed said they had an orable view of Islam—a higher percentage than registered milar poll four years earlier.

itish Muslim leaders also say they feel increasingly hos- nti-Muslim sentiments from the general public and gov- nt officials. "Muslims are very fearful, frustrated, upset, ," says Asghar Bukhari, a spokesman for the Muslim Pub- fairs Committee in London. "It's been almost like a mental t on the Muslim psyche here."

the face-veil debate illustrates, the distrust stems in part an array of differences between today's Christianity and as variously practiced in the so-called Muslim world, ing the growing Muslim diaspora in Europe and North ca.

broad terms, Islam generally regards religion as a more ive presence in daily life and a more important source vil law than contemporary Christianity, according to the author Paul Grieve, who wrote a comprehensive guide m after studying Islamic history and thought for more hree years. "Islam is a system of rules for all aspects of Grieve writes, while Western liberalism limits regulation sonal behavior. In contrast to the secular nation-states of est, he explains, Islam views the ideal Muslim society as ersal community—such as the *ummah* established by the et Muhammed in the seventh century.

se theological and cultural differences are reflected, says, in Westerners' widespread view of Muslims as -minded and extremist. Many Muslims correspondingly Vesterners as decadent and immoral.

differences also can be seen in the debates over the role plays in motivating terrorist violence by Islamic extremist s such as al Qaeda and the objections raised by Muslims to ney consider unflattering and unfair descriptions of Islam West.

slim leaders generally deny responsibility for the violence tted by Islamic terrorists, including the 9/11 terrorist in the United States and subsequent attacks in Indonesia, nd England. "Muslim organizations have done more than efore in trying to advance community cohesion," Anwar They also deny any intention to deny freedom of expres- ven though Muslims worldwide denounced a Danish car- 's satirical portrayal of Muhammad and Pope Benedict citation of a medieval Christian emperor's description of s a violent religion.

many Westerners, however, Islam is associated with Muslims—known as Islamists—who either advocate ear to condone violence and who take to the streets to unfavorable depictions of Islam. "A lot of traditional or te Islam is inert," says Paul Marshall, a senior fellow at m House's Center for Religious Freedom in Washington. of the people who disagree with radicals don't have a bed position. They keep their heads down."

nwhile, many Muslims and non-Muslims alike despair n's sometimes fratricidal intrafaith disputes. Islam split the first decades of its founding in the seventh century into the Sunni and Shiite (Shia) branches. The Sunni-Shiite conflict helps drive the escalating insurgency in Iraq three years after the U.S.-led invasion ousted Saddam Hussein, a Sunni who pursued generally secularist policies. "A real geopolitical fracturing has taken place in the Muslim world since the end of the colonial era," says Reza Aslan, an Iranian-born Shiite Muslim now a U.S. citizen and author of the book *No god but God.*

The tensions between Islam and the West are on the rise as Islam is surging around the world, growing at an annual rate of about 7 percent. John Voll associate director of the Prince Alwaleed bin Talal Centre for Christrian-Muslim Understanding at Georgetown University, notes that the growth is due largely to conversions, not the high birth rates that are driving Hinduism's faster growth.

Moreover, Voll says, Muslims are growing more assertive. "There has been an increase in intensity and an increase in strength in the way Muslims view their place in the world and their place in society," he says.

Teaching assistant Azmi's insistence on wearing the *niqab* exemplifies the new face of Islam in parts of the West. But her choice is not shared by all, or even, most of her fellow Muslim women. "I don't see why she needs to wear it," says Anwar. "She's teaching young children under 11." (Azmi says she wears it because she works with a male classroom teacher.)

Muslim experts generally agree the Koran does not require veils, only modest dress. Observant Muslim women generally comply with the admonition with a head scarf and loose-fitting attire. In particularly conservative cultures, such as Afghanistan under Taliban rule, women cover their entire bodies, including their eyes.

Still, despite the varying practices, many Muslim groups see a disconnect between the West's self-proclaimed tolerance and its pressure on Muslims to conform. "It's a Muslim woman's right to dress as she feels appropriate, given her religious views," says Ibrahim Hooper, director of communications for the Council on American-Islamic Relations in Washington. "But then when somebody actually makes a choice, they're asked not to do that."

Indeed, in Hamtramck, Mich., a judge recently came under fire for throwing out a small-claims case because the Muslim plaintiff refused to remove her full-face veil.

As the debates continue, here are some of the questions being considered:

Is Islam a Religion That Promotes Violence?

Within hours of the London subway and bus bombings on July 7, 2005, the head of the Muslim World League condemned the attacks as un-Islamic. "The heavenly religions, notably Islam, advocate peace and security," said Abdallah al-Turki, secretary-general of the Saudi-funded organization based in Mecca.

The league's statement echoed any number of similar denunciations of Islamist-motivated terrorist attacks issued since 9/11 by Muslims in the United States and around the world. Yet many non-Muslim public officials, commentators, experts and others say Muslims have not done enough to speak out against terrorism committed in the name of their religion.

"Mainstream Muslims have not stepped up to the plate, by and large," says Angel Rabasa, a senior fellow at the Rand Corp., a California think tank, and lead author of a U.S. Air Force-sponsored study, *The Muslim World after 9/11.*

Muslim organizations voice indignant frustration in disputing the accusation. "We can always do more," says Hooper. "The problem is that it never seems to be enough. But that doesn't keep us from trying."

Many Americans, in fact, believe Islam actually encourages violence among its adherents. A CBS poll in April 2006 found that 46 percent of those surveyed believe Islam encourages violence more than other religions. A comparable poll four years earlier registered a lower figure: 32 percent.

Those perceptions are sometimes inflamed by U.S. evangelical leaders. Harsh comments about Islam have come from religious leaders like Franklin Graham, Jerry Falwell, Pat Robertson and Jerry Vines, the former president of the Southern Baptist Convention. Graham called Islam "a very evil and wicked religion," and Vines called Muhammad, Islam's founder and prophet, a "demon-possessed pedophile." Falwell, on the CBS news magazine "60 Minutes" in October 2002, declared, "I think Muhammad was a terrorist."

Mainstream Muslims insist Islam is a peaceful religion and that terrorist organizations distort its tenets and teachings in justifying attacks against the West or other Muslims. But Islamic doctrine and history sometimes seem to justify the use of violence in propagating or defending the faith. The dispute revolves around the meaning of *jihad,* an Arabic word used in the Koran and derived from a root meaning "to strive" or "to make an effort for." Muslim scholars can point to verses in the Koran that depict *jihad* merely as a personal, spiritual struggle and to others that describe *jihad* as encompassing either self-defense or conquest against non-believers.

Georgetown historian Voll notes that, in contrast to Christianity, Islam achieved military success during Muhammad's life and expanded into a major world empire within decades afterward. That history "reinforces the idea that militancy and violence can, in fact, be part of the theologically legitimate plan of the Muslim believer," says Voll.

"Islam, like all religions, has its historical share of violence," acknowledges Stephen Schwartz, an adult convert to Islam and executive director of the Center for Islamic Pluralism in Washington. "But there's no reason to single out Islam."

Modern-day jihadists pack their public manifestos with Koranic citations and writings of Islamic theologians to portray themselves as warriors for Allah and defenders of true Islam. But Voll and others stress that the vast majority of Muslims do not subscribe to their views. "You have a highly visible minority that represents a theologically extreme position in the Muslim world," Voll says.

In particular, writes Seyyed Hossein Nasr, a professor of Islamic studies at George Washington University, Islamic law prohibits the use of force against women, children or civilians—even during war. "Inflicting injuries outside of this context," he writes, "is completely forbidden by Islamic law."

Rabasa says, however, that Muslims who disapprove of terrorism have not said enough or done enough to mobilize opposition to terrorist attacks. "Muslims see themselves as part of a c nity and are reluctant to criticize radical Muslims," he say

In addition, many Muslims are simply intimidated from ing out, he explains. "Radicals are not reluctant to use v and the threat of violence," he says. Liberal and moderat lims are known to receive death threats on their cell phone in relatively peaceful Muslim countries such as Indonesia

Voll also notes that Islamic radicals have simply o nized the moderates. "There is no moderate organizati even begins to resemble some of the radical organizatio have developed," he says.

In Britain, Bukhari of the Muslim Public Affairs C tee criticizes Muslim leaders themselves for failing to c young people opposed to Britain's pro-U.S. foreign poli non-violent political action. "Children who could hav peaceful react to that foreign policy in a way that they selves become criminals," he says.

The Council on American-Islamic Relations' Hooper several anti-terrorism pronouncements and drives issu lowing the London bombings by various Muslim grou leaders in Britain and in the United States, including *fat* legal opinions, rejecting terrorism and extremism.

For his part, Omid Safi, an associate professor of studies at the University of North Carolina in Chapel Hill out that virtually every Muslim organization in the Unitec issued condemnations of violence almost immediately a 9/11 terrorist attacks.

"How long must we keep answering this question asks in exasperation. But he concedes a few momen that the issue is more than perception. "Muslims must c terms with our demons," he says, "and one of those der violence."

Is Islam Compatible with Secular, Pluralistic Societies?

In 2003, Germany's famed Deutsche Oper staged an garde remake of Mozart's opera "Idomeneo," which dra the composer's criticism of organized religion, with depicting the severed heads of Muhammad, Jesus, Budc Poseidon. That production was mounted without incid the company dropped plans to restage it in Novembe after police warned of a possible violent backlash from fundamentalists.

The cancellation prompted protests from German c and artistic-freedom advocates in Europe and in the States, who saw the move as appeasement toward te Wolfgang Bornsen, a spokesman for conservative Cha Angela Merkel, said the cancellation was "a signal" t artistic companies to avoid any works critical of Islam.

The debate continued even after plans were discu mount the production after all—with enhanced secur the blessing of German Muslim leaders. "We live in where democracy was based on criticizing religion," re Philippe Val, editor of the French satirical magazine *Hebdo.* "If we lose the right to criticize or attack religion free countries . . . we are doomed."

vith the issue of violence, Islam's doctrines and history viewed as pointing both ways on questions of pluralism erance. "There are a great many passages [in the Koran] pport a pluralistic interpretation of Islam," says the Rand Rabasa. "But you also find a great many that would sup- intolerant interpretation."

tellectual pluralism is traditional Islam," says Schwartz Center for Islamic Pluralism. An oft-quoted verse from an specifically prohibits compulsion in religion, he says. d other historians agree that Muslim countries generally d Christians and Jews, though they were often subject to taxes or other restrictions.

lam is the only major religious system that has built- ections for minorities," says Hooper at the Council on an-Islamic Relations. "You don't see the kind of perse- of minorities that we often saw in Europe for hundreds s. Many members of the Jewish community fled to find vithin the Muslim world."

n so, Islam's view of religion and politics as inseparable difficult issues. Outside the Arab world, most Muslims practicing democracies with fair to good human-rights . But some Muslim countries—Arab and non-Arab— her adopted or been urged to adopt provisions of Islamic *haria*—that are antithetical to modern ideas of human such as limiting women's rights and prescribing stoning itations as criminal penalties.

lims participating in a society as a minority population ferent issues, according to author Grieve. "Islam is diffi- accommodate in a determinedly secular Western society almost all views are equally respected, and none is seen r right or wrong," he writes.

tensions played out in a number of controversies in years were provoked by unflattering depictions of Islam pe. A Danish cartoonist's satirical view of Muhammad ed worldwide protests from Muslim leaders and groups ey were publicized in early 2006. Scattered violence l in property damage and more than 30 deaths.

ewhat similarly, Pope Benedict XVI drew sharp criti- er a Sept. 12, 2006, lecture quoting a medieval Christian r's description of Islam as "evil and inhuman." Along rbal denunciations, protesters in Basra, Iraq, burned an f the pope. Within a week, he disclaimed the remarks logized.

dom House's Marshall says such controversies, as well cancellation of the opera in Berlin, strengthens radical elements. "Bending to more radical demands marginal- voices of moderate Muslims and hands over leadership adicals," he says.

y Muslims in European countries, however, view the ersies—including the current debate over the veil in l—as evidence of pervasive hostility from the non- majorities. "There is a growing hatred of Muslims in and anybody who bashes Muslims can only get brownie says Bukhari of the Muslim Public Affairs Committee. ese are not friendly times for Western Muslims," says the University of North Carolina. "Whenever people find themselves under assault, opening their arms and opening their hearts is difficult."

Basic Tenets of Islam

Islam is the youngest of the world's three major monotheistic religions. Like the other two, Judaism and Christianity, Islam (the word means both "peace" and "submission") holds there is but one God (Allah). Muslims believe God sent a number of prophets to teach mankind how to live according to His law. Muslims consider Jesus, Moses and Abraham as prophets of God and hold the Prophet Muhammad as his final and most sacred messenger. Many accounts found in Islam's sacred book, the Koran (Qur'an), are also found in sacred writings of Jews and Christians.

There are five basic pillars of Islam:

- Creed—Belief in God and Muhammad as his Prophet.
- Almsgiving—Giving money to charity is considered a sacred duty.
- Fasting—From dawn to dusk during the month of Ramadan.
- Prayer—Five daily prayers must be given facing Mecca, Islam's holiest city.
- Pilgrimage—All Muslims must make a baff to Mecca at least once during their lifetime, if they are physically able.

Does Islam Need a "Reformation"?

If Pakistan's Punjab University expected a chorus of approval when it decided to launch a master's program in musicology in fall 2006, it was in for a surprise. At the Lahore campus, the conservative Islamic Assembly of Students, known as I.J.T., rose up in protest.

Handbills accused school authorities of forsaking Islamic ideological teachings in favor of "the so-called enlightened moderation" dictated by "foreign masters." Undeterred, administrators opened the program for enrollment in September. When fewer students applied than expected, they blamed the poor response in part on the I.J.T. campaign.

The episode reflects how Islam today is evolving differently in the West and in some parts of the Muslim world. Many Muslim writers and scholars in the United States and Europe are calling for Islam to adapt to modern times by, for example, embracing pluralism and gender equality. Introducing a collection of essays by "progressive" Muslims, the University of North Carolina's Safi says the movement seeks to "start swimming through the rising waters of Islam and modernity, to strive for justice in the midst of society."

In much of the Muslim world, however, Islam is growing—in numbers and intensity—on the strength of literal interpretations of the Koran and exclusivist attitudes toward the non-Muslim world. "In the Muslim world in general, more extreme or reactionary forms of Islam are getting stronger—in Africa, Asia and the Middle East," says Freedom House's Marshall, who has previously worked on issues pertaining to persecution of Christians around the world.

Islamist groups such as I.J.T. talk about "reforming" or "purifying" Islam and adopting Islamic law as the primary or exclusive source of civil law. In fact, one version of reformed Islam—Wahhabism* or the currently preferred term Salafism—espouses a literalistic reading of the Koran and a puritanical stance toward such modern practices as listening to music or watching television. It has been instituted in Saudi Arabia and has advanced worldwide because of financial backing from the oil-rich kingdom and its appeal to new generations of Muslims.

"The Salafi movement is a fringe," says the Rand Corp.'s Rabasa. "But it's growing because it's dynamic and revolutionary, whereas traditional Islam tends to be conservative. It has this appeal to young people looking for identity."

But the Center for Islamic Pluralism's Schwartz, an outspoken critic of Salafism, says many Muslims are rejecting it because of its tendency to view other branches of Islam as apostasy. "People are getting sick of this," he says. "They're tired of the social conflict and upheaval."

Voll at the Center for Christian-Muslim Understanding also says some Muslim legal scholars are disputing literalistic readings of *sharia* by contending that the Islamic law cited as divinely ordained is actually "a human construct subject to revision."

Some Western commentators refer to a "reformation" in calling for a more liberal form of Islam. Nicholas D. Kristof, a *New York Times* columnist who focuses on global human-rights issues, sees "hopeful rumblings . . . of steps toward a Muslim Reformation," especially on issues of gender equality. He notes that feminist Muslim scholars are reinterpreting passa the Koran that other Muslims cite in justifying restricti women, such as the Saudi ban on women driving.

Safi says he avoids the term reformation because it ha adopted by Salafists and also because it suggests a need t from traditional Islam. He says "progressive" Muslims to the Prophet's vision of the common humanity of all beings and seek "to hold Muslim societies accountable tice and pluralism."

Rabasa also says reformation is historically inapprop a goal for liberal or progressive Muslims. "What is ne not an Islamic reformation but an Islamic enlightenmen Rabasa. The West's liberal tradition, he notes, was produ by the Reformation but by the Enlightenment—the 18th-c movement that used reason to search for objective truth.

Whatever terms are used, the clash between different of Islam will be less susceptible to resolution than analog putes within most branches of Christianity because Islam la recognized hierarchical structure. Islam has no pope or go council. Instead, each believer is regarded as having a dire tionship with God, or Allah, with no ecclesiastical interme

"In the face of contemporary Islam, there is absolut sense of an authority vacuum," says Safi. Islam's fut adds, "is a question that can only be answered by Musli

Note

*Wahhabism originated in the Arabian peninsula in the late 17 from the teachings of Arabian theologian Muhammand ibn Ab Wahhab (1703–1792).

he Secrets of Haiti's Living Dead

arvard botanist investigates mystic potions, voodoo rites, the making of zombies.

o Del Guercio

ive years ago, a man walked into l'Estère, a village in central Haiti, approached a peasant woman named Angelina Narcisse, and identified himself as her brother Clairvius. ad not introduced himself using a boyhood nickname and oned facts only intimate family members knew, she would ve believed him. Because, eighteen years earlier, Angelina ood in a small cemetery north of her village and watched brother Clairvius was buried.

e man told Angelina he remembered that night well. He when he was lowered into his grave, because he was fully ous, although he could not speak or move. As the earth rown over his coffin, he felt as if he were floating over ave. The scar on his right cheek, he said, was caused by a iven through his casket.

e night he was buried, he told Angelina, a voodoo priest him from the grave. He was beaten with a sisal whip and d off to a sugar plantation in northern Haiti where, with zombies, he was forced to work as a slave. Only with the of the zombie master were they able to escape, and Narventually returned home.

gend has it that zombies are the living dead, raised from raves and animated by malevolent voodoo sorcerers, usur some evil purpose. Most Haitians believe in zombies, arcisse's claim is not unique. At about the time he reapl, in 1980, two women turned up in other villages saying ere zombies. In the same year, in northern Haiti, the local nts claimed to have found a group of zombies wandering ssly in the fields.

t Narcisse's case was different in one crucial respect; it ocumented. His death had been recorded by doctors at nerican-directed Schweitzer Hospital in Deschapelles. On 30, 1962, hospital records show, Narcisse walked into the al's emergency room spitting up blood. He was feverish ll of aches. His doctors could not diagnose his illness, and mptoms grew steadily worse. Three days after he entered spital, according to the records, he died. The attending cians, an American among them, signed his death certifiHis body was placed in cold storage for twenty hours, and e was buried. He said he remembered hearing his doctors unce him dead while his sister wept at his bedside.

At the Centre de Psychiatrie et Neurologie in Port-au-Prince, Dr. Lamarque Douyon, a Haitian-born, Canadian-trained psychiatrist, has been systematically investigating all reports of zombies since 1961. Though convinced zombies were real, he had been unable to find a scientific explanation for the phenomenon. He did not believe zombies were people raised from the dead, but that did not make them any less interesting. He speculated that victims were only made to *look* dead, probably by means of a drug that dramatically slowed metabolism. The victim was buried, dug up within a few hours, and somehow reawakened.

The Narcisse case provided Douyon with evidence strong enough to warrant a request for assistance from colleagues in New York. Douyon wanted to find an ethnobotanist, a traditional-medicines expert, who could track down the zombie potion he was sure existed. Aware of the medical potential of a drug that could dramatically lower metabolism, a group organized by the late Dr. Nathan Kline—a New York psychiatrist and pioneer in the field of psychopharmacology—raised the funds necessary to send someone to investigate.

The search for that someone led to the Harvard Botanical Museum, one of the world's foremost institutes of ethnobiology. Its director, Richard Evans Schultes, Jeffrey professor of biology, had spent thirteen years in the tropics studying native medicines. Some of his best-known work is the investigation of curare, the substance used by the nomadic people of the Amazon to poison their darts. Refined into a powerful muscle relaxant called D-tubocurarine, it is now an essential component of the anesthesia used during almost all surgery.

Schultes would have been a natural for the Haitian investigation, but he was too busy. He recommended another Harvard ethnobotanist for the assignment, Wade Davis, a 28-year-old Canadian pursuing a doctorate in biology.

Davis grew up in the tall pine forests of British Columbia and entered Harvard in 1971, influenced by a *Life* magazine story on the student strike of 1969. Before Harvard, the only Americans he had known were draft dodgers, who seemed very exotic. "I used to fight forest fires with them," Davis says. "Like everybody else, I thought America was where it was at. And I wanted to go to Harvard because of that Life article. When I got there, I realized it wasn't quite what I had in mind."

Davis took a course from Schultes, and when he decided to go to South America to study plants, he approached his professor for guidance. "He was an extraordinary figure," Davis remembers. "He was a man who had done it all. He had lived alone for years in the Amazon." Schultes sent Davis to the rain forest with two letters of introduction and two pieces of advice: wear a pith helmet and try ayahuasca, a powerful hallucinogenic vine. During that expedition and others, Davis proved himself an "outstanding field man," says his mentor. Now, in early 1982, Schultes called him into his office and asked if he had plans for spring break.

"I always took to Schultes's assignments like a plant takes to water," says Davis, tall and blond, with inquisitive blue eyes. "Whatever Schultes told me to do, I did. His letters of introduction opened up a whole world." This time the world was Haiti.

Davis knew nothing about the Caribbean island—and nothing about African traditions, which serve as Haiti's cultural basis. He certainly did not believe in zombies. "I thought it was a lark," he says now.

Davis landed in Haiti a week after his conversation with Schultes, armed with a hypothesis about how the zombie drug—if it existed—might be made. Setting out to explore, he discovered a country materially impoverished, but rich in culture and mystery. He was impressed by the cohesion of Haitian society; he found none of the crime, social disorder, and rampant drug and alcohol abuse so common in many of the other Caribbean islands. The cultural wealth and cohesion, he believes, spring from the country's turbulent history.

During the French occupation of the late eighteenth century, 370,000 African-born slaves were imported to Haiti between 1780 and 1790. In 1791, the black population launched one of the few successful slave revolts in history, forming secret societies and overcoming first the French plantation owners and then a detachment of troops from Napoleon's army, sent to quell the revolt. For the next hundred years Haiti was the only independent black republic in the Caribbean, populated by people who did not forget their African heritage. "You can almost argue that Haiti is more African than Africa," Davis says. "When the west coast of Africa was being disrupted by colonialism and the slave trade, Haiti was essentially left alone. The amalgam of beliefs in Haiti is unique, but it's very, very African."

Davis discovered that the vast majority of Haitian peasants practice voodoo, a sophisticated religion with African roots. Says Davis, "It was immediately obvious that the stereotypes of voodoo weren't true. Going around the countryside, I found clues to a whole complex social world." Vodounists believe they communicate directly with, indeed are often possessed by, the many spirits who populate the everyday world. Vodoun society is a system of education, law, and medicine; it embodies a code of ethics that regulates social behavior. In rural areas, secret vodoun societies, much like those found on the west coast of Africa, are as much or more in control of everyday life as the Haitian government.

Although most outsiders dismissed the zombie phenomenon as folklore, some early investigators, convinced of its reality, tried to find a scientific explanation. The few who sought a zombie drug failed. Nathan Kline, who helped finance Davis's expedition, had searched unsuccessfully, as had Lam Douyon, the Haitian psychiatrist. Zora Neale Hurstc American black woman, may have come closest. An antl logical pioneer, she went to Haiti in the Thirties, studied v society, and wrote a book on the subject, *Tell My Hors* published in 1938. She knew about the secret societies ar convinced zombies were real, but if a power existed, s failed to obtain it.

Davis obtained a sample in a few weeks.

He arrived in Haiti with the names of several conta BBC reporter familiar with the Narcisse case had sugges talk with Marcel Pierre. Pierre owned the Eagle Bar, a bo in the city of Saint Marc. He was also a voodoo sorcer had supplied the BBC with a physiologically active pow unknown ingredients. Davis found him willing to negotia told Pierre he was a representative of "powerful but anon interests in New York," willing to pay generously for the p services, provided no questions were asked. Pierre agree helpful for what Davis will only say was a "sizable sum." spent a day watching Pierre gather the ingredients—inc human bones—and grind them together with mortar and However, from his knowledge of poison, Davis knew im ately that nothing in the formula could produce the po effects of zombification.

Three weeks later, Davis went back to the Eagle Bar, he found Pierre sitting with three associates. Davis chall him. He called him a charlatan. Enraged, the priest gave second vial, claiming that this was the real poison. Davi tended to pour the powder into his palm and rub it into hi "You're a dead man," Pierre told him, and he might have because this powder proved to be genuine. But, as the sub had not actually touched him, Davis was able to mainta bravado, and Pierre was impressed. He agreed to make th son and show Davis how it was done.

The powder, which Davis keeps in a small vial, look dry black dirt. It contains parts of toads, sea worms, li tarantulas, and human bones. (To obtain the last ingredie and Pierre unearthed a child's grave on a nocturnal trip cemetery.) The poison is rubbed into the victim's skin. hours he begins to feel nauseated and has difficulty brea A pins-and-needles sensation afflicts his arms and legs progresses to the whole body. The subject becomes para his lips turn blue for lack of oxygen. Quickly—som within six hours—his metabolism is lowered to a level indistinguishable from death.

As Davis discovered, making the poison is an inexact sc Ingredients varied in the five samples he eventually acc although the active agents were always the same. And the came with no guarantee. Davis speculates that sometimes i of merely paralyzing the victim, the compound kills him. times the victim suffocates in the coffin before he can be rected. But clearly the potion works well enough often eno make zombies more than a figment of Haitian imaginatior

Analysis of the powder produced another surprise. "W went down to Haiti originally," says Davis, "my hypothes that the formula would contain *concombre zombi,* the 'zo cucumber,' which is a *Datura* plant. I thought somehow *L*

ichard Schultes

is students continue his tradition of pursuing botanical esearch in the likeliest of unlikely places.

ichard Evans Schultes, Jeffrey professor of biology emeri-
ıs, has two homes, and they could not be more different. he first is Cambridge, where he served as director of the arvard Botanical Museum from 1970 until last year, when e became director emeritus. During his tenure he interested enerations of students in the exotic botany of the Amazon ain forest. His impact on the field through his own research ; worldwide. The scholarly ethnobotanist with steel-rimmed lasses, bald head, and white lab coat is as much a part of e Botanical Museum as the thousands of plant specimens nd botanical texts on the museum shelves.

In his austere office is a picture of a crew-cut, younger ıan stripped to the waist, his arms decorated with tribal aint. This is Schultes's other persona. Starting in 1941, he pent thirteen years in the rain forests of South America, ving with the Indians and studying the plants they use for edicinal and spiritual purposes.

Schultes is concerned that many of the people he has tudied are giving up traditional ways. "The people of so-alled primitive societies are becoming civilized and losing l their forefathers' knowledge of plant lore," he says. "We'll e losing the tremendous amounts of knowledge they've ained over thousands of years. We're interested in the ractical aspects with the hope that new medicines and ther things can be developed for our own civilization."

Schultes's exploits are legendary in the biology department. Once, while gathering South American plant specimens hundreds of miles from civilization, he contracted beri-beri. For forty days he fought creeping paralysis and overwhelming fatigue as he paddled back to a doctor. "It was an extraordinary feat of endurance," says disciple Wade Davis. "He is really one of the last nineteenth-century naturalists."

Hallucinogenic plants are one of Schultes's primary interests. As a Harvard undergraduate in the Thirties, he lived with Oklahoma's Kiowa Indians to observe their use of plants. He participated in their peyote ceremonies and wrote his thesis on the hallucinogenic cactus. He has also studied other hallucinogens, such as morning glory seeds, sacred mushrooms, and ayahuasca, a South American vision vine. Schultes's work has led to the development of anesthetics made from curare and alternative sources of natural rubber.

Schultes's main concern these days is the scientific potential of plants in the rapidly disappearing Amazon jungle. "If chemists are going to get material on 80,000 species and then analyze them, they'll never finish the job before the jungle is gone," he says. "The short cut is to find out what the [native] people have learned about the plant properties during many years of living in the very rich flora."

—G.D.G.

sed in putting people down." *Datura* is a powerful psycho- plant, found in West Africa as well as other tropical areas sed there in ritual as well as criminal activities. Davis had *Datura* growing in Haiti. Its popular name suggested the was used in creating zombies.

t, says Davis, "there were a lot of problems with the *Dat-* ypothesis. Partly it was a question of how the drug was iistered. *Datura* would create a stupor in huge doses, but wouldn't produce the kind of immobility that was key. people had to appear dead, and there aren't many drugs ill do that."

e of the ingredients Pierre included in the second formula dried fish, a species of puffer or blowfish, common to parts of the world. It gets its name from its ability to fill with water and swell to several times its normal size when ened by predators. Many of these fish contain a powerful n known as tetrodotoxin. One of the most powerful non-n poisons known to man, tetrodotoxin turned up in every e of zombie powder that Davis acquired.

merous well-documented accounts of puffer fish poison-ist, but the most famous accounts come from the Orient, *fugu* fish, a species of puffer, is considered a delicacy. an, special chefs are licensed to prepare *fugu*. The chef es enough poison to make the fish nonlethal, yet enough ns to create exhilarating physiological effects—tingles d down the spine, mild prickling of the tongue and lips, euphoria. Several dozen Japanese die each year, having bitten off more than they should have.

"When I got hold of the formula and saw it was the *fugu* fish, that suddenly threw open the whole Japanese literature," says Davis. Case histories of *fugu* poisoning read like accounts of zombification. Victims remain conscious but unable to speak or move. A man who had "died" after eating *fugu* recovered seven days later in the morgue. Several summers ago, another Japanese poisoned by *fugu* revived after he was nailed into his coffin. "Almost all of Narcisse's symptoms correlated. Even strange things such as the fact that he said he was conscious and could hear himself pronounced dead. Stuff that I thought had to be magic, that seemed crazy. But, in fact, that is what people who get *fugu*-fish poisoning experience."

Davis was certain he had solved the mystery. But far from being the end of his investigation, identifying the poison was, in fact, its starting point. "The drug alone didn't make zombies," he explains. "Japanese victims of puffer-fish poisoning don't become zombies, they become poison victims. All the drug could do was set someone up for a whole series of psychological pressures that would be rooted in the culture. I wanted to know why zombification was going on," he says.

He sought a cultural answer, an explanation rooted in the structure and beliefs of Haitian society. Was zombification simply a random criminal activity? He thought not. He had discovered that Clairvius Narcisse and "Ti Femme," a second victim he interviewed, were village pariahs. Ti Femme was regarded as a thief. Narcisse had abandoned his children and deprived his brother of land that was rightfully his. Equally suggestive, Narcisse claimed that his aggrieved brother had sold him to a *bokor,* a voodoo priest who dealt in black magic; he made cryptic reference to having been tried and found guilty by the "masters of the land."

Gathering poisons from various parts of the country, Davis had come into direct contact with the vodoun secret societies. Returning to the anthropological literature on Haiti and pursuing his contacts with informants, Davis came to understand the social matrix within which zombies were created.

Davis's investigations uncovered the importance of the secret societies. These groups trace their origins to the bands of escaped slaves that organized the revolt against the French in the late eighteenth century. Open to both men and women, the societies control specific territories of the country. Their meetings take place at night, and in many rural parts of Haiti the drums and wild celebrations that characterize the gatherings can be heard for miles.

Davis believes the secret societies are responsible for policing their communities, and the threat of zombification is one way they maintain order. Says Davis, "Zombification has a material basis, but it also has a societal logic." To the uninitiated, the practice may appear a random criminal activity, but in rural vodoun society, it is exactly the opposite—a sanction imposed by recognized authorities, a form of capital punishment. For rural Haitians, zombification is an even more severe punishment than death, because it deprives the subject of his most valued possessions: his free will and independence.

The vodounists believe that when a person dies, his spirit splits into several different parts. If a priest is powerful enough, the spiritual aspect that controls a person's character and individuality, known as *ti bon ange,* the "good little angel," can be captured and the corporeal aspect, deprived of its will, held as a slave.

From studying the medical literature on tetrodotoxin poisoning, Davis discovered that if a victim survives the first few hours of the poisoning, he is likely to recover fully from the ordeal. The subject simply revives spontaneously. But zombies remain without will, in a trance-like state, a condition vodounists attribute to the power of the priest. Davis thinks it possible that the psychological trauma of zombification may be augmented by *Datura* or some other drug; he thinks zombies may be fed a *Datura* paste that accentuates their disorientation. Still, h the material basis of zombification in perspective: "Te toxin and *Datura* are only templates on which cultural and beliefs may be amplified a thousand times."

Davis has not been able to discover how prevalent z fication is in Haiti. "How many zombies there are is n question," he says. He compares it to capital punishment United States: "It doesn't really matter how many peop electrocuted, as long as it's a possibility." As a sanction in the fear is not of zombies, it's of becoming one.

Davis attributes his success in solving the zombie mys his approach. He went to Haiti with an open mind and imm himself in the culture. "My intuition unhindered by biases me well," he says. "I didn't make any judgments." He com this attitude with what he had learned earlier from his e ences in the Amazon. "Schultes's lesson is to go and liv the Indians as an Indian." Davis was able to participate vodoun society to a surprising degree, eventually even pe ing one of the Bizango societies and dancing in their noc rituals. His appreciation of Haitian culture is apparent. "I body asks me how did a white person get this informatic ask the question means you don't understand Haitians- don't judge you by the color of your skin."

As a result of the exotic nature of his discoveries, Dav gained a certain notoriety. He plans to complete his disse soon, but he has already finished writing a popular acco his adventures. To be published in January by Simon and S ter, it is called *The Serpent and the Rainbow,* after the s that vodounists believe created the earth and the rainbow it married. Film rights have already been optioned; in O Davis went back to Haiti with a screenwriter. But Davis the notoriety in stride. "All this attention is funny," he says years, not just me, but all Schultes's students have had extr nary adventures in the line of work. The adventure is not t point, it's just along the way of getting the data. At the Bot Museum, Schultes created a world unto itself. We didn't we were doing anything above the ordinary. I still don't thi do. And you know," he adds, "the Haiti episode does not be compare to what others have accomplished—particularly S tes himself."

Gino Del Guercio is a national science writer for Unitec International.

ody Ritual among the Nacirema

ACE MINER

he anthropologist has become so familiar with the diversity of ways in which different peoples behave in similar situations that he is not apt to be surprised by even st exotic customs. In fact, if all of the logically possible nations of behavior have not been found somewhere in rld, he is apt to suspect that they must be present in some described tribe. This point has, in fact, been expressed spect to clan organization by Murdock (1949: 71). In this he magical beliefs and practices of the Nacirema present nusual aspects that it seems desirable to describe them as mple of the extremes to which human behavior can go.

fessor Linton first brought the ritual of the Nacirema to ention of anthropologists twenty years ago (1936: 326), culture of this people is still very poorly understood. re a North American group living in the territory between nadian Cree, the Yaqui and Tarahumare of Mexico, and rib and Arawak of the Antilles. Little is known of their though tradition states that they came from the east. ding to Nacirema mythology, their nation was originated ulture hero, Notgnishaw, who is otherwise known for two eats of strength—the throwing of a piece of wampum the river Pa-To-Mac and the chopping down of a cherry which the Spirit of Truth resided.

irema culture is characterized by a highly developed economy which has evolved in a rich natural habitat. much of the people's time is devoted to economic pur- large part of the fruits of these labors and a considerable n of the day are spent in ritual activity. The focus of this y is the human body, the appearance and health of which as a dominant concern in the ethos of the people. While concern is certainly not unusual, its ceremonial aspects sociated philosophy are unique.

fundamental belief underlying the whole system appears nat the human body is ugly and that its natural tendency is ility and disease. Incarcerated in such a body, man's only s to avert these characteristics through the use of the pow- nfluences of ritual and ceremony. Every household has more shrines devoted to this purpose. The more powerful luals in the society have several shrines in their houses fact, the opulence of a house is often referred to in terms number of such ritual centers it possesses. Most houses wattle and daub construction, but the shrine rooms of the more wealthy are walled with stone. Poorer families imitate the rich by applying pottery plaques to their shrine walls.

While each family has at least one such shrine, the rituals associated with it are not family ceremonies but are private and secret. The rites are normally only discussed with children, and then only during the period when they are being initiated into these mysteries. I was able, however, to establish sufficient rapport with the natives to examine these shrines and to have the rituals described to me.

The focal point of the shrine is a box or chest which is built into the wall. In this chest are kept the many charms and magical potions without which no native believes he could live. These preparations are secured from a variety of specialized practitioners. The most powerful of these are the medicine men, whose assistance must be rewarded with substantial gifts. However, the medicine men do not provide the curative potions for their clients, but decide what the ingredients should be and then write them down in an ancient and secret language. This writing is understood only by the medicine men and by the herbalists who, for another gift, provide the required charm.

The charm is not disposed of after it has served its purpose, but is placed in the charm-box of the household shrine. As these magical materials are specific for certain ills, and the real or imagined maladies of the people are many, the charm-box is usually full to overflowing. The magical packets are so numerous that people forget what their purposes were and fear to use them again. While the natives are very vague on this point, we can only assume that the idea in retaining all the old magical materials is that their presence in the charm-box, before which the body rituals are conducted, will in some way protect the worshipper.

Beneath the charm-box is a small font. Each day every member of the family, in succession, enters the shrine room, bows his head before the charm-box, mingles different sorts of holy water in the font, and proceeds with a brief rite of ablution. The holy waters are secured from the Water Temple of the community, where the priests conduct elaborate ceremonies to make the liquid ritually pure.

In the hierarchy of magical practitioners, and below the medicine men in prestige, are specialists whose designation is best translated "holy-mouth-men." The Nacirema have an almost pathological horror and fascination with the mouth, the condition of which is believed to have a supernatural influence on all social relationships. Were it not for the rituals of the mouth, they believe that their teeth would fall out, their gums bleed, their jaws shrink, their friends desert them, and their lovers reject them. (They also believe that a strong relationship exists between oral and moral characteristics. For example, there is a ritual ablution of the mouth for children which is supposed to improve their moral fiber.)

The daily body ritual performed by everyone includes a mouth-rite. Despite the fact that these people are so punctilious about care of the mouth, this rite involves a practice which strikes the uninitiated stranger as revolting. It was reported to me that the ritual consists of inserting a small bundle of hog hairs into the mouth, along with certain magical powders, and then moving the bundle in a highly formalized series of gestures.

In addition to the private mouth-rite, the people seek out a holy-mouth-man once or twice a year. These practitioners have an impressive set of paraphernalia, consisting of a variety of augers, awls, probes, and prods. The use of these objects in the exorcism of the evils of the mouth involves almost unbelievable ritual torture of the client. The holy-mouth-man opens the client's mouth and, using the above mentioned tools, enlarges any holes which decay may have created in the teeth. Magical materials are put into these holes. If there are no naturally occurring holes in the teeth, large sections of one or more teeth are gouged out so that the supernatural substance can be applied. In the client's view, the purpose of these ministrations is to arrest decay and to draw friends. The extremely sacred and traditional character of the rite is evident in the fact that the natives return to the holy-mouth-men year after year, despite the fact that their teeth continue to decay.

It is to be hoped that, when a thorough study of the Nacirema is made, there will be a careful inquiry into the personality structure of these people. One has but to watch the gleam in the eye of a holy-mouth-man, as he jabs an awl into an exposed nerve, to suspect that a certain amount of sadism is involved. If this can be established, a very interesting pattern emerges, for most of the population shows definite masochistic tendencies. It was to these that Professor Linton referred in discussing a distinctive part of the daily body ritual which is performed only by men. This part of the rite involves scraping and lacerating the surface of the face with a sharp instrument. Special women's rites are performed only four times during each lunar month, but what they lack in frequency is made up in barbarity. As part of this ceremony, women bake their heads in small ovens for about an hour. The theoretically interesting point is that what seems to be a preponderantly masochistic people have developed sadistic specialists.

The medicine men have an imposing temple, or *latipso,* in every community of any size. The more elaborate ceremonies required to treat very sick patients can only be performed at this temple. These ceremonies involve not only the thaumaturge but a permanent group of vestal maidens who move sedately about the temple chambers in distinctive costume and headdress.

The *latipso* ceremonies are so harsh that it is phenomenal that a fair proportion of the really sick natives who enter the temple ever recover. Small children whose indoctrination is still incomplete have been known to resist attempts to take t the temple because "that is where you go to die." Desp fact, sick adults are not only willing but eager to unde protracted ritual purification, if they can afford to do matter how ill the supplicant or how grave the emergen guardians of many temples will not admit a client if h not give a rich gift to the custodian. Even after one has admission and survived the ceremonies, the guardians w permit the neophyte to leave until he makes still another

The supplicant entering the temple is first stripped of or her clothes. In every-day life the Nacirema avoids ex of his body and its natural functions. Bathing and ex acts are performed only in the secrecy of the household where they are ritualized as part of the body-rites. Psycl cal shock results from the fact that body secrecy is su lost upon entry into the *latipso.* A man, whose own w never seen him in an excretory act, suddenly finds h naked and assisted by a vestal maiden while he perfor natural functions into a sacred vessel. This sort of cere treatment is necessitated by the fact that the excreta are u a diviner to ascertain the course and nature of the client' ness. Female clients, on the other hand, find their naked are subjected to the scrutiny, manipulation, and prodding medicine men.

Few supplicants in the temple are well enough to do an but lie on their hard beds. The daily ceremonies, like th of the holy-mouth-men, involve discomfort and torture ritual precision, the vestals awaken their miserable charge dawn and roll them about on their beds of pain while pe ing ablutions, in the formal movements of which the m are highly trained. At other times they insert magic wa the supplicant's mouth or force him to eat substances wh supposed to be healing. From time to time the medicin come to their clients and jab magically treated needles in flesh. The fact that these temple ceremonies may not cu may even kill the neophyte, in no way decreases the pe faith in the medicine men.

There remains one other kind of practitioner, know "listener." This witch-doctor has the power to exorcise th ils that lodge in the heads of people who have been bew The Nacirema believe that parents bewitch their own ch Mothers are particularly suspected of putting a curse on cl while teaching them the secret body rituals. The counter- of the witch-doctor is unusual in its lack of ritual. The simply tells the "listener" all his troubles and fears, beg with the earliest difficulties he can remember. The m displayed by the Nacirema in these exorcism sessions i remarkable. It is not uncommon for the patient to b the rejection he felt upon being weaned as a babe, and individuals even see their troubles going back to the tra effects of their own birth.

In conclusion, mention must be made of certain pr which have their base in native esthetics but which depen the pervasive aversion to the natural body and its fun There are ritual fasts to make fat people thin and cere feasts to make thin people fat. Still other rites are used tc women's breasts large if they are small, and smaller if th

. General dissatisfaction with breast shape is symbolized e fact that the ideal form is virtually outside the range of in variation. A few women afflicted with almost inhuman rmammary development are so idolized that they make a some living by simply going from village to village and itting the natives to stare at them for a fee.

eference has already been made to the fact that excretory ions are ritualized, routinized, and relegated to secrecy. ral reproductive functions are similarly distorted. Inter- se is taboo as a topic and scheduled as an act. Efforts are to avoid pregnancy by the use of magical materials or by ing intercourse to certain phases of the moon. Conception ually very infrequent. When pregnant, women dress so as le their condition. Parturition takes place in secret, without ds or relatives to assist, and the majority of women do not their infants.

ur review of the ritual life of the Nacirema has certainly n them to be a magic-ridden people. It is hard to under- how they have managed to exist so long under the burdens which they have imposed upon themselves. But even such exotic customs as these take on real meaning when they are viewed with the insight provided by Malinowski when he wrote (1948:70):

> Looking from far and above, from our high places of safety in the developed civilization, it is easy to see all the crudity and irrelevance of magic. But without its power and guidance early man could not have mastered his practical difficulties as he has done, nor could man have advanced to the higher stages of civilization.

References

Linton, Ralph. 1936. *The Study of Man.* New York, D. Appleton-Century Co.

Malinowski, Bronislaw. 1948. *Magic, Science, and Religion.* Glencoe, The Free Press.

Murdock, George P. 1949. *Social Structure.* New York, The Macmillan Co.

merican Anthropologist, by Horace Miner, June 1956, pp. 503–507.

Baseball Magic

George Gmelch

On each pitching day for the first three months of a winning season, Dennis Grossini, a pitcher on a Detroit Tiger farm team, arose from bed at exactly 10:00 a.m. At 1:00 p.m. he went to the nearest restaurant for two glasses of iced tea and a tuna fish sandwich. When he got to the ballpark at 3:00 p.m., he put on the sweatshirt and jock he wore during his last winning game; one hour before the game he chewed a wad of Beech-Nut chewing tobacco. After each pitch during the game he touched the letters on his uniform and straightened his cap after each ball. Before the start of each inning he replaced the pitcher's rosin bag next to the spot where it was the inning before. And after every inning in which he gave up a run, he washed his hands.

When I asked which part of his ritual was most important, he said, "You can't really tell what's most important so it all becomes important. I'd be afraid to change anything. As long as I'm winning, I do everything the same."

Trobriand Islanders, according to anthropologist Bronislaw Malinowski, felt the same way about their fishing magic. Trobrianders fished in two different settings: in the *inner lagoon* where fish were plentiful and there was little danger, and on the *open sea* where fishing was dangerous and yields varied widely. Malinowski found that magic was not used in lagoon fishing, where men could rely solely on their knowledge and skill. But when fishing on the open sea, Trobrianders used a great deal of magical ritual to ensure safety and increase their catch.

Baseball, America's national pastime, is an arena in which players behave remarkably like Malinowski's Trobriand fishermen. To professional ballplayers, baseball is more than just a game, it is an occupation. Since their livelihoods depend on how well they perform, many use magic in an attempt to control the chance that is built into baseball. There are three essential activities of the game—pitching, hitting, and fielding. In the first two, chance can play a surprisingly important role. The pitcher is the player least able to control the outcome of his efforts. He may feel great and have good stuff warming up in the bullpen and then get in the game and get clobbered. He may make a bad pitch and see the batter miss it for a strike or see it hit hard but right into the hands of a fielder for an out. Conversely best pitch may be blooped for a base hit. He may limi opposing team to just a few hits yet lose the game, he may give up many hits and win. And the good and luck don't always average out over the course of a sea For instance, this past season (2007) Matt Cain gav fewer runs per game than his teammate Noah Lowry only won 7 games while losing 16 while Lowry wo games and only lost 8. Both pitched for the same tea the San Francisco Giants—which meant they had the s fielders behind them. By chance, when Cain pitche Giants scored few runs while his teammate Lowry enj considerable run support. Regardless of how well a pi performs, the outcome of the game also depends upo proficiency of his teammates, the ineptitude of the op tion, and luck.

Hitting, which many observers call the single mos ficult task in the world of sports, is also full of uncerta Unless it's a home run, no matter how hard the batter the ball, fate determines whether it will go into a wa glove or find a gap between the fielders. The uncerta is compounded by the low success rate of hitting: the a age hitter gets only one hit in every four trips to the p while the very best hitters average only one hit in e three trips. Fielding, which we will return to later, i one part of baseball where chance does not play mu a role.

How does the risk and uncertainty in pitching and hi affect players? How do they try to control the outcom their performance? These are questions that I first be interested in many years ago both as a ballplayer and anthropology student. I had devoted much of my you baseball, and played professionally as a first baseman i Detroit Tiger organization in the 1960s. It was shortly the end of one baseball season that I took an anthr ogy course called "Magic, Religion, and Witchcraft." listened to my professor describe the magical rituals o Trobriand Islanders, it occurred to me that what thes called "primitive" people did wasn't all that different what my teammates and I did for luck and confiden the ballpark.

›utines and Rituals

most common way players attempt to reduce chance and feelings of uncertainty is to develop a routine—a course of n which is regularly followed. Talking about the routines of layers, Pittsburgh Pirates coach Rich Donnelly said:

> hey're like trained animals. They come out here [ball-ırk] and everything has to be the same, they don't like ything that knocks them off their routine. Just look the dugout and you'll see every guy sitting in the ıme spot every night. It's amazing, everybody in the ıme spot. And don't you dare take someone's seat. If guy comes up from the minors and sits here, they'll y, 'Hey, Jim sits here, find another seat.' You watch e pitcher warm up and he'll do the same thing every ne... You got a routine and you adhere to it and you ɔn't want anybody knocking you off it.

outines are comforting, they bring order into a world in h players have little control. The varied elements in rou- can produce the tangible benefit of helping the player entrate. All ballplayers know that it is difficult to think hit at the same time, and that following a routine can them from thinking too much. But often what players oes beyond mere routine. These actions become what opologists define as *ritual*—prescribed behaviors in h there is no empirical connection between the means tapping home plate three times) and the desired end getting a base hit). Because there is no real connection een the two, rituals are not rational. Sometimes they are irrational. Similar to rituals are the nonrational beliefs orm the basis of taboos and fetishes, which players also ɔ bring luck to their side. But first let's take a close look ıals.

ıseball rituals are infinitely varied. Most are personal, ıre performed by individuals rather than by a team or ɔ. Most are done in a private and unemotional manner, ıch the same way players apply pine tar and rosin to bats to improve the grip. A ballplayer may ritualize any ity that he considers important or somehow linked to performance. Recall the variety of things that Dennis sini does, from specific times for waking and eating to ; and dress. Many pitchers listen to the same song on I-pods on the day they are scheduled to start. Pitcher olland always played with two dollar bills in his back ɛt. The Oriole's Glenn Davis used to chew the same every day during hitting streaks, saving it under his Astros infielder Julio Gotay always played with a cheese wich in his back pocket (he had a big appetite, so there t also have been a measure of practicality here). Red Wade Boggs ate chicken before every game during his r, and that was just one of many elements in his pre- and game routine, which also included leaving his house for allpark at precisely the same time each day (1:47 for a night game), running wind sprints at 7:17 for a 7:35 start, and drawing a chai—the Hebrew symbol for life—upon entering the batter's box.

Many hitters go through a series of preparatory rituals before stepping into the batter's box. These include tugging on their caps, touching their uniform letters or medallions, crossing themselves, and swinging, tapping, or bouncing the bat on the plate a prescribed number of times. Consider the Dodger's Nomar Garciaparra. After each pitch he steps out of the batters box, kicks the dirt with each toe, adjusts his right batting glove, adjusts his left batting glove, and touches his helmet before getting back into the box. He insists that it is a routine, not superstition. "I'm just doing it to get everything tight. I like everything tight, that's all it is, really." Mike Hargrove, former Cleveland Indian first baseman, had so many time-consuming elements in his batting ritual that he was nicknamed "the human rain delay." Both players believe their batting rituals helped them regain their concentration after each pitch. But others wondered if the two had become prisoners of their elaborate superstitions.

Players who have too many or particularly bizarre rituals risk being labeled as flakes, and not just by teammates but by fans and the media as well. For example, ex-Mets pitcher Turk Wendell's eccentric rituals, which include chewing black licorice while pitching, only to spit it out, brush his teeth and reload the candy between innings, and wearing a necklace of teeth from animals he has killed, made him a cover story subject in the *New York Times Sunday Magazine.*

Baseball fans observe a lot of this ritual behavior, such as pitchers smoothing the dirt on the mound before each new batter and position players tagging a base when leaving and returning to the dugout between innings, never realizing its importance to the player. The one ritual many fans do recognize, largely because it's a favorite of TV cameramen, is the "rally cap"—players in the dugout folding their caps and wearing them bill up in hopes of sparking a rally.

Rituals grow out of exceptionally good performances. When a player does well, he seldom attributes his success to skill alone; he knows that his skills don't change much from day to day. So, then, what was different about today which can explain his three hits? He makes a correlation. That is, he attributes his success, in part, to an object, a food he ate, not having shaved, a new shirt he bought that day, or just about any behavior out of the ordinary. By repeating those behaviors, the player seeks to gain control over his performance, to bring more good luck. Outfielder John White explained how one of his rituals started:

> I was jogging out to centerfield after the national anthem when I picked up a scrap of paper. I got some good hits that night and I guess I decided that the paper had something to do with it. The next night I picked up a gum wrapper and had another good night at the plate . . . I've been picking up paper every night since.

When outfielder Ron Wright played for the Calgary Cannons he shaved his arms once a week. It all began two years before when after an injury he shaved his arm so it could be taped, and then hit three homers. Now he not only has one of the smoothest swings in the minor leagues, but two of the smoothest forearms. Wade Boggs' routine of eating chicken before every game began when he was a rookie in 1982 and noticed a correlation between multiple-hit games and poultry plates (his wife has 40 chicken recipes). One of Montreal Expo farmhand Mike Saccocio's rituals also concerned food: "I got three hits one night after eating at Long John Silver's. After that when we'd pull into town, my first question would be, "Do you have a Long John Silver's?" Unlike Boggs, Saccocio abandoned his ritual and looked for a new one when he stopped hitting well.

During one game New York Yankee manager Joe Torre stood on the dugout steps instead of sitting on the bench when his team was batting. The Yankees scored a few runs, so he decided to keep on doing it. As the Yankees won nine games in a row, Torre kept standing. Torre explained, "I have a little routine going now . . . As long as we score, I'll be doing the same thing."

When in a slump, most players make a deliberate effort to change their routines and rituals in an attempt to shake off their bad luck. One player tried taking different routes to the ballpark, another tried sitting in a different place in the dugout, another shaved his head, and several reported changing what they ate before the game. I had one manager who would rattle the bat bin when the team was not hitting well, as if the bats were in a stupor and could be aroused by a good shaking. Some of my teammates rubbed their hands along the handles of the bats protruding from the bat bin in hopes of picking up some luck from the bats of others. Diamondbacks left fielder Luis Gonzalez sometimes places his bats in the room where Baseball Chapel – a Sunday church service—is about to get underway. Gonzalez hopes his bats will get some benefit, though he doesn't usually attend the service himself.

Taboo

Taboos (the word comes from a Polynesian term meaning prohibition) are the opposite of rituals. These are things you shouldn't do. Breaking a taboo, players believe, leads to undesirable consequences or bad luck. Most players observe at least a few taboos, such as never stepping on the chalk foul lines. A few, like Nomar Garciaparra, leap over the entire base path. One teammate of mine would never watch a movie on a game day, despite our playing virtually every day from April to September. Another teammate refused to read anything before a game because he believed it weakened his batting eye.

Many taboos take place off the field, out of public v On the day a pitcher is scheduled to start, he is like avoid activities he believes will sap his strength and de from his effectiveness. On the day they are to start, s pitchers avoid shaving, eating certain foods and even ing sex (this nostrum is probably based on an 18th ce belief about preserving vital body fluids, but experts agree there is no ill effect and there may actually be a s benefit).

Taboos usually grow out of exceptionally poor perf ances, which players attribute to a particular behavior. ing my first season of pro ball I ate pancakes before a g in which I struck out three times. A few weeks later I another terrible game, again after eating pancakes. result was a pancake taboo: I never again ate pancakes ing the season. (Conversely, Orioles pitcher Jim Palmer, some success, insisted on eating pancakes before each c starts).

While most taboos are idiosyncratic, there are a few all ballplayers hold and that do not develop out of indiv experience or misfortune. These form part of the cultu baseball, and are sometimes learned as early as Little Le Mentioning a no-hitter while one is in progress is a known example. The origins of such shared beliefs ar in time, though some scholars have proposed theories example, the taboo against stepping on the chalk foul when running onto or off the field between innings, sug National Baseball Hall of Fame research director Tim W may be rooted in the children's superstition, "step on a c break your mother's back."

Fetishes

Fetishes are charms, material objects believed to em supernatural power that can aid or protect the owner. C luck charms are standard equipment for some ballpla These include a wide assortment of objects from c chains, and crucifixes to a favorite baseball hat. The fetis object may be a new possession or something a player f that coincided with the start of a streak and which he responsible for his good fortune. While playing in the Pa Coast League, Alan Foster forgot his baseball shoes road trip and borrowed a pair from a teammate. That he pitched a no-hitter, which he attributed to the shoes. A wards he bought them from his teammate and they be a fetish. Expo farmhand Mark LaRosa's rock has a diff origin and use:

> I found it on the field in Elmira after I had gott bombed. It's unusual, perfectly round, and it caught r attention. I keep it to remind me of how important it to concentrate. When I am going well I look at the ro and remember to keep my focus. The rock reminds r of what can happen when I lose my concentration.

one season Marge Schott, former owner of the Cincin-
ɜds, insisted that her field manager rub her St. Bernard
:zie" for good luck before each game. When the Reds
n the road, Schott would sometimes send a bag of the
hair to the field manager's hotel room. Religious medal-
which many Latino players wear around their necks
metimes touch before going to the plate or mound, are
tishes, though tied to their Roman Catholicism. Also
g to their religion, some players some make the sign of
oss or bless themselves before every at bat (a few like
Rodriguez do so before every pitch), and a few point
v a kiss to the heavens after hitting a home run.

ne players regard certain uniform numbers as lucky.
Ricky Henderson came to the Blue Jays in 1993, he paid
ate Turner Ward $25,000 for the right to wear number
on Sutton got off cheaper. When he joined the Dodgers
vinced teammate Bruce Boche to give up number 20 in
ıge for a new set of golf clubs. Oddly enough, there is no
ısus about the effect of wearing number 13. Some play-
n it, while a few request it. When Jason Giambi arrived
ie Oakland A's his favorite number 7 was already taken,
settled for 16 (the two numbers add up to 7). When he
with the Yankees, number 7 (Mickey Mantle's old
r) was retired and 16 was taken, so he settled for 25
, the numbers add up to 7).

mber preferences emerge in different ways. A young
may request the number of a former star, sometimes
g that it will bring him the same success. Or he may
t a number he associates with good luck. Colorado
es' Larry Walker's fixation with the number 3 has
e well known to baseball fans. Besides wearing 33,
es three practice swings before stepping into the box,
owers from the third nozzle, sets his alarm for three
es past the hour and he was wed on November 3 at
).m.[1] Fans in ballparks all across America rise from
seats for the seventh-inning stretch before the home
omes to bat because the number 7 is lucky, although
ecific origin of this tradition has been lost.[2]

thing, both the choice and the order in which it is put
mbine elements of both ritual and fetish. Some players
the part of their uniform in a particular order. Expos
and Jim Austin always puts on his left sleeve, left pants
d left shoe before the right. Most players, however, sin-
t one or two lucky articles or quirks of dress for rit-
aboration. After hitting two home runs in a game, for
le, ex-Giant infielder Jim Davenport discovered that he
issed a buttonhole while dressing for the game. For the
nder of his career he left the same button undone. Phil-
en Dykstra would discard his batting gloves if he failed
a hit in a single at-bat. In a hitless game, he might go
h four pair of gloves. For outfielder Brian Hunter the
is shoes: "I have a pair of high tops and a pair of low
Whichever shoes don't get a hit that game, I switch to the
pair." At the time of our interview, he was struggling at the plate and switching shoes almost every day. For Birmingham Baron pitcher Bo Kennedy the arrangement of the different pairs of baseball shoes in his locker is critical:

> I tell the clubbies [clubhouse boys] when you hang stuff in my locker don't touch my shoes. If you bump them move them back. I want the Ponys in front, the turfs to the right, and I want them nice and neat with each pair touching each other . . . Everyone on the team knows not to mess with my shoes when I pitch.

During hitting or winning streaks players may wear the same clothes day after day. Once I changed sweatshirts midway through the game for seven consecutive nights to keep a hitting streak going. Clothing rituals, however, can become impractical. Catcher Matt Allen was wearing a long sleeve turtle neck shirt on a cool evening in the New York-Penn League when he had a three-hit game. "I kept wearing the shirt and had a good week," he explained. "Then the weather got hot as hell, 85 degrees and muggy, but I would not take that shirt off. I wore it for another ten days—catching—and people thought I was crazy." Former Phillies, Expos, Twins, and perhaps taking a ritual to the extreme, Leo Durocher, managing the Brooklyn Dodgers to a pennant in 1941, spent three and a half weeks in the same gray slacks, blue coat, and knitted blue tie. Losing streaks often produce the opposite effect, such as the Oakland A's players who went out and bought new street clothes after losing 14 in a row.

Former Oakland A's manager Art Howe often wouldn't wash his socks after the A's were victorious; and he would also write the line up card with the same pen, and tape the pregame radio show in the same place on the field. In the words of one veteran, "It all comes down to the philosophy of not messing with success—or deliberately messing with failure."

Baseball's superstitions, like most everything else, change over time. Many of the rituals and beliefs of early baseball are no longer observed. In the 1920s-30s sportswriters reported that a player who tripped en route to the field would often retrace his steps and carefully walk over the stumbling block for "insurance." A century ago players spent time on and off the field intently looking for items that would bring them luck. To find a hairpin on the street, for example, assured a batter of hitting safely in that day's game. A few managers were known to strategically place a hairpin on the ground where a slumping player would be sure to find it. Today few women wear hairpins—a good reason the belief has died out. In the same era, Philadelphia Athletics manager Connie Mack hoped to ward off bad luck by employing a hunchback as a mascot. Hall of Famer Ty Cobb took on a young black boy as a good luck charm, even taking him on the road during the 1908 season. It was a not uncommon then for players to rub the head of a black child for good luck.

To catch sight of a white horse or a wagon-load of barrels were also good omens. In 1904 the manager of the New

York Giants, John McGraw, hired a driver with a team of white horses to drive past the Polo Grounds around the time his players were arriving at the ballpark. He knew that if his players saw white horses, they would have more confidence and that could only help them during the game. Belief in the power of white horses survived in a few backwaters until the 1960s. A gray-haired manager of a team I played for in Drummondville, Quebec, would drive around the countryside before important games and during the playoffs looking for a white horse. When he was successful, he would announce it to everyone in the clubhouse.

One belief that appears to have died out recently is a taboo about crossed bats. Several of my Latino teammates in the 1960s took it seriously. I can still recall one Dominican player becoming agitated when another player tossed a bat from the batting cage and it landed on top of his bat. He believed that the top bat might steal hits from the lower one. In his view, bats contained a finite number of hits. It was once commonly believed that when the hits in a bat were used up no amount of good hitting would produce any more. Hall of Famer Honus Wagner believed each bat contained only 100 hits. Regardless of the quality of the bat, he would discard it after its 100th hit. This belief would have little relevance today, in the era of light bats with thin handles—so thin that the typical modern bat is lucky to survive a dozen hits without being broken. Other superstitions about bats do survive, however. Position players on the Class A Asheville Tourists would not let pitchers touch or swing their bats, not even to warm up. Poor-hitting players, as most pitchers are, were said to pollute or weaken the bats.

While the elements in many rituals have changed over time, the reliance of players on them has not. Moreover, that reliance seems fairly impervious to advances in education. Way back in the 1890s, in an article I found in the archives of the National Baseball Hall of Fame, one observer predicted that the current influx of better educated players into the game and the "gradual weeding out of bummers and thugs" would raise the intellectual standard of the game and reduce baseball's rampant superstitions. It didn't. I first researched baseball magic in the late 1960s; when I returned 30 years later to study the culture of baseball, I expected to find less superstition. After all, I reasoned, unlike in my playing days most of today's players have had some college. I did find that today's players are less willing to admit to having superstitions, but when I asked instead about their "routines" they described rituals and fetishes little different from my teammates in the 60s.

Uncertainty and Magic

The best evidence that players turn to rituals, taboos, and fetishes to control chance and uncertainty is found in their uneven application. They are associated mainly with pitching and hitting—the activities with the highest degree of chance—and not fielding. I met only one player who had any ritual in connection with fielding, and he was an error shortstop. Unlike hitting and pitching, a fielder has complete control over the outcome of his performance a ball has been hit in his direction, no one can int and ruin his chances of catching it for an out (except unlikely event of two fielders colliding). Compared w pitcher or the hitter, the fielder has little to worry abo knows that in better than 9.7 times out of 10 he will e his task flawlessly. With odds like that there is little ne ritual.

Clearly, the rituals of American ballplayers are not those of the Trobriand Islanders studied by Malinowski years ago.[3] In professional baseball, fielding is the equi of the inner lagoon while hitting and pitching are li open sea.

While Malinowski helps us understand how ballp respond to chance and uncertainty, behavioral psych B. F. Skinner sheds light on why personal rituals get lished in the first place.[4] With a few grains of seed S could get pigeons to do anything he wanted. He merely for the desired behavior (e.g. pecking) and then rewa with some food. Skinner then decided to see what happen if pigeons were rewarded with food pellets reg every fifteen seconds, regardless of what they did. He that the birds associate the arrival of the food with a p lar action, such as tucking their head under a wing or w in clockwise circles. About ten seconds after the arri the last pellet, a bird would begin doing whatever it a ated with getting the food and keep doing it until th pellet arrived. In short, the pigeons behaved as if their a made the food appear. They learned to associate par behaviors with the reward of being given seed.

Ballplayers also associate a reward—successful pe ance—with prior behavior. If a player touches his cr and then gets a hit, he may decide the gesture was respo for his good fortune and touch his crucifix the next ti comes to the plate. Unlike pigeons, however, most ba ers are quicker to change their rituals once they no seem to work. Skinner found that once a pigeon asso one of its actions with the arrival of food or water, onl radic rewards were necessary to keep the ritual going pigeon, believing that hopping from side to side broug lets into its feeding cup, hopped ten thousand times w a pellet before finally giving up. But, then, Wade Bog chicken before every game, through slumps and good for seventeen years.

Obviously the rituals and superstitions of baseb not make a pitch travel faster or a batted ball find th between the fielders, nor do the Trobriand rituals ca seas or bring fish. What both do, however, is give thei titioners a sense of control, and with that added confi And we all know how important that is. If you really b eating chicken or hopping over the foul lines will mak a better hitter, it probably will.

ferences

ch, G. *Inside Pitch: Life in Professional Baseball* (Smithsonian nstitution Press, 2001).

owski, B. *Magic, Science and Religion and Other Essays* Glencoe, III., 1948).

er, B.F. *Behavior of Organisms: An Experimental Analysis* D. Appleton-Century Co., 1938).

er, B.F. *Science and Human Behavior* (New York: Macmillan, 1953).

z, D. *High Inside: Memoirs of a Baseball Wife* (New York: G.P. Putnam's Sons, 1983.)

Notes

1. *Sports Illustrated . . .* , 48
2. Allen, *The Superstitions of Baseball Players,* 104.
3. Malinowski, B., *Magic, Science and Religion and Other Essays*
4. Skinner, B.F., *Behavior of Organisms: An Experimental Analysis*
5. Skinner, B.F., *Science and Human Behavior*

UNIT 7

Sociocultural Change

Unit Selections

31. **Why Can't People Feed Themselves?,** Frances Moore Lappé and Joseph Collins
32. **The Arrow of Disease,** Jared Diamond
33. **The Price of Progress,** John Bodley
34. **Of Ice and Men,** Cameron M. Smith
35. **Inundation,** Austin Blair and Casey Beck
36. **Isolation,** Lucas Bessire
37. **Seeing Conservation through the Global Lens,** Jim Igoe
38. **What Native Peoples Deserve,** Roger Sandall

Key Points to Consider

- What is a subsistence system? What have been the effects of colonialism on former subsistence-oriented socioeconomic systems?
- How does the production of cash crops inevitably lead to class distinctions and poverty?
- What ethical obligations do you think industrial societies have toward human rights and the cultural diversity of traditional communities?
- Are the hunting and gathering Iñupiat a threat to the polar bear?
- If island nations are inundated as a result of global warming, what obligations does the rest of the world have toward them?
- Should people who choose isolation be left alone?
- Why do so many indigenous people look upon conservation with disdain?
- Are wealth and power distributed fairly across the world?
- What should your nation's policy be towards genocidal practices in other countries?
- How has exploitation of indigenous people persisted in Africa even after political independence?

Student Website

www.mhcls.com

Internet References

Association for Political and Legal Anthropology
http://www.aaanet.org/apla/index.htm

Human Rights and Humanitarian Assistance
http://www.etown.edu/vl/humrts.html

The Indigenous Rights Movement in the Pacific
http://www.inmotionmagazine.com/pacific.html

Murray Research Center
http://www.radcliffe.edu/murray_redirect/index.php

RomNews Network—Online
http://www.romnews.com/community/index.php

WWW Virtual Library: Indigenous Studies
http://www.cwis.org/wwwvl/indig-vl.html

ıe origins of academic anthropology lie in the colonial and ›rial ventures of the past five hundred years. During this ›d, many people of the world were brought into a relationship Europe and the United States that was usually exploitative often socially and culturally disruptive. For over a century, ropologists have witnessed this process, and the transforons that have taken place in those social and cultural sys- ; brought under the umbrella of a world economic order. / anthropological studies—even those widely regarded as research—directly or indirectly served colonial interests. y anthropologists certainly believed that they were extendhe benefits of Western technology and society, while preing the cultural rights of those people whom they studied. epresentatives of poor nations challenge this view, and are ›ss generous in describing the past role of the anthropolo- Most contemporary anthropologists, however, have a deep ıl commitment to defending the legal, political, and eco- 'c rights of the people with whom they work.

'hen anthropologists discuss social change, they usumean the change brought about in pre-industrial societhrough longstanding interaction with the nation-states of ndustrialized world. In early anthropology, contact between Vest and the remainder of the world was characterized e terms "acculturation" and "culture contact." These terms used to describe the diffusion of cultural traits between the loped and the less-developed countries. Often this was /zed as a one-way process, in which cultures of the less loped world were seen, for better or worse, as receptacles Vestern cultural traits. Nowadays, many anthropologists ve that the diffusion of cultural traits across social, political, economic boundaries was emphasized at the expense of eal issues of dominance, subordination, and dependence characterized the colonial experience. Just as important, / anthropologists recognize that the present-day forms of ral, economic, and political interaction between the devel- and the so-called underdeveloped world are best charac- ›d as neocolonial. Most of the authors represented in this ake the perspective that anthropology should be critical as as descriptive. They raise questions about cultural contact subsequent economic and social disruption.

keeping with the notion that the negative impact of the on traditional cultures began with colonial domination, nit opens with "Why Can't People Feed Themselves?" and des "The Arrow of Disease." Continuing with "The Price of ress" we see that "progress" for the West has often meant rty, hunger, disease, and death for traditional peoples.

course, traditional peoples from Alaska ("Of Ice and ") to the South Pacific ("Inundation") and to South America

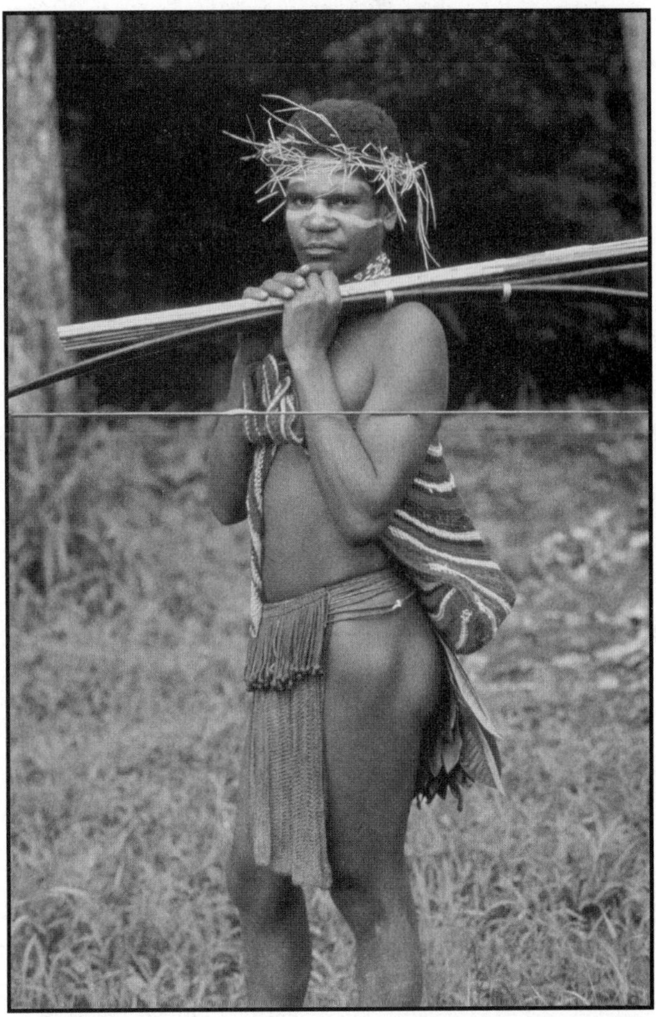

("Isolation" and "What Native Peoples Deserve") are not the only losers in the process of cultural destruction. In "Seeing Conservation through the Global Lens," we learn that the more we deprive the traditional stewards (the Indigenous peoples) of their land, the greater the loss in overall biodiversity. All of humanity stands to suffer, as a vast store of human knowledge—embodied in tribal subsistence practices, language, medicine, and folklore—is obliterated, in a manner not unlike the burning of the library of Alexandria 1,600 years ago. We can only hope that it is not too late to save what is left.

Why Can't People Feed Themselves?

FRANCES MOORE LAPPÉ AND JOSEPH COLLINS

Question: You have said that the hunger problem is not the result of overpopulation. But you have not yet answered the most basic and simple question of all: Why can't people feed themselves? As Senator Daniel P. Moynihan put it bluntly, when addressing himself to the Third World, "Food growing is the first thing you do when you come down out of the trees. The question is, how come the United States can grow food and you can't?"

Our Response: In the very first speech I, Frances, ever gave after writing *Diet for a Small Planet,* I tried to take my audience along the path that I had taken in attempting to understand why so many are hungry in this world. Here is the gist of that talk that was, in truth, a turning point in my life:

> When I started I saw a world divided into two parts: a *minority* of nations that had "taken off" through their agricultural and industrial revolutions to reach a level of unparalleled material abundance and a *majority* that remained behind in a primitive, traditional, undeveloped state. This lagging behind of the majority of the world's peoples must be due, I thought, to some internal deficiency or even to several of them. It seemed obvious that the underdeveloped countries must be deficient in natural resources—particularly good land and climate—and in cultural development, including modern attitudes conducive to work and progress.
>
> But when looking for the historical roots of the predicament, I learned that my picture of these two separate worlds was quite false. My two separate worlds were really just different sides of the same coin. One side was on top largely because the other side was on the bottom. Could this be true? How were these separate worlds related?
>
> Colonialism appeared to me to be the link. Colonialism destroyed the cultural patterns of production and exchange by which traditional societies in "underdeveloped" countries previously had met the needs of the people. Many precolonial social structures, while dominated by exploitative elites, had evolved a system of mutual obligations among the classes that helped to ensure at least a minimal diet for all. A friend of mine once said: "Precolonial village existence in subsistence agriculture was a limited life indeed, but it's certainly not Calcutta."
>
> The misery of starvation in the streets of Calcutta can onl be understood as the end-point of a long historical proc ess—one that has destroyed a traditional social system.
>
> "Underdeveloped," instead of being an adjective th evokes the picture of a static society, became for me verb (to "underdevelop") meaning the *process* by whic the minority of the world has transformed—indeed ofte robbed and degraded—the majority.

That was in 1972. I clearly recall my thoughts on my re home. I had stated publicly for the first time a world view had taken me years of study to grasp. The sense of relief wa mendous. For me the breakthrough lay in realizing that toc "hunger crisis" could not be described in static, descri terms. Hunger and underdevelopment must always be thc of as a *process.*

To answer the question "why hunger?" it is counterprc tive to simply *describe* the conditions in an underdevel country today. For these conditions, whether they be the de of malnutrition, the levels of agricultural production, or the country's ecological endowment, are not static fact they are not "givens." They are rather the *results* of an ong historical process. As we dug ever deeper into that histc process for the preparation of this book, we began to disc the existence of scarcity-creating mechanisms that we had vaguely intuited before.

We have gotten great satisfaction from probing into the since we recognized it is the only way to approach a soluti hunger today. We have come to see that it is the *force* cre the condition, not the condition itself, that must be the targ change. Otherwise we might change the condition today, o find tomorrow that it has been recreated—with a vengeanc

Asking the question "Why can't people feed themsel carries a sense of bewilderment that there are so many ple in the world not able to feed themselves adequately. astonished us, however, is that there are not *more* people i world who are hungry—considering the weight of the cen of effort by the few to undermine the capacity of the m ity to feed themselves. No, we are not crying "conspirac these forces were entirely conspiratorial, they would be e to detect and many more people would by now have risen resist. We are talking about something more subtle and i ous; a heritage of a colonial order in which people wit ıtage of considerable power sought their own self-interest, arrogantly believing they were acting in the interest of the le whose lives they were destroying.

e Colonial Mind

colonizer viewed agriculture in the subjugated lands as tive and backward. Yet such a view contrasts sharply with ments from the colonial period now coming to light. For ple, A. J. Voelker, a British agricultural scientist assigned lia during the 1890s wrote:

> owhere would one find better instances of keeping land rupulously clean from weeds, of ingenuity in device of ater-raising appliances, of knowledge of soils and their pabilities, as well as of the exact time to sow and reap, one would find in Indian agriculture. It is wonderful o, how much is known of rotation, the system of "mixed ops" and of fallowing. . . . I, at least, have never seen a ore perfect picture of cultivation."[1]

one the less, viewing the agriculture of the vanquished as tive and backward reinforced the colonizer's rationale for oying it. To the colonizers of Africa, Asia, and Latin Amer- agriculture became merely a means to extract wealth— as gold from a mine—on behalf of the colonizing power. ulture was no longer seen as a source of food for the local lation, nor even as their livelihood. Indeed the English omist John Stuart Mill reasoned that colonies should not be ht of as civilizations or countries at all but as "agricultural lishments" whose sole purpose was to supply the "larger unity to which they belong." The colonized society's agri- re was only a subdivision of the agricultural system of the politan country. As Mill acknowledged, "Our West India ies, for example, cannot be regarded as countries. . . . The Indies are the place where England *finds it convenient* to on the production of sugar, coffee and a few other tropical nodities."[2]

ior to European intervention, Africans practiced a diver- agriculture that included the introduction of new food s of Asian or American origin. But colonial rule simplified iversified production to single cash crops—often to the sion of staple foods—and in the process sowed the seeds nine.[3] Rice farming once had been common in Gambia. vith colonial rule so much of the best land was taken over anuts (grown for the European market) that rice had to be rted to counter the mounting prospect of famine. North- hana, once famous for its yams and other foodstuffs, was d to concentrate solely on cocoa. Most of the Gold Coast ecame dependent on cocoa. Liberia was turned into a vir- lantation subsidiary of Firestone Tire and Rubber. Food ction in Dahomey and southeast Nigeria was all but aban- l in favor of palm oil; Tanganyika (now Tanzania) was d to focus on sisal and Uganda on cotton.

e same happened in Indochina. About the time of the ican Civil War the French decided that the Mekong Delta tnam would be ideal for producing rice for export. Through duction system based on enriching the large landowners, Vietnam became the world's third largest exporter of rice by the 1930s; yet many landless Vietnamese went hungry.[4]

Rather than helping the peasants, colonialism's public works programs only reinforced export crop production. British irrigation works built in nineteenth-century India did help increase production, but the expansion was for spring export crops at the expense of millets and legumes grown in the fall as the basic local food crops.

Because people living on the land do not easily go against their natural and adaptive drive to grow food for themselves, colonial powers had to force the production of cash crops. The first strategy was to use physical or economic force to get the local population to grow cash crops instead of food on their own plots and then turn them over to the colonizer for export. The second strategy was the direct takeover of the land by large-scale plantations growing crops for export.

Forced Peasant Production

As Walter Rodney recounts in *How Europe Underdeveloped Africa,* cash crops were often grown literally under threat of guns and whips.[5] One visitor to the Sahel commented in 1928: "Cotton is an artificial crop and one the value of which is not entirely clear to the natives . . . " He wryly noted the "enforced enthusiasm with which the natives . . . have thrown themselves into . . . planting cotton."[6] The forced cultivation of cotton was a major grievance leading to the Maji Maji wars in Tanzania (then Tanganyika) and behind the nationalist revolt in Angola as late as 1960.[7]

Although raw force was used, taxation was the preferred colonial technique to force Africans to grow cash crops. The colonial administrations simply levied taxes on cattle, land, houses, and even the people themselves. Since the tax had to be paid in the coin of the realm, the peasants had either to grow crops to sell or to work on the plantations or in the mines of the Europeans.[8] Taxation was both an effective tool to "stimulate" cash cropping and a source of revenue that the colonial bureaucracy needed to enforce the system. To expand their production of export crops to pay the mounting taxes, peasant producers were forced to neglect the farming of food crops. In 1830, the Dutch administration in Java made the peasants an offer they could not refuse; if they would grow government owned export crops on one fifth of their land, the Dutch would remit their land taxes.[9] If they refused and thus could not pay the taxes, they lost their land.

Marketing boards emerged in Africa in the 1930s as another technique for getting the profit from cash crop production by native producers into the hands of the colonial government and international firms. Purchases by the marketing boards were well below the world market price. Peanuts bought by the boards from peasant cultivators in West Africa were sold in Britain for more than *seven times* what the peasants received.[10]

The marketing board concept was born with the "cocoa hold-up" in the Gold Coast in 1937. Small cocoa farmers refused to sell to the large cocoa concerns like United Africa Company (a subsidiary of the Anglo-Dutch firm, Unilever—which we know as Lever Brothers) and Cadbury until they got a higher price. When the British government stepped in and agreed to buy the cocoa directly in place of the big business concerns, the smallholders must have thought they had scored at least a minor victory. But had they really? The following year the British formally set up the West African Cocoa Control Board. Theoretically, its purpose was to pay the peasants a reasonable price for their crops. In practice, however, the board, as sole purchaser, was able to hold down the prices paid the peasants for their crops when the world prices were rising. Rodney sums up the real "victory":

> None of the benefits went to Africans, but rather to the British government itself and to the private companies. . . . Big companies like the United African Company and John Holt were given . . . quotas to fulfill on behalf of the boards. As agents of the government, they were no longer exposed to direct attack, and their profits were secure.[11]

These marketing boards, set up for most export crops, were actually controlled by the companies. The chairman of the Cocoa Board was none other than John Cadbury of Cadbury Brothers (ever had a Cadbury chocolate bar?) who was part of a buying pool exploiting West African cocoa farmers.

The marketing boards funneled part of the profits from the exploitation of peasant producers indirectly into the royal treasury. While the Cocoa Board sold to the British Food Ministry at low prices, the ministry upped the price for British manufacturers, thus netting a profit as high as 11 million pounds in some years.[12]

These marketing boards of Africa were only the institutionalized rendition of what is the essence of colonialism—the extraction of wealth. While profits continued to accrue to foreign interests and local elites, prices received by those actually growing the commodities remained low.

Plantations

A second approach was direct takeover of the land either by the colonizing government or by private foreign interests. Previously self-provisioning farmers were forced to cultivate the plantation fields through either enslavement or economic coercion.

After the conquest of the Kandyan Kingdom (in present day Sri Lanka), in 1815, the British designated all the vast central part of the island as crown land. When it was determined that coffee, a profitable export crop, could be grown there, the Kandyan lands were sold off to British investors and planters at a mere five shillings per acre, the government even defraying the cost of surveying and road building.[13]

Java is also a prime example of a colonial government seizing territory and then putting it into private foreign hands. In 1870, the Dutch declared all uncultivated land—called waste land—property of the state for lease to Dutch plantation enterprises. In addition, the Agrarian Land Law of 1870 authorized foreign companies to lease village-owned land. The peasants, in chronic need of ready cash for taxes and foreign consumer goods, were only too willing to lease their land to the foreign companies for very modest sums and under terms dictated by the firms. Where land was still held communally, the village headman was tempted by high cash commissions offere plantation companies. He would lease the village land more cheaply than would the individual peasant or, as wa quently the case, sell out the entire village to the company

The introduction of the plantation meant the divorce of culture from nourishment, as the notion of food value wa to the overriding claim of "market value" in international Crops such as sugar, tobacco, and coffee were selected, n the basis of how well they feed people, but for their high value relative to their weight and bulk so that profit ma could be maintained even after the costs of shipping to Eu

Suppressing Peasant Farming

The stagnation and impoverishment of the peasant food-prod sector was not the mere by-product of benign neglect, that i unintended consequence of an overemphasis on export produ Plantations—just like modern "agro-industrial complex needed an abundant and readily available supply of low- agricultural workers. Colonial administrations thus de a variety of tactics, all to undercut self-provisioning ag ture and thus make rural populations dependent on p tion wages. Government services and even the most mi infrastructure (access to water, roads, seeds, credit, pes disease control information, and so on) were systemati denied. Plantations usurped most of the good land, either ing much of the rural population landless or pushing them marginal soils. (Yet the plantations have often held mu their land idle simply to prevent the peasants from usin even to this day. Del Monte owns 57,000 acres of Guate but plants only 9000. The rest lies idle except for a few sand head of grazing cattle.)[15]

In some cases a colonial administration would go even f to guarantee itself a labor supply. In at least twelve countr the eastern and southern parts of Africa the exploitation of eral wealth (gold, diamonds, and copper) and the establish of cash-crop plantations demanded a continuous supply o cost labor. To assure this labor supply, colonial administr simply expropriated the land of the African communiti violence and drove the people into small reserves.[16] Wit ther adequate land for their traditional slash-and-burn me nor access to the means—tools, water, and fertilizer—to continuous farming of such limited areas viable, the indig population could scarcely meet subsistence needs, muc produce surplus to sell in order to cover the colonial taxes. dreds of thousands of Africans were forced to become the labor source so "needed" by the colonial plantations. Or laboring on plantations and in the mines could they hope the colonial taxes.

The tax scheme to produce reserves of cheap plantatio mining labor was particularly effective when the Great D sion hit and the bottom dropped out of cash crop economi 1929 the cotton market collapsed, leaving peasant cotto ducers, such as those in Upper Volta, unable to pay their co taxes. More and more young people, in some years as ma 80,000, were thus forced to migrate to the Gold Coast to pete with each other for low-wage jobs on cocoa plantatio

ne forced migration of Africa's most able-bodied workers—
oing village food farming of needed hands—was a recur-
feature of colonialism. As late as 1973 the Portuguese
orted" 400,000 Mozambican peasants to work in South
a in exchange for gold deposited in the Lisbon treasury.

he many techniques of colonialism to undercut self-
sioning agriculture in order to ensure a cheap labor supply
o better illustrated than by the story of how, in the mid-
eenth century, sugar plantation owners in British Guiana
d with the double blow of the emancipation of slaves and
rash in the world sugar market. The story is graphically
nted by Alan Adamson in *Sugar Without Slaves.*[18]

'ould the ex-slaves be allowed to take over the plantation
and grow the food they needed? The planters, many ruined
ne sugar slump, were determined they would not. The
er-dominated government devised several schemes for
rting food self-sufficiency. The price of crown land was
artificially high, and the purchase of land in parcels smaller
100 acres was outlawed—two measures guaranteeing that
y organized ex-slave cooperatives could not hope to gain
s to much land. The government also prohibited cultiva-
on as much as 400,000 acres—on the grounds of "uncer-
property titles." Moreover, although many planters held
of their land out of sugar production due to the depressed
l price, they would not allow any alternative production on
. They feared that once the ex-slaves started growing food
uld be difficult to return them to sugar production when
l market prices began to recover. In addition, the govern-
taxed peasant production, then turned around and used
inds to subsidize the immigration of laborers from India
Malaysia to replace the freed slaves, thereby making sugar
iction again profitable for the planters. Finally, the gov-
ent neglected the infrastructure for subsistence agriculture
enied credit for small farmers.

rhaps the most insidious tactic to "lure" the peasant away
food production—and the one with profound historical
quences—was a policy of keeping the price of imported
low through the removal of tariffs and subsidies. The policy
louble-edged: first, peasants were told they need not grow
because they could always buy it cheaply with their planta-
vages; second, cheap food imports destroyed the market for
stic food and thereby impoverished local food producers.

lamson relates how both the Governor of British Guiana and
ecretary for the Colonies Earl Grey favored low duties on
rts in order to erode local food production and thereby release
for the plantations. In 1851 the governor rushed through a
tion of the duty on cereals in order to "divert" labor to the
estates. As Adamson comments, "Without realizing it, he
overnor] had put his finger on the most mordant feature of
culture: . . . its convulsive need to destroy any other sector
economy which might compete for 'its' labor."[19]

any colonial governments succeeded in establishing
dence on imported foodstuffs. In 1647 an observer in the
Indies wrote to Governor Winthrop of Massachusetts:
are so intent upon planting sugar that they had rather buy
at very dear rates than produce it by labour, so infinite is
ofitt of sugar workes. . . ."[20] By 1770, the West Indies were importing most of the continental colonies' exports of dried fish, grain, beans, and vegetables. A dependence on imported food made the West Indian colonies vulnerable to any disruption in supply. This dependence on imported food stuffs spelled disaster when the thirteen continental colonies gained independence and food exports from the continent to the West Indies were interrupted. With no diversified food system to fall back on, 15,000 plantation workers died of famine between 1780 and 1787 in Jamaica alone.[21] The dependence of the West Indies on imported food persists to this day.

Suppressing Peasant Competition

We have talked about the techniques by which indigenous populations were forced to cultivate cash crops. In some countries with large plantations, however, colonial governments found it necessary to *prevent* peasants from independently growing cash crops not out of concern for their welfare, but so that they would not compete with colonial interests growing the same crop. For peasant farmers, given a modicum of opportunity, proved themselves capable of outproducing the large plantations not only in terms of output per unit of land but, more important, in terms of capital cost per unit produced.

In the Dutch East Indies (Indonesia and Dutch New Guinea) colonial policy in the middle of the nineteenth century forbade the sugar refineries to buy sugar cane from indigenous growers and imposed a discriminatory tax on rubber produced by native smallholders.[22] A recent unpublished United Nations study of agricultural development in Africa concluded that large-scale agricultural operations owned and controlled by foreign commercial interests (such as the rubber plantations of Liberia, the sisal estates of Tanganyika [Tanzania], and the coffee estates of Angola) only survived the competition of peasant producers because "the authorities actively supported them by suppressing indigenous rural development."[23]

The suppression of indigenous agricultural development served the interests of the colonizing powers in two ways. Not only did it prevent direct competition from more efficient native producers of the same crops, but it also guaranteed a labor force to work on the foreign-owned estates. Planters and foreign investors were not unaware that peasants who could survive economically by their own production would be under less pressure to sell their labor cheaply to the large estates.

The answer to the question, then, "Why can't people feed themselves?" must begin with an understanding of how colonialism actively prevented people from doing just that.

Colonialism

- forced peasants to replace food crops with cash crops that were then expropriated at very low rates;
- took over the best agricultural land for export crop plantations and then forced the most able-bodied workers to leave the village fields to work as slaves or for very low wages on plantations;

- encouraged a dependence on imported food;
- blocked native peasant cash crop production from competing with cash crops produced by settlers or foreign firms.

These are concrete examples of the development of underdevelopment that we should have perceived as such even as we read our history schoolbooks. Why didn't we? Somehow our schoolbooks always seemed to make the flow of history appear to have its own logic—as if it could not have been any other way. I, Frances, recall, in particular, a grade-school, social studies pamphlet on the idyllic life of Pedro, a nine-year-old boy on a coffee plantation in South America. The drawings of lush vegetation and "exotic" huts made his life seem romantic indeed. Wasn't it natural and proper that South America should have plantations to supply my mother and father with coffee? Isn't that the way it was *meant* to be?

Notes

1. Radha Sinha, *Food and Poverty* (New York: Holmes and Meier, 1976), p. 26.
2. John Stuart Mill, *Political Economy,* Book 3, Chapter 25 (emphasis added).
3. Peter Feldman and David Lawrence, "Social and Economic Implications of the Large-Scale Introduction of New Varieties of Foodgrains," Africa Report, preliminary draft (Geneva: UNRISD, 1975), pp. 107–108.
4. Edgar Owens, *The Right Side of History,* unpublished manuscript, 1976.
5. Walter Rodney, *How Europe Underdeveloped Africa* (London: Bogle-L'Ouverture Publications, 1972), pp. 171–172.
6. Ferdinand Ossendowski, *Slaves of the Sun* (New York: Dutton, 1928), p. 276.
7. Rodney, *How Europe Underdeveloped Africa,* pp. 171–172.
8. Ibid., p. 181.
9. Clifford Geertz, *Agricultural Involution* (Berkeley and Los Angeles: University of California Press, 1963), pp. 52–53.
10. Rodney, *How Europe Underdeveloped Africa,* p. 185.
11. Ibid., p. 184.
12. Ibid., p. 186.
13. George L. Beckford, *Persistent Poverty: Underdevelopment Plantation Economies of the Third World* (New York: Oxfor University Press, 1972), p. 99.
14. Ibid., p. 99, quoting from Erich Jacoby, *Agrarian Unrest in Southeast Asia* (New York: Asia Publishing House, 1961), p. 66.
15. Pat Flynn and Roger Burbach, North American Congress or Latin America, Berkely, California, recent investigation.
16. Feldman and Lawrence, "Social and Economic Implications p. 103.
17. Special Sahelian Office Report, Food and Agriculture Organization, March 28, 1974, pp. 88–89.
18. Alan Adamson, *Sugar Without Slaves: The Political Econor of British Guiana, 1838–1904* (New Haven and London: Ya University Press, 1972).
19. Ibid., p. 41.
20. Eric Williams, *Capitalism and Slavery* (New York: Putnam, 1966), p. 110.
21. Ibid., p. 121.
22. Gunnar Myrdal, *Asian Drama,* vol. 1 (New York: Pantheon, 1966), pp. 448–449.
23. Feldman and Lawrence, "Social and Economic Implication p. 189.

Frances Moore Lappé and **Dr. Joseph Collins** are founde directors of the Institute for Food and Development Policy, loca San Francisco and New York.

he Arrow of Disease

ien Columbus and his successors invaded the Americas, the most tent weapon they carried was their germs. But why didn't deadly ease flow in the other direction, from the New World to the Old?

RED DIAMOND

he three people talking in the hospital room were already stressed out from having to cope with a mysterious illness, and it didn't help at all that they were having trouble com- icating. One of them was the patient, a small, timid man, sick pneumonia caused by an unidentified microbe and with only ited command of the English language. The second, acting as lator, was his wife, worried about her husband's condition and tened by the hospital environment. The third person in the trio n inexperienced young doctor, trying to figure out what might brought on the strange illness. Under the stress, the doctor was tting everything he had been taught about patient confidenti- He committed the awful blunder of requesting the woman k her husband whether he'd had any sexual experiences that t have caused the infection.

s the young doctor watched, the husband turned red, pulled elf together so that he seemed even smaller, tried to disap- under his bed sheets, and stammered in a barely audible voice. vife suddenly screamed in rage and drew herself up to tower him. Before the doctor could stop her, she grabbed a heavy bottle, slammed it onto her husband's head, and stormed out e room. It took a while for the doctor to elicit, through the s broken English, what he had said to so enrage his wife. The er slowly emerged: he had admitted to repeated intercourse sheep on a recent visit to the family farm; perhaps that was he had contracted the mysterious microbe.

is episode, related to me by a physician friend involved in ase, sounds so bizarrely one of a kind as to be of no pos- broader significance. But in fact it illustrates a subject of great rtance: human diseases of animal origins. Very few of us may sheep in the carnal sense. But most of us platonically love our nimals, like our dogs and cats; and as a society, we certainly r to have an inordinate fondness for sheep and other livestock, ge from the vast numbers of them that we keep.

me of us—most often our children—pick up infectious ses from our pets. Usually these illnesses remain no more a nuisance, but a few have evolved into far more. The major s of humanity throughout our recent history—smallpox, flu, culosis, malaria, plague, measles, and cholera—are all infec- diseases that arose from diseases of animals. Until World I more victims of war died of microbes than of gunshot or sword wounds. All those military histories glorifying Alexander the Great and Napoleon ignore the ego-deflating truth: the winners of past wars were not necessarily those armies with the best generals and weapons, but those bearing the worst germs with which to smite their enemies.

The grimmest example of the role of germs in history is much on our minds this month, as we recall the European conquest of the Americas that began with Columbus's voyage of 1492. Numerous as the Indian victims of the murderous Spanish conquistadores were, they were dwarfed in number by the victims of murderous Spanish microbes. These formidable conquerors killed an estimated 95 percent of the New World's pre-Columbian Indian population.

Why was the exchange of nasty germs between the Americas and Europe so unequal? Why didn't the reverse happen instead, with Indian diseases decimating the Spanish invaders, spreading back across the Atlantic, and causing a 95 percent decline in *Europe's* human population?

Similar questions arise regarding the decimation of many other native peoples by European germs, and regarding the decimation of would-be European conquistadores in the tropics of Africa and Asia.

Naturally, we're disposed to think about diseases from our own point of view: What can we do to save ourselves and to kill the microbes? Let's stamp out the scoundrels, and never mind what *their* motives are!

In life, though, one has to understand the enemy to beat him. So for a moment, let's consider disease from the microbes' point of view. Let's look beyond our anger at their making us sick in bizarre ways, like giving us genital sores or diarrhea, and ask why it is that they do such things. After all, microbes are as much a product of natural selection as we are, and so their actions must have come about because they confer some evolutionary benefit.

Basically, of course, evolution selects those individuals that are most effective at producing babies and at helping those babies find suitable places to live. Microbes are marvels at this latter requirement. They have evolved diverse ways of spreading from one person to another, and from animals to people. Many of our symptoms of disease actually represent ways in which some clever bug modifies our bodies or our behavior such that we become enlisted to spread bugs.

The most effortless way a bug can spread is by just waiting to be transmitted passively to the next victim. That's the strategy practiced by microbes that wait for one host to be eaten by the next—salmonella bacteria, for example, which we contract by eating already-infected eggs or meat; or the worm responsible for trichinosis, which waits for us to kill a pig and eat it without properly cooking it.

As a slight modification of this strategy; some microbes don't wait for the old host to die but instead hitchhike in the saliva of an insect that bites the old host and then flies to a new one. The free ride may be provided by mosquitoes, fleas, lice, or tsetse flies, which spread malaria, plague, typhus, and sleeping sickness, respectively. The dirtiest of all passive-carriage tricks is perpetrated by microbes that pass from a woman to her fetus—microbes such as the ones responsible for syphilis, rubella (German measles), and AIDS. By their cunning these microbes can already be infecting an infant before the moment of its birth.

Other bugs take matters into their own hands, figuratively speaking. They actively modify the anatomy or habits of their host to accelerate their transmission. From our perspective, the open genital sores caused by venereal diseases such as syphilis are a vile indignity. From the microbes' point of view, however, they're just a useful device to enlist a host's help in inoculating the body cavity of another host with microbes. The skin lesions caused by smallpox similarly spread microbes by direct or indirect body contact (occasionally very indirect, as when U.S. and Australian whites bent on wiping out "belligerent" native peoples sent them gifts of blankets previously used by smallpox patients).

More vigorous yet is the strategy practiced by the influenza, common cold, and pertussis (whooping cough) microbes, which induce the victim to cough or sneeze, thereby broadcasting the bugs toward prospective new hosts. Similarly the cholera bacterium induces a massive diarrhea that spreads bacteria into the water supplies of potential new victims. For modification of a host's behavior, though, nothing matches the rabies virus, which not only gets into the saliva of an infected dog but drives the dog into a frenzy of biting and thereby infects many new victims.

Thus, from our viewpoint, genital sores, diarrhea, and coughing are "symptoms" of disease. From a bug's viewpoint, they're clever evolutionary strategies to broadcast the bug. That's why it's in the bug's interests to make us "sick." But what does it gain by killing us? That seems self-defeating, since a microbe that kills its host kills itself.

Though you may well think it's of little consolation, our death is really just an unintended by-product of host symptoms that promote the efficient transmission of microbes. Yes, an untreated cholera patient may eventually die from producing diarrheal fluid at a rate of several gallons a day. While the patient lasts, though, the cholera bacterium profits from being massively disseminated into the water supplies of its next victims. As long as each victim thereby infects, on average, more than one new victim, the bacteria will spread, even though the first host happens to die.

So much for the dispassionate examination of the bug's interests. Now let's get back to considering our own selfish interests: to stay alive and healthy, best done by killing the damned bugs. One common response to infection is to develop a fever. Again, we consider fever a "symptom" of disease, as if it developed inevitably without serving any function. But regulation of body temperature is under our genetic control, and a f doesn't just happen by accident. Because some microbes are r sensitive to heat than our own bodies are, by raising our body perature we in effect try to bake the bugs to death before we baked ourselves.

We and our pathogens are now locked in an escalating evolutionary contest, with the death of one contestant the price of defeat, and with natural selection playi the role of umpire.

Another common response is to mobilize our immune sys White blood cells and other cells actively seek out and kill fo microbes. The specific antibodies we gradually build up agai particular microbe make us less likely to get reinfected onc are cured. As we all know there are some illnesses, such as flu the common cold, to which our resistance is only temporary can eventually contract the illness again. Against other illne though—including measles, mumps, rubella, pertussis, and now-defeated menace of smallpox—antibodies stimulated by infection confer lifelong immunity. That's the principle be vaccination—to stimulate our antibody production without having to go through the actual experience of the disease.

Alas, some clever bugs don't just cave in to our immune defe Some have learned to trick us by changing their antigens, t molecular pieces of the microbe that our antibodies recognize constant evolution or recycling of new strains of flu, with diff antigens, explains why the flu you got two years ago didn't pr you against the different strain that arrived this year. Sleeping ness is an even more slippery customer in its ability to chang antigens rapidly.

Among the slipperiest of all is the virus that causes AIDS, w evolves new antigens even as it sits within an individual pa until it eventually overwhelms the immune system.

Our slowest defensive response is through natural selec which changes the relative frequency with which a gene ap from generation to generation. For almost any disease some pe prove to be genetically more resistant than others. In an epide those people with genes for resistance to that particular mic are more likely to survive than are people lacking such gene a result, over the course of history human populations repea exposed to a particular pathogen tend to be made up of indivi with genes that resist the appropriate microbe just because unf nate individuals without those genes were less likely to survi pass their genes on to their children.

Fat consolation, you may be thinking. This evolutionary res is not one that does the genetically susceptible dying individua good. It does mean, though, that a human population as a w becomes better protected.

In short, many bugs have had to evolve tricks to let them s among potential victims. We've evolved counter-tricks, to w the bugs have responded by evolving counter-counter-tricks and our pathogens are now locked in an escalating evolutio contest, with the death of one contestant the price of defeat with natural selection playing the role of umpire.

he form that this deadly contest takes varies with the pathogens: for some it is like a guerrilla war, while for others it is a blitzkrieg. With certain diseases, like malaria or worm, there's a more or less steady trickle of new cases in fected area, and they will appear in any month of any year. mic diseases, though, are different: they produce no cases for g time, then a whole wave of cases, then no more cases again while.

mong such epidemic diseases, influenza is the most familiar nericans, this year having been a particularly bad one for us great year for the influenza virus). Cholera epidemics come ger intervals, the 1991 Peruvian epidemic being the first one ch the New World during the twentieth century. Frightening lay's influenza and cholera epidemics are, though, they pale e the far more terrifying epidemics of the past, before the rise odern medicine. The greatest single epidemic in human hisvas the influenza wave that killed 21 million people at the end First World War. The black death, or bubonic plague, killed uarter of Europe's population between 1346 and 1352, with tolls up to 70 percent in some cities.

e infectious diseases that visit us as epidemics share several cteristics. First, they spread quickly and efficiently from an ed person to nearby healthy people, with the result that the population gets exposed within a short time. Second, they're e" illnesses: within a short time, you either die or recover letely. Third, the fortunate ones of us who do recover develop odies that leave us immune against a recurrence of the disease long time, possibly our entire lives. Finally, these diseases o be restricted to humans; the bugs causing them tend not e in the soil or in other animals. All four of these characterapply to what Americans think of as the once more-familiar epidemic diseases of childhood, including measles, rubella, os, pertussis, and smallpox.

s easy to understand why the combination of those four charstics tends to make a disease run in epidemics. The rapid d of microbes and the rapid course of symptoms mean that oody in a local human population is soon infected, and thereither dead or else recovered and immune. No one is left alive ould still be infected. But since the microbe can't survive t in the bodies of living people, the disease dies out until a rop of babies reaches the susceptible age—and until an infecperson arrives from the outside to start a new epidemic.

classic illustration of the process is given by the history of es on the isolated Faeroe Islands in the North Atlantic. A epidemic of the disease reached the Faeroes in 1781, then ut, leaving the islands measles-free until an infected carpenived on a ship from Denmark in 1846. Within three months t the whole Faeroes population—7,782 people—had gotten es and then either died or recovered, leaving the measles virus ppear once again until the next epidemic. Studies show that es is likely to die out in any human population numbering less alf a million people. Only in larger populations can measles rom one local area to another, thereby persisting until enough have been born in the originally infected area to permit the e's return.

bella in Australia provides a similar example, on a much scale. As of 1917 Australia's population was still only 5 milvith most people living in scattered rural areas. The sea voy-Britain took two months, and land transport within Australia itself was slow. In effect, Australia didn't even consist of a population of 5 million, but of hundreds of much smaller populations. As a result, rubella hit Australia only as occasional epidemics, when an infected person happened to arrive from overseas and stayed in a densely populated area. By 1938, though, the city of Sydney alone had a population of over one million, and people moved frequently and quickly by air between London, Sydney, and other Australian cities. Around then, rubella for the first time was able to establish itself permanently in Australia.

What's true for rubella in Australia is true for most familiar acute infectious diseases throughout the world. To sustain themselves, they need a human population that is sufficiently numerous and densely packed that a new crop of susceptible children is available for infection by the time the disease would otherwise be waning. Hence the measles and other such diseases are also known as "crowd diseases."

Crowd diseases could not sustain themselves in small bands of hunter-gatherers and slash-and-burn farmers. As tragic recent experience with Amazonian Indians and Pacific Islanders confirms, almost an entire tribelet may be wiped out by an epidemic brought by an outside visitor, because no one in the tribelet has any antibodies against the microbe. In addition, measles and some other "childhood" diseases are more likely to kill infected adults than children, and all adults in the tribelet are susceptible. Having killed most of the tribelet, the epidemic then disappears. The small population size explains why tribelets can't sustain epidemics introduced from the outside; at the same time it explains why they could never evolve epidemic diseases of their own to give back to the visitors.

That's not to say that small human populations are free from all infectious diseases. Some of their infections are caused by microbes capable of maintaining themselves in animals or in soil, so the disease remains constantly available to infect people. For example, the yellow fever virus is carried by African wild monkeys and is constantly available to infect rural human populations of Africa. It was also available to be carried to New World monkeys and people by the transAtlantic slave trade.

Other infections of small human populations are chronic diseases, such as leprosy and yaws, that may take a very long time to kill a victim. The victim thus remains alive as a reservoir of microbes to infect other members of the tribelet. Finally, small human populations are susceptible to nonfatal infections against which we don't develop immunity, with the result that the same person can become reinfected after recovering. That's the case with hookworm and many other parasites.

All these types of diseases, characteristic of small, isolated populations, must be the oldest diseases of humanity. They were the ones that we could evolve and sustain through the early millions of years of our evolutionary history, when the total human population was tiny and fragmented. They are also shared with, or are similar to the diseases of, our closest wild relatives, the African great apes. In contrast, the evolution of our crowd diseases could only have occurred with the buildup of large, dense human populations, first made possible by the rise of agriculture about 10,000 years ago, then by the rise of cities several thousand years ago. Indeed, the first attested dates for many familiar infectious diseases are surprisingly recent: around 1600 B.C. for smallpox (as deduced from pockmarks on an Egyptian mummy), 400 B.C. for mumps, 1840 for polio, and 1959 for AIDS.

Agriculture sustains much higher human population densities than do hunting and gathering—on average, 10 to 100 times higher. In addition, hunter-gatherers frequently shift camp, leaving behind their piles of feces with their accumulated microbes and worm larvae. But farmers are sedentary and live amid their own sewage, providing microbes with a quick path from one person's body into another person's drinking water. Farmers also become surrounded by disease-transmitting rodents attracted by stored food.

The explosive increase in world travel by Americans, and in immigration to the United States, is turning us into another melting pot—this time of microbes that we'd dismissed as causing disease in far-off countries.

Some human populations make it even easier for their own bacteria and worms to infect new victims, by intentionally gathering their feces and urine and spreading it as fertilizer on the fields where people work. Irrigation agriculture and fish farming provide ideal living conditions for the snails carrying schistosomes, and for other flukes that burrow through our skin as we wade through the feces-laden water.

If the rise of farming was a boon for our microbes, the rise of cities was a veritable bonanza, as still more densely packed human populations festered under even worse sanitation conditions. (Not until the beginning of the twentieth century did urban populations finally become self-sustaining; until then, constant immigration of healthy peasants from the countryside was necessary to make good the constant deaths of city dwellers from crowd diseases.) Another bonanza was the development of world trade routes, which by late Roman times effectively joined the populations of Europe, Asia, and North Africa into one giant breeding ground for microbes. That's when smallpox finally reached Rome as the "plague of Antonius," which killed millions of Roman citizens between A.D. 165 and 180.

Similarly, bubonic plague first appeared in Europe as the plague of Justinian (A.D. 542–543). But plague didn't begin to hit Europe with full force, as the black death epidemics, until 1346, when new overland trading with China provided rapid transit for flea-infested furs from plague-ridden areas of Central Asia. Today our jet planes have made even the longest intercontinental flights briefer than the duration of any human infectious disease. That's how an Aerolíneas Argentinas airplane, stopping in Lima, Peru, earlier this year, managed to deliver dozens of cholera-infected people the same day to my city of Los Angeles, over 3,000 miles away. The explosive increase in world travel by Americans, and in immigration to the United States, is turning us into another melting pot—this time of microbes that we previously dismissed as just causing exotic diseases in far-off countries.

When the human population became sufficiently large and concentrated, we reached the stage in our history when we could at last sustain crowd diseases confined to our species. But that presents a paradox: such diseases could never have existed before. Instead they had to evolve as nev eases. Where did those new diseases come from?

Evidence emerges from studies of the disease-causing mic themselves. In many cases molecular biologists have identifie microbe's closest relative. Those relatives also prove to be age infectious crowd diseases—but ones confined to various spec domestic animals and pets! Among animals too, epidemic dis require dense populations, and they're mainly confined to animals that provide the necessary large populations. Hence we domesticated social animals such as cows and pigs, they already afflicted by epidemic diseases just waiting to be trans to us.

For example, the measles virus is most closely related to the causing rinderpest, a nasty epidemic disease of cattle and wild cud-chewing mammals. Rinderpest doesn't affect hu Measles, in turn, doesn't affect cattle. The close similarity measles and rinderpest viruses suggests that the rinderpest transferred from cattle to humans, then became the measles by changing its properties to adapt to us. That transfer isn't su ing, considering how closely many peasant farmers live and next to cows and their accompanying feces, urine, breath, and blood. Our intimacy with cattle has been going on for years since we domesticated them—ample time for the rind virus to discover us nearby. Other familiar infectious disease similarly be traced back to diseases of our animal friends.

Given our proximity to the animals we love, we must cons be getting bombarded by animal microbes. Those invaders ge nowed by natural selection, and only a few succeed in establi themselves as human diseases. A quick survey of current di lets us trace four stages in the evolution of a specialized h disease from an animal precursor.

In the first stage, we pick up animal-borne microbes that a at an early stage in their evolution into specialized human path They don't get transmitted directly from one person to anothe even their transfer from animals to us remains uncommon. are dozens of diseases like this that we get directly from pe domestic animals. They include cat scratch fever from cats, lep rosis from dogs, psittacosis from chickens and parrots, and b losis from cattle. We're similarly susceptible to picking up di from wild animals, such as the tularemia that hunters occasi get from skinning wild rabbits.

In the second stage, a former animal pathogen evolves point where it does get transmitted directly between peop causes epidemics. However, the epidemic dies out for sever sons—being cured by modern medicine, stopping when body has been infected and died, or stopping when ever has been infected and become immune. For example, a prev unknown disease termed *o'nyong-nyong* fever appeared i Africa in 1959 and infected several million Africans. It pr arose from a virus of monkeys and was transmitted to hum mosquitoes. The fact that patients recovered quickly and b immune to further attack helped cause the new disease to c quickly.

The annals of medicine are full of diseases that sound known disease today but that once caused terrifying epic before disappearing as mysteriously as they had come. Wh today remembers the "English sweating sickness" that swe terrified Europe between 1485 and 1578, or the "Picardy s of eighteenth- and nineteenth-century France?

ird stage in the evolution of our major diseases is represented ner animal pathogens that establish themselves in humans t do not die out; until they do, the question of whether they come major killers of humanity remains up for grabs. The s still very uncertain for Lassa fever, first observed in 1969 eria and caused by a virus probably derived from rodents. established is Lyme disease, caused by a spirochete that we m the bite of a tick. Although the first known human cases Jnited States appeared only as recently as 1962, Lyme dis- already reaching epidemic proportions in the Northeast, on st Coast, and in the upper Midwest. The future of AIDS, from monkey viruses, is even more secure, from the virus's ctive.

final stage of this evolution is represented by the major, stablished epidemic diseases confined to humans. These dis- nust have been the evolutionary survivors of far more patho- at tried to make the jump to us from animals—and mostly

eases represent evolution in progress, as microbes adapt ural selection to new hosts. Compared with cows' bodies, , our bodies offer different immune defenses and different try. In that new environment, a microbe must evolve new) live and propagate itself.

best-studied example of microbes evolving these new ways s myxomatosis, which hit Australian rabbits in 1950. The na virus, native to a wild species of Brazilian rabbit, was to cause a lethal epidemic in European domestic rabbits, are a different species. The virus was intentionally intro- o Australia in the hopes of ridding the continent of its plague opean rabbits, foolishly introduced in the nineteenth cen- the first year, myxoma produced a gratifying (to Australian s) 99.8 percent mortality in infected rabbits. Fortunately for bits and unfortunately for the farmers, the death rate then d in the second year to 90 percent and eventually to 25 per- ustrating hopes of eradicating rabbits completely from Aus- The problem was that the myxoma virus evolved to serve its terest, which differed from the farmers' interests and those rabbits. The virus changed to kill fewer rabbits and to per- nally infected ones to live longer before dying. The result d for Australian farmers but good for the virus: a less lethal na virus spreads baby viruses to more rabbits than did the l, highly virulent myxoma.

a similar example in humans, consider the surprising evolu- syphilis. Today we associate syphilis with genital sores and slowly developing disease, leading to the death of untreated only after many years. However, when syphilis was first ly recorded in Europe in 1495, its pustules often covered the om the head to the knees, caused flesh to fall off people's nd led to death within a few months. By 1546 syphilis had l into the disease with the symptoms known to us today. ntly, just as with myxomatosis, those syphilis spirochetes l to keep their victims alive longer in order to transmit their ete offspring into more victims.

ow, then, does all this explain the outcome of 1492—that Europeans conquered and depopulated the New World, instead of Native Americans conquering and depopulat- ope?

In the century or two following Columbus's arrival in the New World, the Indian population declined by about 95 percent. The main killers were European germs, to which the Indians had never been exposed.

Part of the answer, of course, goes back to the invaders' technological advantages. European guns and steel swords were more effective weapons than Native American stone axes and wooden clubs. Only Europeans had ships capable of crossing the ocean and horses that could provide a decisive advantage in battle. But that's not the whole answer. Far more Native Americans died in bed than on the battlefield—the victims of germs, not of guns and swords. Those germs undermined Indian resistance by killing most Indians and their leaders and by demoralizing the survivors.

The role of disease in the Spanish conquests of the Aztec and Inca empires is especially well documented. In 1519 Cortés landed on the coast of Mexico with 600 Spaniards to conquer the fiercely militaristic Aztec Empire, which at the time had a population of many millions. That Cortés reached the Aztec capital of Tenochtitlán, escaped with the loss of "only" two-thirds of his force, and managed to fight his way back to the coast demonstrates both Spanish military advantages and the initial naïveté of the Aztecs. But when Cortés's next onslaught came, in 1521, the Aztecs were no longer naïve; they fought street by street with the utmost tenacity.

What gave the Spaniards a decisive advantage this time was smallpox, which reached Mexico in 1520 with the arrival of one infected slave from Spanish Cuba. The resulting epidemic proceeded to kill nearly half the Aztecs. The survivors were demoralized by the mysterious illness that killed Indians and spared Spaniards, as if advertising the Spaniards' invincibility. By 1618 Mexico's initial population of 20 million had plummeted to about 1.6 million.

Pizarro had similarly grim luck when he landed on the coast of Peru in 1531 with about 200 men to conquer the Inca Empire. Fortunately for Pizarro, and unfortunately for the Incas, smallpox had arrived overland around 1524, killing much of the Inca population, including both Emperor Huayna Capac and his son and designated successor, Ninan Cuyoche. Because of the vacant throne, two other sons of Huayna Capac, Atahuallpa and Huáscar, became embroiled in a civil war that Pizarro exploited to conquer the divided Incas.

When we in the United States think of the most populous New World societies existing in 1492, only the Aztecs and Incas come to mind. We forget that North America also supported populous Indian societies in the Mississippi Valley. Sadly, these societies too would disappear. But in this case conquistadores contributed nothing directly to the societies' destruction; the conquistadores' germs, spreading in advance, did everything. When De Soto marched through the Southeast in 1540, he came across Indian towns abandoned two years previously because nearly all the inhabitants had died in epidemics. However, he was still able to see some of the densely populated towns lining the lower Mississippi. By a century and a half later, though, when French settlers returned to the lower Mississippi, almost all those towns had vanished. Their relics are the great mound sites of the Mississippi Valley. Only recently have we come to realize that the mound-building societies were still largely intact when Columbus arrived, and that they collapsed between 1492 and the systematic European exploration of the Mississippi.

When I was a child in school, we were taught that North America had originally been occupied by about one million Indians. That low number helped justify the white conquest of what could then be viewed as an almost empty continent. However, archeological excavations and descriptions left by the first European explorers on our coasts now suggest an initial number of around 20 million. In the century or two following Columbus's arrival in the New World, the Indian population is estimated to have declined by about 95 percent.

The main killers were European germs, to which the Indians had never been exposed and against which they therefore had neither immunologic nor genetic resistance. Smallpox, measles, influenza, and typhus competed for top rank among the killers. As if those were not enough, pertussis, plague, tuberculosis, diphtheria, mumps, malaria, and yellow fever came close behind. In countless cases Europeans were actually there to witness the decimation that occurred when the germs arrived. For example, in 1837 the Mandan Indian tribe, with one of the most elaborate cultures in the Great Plains, contracted smallpox thanks to a steamboat traveling up the Missouri River from St. Louis. The population of one Mandan village crashed from 2,000 to less than 40 within a few weeks.

The one-sided exchange of lethal germs between the Old and New Worlds is among the most striking and consequence-laden facts of recent history. Whereas over a dozen major infectious diseases of Old World origins became established in the New World, not a single major killer reached Europe from the Americas. The sole possible exception is syphilis, whose area of origin still remains controversial.

That one-sidedness is more striking with the knowledge that large, dense human populations are a prerequisite for the evolution of crowd diseases. If recent reappraisals of the pre-Columbian New World population are correct, that population was not far below the contemporaneous population of Eurasia. Some New World cities, like Tenochtitlán, were among the world's most populous cities at the time. Yet Tenochtitlán didn't have awful germs waiting in store for the Spaniards. Why not?

One possible factor is the rise of dense human populations began somewhat later in the New World than in the Old. Another is that the three most populous American centers—the Andes, Mexico, and the Mississippi Valley—were never connected by regular fast trade into one gigantic breeding ground for microbes, in the way that Europe, North Africa, India, and China became connected in late Roman times.

The main reason becomes clear, however, if we ask a simple question: From what microbes could any crowd diseases of the Americas have evolved? We've seen that Eurasian crowd diseases evolved from diseases of domesticated herd animals. Significantly, there were many such animals in Eurasia. But there were only five animals that became domesticated in the Americas: the turkey in Mexico and parts of North America, the guinea pig and llama/alpaca (probably derived from the same original wild species) in the Andes, and Muscovy duck in tropical South America, and the dog throughout the Americas.

That extreme paucity of New World domestic animals reflects the paucity of wild starting material. About 80 percent of the big wild mammals of the Americas became extinct at the end of the last ice age, around 11,000 years ago, at approximately the same time that the first well-attested wave of Indian hunters spread the Americas. Among the species that disappeared were one would have yielded useful domesticates, such as American h and camels. Debate still rages as to whether those extinctions due to climate changes or to the impact of Indian hunters on that had never seen humans. Whatever the reason, the extinc removed most of the basis for Native American animal dome tion—and for crowd diseases.

The few domesticates that remained were not likely sourc such diseases. Muscovy ducks and turkeys don't live in enor flocks, and they're not naturally endearing species (like lambs) with which we have much physical contact. Guinea may have contributed a trypanosome infection like Chagas' di or leishmaniasis to our catalog of woes, but that's uncertain.

Initially the most surprising absence is of any human di derived from llamas (or alpacas), which are tempting to consi the Andean equivalent of Eurasian livestock. However, llama three strikes against them as a source of human pathogens: wild relatives don't occur in big herds as do wild sheep, goat pigs; their total numbers were never remotely as large as the asian populations of domestic livestock, since llamas never s beyond the Andes; and llamas aren't as cuddly as piglets and and aren't kept in such close association with people. (You m think of piglets as cuddly, but human mothers in the New G highlands often nurse them, and they frequently live right huts of peasant farmers.)

The importance of animal-derived diseases for human h extends far beyond the Americas. Eurasian germs played a ke in decimating native peoples in many other parts of the wo well, including the Pacific islands, Australia, and southern A Racist Europeans used to attribute those conquests to thei posedly better brains. But no evidence for such better brai been forthcoming. Instead, the conquests were made possi Europeans' nastier germs, and by the technological advanc denser populations that Europeans ultimately acquired by me their domesticated plants and animals.

So on this 500th anniversary of Columbus's discovery, le to regain our sense of perspective about his hotly debated ac ments. There's no doubt that Columbus was a great visionar man, and leader. There's also no doubt that he and his succ often behaved as bestial murderers. But those facts alone don explain why it took so few European immigrants to initiall quer and ultimately supplant so much of the native popula the Americas. Without the germs Europeans brought with th germs that were derived from their animals—such conquests have been impossible.

Jared Diamond is a contributing editor of *Discover,* a profe physiology at the UCLA School of Medicine, a recipient of a M thur genius award, and a research associate in ornithology American Museum of Natural History. Expanded versions o of his *Discover* articles appear in his book *The Third Chimp The Evolution and Future of the Human Animal,* which won B 1992 COPUS prize for best science book. Not least among hi accomplishments was his rediscovery in 1981 of the long-lost bird of New Guinea. Diamond wrote about pseudo-hermaphroc *Discover's* special June issue on the science of sex.

he Price of Progress

IN BODLEY

aiming at progress . . . you must let no one suffer by too rastic a measure, nor pay too high a price in upheaval nd devastation, for your innovation.

Maunier, 1949: 725

Until recently, government planners have always considered economic development and progress beneficial goals that all societies should want to strive toward. social advantage of progress—as defined in terms of ased incomes, higher standards of living, greater security, etter health—are thought to be positive, *universal* goods, obtained at any price. Although one may argue that tribal les must sacrifice their traditional cultures to obtain these fits, government planners generally feel that this is a small to pay for such obvious advantages.

earlier chapters [in *Victims of Progress,* 3rd ed.], evidence resented to demonstrate that autonomous tribal peoples not *chosen* progress to enjoy its advantages, but that nments have *pushed* progress upon them to obtain tribal rces, not primarily to share with the tribal peoples the benof progress. It has also been shown that the price of forcrogress on unwilling recipients has involved the deaths of ns of tribal people, as well as their loss of land, political eignty, and the right to follow their own life style. This er does not attempt to further summarize that aspect of the f progress, but instead analyzes the specific effects of the ipation of tribal peoples in the world-market economy. In opposition to the usual interpretation, it is argued here he benefits of progress are often both illusory and detril to tribal peoples when they have not been allowed to l their own resources and define their relationship to the t economy.

gress and the Quality of Life

of the primary difficulties in assessing the benefits of ss and economic development for any culture is that of ishing a meaningful measure of both benefit and detri- It is widely recognized that *standard of living,* which is ost frequently used measure of progress, is an intrinsically centric concept relying heavily upon indicators that lack universal cultural relevance. Such factors as GNP, per capita income, capital formation, employment rates, literacy, formal education, consumption of manufactured goods, number of doctors and hospital beds per thousand persons, and the amount of money spent on government welfare and health programs may be irrelevant measures of actual *quality* of life for autonomous or even semiautonomous tribal cultures. In its 1954 report, the Trust Territory government indicated that since the Micronesian population was still largely satisfying its own needs within a cashless subsistence economy, "Money income is not a significant measure of living standards, production, or well-being in this area" (TTR, 1953: 44). Unfortunately, within a short time the government began to rely on an enumeration of certain imported consumer goods as indicators of a higher standard of living in the islands, even though many tradition-oriented islanders felt that these new goods symbolized a lowering of the quality of life.

A more useful measure of the benefits of progress might be based on a formula for evaluating cultures devised by Goldschmidt (1952: 135). According to these less ethnocentric criteria, the important question to ask is: Does progress or economic development increase or decrease a given culture's ability to satisfy the physical and psychological needs of its population, or its stability? This question is a far more direct measure of quality of life than are the standard economic correlates of development, and it is universally relevant. Specific indication of this *standard* of living could be found for any society in the nutritional status and general physical and mental health of its population, the incidence of crime and delinquency, the demographic structure, family stability, and the society's relationship to its natural resource base. A society with high rates of malnutrition and crime, and one degrading its natural environment to the extent of threatening its continued existence, might be described as at a lower standard of living than is another society where these problems did not exist.

Careful examination of the data, which compare, on these specific points, the former condition of self-sufficient tribal peoples with their condition following their incorporation into the world-market economy, leads to the conclusion that their standard of living is *lowered,* not raised, by economic progress—and often to a dramatic degree. This is perhaps the most outstanding and inescapable fact to emerge from the years of research that anthropologists have devoted to the study of culture change and modernization. Despite the best intentions of those who have promoted change and improvement, all too often the results have been poverty, longer working hours, and much greater physical exertion, poor health, social disorder, discontent, discrimination, overpopulation, and environmental deterioration—combined with the destruction of the traditional culture.

Diseases of Development

> *Perhaps it would be useful for public health specialists to start talking about a new category of diseases. . . . Such diseases could be called the "diseases of development" and would consist of those pathological conditions which are based on the usually unanticipated consequences of the implementation of developmental schemes.*
>
> Hughes & Hunter, 1972: 93

Economic development increases the disease rate of affected peoples in at least three ways. First, to the extent that development is successful, it makes developed populations suddenly become vulnerable to all of the diseases suffered almost exclusively by "advanced" peoples. Among these are diabetes, obesity, hypertension, and a variety of circulatory problems. Second, development disturbs traditional environmental balances and may dramatically increase certain bacterial and parasite diseases. Finally, when development goals prove unattainable, an assortment of poverty diseases may appear in association with the crowded conditions of urban slums and the general breakdown in traditional socioeconomic systems.

Outstanding examples of the first situation can be seen in the Pacific, where some of the most successfully developed native peoples are found. In Micronesia, where development has progressed more rapidly than perhaps anywhere else, between 1958 and 1972 the population doubled, but the number of patients treated for heart disease in the local hospitals nearly tripled, mental disorder increased eightfold, and by 1972 hypertension and nutritional deficiencies began to make significant appearances for the first time (TTR, 1959, 1973, statistical tables).

Although some critics argue that the Micronesian figures simply represent better health monitoring due to economic progress, rigorously controlled data from Polynesia show a similar trend. The progressive acquisition of modern degenerative diseases was documented by an eight-member team of New Zealand medical specialists, anthropologists, and nutritionists, whose research was funded by the Medical Research Council of New Zealand and the World Health Organization. These researchers investigated the health status of a genetically related population at various points along a continuum of increasing cash income, modernizing diet, and urbanization. The extremes on this acculturation continuum were represented by the relatively traditional Pukapukans of the Cook Islands and the essentially Europeanized New Zealand Maori, while the busily developing Rarotongans, also of the Cook Islands, occupied the intermediate position. In 1971, after eight years of work, the team's preliminary findings were summarized by Dr. Ian P cardiologist and leader of the research, as follows:

> *We are beginning to observe that the more an island takes on the ways of the West, the more prone he is t succumb to our degenerative diseases. In fact, it does n seem too much to say our evidence now shows that th farther the Pacific natives move from the quiet, carefre life of their ancestors, the closer they come to gout, diab tes, atherosclerosis, obesity, and hypertension.*
>
> Prior, 1971:

In Pukapuka, where progress was limited by the isl small size and its isolated location some 480 kilometers the nearest port, the annual per capita income was only a thirty-six dollars and the economy remained essentially subsistence level. Resources were limited and the area was ited by trading ships only three or four times a year; thus, was little opportunity for intensive economic developm Predictably, the population of Pukapuka was characterize relatively low levels of imported sugar and salt intake, a presumably related low level of heart disease, high blood sure, and diabetes. In Rarotonga, where economic success introducing town life, imported food, and motorcycles, and salt intakes nearly tripled, high blood pressure incre approximately ninefold, diabetes two- to threefold, and disease doubled for men and more than quadrupled for wo while the number of grossly obese women increased than tenfold. Among the New Zealand Maori, sugar i was nearly eight times that of the Pukapukans, gout in me nearly double its rate on Pukapuka, and diabetes in me more than fivefold higher, while heart disease in wome increased more than sixfold. The Maori were, in fact, dyi "European" diseases at a greater rate than was the average Zealand European.

Government development policies designed to bring changes in local hydrology, vegetation, and settlement pa and to increase population mobility, and even programs at reducing certain diseases, have frequently led to dra increases in disease rates because of the unforeseen effe disturbing the preexisting order. Hughes and Hunter (published an excellent survey of cases in which develop led directly to increased disease rates in Africa. They conc that hasty development intervention in relatively balanced cultures and environments resulted in "a drastic deteriorat the social and economic conditions of life."

Traditional populations in general have presumably lear live with the endemic pathogens of their environments, and in cases they have evolved genetic adaptations to specific dis such as the sickle-cell trait, which provided an immunity to m Unfortunately, however, outside intervention has entirely ch this picture. In the late 1960s, sleeping sickness suddenly inc in many areas of Africa and even spread to areas where it c formerly occur, due to the building of new roads and mig labor, both of which caused increased population movement. scale relocation schemes, such as the Zande Scheme, had dis s when natives were moved from their traditional disease-free es into infected areas. Dams and irrigation developments inad- ıtly created ideal conditions for the rapid proliferation of snails ing schistosomiasis (a liver fluke disease), and major epidem- ıddenly occurred in areas where this disease had never before a problem. DDT spraying programs have been temporarily ssful in controlling malaria, but there is often a rebound effect ncreases the problem when spraying is discontinued, and the ial mosquitoes are continually evolving resistant strains.

rbanization is one of the prime measures of development, is a mixed blessing for most former tribal peoples. Urban h standards are abysmally poor and generally worse than al areas for the detribalized individuals who have crowded the towns and cities throughout Africa, Asia, and Latin rica seeking wage employment out of new economic neces- nfectious diseases related to crowding and poor sanitation ımpant in urban centers, while greatly increased stress and nutrition aggravate a variety of other health problems. ıtrition and other diet-related conditions are, in fact, one characteristic hazards of progress faced by tribal peoples re discussed in the following sections.

Hazards of Dietary Change

raditional diets of tribal peoples are admirably adapted to utritional needs and available food resources. Even though diets may seem bizarre, absurd, and unpalatable to outsid- ey are unlikely to be improved by drastic modifications. the delicate balances and complexities involved in any tence system, change always involves risks, but for tribal e the effects of dietary change have been catastrophic.

der normal conditions, food habits are remarkably resist- change, and indeed people are unlikely to abandon their onal diets voluntarily in favor of dependence on difficult- ain exotic imports. In some cases it is true that imported may be identified with powerful outsiders and are there- ought as symbols of greater prestige. This may lead to ıbsurdities as Amazonian Indians choosing to consume ted canned tunafish when abundant high-quality fish is ble in their own rivers. Another example of this situation s in tribes where mothers prefer to feed their infants expen- utritionally inadequate canned milk from unsanitary, but *tatus,* baby bottles. The high status of these items is often ›ted by clever traders and clever advertising campaigns.

ide from these apparently voluntary changes, it appears ore often dietary changes are forced upon unwilling tribal s by circumstances beyond their control. In some areas, ›od crops have been introduced by government decree, or nsequence of forced relocation or other policies designed hunting, pastoralism, or shifting cultivation. Food habits ılso been modified by massive disruption of the natural nment by outsiders—as when sheepherders transformed stralian Aborigines' foraging territory or when European rs destroyed the bison herds that were the primary ele- n the Plains Indians' subsistence patterns. Perhaps the requent cause of diet change occurs when formerly self- ent peoples find that wage labor, cash cropping, and other economic development activities that feed tribal resources into the world-market economy must inevitably divert time and energy away from the production of subsistence foods. Many developing peoples suddenly discover that, like it or not, they are unable to secure traditional foods and must spend their newly acquired cash on costly, and often nutritionally inferior, manufactured foods.

Overall, the available data seem to indicate that the dietary changes that are linked to involvement in the world-market economy have tended to *lower* rather than raise the nutritional levels of the affected tribal peoples. Specifically, the vitamin, mineral, and protein components of their diets are often drastically reduced and replaced by enormous increases in starch and carbohydrates, often in the form of white flour and refined sugar.

Any deterioration in the quality of a given population's diet is almost certain to be reflected in an increase in deficiency diseases and a general decline in health status. Indeed, as tribal peoples have shifted to a diet based on imported manufactured or processed foods, there has been a dramatic rise in malnutrition, a massive increase in dental problems, and a variety of other nutritional-related disorders. Nutritional physiology is so complex that even well-meaning dietary changes have had tragic consequences. In many areas of Southeast Asia, government-sponsored protein supplementation programs supplying milk to protein-deficient populations caused unexpected health problems and increased mortality. Officials failed to anticipate that in cultures where adults do not normally drink milk, the enzymes needed to digest it are no longer produced and milk *intolerance* results (Davis & Bolin, 1972). In Brazil, a similar milk distribution program caused an epidemic of permanent blindness by aggravating a preexisting vitamin A deficiency (Bunce, 1972).

Teeth and Progress

> *There is nothing new in the observation that savages, or peoples living under primitive conditions, have, in general, excellent teeth. . . . Nor is it news that most civilized populations possess wretched teeth which begin to decay almost before they have erupted completely, and that dental caries is likely to be accompanied by periodontal disease with further reaching complications.*
>
> Hooton, 1945: xviii

Anthropologists have long recognized that undisturbed tribal peoples are often in excellent physical condition. And it has often been noted specifically that dental caries and the other dental abnormalities that plague industrialized societies are absent or rare among tribal peoples who have retained their traditional diets. The fact that tribal food habits may contribute to the development of sound teeth, whereas modernized diets may do just the opposite, was illustrated as long ago as 1894 in an article in the *Journal of the Royal Anthropological Institute* that described the results of a comparison between the teeth of ten Sioux Indians who were examined when they came to London as members of Buffalo Bill's Wild West Show and were found to be completely free of caries and in possession of all their teeth, even though half of the group were over thirty-nine years of age. Londoners' teeth were conspicuous for both their caries and their steady reduction in number with advancing age. The difference was attributed primarily to the wear and polishing caused by the traditional Indian diet of coarse food and the fact that they chewed their food longer, encouraged by the absence of tableware.

One of the most remarkable studies of the dental conditions of tribal peoples and the impact of dietary change was conducted in the 1930s by Weston Price (1945), an American dentist who was interested in determining what caused normal, healthy teeth. Between 1931 and 1936, Price systematically explored tribal areas throughout the world to locate and examine the most isolated peoples who were still living on traditional foods. His fieldwork covered Alaska, the Canadian Yukon, Hudson Bay, Vancouver Island, Florida, the Andes, the Amazon, Samoa, Tahiti, New Zealand, Australia, New Caledonia, Fiji, the Torres Strait, East Africa, and the Nile. The study demonstrated both the superior quality of aboriginal dentition and the devastation that occurs as modern diets are adopted. In nearly every area where traditional foods were still being eaten, Price found perfect teeth with normal dental arches and virtually no decay, whereas caries and abnormalities increased steadily as new diets were adopted. In many cases the change was sudden and striking. Among Eskimo groups subsisting entirely on traditional food he found caries totally absent, whereas in groups eating a considerable quantity of store-bought food approximately 20 percent of their teeth were decayed. This figure rose to more than 30 percent with Eskimo groups subsisting almost exclusively on purchased or government-supplied food, and reached an incredible 48 percent among the Vancouver Island Indians. Unfortunately for many of these people, modern dental treatment did not accompany the new food, and their suffering was appalling. The loss of teeth was, of course, bad enough in itself, and it certainly undermined the population's resistance to many new diseases, including tuberculosis. But new foods were also accompanied by crowded, misplaced teeth, gum diseases, distortion of the face, and pinching of the nasal cavity. Abnormalities in the dental arch appeared in the new generation following the change in diet, while caries appeared almost immediately even in adults.

Price reported that in many areas the affected peoples were conscious of their own physical deterioration. At a mission school in Africa, the principal asked him to explain to the native schoolchildren why they were not physically as strong as children who had had no contact with schools. On an island in the Torres Strait the natives knew exactly what was causing their problems and resisted—almost to the point of bloodshed—government efforts to establish a store that would make imported food available. The government prevailed, however, and Price was able to establish a relationship between the length of time the government store had been established and the increasing incidence of caries among a population that showed an almost 100 percent immunity to them before the store had been opened.

In New Zealand, the Maori, who in their aboriginal sta often considered to have been among the healthiest, mos fectly developed of people, were found to have "advanced furthest. According to Price:

> *Their modernization was demonstrated not only by t high incidence of dental caries but also by the fact th 90 percent of the adults and 100 percent of the childr had abnormalities of the dental arches.*
>
> Price, 1945: 2

Malnutrition

Malnutrition, particularly in the form of protein deficienc become a critical problem for tribal peoples who must new economic patterns. Population pressures, cash crop and government programs all have tended to encourag replacement of traditional crops and other food source were rich in protein with substitutes, high in calories bu in protein. In Africa, for example, protein-rich staples as millet and sorghum are being replaced systematica high-yielding manioc and plantains, which have insigni amounts of protein. The problem is increased for cash cro and wage laborers whose earnings are too low and unpredi to allow purchase of adequate amounts of protein. In some areas, agricultural laborers have been forced systematica deprive nonproductive members (principally children) of households of their minimal nutritional requirements to s the need of the productive members. This process has documented in northeastern Brazil following the introdu of large-scale sisal plantations (Gross & Underwood, 197 urban centers the difficulties of obtaining nutritionally ade diets are even more serious for tribal immigrants, because are higher and poor quality foods are more tempting.

One of the most tragic, and largely overlooked, aspe chronic malnutrition is that it can lead to abnormally unde brain development and apparently irreversible brain dam has been associated with various forms of mental impairn retardation. Malnutrition has been linked clinically with r retardation in both Africa and Latin America (see, for ex Mönckeberg, 1968), and this appears to be a worldwid nomenon with serious implications (Montagu, 1972).

Optimistic supporters of progress will surely say that these new health problems are being overstressed and th introduction of hospitals, clinics, and the other modern institutions will overcome or at least compensate for all o difficulties. However, it appears that uncontrolled popu growth and economic impoverishment probably will kee of these benefits out of reach for many tribal peoples, a intervention of modern medicine has at least partly contr to the problem in the first place.

The generalization that civilization frequently has a negative impact on tribal health has found broad e cal support (see especially Kroeger & Barbira-Fre [1982] on Amazonia; Reinhard [1976] on the Arctic; and W

] globally), but these conclusions have not gone unchal- d. Some critics argue that tribal health was often poor e modernization, and they point specifically to tribals' low xpectancy and high infant mortality rates. Demographic tics on tribal populations are often problematic because se data are scarce, but they do show a less favorable pro- ıan that enjoyed by many industrial societies. However, it d be remembered that our present life expectancy is a recent ›menon that has been very costly in terms of medical ·ch and technological advances. Furthermore, the benefits r health system are not enjoyed equally by all members r society. High infant mortality could be viewed as a rela- inexpensive and egalitarian tribal public health program ffered the reasonable expectation of a healthy and produc- fe for those surviving to age fifteen.

me critics also suggest that certain tribal populations, such New Guinea highlanders, were "stunted" by nutritional encies created by tribal culture and are "improved" by lturation" and cash cropping (Dennett & Connell, 1988). ugh this argument does suggest that the health question es careful evaluation, it does not invalidate the empiri- neralizations already established. Nutritional deficiencies ıbtedly occurred in densely populated zones in the central Guinea highlands. However, the specific case cited above ot be widely representative of other tribal groups even in Guinea, and it does not address the facts of outside intru- r the inequities inherent in the contemporary development ss.

›cide

ow is it," asked a herdsman . . . "how is it that these s can no longer give pasture to my cattle? In my father's they were green and cattle thrived there; today there o grass and my cattle starve." As one looked one saw what had once been a green hill had become a raw rock.

Jones, 1934

ss not only brings new threats to the health of tribal peo- ut it also imposes new strains on the ecosystems upon they must depend for their ultimate survival. The intro- n of new technology, increased consumption, lowered ity, and the eradication of all traditional controls have ıed to replace what for most tribal peoples was a rela- stable balance between population and natural resources, new system that is imbalanced. Economic development ng *ecocide* on peoples who were once careful stewards r resources. There is already a trend toward widespread mental deterioration in tribal areas, involving resource on, erosion, plant and animal extinction, and a disturbing of other previously unforeseen changes.

r the initial depopulation suffered by most tribal peoples their engulfment by frontiers of national expansion, most opulations began to experience rapid growth. Authori- ıerally attribute this growth to the introduction of mod- dicine and new health measures and the termination of intertribal warfare, which lowered morality rates, as well as to new technology, which increased food production. Certainly all of these factors played a part, but merely lowering mortality rates would not have produced the rapid population growth that most tribal areas have experienced if traditional birth-spacing mechanisms had not been eliminated at the same time. Regardless of which factors were most important, it is clear that all of the natural and cultural checks on population growth have suddenly been pushed aside by culture change, while tribal lands have been steadily reduced and consumption levels have risen. In many tribal areas, environmental deterioration due to overuse of resources has set in, and in other areas such deterioration is imminent as resources continue to dwindle relative to the expanding population and increased use. Of course, population expansion by tribal peoples may have positive political consequences, because where tribals can retain or regain their status as local majorities they may be in a more favorable position to defend their resources against intruders.

Swidden systems and pastoralism, both highly successful economic systems under traditional conditions, have proved particularly vulnerable to increased population pressures and outside efforts to raise productivity beyond its natural limits. Research in Amazonia demonstrates that population pressures and related resource depletion can be created indirectly by official policies that restrict swidden peoples to smaller territories. Resource depletion itself can then become a powerful means of forcing tribal people into participating in the world-market economy—thus leading to further resource depletion. For example, Bodley and Benson (1979) showed how the Shipibo Indians in Peru were forced to further deplete their forest resources by cash cropping in the forest area to replace the resources that had been destroyed earlier by the intensive cash cropping necessitated by the narrow confines of their reserve. In this case, certain species of palm trees that had provided critical housing materials were destroyed by forest clearing and had to be replaced by costly purchased materials. Research by Gross (1979) and others showed similar processes at work among four tribal groups in central Brazil and demonstrated that the degree of market involvement increases directly with increases in resource depletion.

The settling of nomadic herders and the removal of prior controls on herd size have often led to serious overgrazing and erosion problems where these had not previously occurred. There are indications that the desertification problem in the Sahel region of Africa was aggravated by programs designed to settle nomads. The first sign of imbalance in a swidden system appears when the planting cycles are shortened to the point that garden plots are reused before sufficient forest regrowth can occur. If reclearing and planting continue in the same area, the natural patterns of forest succession may be disturbed irreversibly and the soil can be impaired permanently. An extensive tract of tropical rainforest in the lower Amazon of Brazil was reduced to a semiarid desert in just fifty years through such a process (Ackermann, 1964). The soils in the Azande area are also now seriously threatened with laterization and other problems as a result of the government-promoted cotton development scheme (McNeil, 1972).

The dangers of overdevelopment and the vulnerability of local resource systems have long been recognized by both anthropologists and tribal peoples themselves. But the pressures for change have been overwhelming. In 1948 the Maya villagers of Chan Kom complained to Redfield (1962) about the shortening of their swidden cycles, which they correctly attributed to increasing population pressures. Redfield told them, however, that they had no choice but to go "forward with technology" (Redfield, 1962: 178). In Assam, swidden cycles were shortened from an average of twelve years to only two or three within just twenty years, and anthropologists warned that the limits of swiddening would soon be reached (Burling, 1963: 311–312). In the Pacific, anthropologists warned of population pressures on limited resources as early as the 1930s (Keesing, 1941: 64–65). These warnings seemed fully justified, considering the fact that the crowded Tikopians were prompted by population pressures on their tiny island to suggest that infanticide be legalized. The warnings have been dramatically reinforced since then by the doubling of Micronesia's population in just the fourteen years between 1958 and 1972, from 70,600 to 114,645, while consumption levels have soared. By 1985 Micronesia's population had reached 162,321.

The environmental hazards of economic development and rapid population growth have become generally recognized only since worldwide concerns over environmental issues began in the early 1970s. Unfortunately, there is as yet little indication that the leaders of the new developing nations are sufficiently concerned with environmental limitations. On the contrary, governments are forcing tribal peoples into a self-reinforcing spiral of population growth and intensified resource exploitation, which may be stopped only by environmental disaster or the total impoverishment of the tribals.

The reality of ecocide certainly focuses attention on the fundamental contrasts between tribal and industrial systems in their use of natural resources, who controls them, and how they are managed. Tribal peoples are victimized because they control resources that outsiders demand. The resources exist because tribals managed them conservatively. However, as with the issue of the health consequences of detribalization, some anthropologists minimize the adaptive achievements of tribal groups and seem unwilling to concede that ecocide might be a consequence of cultural change. Critics attack an exaggerated "noble savage" image of tribals living in perfect harmony with nature and having no visible impact on their surroundings. They then show that tribals do in fact modify the environment, and they conclude that there is no significant difference between how tribals and industrial societies treat their environments. For example, Charles Wagley declared that Brazilian Indians such as the Tapirape

> *are not "natural men." They have human vices just as we do.... They do not live "in tune" with nature any more than I do; in fact, they can often be as destructive of their environment, within their limitations, as some civilized men. The Tapirape are not innocent or childlike in any way.*
>
> Wagley, 1977: 302

Anthropologist Terry Rambo demonstrated that the Se of the Malaysian rain forests have a measurable impact on environment. In his monograph *Primitive Polluters,* R (1985) reported that the Semang live in smoke-filled hc They sneeze and spread germs, breathe, and thus emit c dioxide. They clear small gardens, contributing "particulate ter" to the air and disturbing the local climate because cl areas proved measurably warmer and drier than the shady f Rambo concluded that his research "demonstrates the ess functional similarity of the environmental interactions of p tive and civilized societies" (1985: 78) in contrast to a "nobl age" view (Bodley, 1983) which, according to Rambo (198 mistakenly "claims that traditional peoples almost alway in essential harmony with their environment."

This is surely a false issue. To stress, as I do, that tribal to manage their resources for sustained yield within rela self-sufficient subsistence economies is not to make them innocent children or natural men. Nor is it to deny that "disrupt" their environment and may never be in absolute ance" with nature.

The ecocide issue is perhaps most dramatically illus by two sets of satellite photos taken over the Brazilian rai ests of Rôndonia (Allard & McIntyre, 1988: 780–781). I taken in 1973, when Rôndonia was still a tribal domain, virtually unbroken rain forest. The 1987 satellite photos, after just fifteen years of highway construction and "de ment" by outsiders, show more than 20 percent of the destroyed. The surviving Indians were being concentra FUNAI (Brazil's national Indian foundation) into what soon become mere islands of forest in a ravaged landsc is irrelevant to quibble about whether tribals are noble, like, or innocent, or about the precise meaning of balanc nature, carrying capacity, or adaptation, to recognize that past 200 years rapid environmental deterioration on an u edented global scale has followed the wresting of con vast areas of the world from tribal groups by resource-l industrial societies.

Deprivation and Discriminatio

> *Contact with European culture has given them a kno edge of great wealth, opportunity and privilege, but very limited avenues by which to acquire these things*
>
> Crocombe, 1

Unwittingly, tribal peoples have had the burden of pe relative deprivation thrust upon them by acceptance—ei themselves or by the governments administering them— standards of socioeconomic progress set for them by inc civilizations. By comparison with the material wealth of trial societies, tribal societies become, by definition, i erished. They are then forced to transform their cultu work to achieve what many economists now acknowledg unattainable goals. Even though in many cases the mod goals set by development planners for the developing during the "development decade" of the 1960s were oft the results were hardly noticeable for most of the tribal olved. Population growth, environmental limitations, inequi-le distribution of wealth, and the continued rapid growth of industrialized nations have all meant that both the absolute l the relative gap between the rich and poor in the world is adily widening. The prospect that tribal peoples will actually able to attain the levels of resource consumption to which y are being encouraged to aspire is remote indeed except those few groups who have retained effective control over ategic mineral resources.

Tribal peoples feel deprivation not only when the economic ls they have been encouraged to seek fail to materialize, but o when they discover that they are powerless, second-class zens who are discriminated against and exploited by the dom-nt society. At the same time, they are denied the satisfactions their traditional cultures, because these have been sacrificed he process of modernization. Under the impact of major eco-nic change family life is disrupted, traditional social controls often lost, and many indicators of social anomie such as alco-ism, crime, delinquency, suicide, emotional disorders, and pair may increase. The inevitable frustration resulting from continual deprivation finds expression in the cargo cults, italization movements, and a variety of other political and gious movements that have been widespread among tribal ples following their disruption by industrial civilization.

eferences

:ermann, F. L. 1964. *Geologia e Fisiografia da Região Bragantina, Estado do Pará.* Manaus, Brazil: Conselho Nacional de Pesquisas, Instituto Nacional de Pesquisas da Amazonia.

rd, William Albert, and Loren McIntyre. 1988. Rondônia's settlers invade Brazil's imperiled rain forest. *National Geographic* 174(6):772–799.

lley, John H. 1970. *Campa Socio-Economic Adaptation.* Ann Arbor: University Microfilms.

___. 1983. *Der Weg der Zerstörung: Stammesvölker und die industrielle Zivilization.* Munich: Trickster-Verlag. (Translation of *Victims of Progress.*)

ley, John H., and Foley C. Benson. 1979. Cultural ecology of Amazonian palms. *Reports of Investigations,* no. 56. Pullman: Laboratory of Anthropology, Washington State University.

ce, George E. 1972. Aggravation of vitamin A deficiency following distribution of non-fortified skim milk: An example of nutrient interaction. In *The Careless Technology: Ecology and International Development,* ed. M. T. Farvar and John P. Milton, pp. 53–60. Garden City, N.Y.: Natural History Press.

ing, Robbins. 1963. *Rengsanggri: Family and Kinship in a Garo Village.* Philadelphia: University of Pennsylvania Press.

is, A. E., and T. D. Bolin. 1972. Lactose intolerance in Southeast Asia. In *The Careless Technology: Ecology and International Development,* ed. M. T. Farvar and John P. Milton, pp. 61–68. Garden City, N.Y.: Natural History Press.

nett, Glenn, and John Connell. 1988. Acculturation and health in the highlands of Papua New Guinea. *Current Anthropology* 29(2):273–299.

Goldschmidt, Walter R. 1972. The interrelations between cultural factors and the acquisition of new technical skills. In *The Progress of Underdeveloped Areas,* ed. Bert F. Hoselitz, pp. 135–151. Chicago: University of Chicago Press.

Gross, Daniel R., et al. 1979. Ecology and acculturation among native peoples of Central Brazil. *Science* 206(4422): 1043–1050.

Hughes, Charles C., and John M. Hunter. 1972. The role of technological development in promoting disease in Africa. In *The Careless Technology: Ecology and International Development,* ed. M. T. Farvar and John P. Milton, pp. 69–101. Garden City, N.Y.: Natural History Press.

Keesing, Felix M. 1941. *The South Seas in the Modern World.* Institute of Pacific Relations International Research Series. New York: John Day.

Kroeger, Axel, and François Barbira-Freedman. 1982. *Culture Change and Health: The Case of South American Rainforest Indians.* Frankfurt am Main: Verlag Peter Lang. (Reprinted in Bodley, 1988a:221–236.)

McNeil, Mary. 1972. Lateritic soils in distinct tropical environments: Southern Sudan and Brazil. In *The Careless Technology: Ecology and International Development,* ed. M. T. Farvar and John P. Milton, pp. 591–608. Garden City, N.Y.: Natural History Press.

Mönckeberg, F. 1968. Mental retardation from malnutrition. *Journal of the American Medical Association* 206:30–31.

Montagu, Ashley. 1972. Sociogenic brain damage. *American Anthropologist* 74(5):1045–1061.

Rambo, A. Terry. 1985. *Primitive Polluters: Semang Impact on the Malaysian Tropical Rain Forest Ecosystem.* Anthropological Papers no. 76, Museum of Anthropology, University of Michigan.

Redfield, Robert. 1953. *The Primitive World and Its Transformations.* Ithaca, N.Y.: Cornell University Press.

______. 1962. *A Village That Chose Progress: Chan Kom Revisited.* Chicago: University of Chicago Press, Phoenix Books.

Smith, Wilberforce. 1894. The teeth of ten Sioux Indians. *Journal of the Royal Anthropological Institute* 24:109–116.

TTR: *See under* United States.

United States, Department of the Interior, Office of Territories. 1953. *Report on the Administration of the Trust Territory of the Pacific Islands* (by the United States to the United Nations) for the Period July 1, 1951, to June 30, 1952.

______. 1954. *Annual Report, High Commissioner of the Trust Territory of the Pacific Islands to the Secretary of the Interior* (for 1953).

United States, Department of State. 1955. *Seventh Annual Report to the United Nations on the Administration of the Trust Territory of the Pacific Islands* (July 1, 1953, to June 30, 1954).

______. 1959. *Eleventh Annual Report to the United Nations on the Administration of the Trust Territory of the Pacific Islands* (July 1, 1957, to June 30, 1958).

______. 1964. *Sixteenth Annual Report to the United Nations on the Administration of the Trust Territory of the Pacific Islands* (July 1, 1962 to June 30, 1963).

______. 1973. *Twenty-Fifth Annual Report to the United Nations on the Administration of the Trust Territory of the Pacific Islands* (July 1, 1971, to June 30, 1972).

Article 34

Of Ice and Men

In most quarters, the U.S. government decision to list the polar bear as a threatened species was heralded as a milestone in awareness of global warming, but the people you might expect to most rejoice in the decision—the Arctic indigenous peoples who suffer the greatest effects of global warming—are strongly opposed to it.

CAMERON M. SMITH

As the thin end of the global warming wedge begins prying apart the foundations of traditional life in the Alaskan Arctic, you might think that the native people there would welcome the federal listing of the polar bear as a threatened species. After all, everyone loves polar bears (Knud, the Berlin Zoo's über-cute furball, appeared on the cover of the May 2007 *Vanity Fair*, photographed by none other than Annie Leibovitz), and they bring tourism dollars to the Arctic, raising awareness of global warming at the same time. But the Iñupiat—the indigenous people around Barrow, for whom the bears are a cornerstone of their traditional hunting culture, along with whales, seals and caribou—argue that listing the polar bear as threatened won't save it. And as I explored the polar bear's frozen-sea habitat on the north coast of Alaska in the winter of 2007, I came to understand their point of view.

Dragging my supply sled toward my base in Barrow one frigid morning—it had been 30 below the night before, and I didn't dare to check the temperature before I crawled out of my sleeping bag—I recalled the simple wonders of the past week. I'd heard the Arctic described as a wasteland, but nobody who'd taken the time to walk here could call it anything less than a thriving ecosystem. Cold, yes, but without question thriving, electric with life. I wanted to learn what native people thought about what was being done to protect this priceless wilderness in the face of increasing oil and gas exploration, and I thought the proposed listing of the polar bear as a threatened species might help smooth the way.

But Billy Leavitt, an Iñupiat hunter who picked me up on the outskirts of Barrow, blew that idea to pieces with a few words. As we tore down an ice road in his battered pickup truck, and a 60-below windchill blew through an open window—just about killing me but cooling him nicely—Billy gestured at the landscape, speaking in long, flat vowels and drawn-out consonants.

"It's too warm for this time of year," he said, "That global warming is really happening."

"Yeah, I hear the polar bear is in trouble," I replied, tryin[g] sympathize. Billy tensed up.

"No," he said, "That's your Greenpeace people sayin' t[h] That's your conservationists"—he spat the last word—"peo who watch that Discovery Channel and then come up here tell us how to hunt." I considered myself a conservationist, b had no reply to that conversation-stopper. I sat there wonder what else I might be wrong about.

Still, Billy cordially shook my hand when he dropped off in Barrow, inviting me to come to his cabin out on the la "You'll learn a lot," he said. Although I didn't have a chanc visit him, I did take another trek, and learned a little more ab his point of view. On March 7th, the residents of Barrow (c 60 percent Iñupiat) met with representatives of the U.S. F and Wildlife Service, the federal agency then considering lis the polar bear as threatened.

The Iñupiat Heritage Center, where the meeting was hel a modern, multi-million-dollar facility at once a museum playing relics of pre-contact life, a meeting hall, and a work where walrushide boats are sewn together in preparation whale-hunts. Once everyone's snowmobiles had been par it was quiet in the meeting hall, but the atmosphere was te A handful of Fish and Wildlife presenters sat at a table in front of the hall, looking out at a hundred mostly native B row residents, who awaited the government's presentation patience, but no smiles.

The meeting began with the government representat presenting their case for listing the polar bear, supported two main points. First, the polar bear's sea ice habitat has b steadily reduced in the past 30 years, a finding of 5 indepen studies that nobody can deny: today, satellite imagery sh us an Alaska-sized hole in the summer sea ice cover, w 30 years ago it was a solid sheet, and the prediction is tha 2050, most of the Arctic Ocean will be ice-free in the sum driving polar bears either to adapt to land in that season, o ct. The Iñupiat agreed with this, saying in fact that they'd trying to raise the alarm over global warming for years. they let this point slide.

cond, Fish and Wildlife argued that polar bear populations ready in decline, as seen in a study of the western Hudson polar bear population, which they claimed has decreased ver 20 percent in the last 20 years. The Iñupiat weren't re of this; like their Canadian counterparts, the Inuit, they ved that polar bear numbers were actually up, but that the had migrated out of the scientists' survey areas. Still, Fish Wildlife concluded that while over-hunting, disease, and factors do not threaten the polar bear throughout its natunge, it should be listed as threatened because of the well nented decline of sea ice.

en the Iñupiat took the podium. For two hours they pred their own testimony, questioning Fish and Wildlife's nptions and facts, and making a strong case for entrusting urvival of the polar bear not to regulations dictated from ington, D.C., but to the Iñupiat and other native polar e.

s not surprising that the Iñupiat's discussion of polar bear gy, behavior, ecology, habitat, and population was more sticated than that of the Fish and Wildlife representatives; all, the federal representatives had flown in from Washa or Anchorage, and would fly out in a day or two, while upiat lived their entire lives in the polar bear's habitat. were not new to the polar bear, and they weren't impressed -year studies that Fish and Wildlife called "long-term." ñupiat had cultural knowledge about polar bears—and the f their ecosystem—that went back far longer. "As the ice ts," one hunter said, "some bears will follow it, and others et stranded on land, like some of them are now, when the reats in the summer. Those that follow the ice will survive, ose that live on the land will have to adapt, just like their tors did." Glenn Sheehan, executive director of the Barrow Science Consortium, pointed out that the polar bear had iving with climate changes for more than 200,000 years, at it had survived at least one other warming episode, the eval Warm period. "Have you considered that at all?" he the Fish and Wildlife representatives. "Do you even have oing back more than 50 years?"

e Iñupiat speakers included common citizens, native huntveral whaling captains, and North Slope Borough mayor rd S. Itta, all of whom looked hard into the eyes of the Fish Vildlife representatives. After all, in this modest meeting ere doing nothing less than fighting to prevent yet another tant part of their traditional life from being wrested away hem by a distant federal agency.

e Iñupiat based their opposition to polar bear listing on three facts. First, in their experience polar bear numbers were eclining, an observation also noted by native Canadians dson Bay, who say the decline there has been misunderby scientists who drop in from time to time, but fail to stand polar bear migration behavior. One resident pointed at scientists were fond of saying they needed "holistic, erm studies" of the polar bear, but were—insultingly and ly—ignoring exactly that kind of knowledge by relying on studies that "only went back a generation or two." Mayor Itta sharply pointed out that the Fish and Wildlife study did not actually have empirical data for the population increase or decrease of polar bears in northern Alaska, only projections and estimates based on the Hudson Bay population, 4,000 miles away. If the tables were turned, Itta noted, Washington wouldn't respond to hypotheses or hearsay; they'd want real, empirical data, and the Iñupiat deserved the same. In short, Fish and Wildlife's data on the polar bear population was largely theoretical (they had admitted this in their own presentation), and based on no more empirical facts or observations than the Iñupiats' own. The implication was clear to all: who would you rather trust about these numbers—the people who live in the area and observe the polar bear population day by day, or federal government monitors?

The Iñupiats' second point was that they simply don't take enough bears to threaten the species, only about 20 a year. Indeed, Fish and Wildlife's own study concluded that over-hunting was not a threat in Canada (because of sound management policies there) or Alaska (because of the 30-year-old Marine Mammal Protection Act). Barrow Arctic Science Consortium president and native hunter Richard Glenn told Fish and Wildlife, "If you want to address over-hunting, go to Russia, where they poach 200 polar bears a year!"

The third point, mentioned time and again, was summarized by Mayor Itta: "Listing the polar bear does not address the problem!" Whaling captain Charlie Brower said, "The problem—pointed out in your own study—is shrinking sea ice, which is caused by carbon dioxide emissions!" The Iñupiat said that listing the polar bear as threatened does nothing to address sea ice retreat; it's just a measure meant to make people of the Lower 48 feel as though they're "saving the polar bear" when in fact they're doing nothing at all.

Listing a species as threatened or endangered is meant to force federally backed action to preserve that species' critical habitat. If that habitat isn't delineated, however, the listing has little value. In this case, the Fish and Wildlife Department found that the bears' habitat needs were "undeterminable." The proposed listing did not mention greenhouse gas or carbon emissions at all, an omission that was made overt when Secretary of the Interior Dirk Kempthorne announced the official threatened listing for polar bears on May 18, 2008. "The most significant part of today's decision," he said, "is what President Bush observed about climate change policy last month. President Bush noted that 'The Clean Air Act, the Endangered Species Act and the National Environmental Policy Act were never meant to regulate global climate change.'"

If the polar bear's critical sea ice habitat isn't defined, the Iñupiat argued, and its reduction isn't linked to human-induced warming brought about by greenhouse gas emissions, then listing the polar bear will not work as a lever to force action on climate change.

In short, the science brought by the Fish and Wildlife representatives to justify listing the polar bear as threatened looked great on paper, but was incomplete—even to other scientists—and ignored Iñupiat traditional knowledge. And putting the polar bear on the endangered list wouldn't stop illegal poaching in Russia, or the sea ice from retreating, or anything else that was actually affecting polar bear populations. In fact it would mask the real issue of climate change.

The Iñupiat solution was for Washington to address climate change head-on by legislating global warming preventatives, and leave the polar bears to the native peoples of the Arctic. After all, they are subsistence hunters who manage animal populations so that they will be there in the future. The word "sustainable" has been in the American consciousness for about a generation, while it has been the cornerstone of Iñupiat life for millennia. Not taking their lead in this issue would be a te loss of opportunity, especially considering that they are on the front line of global warming, where change is fel and foremost.

Dr. Cameron M. Smith, an archaeologist at Portland State U sity's Department of Anthropology, has recently published *The T Myths About Evolution* (Prometheus, 2006) and has written a for *Scientific American MIND, Archaeology, Spaceflight, Playb* other magazines. He returned to north Alaska in February 2008.

undation

ny news stories have sent up alerts about the imminent wning of Pacific islands. But for people living on bati the real problems are happening right now.

TIN BLAIR AND CASEY BECK

eramira wraps dried pandanus leaves into large rolls. I-Kiribati women use these leaves to weave a variety of household products, such as mats, cur- and traditional clothing. Uriam reclined comfortably s bwia and eyed his son-in-law, who was smiling as uffled up the path of the family's home, struggling to a 15-horsepower Yamaha outboard motor. It was early oon in the family compound, and people gathered d as he set the motor on its stand. Two women lay out ut frond mats on the ground as another man appeared, ng a large sack. Chuckling, he dumped more than h onto the mats.

m his nearby bwia—the large, open-air structure used th living and dining rooms in Kiribati households— ar-old Uriam sat up and adjusted his Coke-bottle glasses. his lips parted into a wide, toothless grin, the head elder of Maiana Island remarked, "Now that's a " and glanced playfully at me. I couldn't help but feel e shy, remembering the glum looks on the family's the day before, when I had returned with my pathetic of six fish. I had to acknowledge that we I-matangs erners) don't share the I-Kiribati knack for fishing.

h is the dietary staple on the island chain nation of ti, and the unloading of fish is a daily scene at Uriam's but the nature of fishing has changed.

efore, you could hang out there under the sun, no m," Uriam told me as his daughter began to prepare "Now, if you're out there fishing you can feel it. Or, 're out working, you just feel the heat. It's very hot."

ile there still may be plenty of fish, hotter temper- on this equatorial atoll are just the beginning of vable climatic and environmental changes.

e previous week, I saw the devastation of another tra- al source of food, the babai tuber crop, which is grown . Torote, Uriam's eldest son, stood over a barren six- eep pit on the family's land and explained that many islanders were having trouble with seawater washing overland and entering pits. It not only kills that crop, he told me; the seawater is tainting the water supply of the people.

And Not a Drop to Drink

Back on Uriam's main property, a three-foot-wide hole awaited construction of the family's new well. In the coming days, a group of neighbors would bring bags of coral, sand, and imported concrete to help Torote build his father a well closer to the center of the island, where water is more abundant. Their old well, across the island's only road, had become increasingly brackish in recent years.

The availability of fresh drinking water is critical on an equatorial coral atoll. Kiribati's slender strips of land, never more than a half-mile across and rarely more than several hundred yards, store rainwater in a freshwater lens—an underground layer of fresh water that floats atop a layer of denser ocean water. As ever-higher high tides penetrate these atolls' porous coral foundations, they foul the only reliable source of fresh water.

When I first arrived on Kuria Island, I met Donna and Katherine, two Peace Corps volunteers, who were teaching in the island's primary and middle schools. I asked for water, desperately hoping to rehydrate after a 26-hour boat ride on the open Pacific, and they looked at each other sheepishly. "I don't think we have any," Donna admitted. I was shocked. "What do people drink?" I asked. They told me that many of the wells were brackish but agreed that the well in the middle of the island near the middle school would probably have water. They lent a bicycle and five-gallon jug to a local boy to investigate the well and retrieve some water if it happened to be there. It hadn't rained, they explained, for the past five months.

Most islanders prefer pure rainwater to brackish well water, but acquiring the several-thousand-gallon tanks to store rainwater is financially impossible for individuals. On Kuria, Peace Corps volunteers worked with local teachers to apply for a grant from New Zealand for two such tanks for their school. They received the grant and were told that the tanks would be sent from Tarawa by boat. But in the few-day journey from Tarawa, one of the tanks slipped off the boat. No replacement would come—the application process had to begin anew.

Today, one water tank sits in the center of the school compound, attached to piping from the roofs of school buildings, which collect rainwater. Without rain, however, the tank remains empty. With marginal water storage capacity, the people of Kuria will continue to rely on wells for the foreseeable future.

"Water is a serious problem," Kiribati's President, Anote Tong, told me. "The likely infringement of the saltwater into the freshwater lens would be a serious problem. Any substantial change in weather patterns would also be a huge problem for us. Water has always been a problem, whether the sea level was rising or not. We are a hearty breed in a sense." He said that the I-Kiribati survive in ways people from the developed world might find hard to understand, particularly on the country's outer islands.

Life on outer islands is so much harder than life in the capital, Tawara, that islanders are increasingly choosing urban life ("urban," here, is a relative term).

A subsistence lifestyle, like that practiced on the outer islands, is necessarily climate dependant. Those who live directly off the land will be most affected by climate change. These people are the world's small-scale farmers, herders, and fishermen—people whose livelihoods depend on annual climatic constants.

The frustrating reality is that those who need protection most from the immediate effects of climate change tend to live in countries like Kiribati that are least equipped to provide it. Whereas the larger, industrialized countries responsible for over 80 percent of all greenhouse gas emissions can develop new technologies or move people to higher altitudes if coastal lands are flooded, the peoples of the small island nations do not have such options.

Though many I-Kiribati are making simple changes like transitioning babai out of their diet because it is increasingly difficult to grow, some islanders are already beginning to feel the more severe environmental and climatic changes.

"Because of the heat," says a woman named Tarai on Kuria Island, "the coconuts dry up in the tree, and it's very hard [for them] to fall." Many islanders like Tarai and her family rely on revenue from the sale of dried coconut meat, or copra, the nation's leading export. The four-day process of producing copra garners roughly $25 for one harvest.

Coconut palms not only generate income but also provide food, both for people and livestock; toddy (a sweet drink used extensively in I-Kiribati cooking that also bec alcoholic when fermented); and materials for mats, thatch, rope, and firewood. Without coconuts, the I-Ki traditional lifestyle becomes impossible.

On southern Maiana, high tides have overrun sea destroying a major coconut plantation and creating ren stretch of land locals call the Lake. Locals compl the increasingly frequent need to repair the handmade seawalls that, in some cases, are their only shield a higher tides. Uriam told me that in the past few dec they have rebuilt the main seawall three times.

In February 2007, a king tide washed up 50 yards i on Kuria. This tide, which brought water up to pe waists, forced islanders like Tarai's daughter to re their families farther inland. Tarai's daughter aban five buildings on her family's property.

While Tarai's family was fortunate to own a large of land on Kuria, for most families on outer islands, ing inland is more difficult. On the more crowded c island, relocation is out of the question.

Today, South Tarawa is reeling under the weight now-more-than 50,000 residents. As half of the na population crowds onto the capital island, its resourc heavily strained. With no functioning sewage system, is ers do as they always have and use the sheltered wat the lagoon as a toilet. With so many people resorting t method, the lagoon now has dangerously high lev bacteria, and there is widespread disease too severe f island's two hospitals to handle. Human rights worker estimated that over 95 percent of children have inte worms.

A People Without a Place

President Tong understands only too well the imn nature of the rising sea level and its predicted effects country. He told me the international community has blind to the current and future problems Kiribati is e encing with rising sea level and threatened water rese

"There's nothing we can do about reversing the p [of global warming]," he told me, "We've screamed, shouted at international fora, but with very little effec in terms of how we will respond to the impact of c change—yes indeed, we do have a number of option must have a number of options."

From what I witnessed, it seemed to me the only would one day be mass migration. I cautiously intro the topic of the I-Kiribati as environmental refugee President Tong. He acknowledged the sensitive nat the issue but added, "I hesitate to call our people ref we would train them, and they would become peopl would contribute to whatever country they choose to with meaningful lives."

:k on Maiana, Uriam also reflected on the fate of Kiri- 'When it's time, I think our people will evacuate the , Kiribati." He grinned and added, "They will prob- o to America or Australia or New Zealand." Immedi- his smile faded and he turned, staring off toward the 1.

astute leader, President Tong fears that the situation each crisis level before the international community notice. "Can we remain nationals of Kiribati when living in Australia?" he asks. "What would be our nship? Do we still have sovereignty of Kiribati when s no longer the country of Kiribati? These are issues think at this point nobody is ready yet to address."

ile President Tong's concerns may remain unad- d for decades, the realities of immigration from ing island nations are surfacing in international poli- Currently, New Zealand is the only country accepting bati immigrants. Speaking to the New Zealand deputy ommissioner to Kiribati, I learned that each year they 75 I-Kiribati along with several hundred other Pacific ers, such as Tongans and Tuvaluans. Immigrants must nstrate a means for supporting themselves, though the Zealand government will help with assimilation. The commissioner stressed that this is a "good neighbor " and, as of now, New Zealand has no official policy rning environmental refugees.

ibati's fishing rights are an important consideration, the prospect of mass migration. Most developed coun- will not accept a significant number of refugees from ation without something in return. However, Kiribati significant natural resource: an ocean of 1.31 million miles that includes very lucrative commercial fish- ounds.

enue from the sale of fishing rights is a critical por- Kiribati's gross national product. Many major coun- n the Pacific Rim, including Australia and Taiwan, tly covet these fishing rights, a situation that brings weight to President Tong's questions of sovereignty face of environmental disaster. Who would control g rights on this massive stretch of ocean, if the zone stion included no habitable land?

night I returned to South Tarawa from Kuria, I d an eerie string of lights on the horizon. They were n vapor work lights of large Taiwanese fishing boats ed in the lagoon to fish for tuna for the next month. the conspicuous ships in the lagoon suggest, the nese have maintained a prominent presence in ti since President Tong established diplomatic ties 3. Like many other Pacific island nations, Kiribati en advantage of tension between Taiwan and China, ging recognition of Taiwan for aid.

e then, Taiwan has built numerous small gardens and fisheries on South Tarawa as part of an agricultural aid program. They have also donated two large trucks and two pickup trucks to each of the outer islands, along with a small fleet of trucks for South Tarawa. These trucks, with "From Taiwan" painted on the doors, serve all transportation needs for outer islanders.

While Taiwanese aid projects may be the most visible, other foreign donors also contribute large sums. Australia, the biggest donor, supplies $15 million a year, with another $4 million coming from New Zealand. Kiribati's national budget, including aid, is about $65 million.

Aid from Japan took a different form. Occupiers of South Tarawa during World War II, the Japanese have since built a two-mile-long concrete berm connecting the most populous islet, Betio (pronounced Base-oh), to the rest of South Tarawa.

A coral atoll, the rim of an extinct volcano, is often a string of islets instead of a continuous strip of land. Unobstructed ocean water filters in and out of an atoll's lagoon, providing a natural cleaning process. In the case of South Tarawa, the berm effectively sealed off the lagoon. While the connection was a boon for business and transportation, the berm has significantly altered currents, making it impossible for the lagoon to flush completely, creating a stinking cesspool.

Another environmental consequence of the berm is the disappearance of Bikeman Island in the center of Tarawa lagoon. Over the past 10 years, changing ocean currents have transformed Bikeman from a verdant, popular, day-trip destination into a desolate patch of sand that only emerges at low tide. Foreigners and environmental activists want to use Bikeman's disintegration as evidence of rising sea levels, but locals tend to blame the causeway.

Because of all the development efforts, life in Kiribati exists within the balance between a desire for modernity and the appeal and comfort of tradition. The influx of televisions and DVD players, modern junk food and Western movies is fueling an exodus from the outer islands. But Kiribati is not suffering from the brain-drain that often accompanies much of the push toward modernity. Certainly, for the vast majority of I-Kiribati on the outer island, who live at a subsistence level, moving out of the country unaided is an economic impossibility. But moving away is not necessarily appealing, anyway.

The lure of the I-Kiribati lifestyle remains undeniable. The slow pace of life on the outer islands, where there is little need for money, possessions, or work, beyond gathering food and tending the land, seems to be enough to keep older generations away from South Tarawa.

Education beyond the middle school level, however, is only available on a few outer islands. The same is true for job opportunities. For outer islanders looking for more education or work for wages, moving to South Tarawa is the only option.

Kiribati Steps Up to the Plate

On my first night on Maiana the town's greeting council, a group of middle-aged women, threw a botaki, or party, for me. Every guest at a botaki is expected to give a speech. When it was my turn, I told the women, who were dressed in matching homemade outfits and garlands of fresh flowers, that I was there to learn about Kiribati culture in the face of climate change. I explained climate change to them, and their immediate reaction shocked me. If burning gas is contributing to climate change, one woman said matter-of-factly, then we should use our generators less. The others nodded in agreement.

Kiribati uses the fourth-smallest amount of oil of any country in the world and both produces and uses the sixth-lowest amount of electricity. Yet, when these w learned that their actions, however insignificant, contribute to climate change and affect others a the world, their first reaction was to reduce thei consumption.

In the face of devastating climatic changes, the I-K people remain optimistic. Most are not ready to discu eventuality of leaving their homes or the realities o they will define their culture once outside their bc Until such a time, the I-Kiribati, like Uriam and T families, will continue to adapt as best they can.

Casey Beck and **Austin Blair** are recent graduates of Tufts sity. See more of their work at www.therisingtidekiribati.org.

olation

outh America's Gran Chaco, voluntarily isolated indigenous ıps are still dodging the rampant development of the on, and with good reason: those that have already come have found that even greater isolation awaits them.

AS BESSIRE

he young Totobiegosode sitting next to me is an "Ishi" for our time. Like the famous Yahi tribesman who suddenly emerged from the California forest almost a y ago, his story poses unsettling questions about what it to be an "isolated person" in our modern world. His black now close-cropped, and he wears a cotton shirt and pants of a plant-fiber woven loincloth. A baseball cap shades que almond-shaped eyes as he sits sipping a warm Coke, ed feet moving in and out of torn plastic flip-flops. In the jungle villages of the Gran Chaco in the heart of South a where I have spent 21 months doing my fieldwork, he unting partner, the one who gives me his first find of the d receives mine.

Totobiegosode ("People-from-the-Place-Where-d-Peccaries-Ate-Their-Gardens") are one of the six l subgroups of seminomadic Ayoreo Indians tradition-nging through the vast dry tropical woodlands on both f the international border between Paraguay and Bolivia. as Ishi was the last survivor of his tribe, my friend, who I l Jnoraine, is a member of the latest Ayoreo band to leave a free life in the shrinking wilderness. His grandfather e leader of a small group first contacted in 1979; his lied in the forest; and his uncle and brother were brought Christian missionaries in 1986. For Jnoraine, as for Ishi, out of isolation has meant deep ruptures as well as new ıships.

"isolation" is a problematic category. By all accounts, gosode bands never existed in pure isolation, but always part of larger social networks spanning across the Chaco. ging hunters, they always knew about remote strangers, ally dangerous "others" lurking on the edges of their tra-l hunting lands. Theirs was and is a life of courage and h in the face of intrusion and terror.

ancestral Ayoreo homeland was invaded by about 0 Bolivian and Paraguayan soldiers fighting each other the Chaco War (1932–1935). It was sliced by the Santa Cruz-Corumba railroad in the following decade and dissected with large-scale exploration and drilling by a U.S. oil company throughout the 1950s. Invading newcomers soon occupied the few permanent fresh water sources, leading to sporadic violent skirmishes with threatened Ayoreo warriors. Frontier slave-raiders carried off Ayoreo children, and well into the 1970s the Paraguayan army offered an exemption from service for anyone who presented a severed "savage" Indian head.

I met Jnoraine in 2004, just five months after his first contact, a time, he says, "when everything was new." He had only seen a handful of *cojnone* (non-Ayoreos, especially whites) up close in his entire life. For weeks, he stared at me on the other side of the fire, pale in the shadows, unblinking and blank, as tense and timid as a deer.

The Trunk of Stories

Jnoraine began speaking to me on our third hunting trip together. I talked back. Although by no means fully fluent, I gradually learned his language, known by few outsiders. Sometimes we didn't understand one another, but often we did. By sharing experiences and stories, we both reached out to forge a link, however fraught and fragile, between his "isolated" community and the wider world beyond our horizons. Perhaps the story of his indigenous community will draw attention to the liminal life they now face, wandering the unfamiliar borderlands betwixt isolation and desolation.

Here is part of what he told me:

> The whites arrived to those places because a shaman named Udodaquide made a road that connected our land to the place the whites were working. The evil spirit told this shaman to make the road in order to make problems for the shaman's people. This shaman wanted to defeat his rival but he was too weak. So he went to heaven to bring coldness to calm and strike fear in his opponent,

but he couldn't kill him. . . . So he sent his soul to Earth's End to see if he could call up large ants to cut a road. But when he spoke of the ants, he referred to the white men. This shaman made a road to bring the white men into his territory and to kill his people. This is his song:

I am going far, to the land of Earth's End,
I spoke to the warriors,
I took out their righteous anger
to fight for their land,
I went and found cold water lilies
I used them to hit my enemies,
But I could not overcome their will.
I went and I spoke to the ants under the earth,
And I sent them here.
I went and we ate the forest,
Now I drive them to all the corners of the world.

This is the trunk of all stories, it tells about our dead world.

By the time Ayoreo made "first contact" with foreigners invading their ancestral homeland, they had already experienced the tremors of a world about to be turned upside down. Growing external pressures, including encroachments on their forests and deadly new diseases, fueled tensions and distrust among themselves, leading to warfare among northern and southern Ayoreo groups. In 1947, already decimated by epidemics and surrounded by enemies, northern Ayoreo bands began taking refuge in new Bolivian mission villages, where Christian missionaries controlling medicine and supplies urged, cajoled, and persuaded them to devalue traditional social practices. Using shotguns obtained from these powerful foreigners—their new allies—the northern Ayoreo then took revenge on their southern neighbors. Many of these, in turn, were lured to Protestant and Roman Catholic missions in Paraguay throughout the 1950s and 60s. Only the Totobiegosode, one of the larger southern Ayoreo groups, avoided such contact and chose to remain isolated. However, those southern Ayoreos who settled in mission villages acquired guns and then staged devastating raids against their "heathen" neighbors still remaining in their seasonal forest villages. One older Totobiegosode woman in Jnoraine's band told me about a massacre she had witnessed:

We died there in that place. I was a young girl. We heard them attack. My mother called to me, she carried me on her shoulder. I remember but I forget. She ran. But she weakened with my weight. Then they killed us. She put me down then they killed her. A gun. They killed my father, my sisters, my brother. Then I began to run. I was afraid of the guns that wanted to release the blood from my body. I ran towards the place I gathered doidie roots with my mother. There one of them struck me, and I fell to the ground. They cut me several times in the head with a machete. The cuts filled with dirt. I passed out. Then I woke up and went to the sandy ground and saw my people. I was very thirsty. They told me that there was no water left. I was weak and couldn't walk. It seemed I would die there in the afternoon, but I began to walk.

In 1975, after widespread Ayoreo conversion to Christ raids against the free-ranging Totobiegosode took on a elytizing slant. Assisted by American Protestant missic who spotted their homes in small forest clearings when low over the Paraguayan Chaco, southern Ayoreos wh already settled on mission lands located and contacted ' egosode bands in the notorious "wild man hunts" of 19 1986. They took their frightened captives back to the n villages and forced them into servitude.

In 1993, the Totobiegosode people captured in 1986 a (still-unresolved) land claim with a Paraguayan nong mental organization. The pioneering effort involves est ing settlements in the ancestral homeland they are claim 2004, while in the process of establishing a second villag encountered 17 of their isolated tribal relatives. These contacted Ayoreos were then brought in and reduced to status—a social degradation the earlier contacted tribes had experienced upon being captured and settled on th sions. Like those before them, the "new people" were s and emotionally pressured into abandoning traditiona then" spirituality, into cutting their long "savage" hair sh adopting new diets. They were taught that such extrem would let them be "born-again," transformed into "civ people saved from their "innate sin."

Feeling powerless to stop what I saw as an indigenous coming, I witnessed the unraveling and remaking of thei their exile from isolation. All along this traumatic journe were (and continue to be) shocks and situations that a ficult, if not impossible, for us to really imagine. For in Jnoraine's wife was put on antidepressant medication b meaning outsiders to help her overcome an inexplicab of deafness soon after first contact. Her hearing returne tually, but her depressing situation did not change. On occasions, she decided to offer me a small window into h telling me of her life "before" in a quick string of sn images.

We saw tracks. White men. Where? It was very hot. ran far. Faaaaar. There was no water. Our tongues w swollen. We cried. We left our things. We ran. Craw low. We watched. No cattle near. There was a water t Full. A white man. Very fat, wearing a red shirt. waited. Trembling. Blood in the water. A lot of blood. didn't sleep. We ran. Crying, we ran.

. . . We were very afraid of the big road. That some would see us and kill us. We thought the vehicles eyes, that they would see our tracks or smell our tr and follow us. We would lie nearby. We waited and wa until we could hear no vehicles, and we would cros night. One would go last and cover our tracks.

Boasting one of the world's highest local deforestatic in a country where official numbers are more fiction th the Gran Chaco is being cleared at a frightening and un rate for extensive cattle-ranching. Many ranchers see the ness and its free-ranging indigenous inhabitants as an o to progress. The thick shrub is almost impossible to cu is cleared with huge caged bulldozers, riding and pushi thing in the way, working around the clock, the metal pol- by the plants. Paraguayans say that driving one makes you *ıtecido,* hard and mean, that it damages your kidneys, your , your brain. A working bulldozer produces a cacophony tal friction, diesel combustion, and exploding tree trunks. ınds as if an unknowable monster is ingesting the forest. nding on the wind, the guttural howl can be heard 10 miles Jnoraine recalled:

> e thought the bulldozers were looking for us because seemed that every time we made a village a bulldozer uld come. We said, "It seems that they are following us cause they always come to our villages. Every village. e have to leave behind our gardens and plants."

rds of cattle came in the bulldozers' wake, wild Zebus and nas, rangy and often pure white, filling up the suddenly ed land with their inquisitive eyes and loud moaning cries ails.

> e tried to talk to the cattle. "Cattle, we are your grand- hers, too! Do not be afraid of us! Listen to us! This is r land. Tell the white men, your fathers, that we are aceful, that this is our home!" We thought they could derstand our language, but they couldn't.

> . We thought that life would be easy with the whites. We ought that everything was free, that they did not have to nt and find their food, that they always had plenty. But w we know that everything is very expensive. We were ngry before, and we are hungry still.

ere Are Not Any Thoughts t for the Old Ways"

ne, his young wife and their infant son (who they named ive") now confront a new kind of isolation, the danger of separated from their orienting ancestral past by a collec- solve to silence most of "the old things." "His memory is l," is a common Ayoreo explanation for choosing to repress rget, to not pass on the sacred ancient stories, songs, and chants. The elders say they saw this new time coming, ne when "the visions stop." To remember now is often too of a burden, an insufferable weight. Many memories are as and have become taboo.

s ironic, in a way, that outsiders like me would seek to into their past in order to record or recover those mem- Their silencing is, after all, a profound reaction to the oing outside world of which I'm part. For many of these o elders, who have already seen one way of life "die" and ormed, the notion of an impending Apocalypse is not a of fear, but of hope for a resolution to the insoluble and ning contradictions they now face.

e old people run up to a visitor in the desolate Protes- ission village not far from where I lived, 10 or 20 or 30 g to the front of a larger crowd, all soft eyes and ravaged and wild gray streaked hair, keening and pulling up their d dust-colored rags and pressing your clean hands to their oard ribs so that you could therefore know that they were not lying when they said they were starving and asked you for food. Many Ayoreo hoped I was one of Jesus's people. "Do you know when Jesus will come?" I was asked more than once. "We don't know when it will be, but he will only take those in his family. Are you one of his people?"

When the price of Paraguayan beef and uncleared land surged in the late 1990s, when the bulldozers worked 24 hours a day 365 days a year, someone decided to help the poor starving Indians by donating them food, subsidized in part by a grant from a European foreign development branch. Once a week for several years, a truck half full of the unusable bovine entrails would drive through the village, make a slow U turn, and dump the wet offal on the dusty ground. The news was shouted among the households, knives were hauled out, skirts hiked up, and the race was on. Old ladies and children trampled and pushed down by other old ladies and children, fighting over the small shreds of foul viscera, covered in bloody mud. This was replaced by a scheme to make charcoal, also sponsored in part by international development aid. This means that most Ayoreo communities—these people who believed that every plant, insect and animal in the universe had once been a member of their tribe—now cut down the trees remaining on the small plots of land they still control and burn them in giant turtle-like clay ovens for about three cents a pound.

"Before, We Believed That Our Thoughts Could Become Reality"

One small group of free-ranging Totobiegosode remains in hiding. Although the total number of still-isolated Ayoreo is hotly contested by NGOs and Ayoreo groups, all agree that there are at least two groups and several lone individuals in this state. Perhaps 60 people total, probably a fraction of that. One band of unknown origin roams near the Bolivia-Paraguay border, and the other band is led by Yocayipie, Jnoraine's father-in-law. His sister and aunt live in this band. We know their names, their fears. We know that they run, far and fast, that they venture to the margins of settlements. They have theories about the people, animals and machines occupying their homeland, and how to best interact with them. They hide their urine from trucks and dogs. On several occasions they attacked the bulldozers they thought were hunting them down. They often enter isolated farm houses, taking metal, buckets, and clothes. They live quietly, often communicating with whistles, signs, and whispers, fleeing long and hard if they hear a noise or see a bootprint. They hide their trails in the thick Chaco underbrush. For these Totobiegosode, as for Ishi as a lonely survivor almost a century ago, life has been reduced to concealment.

Ecological destruction, fear, and genetic limitations will force the "isolated" Ayoreo to make "contact" at some point in the near or very near future. Based on past experiences, it is not difficult to guess what the outcome of the next "first contact" will be if we all do not begin to question the default sequences of contact, and also realize that "isolation" is an attributed description, a label we made, and one that limits the kinds of inter-relationships that otherwise may be imaginable. Meanwhile, ranchers eager to remove the people from their lands on both sides of the border hire Ayoreo workers to initiate contact or scare the isolated people away. For the Totobiegosode, these people are close relatives—their mothers, fathers, lovers, siblings, even children. They are familiar, not alien, and their isolation is an artifice of our culture, not theirs.

Many settled Ayoreo, even among the Totobiegosode, strongly advocate crossing the divide and initiating contact. As one leader rebuked me, "You do not know what it is like to always run and hide in fear." As they struggle to find their way, voluntary isolation is becoming a focal point for discussions of international human rights. In UN regional seminars and the Inter-American system, indigenous organizations and their allies are negotiating isolation as a new category of indigenous rights, one described in the recommendations of the fifth UN Permanent Forum on Indigenous Issues as the right "of these indigenous peoples and their designated territories throughout the world to exist in isolation, should they so choose." Often linked to the right of self-determination, conceptualizing isolation as a human right is an urgent appeal to the international community for crit needed aid in respecting and protecting these extremely nerable groups. Exposed to these discourses by participat international forums, some Ayoreo ideas are slowly char and their tribal organizations are expected to represent th lated groups and defend this right.

But who are the isolated people? Are they those very groups pushed to the last margins of their forest world, liv concealment? Are they those Ayoreo cut off from their ow and struggling to create a viable future? And what abo What does it mean for the Ayoreo and our world if we cho be isolated from such repeated and all-inclusive stories, c from a slice of humanity and a difficult situation that ther is time to change?

Lucas Bessire is a doctoral candidate at New York Universi the director of the film *Asking Ayahai: An Ayoreo Story.* Since he has lived with the Ayoreo and served as an advisor to the research was funded in part by the Wenner-Gren Foundation a Fulbright-Hays Dissertation Research program.

eeing Conservation
rough the Global Lens

IGOE

pular Notions and Painful alities about Conservation d Globalization

probably have some idea of what both conservation and lization are about. A person would have to have been liv- a cave not to have heard of conservation. Indeed, conser- n now enjoys an unquestioned place in American popular re: Earth Day, the Earth Summit, Al Gore's book *Earth Balance*, Sting's rainforest benefits, Green Peace, and reen Party. McDonald's has habitat conservation areas on edian separating their drive through windows from their ng lots. Even George W. Bush, not exactly a noted conser- nist, pays lip service to the environment, while proposing ll for oil in the Alaskan Wilderness Preserve. Although icans might not all agree about what form conservation d take, most are aware that it is important.

e idea of globalization is less well known, but still has a ndous impact on how people think about the world. The that defines globalization is the photograph of Earth taken ronauts in the 1960s. The importance of this image to "one " thinking is evidenced by the fact that it is often used in ls that "we are all in this together." Most Americans are ar with slogans like "space-ship earth," "a green and peace- anet," and "the global village." They are also broadly aware e world is becoming a smaller place, not physically smaller, sier to communicate around and travel over. There's really ce on earth that a person can't reach in a couple of days, ing he or she has the money to pay for the ticket. Americans so aware that localized environmental destruction threat- e entire planet. This is why the Amazon Rainforest is now ed to as "the lungs" of the planet. Clearly, therefore, notions nservation and globalization are interlinked.

balization as a Homogenizing cess

er important aspect of globalization is the fact that it is nogenizing process. Americans might "celebrate diver- but the implicit assumption of globalization is that it will transform other people in the world to become more like the West. So fundamental are these transformations that many Americans do not recognize that they are happening at all. Being a consumer, for instance, is something that Westerners take for granted. However, it is not a "natural" way of being for many peoples. Being a consumer means having money and accumulating things. It also assumes that people are naturally self-interested and acquisitive. As it turns out, however, this ide- ology is frequently incompatible with the ways in which many people live their lives. A large part of the world's people grow their own food, build their houses from materials that they find in their environment, and require little in the way of consumer goods (a situation that is rapidly changing of course). In many of these societies acquisitiveness and competition are frowned on. People share and cooperate. Those who do not are viewed with suspicion. Such cultural proclivities are often seen as a barrier to globalization and progress; people who hold them are said to have the wrong "mind-set."

Many other categories that Americans take for granted imply transformation for others in the process of globalization. A short list might include categories of citizen, entrepreneur, and wage laborer. These categories are part and parcel of globalization, but they are also widely resisted by people around the world. Even Americans sometimes need to be reminded that they are citizens and consumers. In the wake of the 9/11 attacks, the Bush administration reminded Americans constantly that the most patriotic thing they could do was to go shopping. It also discouraged them from thinking about themselves as African Americans, Native Americans, Irish Americans, or what have you, reminding them that they were U.S. citizens first and fore- most. The upshot is that globalization requires people to con- form to certain categories, categories that even Americans need to be actively reminded of from time to time. For people who lack a traditional category of citizen-consumer, this can be an extremely painful process.

Globalization and Indigenous People

. . . The most common definition of indigenous people is the original inhabitants of a particular place. However, this defini- tion is being broadened to include those who have maintained their traditional ways of life in spite of the modernization and social change. Such definitions are necessary for places like Africa, where Europeans and other outsiders make up a small percentage of the population (the exception being South Africa), and so, practically speaking, everyone is indigenous. And yet, in a movie such as *The Gods Must Be Crazy*, the viewer can definitely tell the difference between the bushman who wears a loin cloth and coexists with elephants, and the African who gets up when his alarm clock goes off and stands in a busy intersection directing traffic in a pressed white uniform. The bushman, who remains indigenous, has not been globalized. The man directing traffic has.

Few people, if any, still live the idyllic indigenous lifestyle of the people in *The Gods Must Be Crazy*. The idea shown in the movie that people living in the Kalahari have never seen a bottle of Coca-Cola is simply preposterous. Coca-Cola is so widely available in Africa that it is easier to get than clean drinking water in many places. A more accurate portrayal of the Bushmen (or !Kung as they call themselves) can be seen in the anthropological documentary *N!ai: Portrait of a !Kung Woman* (the explanation point stands for the clicking sound so common in the !Kung language). This film shows the making of *The Gods Must Be Crazy*, and the confusion of the !Kung actors about the ways in which the director wanted to portray their culture. Far from living an idyllic existence in the Kalahari, these actors have been forced to live on a reservation, where they rely on government handouts and tourist money, rather than on hunting antelope as portrayed in the movie. If you haven't seen *N!ai* or *The Gods Must Be Crazy*, I strongly urge you to do so.

Such conditions are typical of indigenous communities around the world: pushed off their land by commercial enterprises and national parks, relegated to government-designated reservations, living in poverty because they have not been fully integrated into the modern economy, and yet no longer able to pursue their traditional economic activities. Through all of this, indigenous communities strive to maintain their traditions after some fashion. I would argue that this effort to maintain tradition in the face of globalization is the foundation of a global indigenous identity. That is to say that until recently groups like the !Kung, the Maasai, the Sherpa, the Kayapo, the Anangu, and the Inuit were first and foremost !Kung or Maasai or what have you. They did not identify strongly with people in similar straits in other parts of the world or even necessarily know of their existence. With globalization, however, came improved communication and a growing recognition of a common problem. Networking by indigenous activists eventually led to the recognition of a global indigenous community by the United Nations (UN) and other transnational institutions. A global indigenous identity began to emerge.

Introducing the Maasai

. . . Like other indigenous peoples, the Maasai are economically, culturally, and politically marginalized. Their traditional culture is distinct from the dominant cultures of Kenya and Tanzania, the two countries in which most Maasai live. U most other Kenyans and Tanzanians, who speak English or Swahili, most Maasai speak their own language. In remote Maasai communities, it is sometimes difficult to anyone who speaks Swahili, the national language of Ta nia, let alone English, which is spoken primarily by edu people in urban areas.

The Maasai have also struggled to maintain their tradit herding economy, which revolves around the ability to large herds of cattle, sheep, and goats. . . .it also requires a tain amount of mobility because the Maasai have traditio moved their herds in search of pasture and water. This m ment was informed by traditional environmental know and seasonal cycles. Traditional Maasai resource manage systems were complex.

My liberal use of the past tense has probably cued you t fact that the Maasai (at least the majority of them) no lo pursue their traditional herding economy.

Increasingly they rely on subsistence farming, even th most of the areas in which they live are too arid to ens successful crop. Most Maasai can no longer be mobile be they have lost their traditional grazing lands to global proc This change began with colonialism, when British settlers over high-quality Maasai pasture for farms and cattle ran More recently the Maasai have lost land to African and fo investors who have claimed large areas for bean farms, mercial hunting safaris, and wildlife viewing. These inve came into East Africa in recent years in response to po designed to transform the economies of Kenya and Tan so that they could become more fully integrated into the economy. The expectation, of course, was that Africans w also be transformed into wage-earning consumers inste subsistence-oriented peasants. For the most part, howeve hasn't happened. The Maasai (in fact most rural Africans) wound up left out of the process altogether. They have los land and their subsistence economy, but they haven't bee to benefit from the integration of their countries into the economy.

Many of the elders I interviewed lamented that these cesses were leading to the demise of their traditional v In Maasai society, cattle are everything, in about the same that money is everything in the United States. That is, alth it may be a bit of an exaggeration to say that "it's everyt people certainly do spend a lot of time thinking about i trying to accumulate it. The fact that Americans need to re themselves that "money isn't everything" reflects the fac they often behave as though it is. However, Americans have money in their creation myth: the Maasai creation holds that when God created the earth He gave cattle Maasai and proclaimed that they were the only people on with the right to own it. Throughout their history the M have used this myth as a justification to raid neighboring groups and take away their cattle by force. If God procla cattle to be the sole property of the Maasai, then other p must have obtained their cattle by less than honorable me may have been generations ago, but that is not importan right, nay the duty, of the Maasai to reclaim their God-given tle whenever possible.

The ability of the Maasai to control large herds of cattle, as ll as to take other people's cattle when they took a fancy to it, s based on their superior military organization. In fact when British arrived in East Africa at the turn of the 20th century, y saw the Maasai as the single biggest threat to their colo- l project. Their initial approach, therefore, was to seek alli- ces with the Maasai, rather than to try and dominate them by litary force. In this respect, the British did not appear terribly ferent to the Maasai than the numerous African groups who d sought similar alliances with them over the years. Because y controlled so many cattle and such a large territory, the aasai were seen as desirable allies and trading partners for nic groups throughout East Africa. While God may have creed that all cattle belonged to the Maasai, almost everyone nted them, meaning that "being Maasai" was one of the most stigious things that someone could achieve in pre-colonial st Africa (Spear and Waller 1993).

The central importance of livestock to the Maasai economy is lected in its traditional (but diminishing) use as a medium of change in Maasai society. Gifts of livestock are presented to ys as they are initiated into warriorhood. Friendships, called ck associations by anthropologists, are cemented by periodic ts of livestock. Wealthy men frequently lend animals to poorer n in an effort to build a loyal following of clients. Perhaps most portant, livestock in Maasai society is used as a medium of mar- ge exchange. When a young man wishes to marry, he presents parents of his potential bride with gifts of livestock. If the gift acceptable, then he will periodically add new gifts of livestock his original gift until the marriage is made official through a ies of rituals, also involving livestock exchange. Even once marriage is complete the husband will continue to present in-laws with livestock for the rest of their lives. These gifts, ich were the intended subject of my original research project, nent relationships between two social groups: the bride givers l the bride takers. If the marriage is dissolved then the livestock st be returned. As you can imagine, this creates huge pressures inst divorce in Maasai society. One of the unfortunate effects his tradition is that it makes it exceedingly difficult for Maasai men to escape abusive marriages.

The social exchange of livestock also serves ecological and up survival functions. One of the defining characteristics Maasai country is its unpredictable weather patterns and iodic lack of rain. Rain may come for seven years to one a, and then not at all for another seven. By giving and loan- livestock to friends and clients, Maasai herders effectively tter their herds all over the place. When the area in which a der lives is dry and several of his animals die, the area of his ck associates may receive abundant rains. Traditionally this ans that this man's stock associates will present him with stock, or if he is wealthy, his clients may return some of animals he lent to them, allowing his herd to recover from drought. The social networks created by these livestock hanges are also useful in that such networks make it pos- e for herders to relocate their entire herd to the country of their stock associates, a greater benefit than all but the most generous gifts of stock.

While herders have always tried to spread their livestock over large areas, certain places have been traditionally recognized as better than others. Some had permanent sources of water; others were at higher elevations and so received more rain. Other areas have ancient wells, which were dug by and belong to specific Maasai clans. My research area, Simanjiro, was once considered an especially great place to keep livestock. Elders who came to Simanjiro from other places told stories about its reputation. During the 1940s and 1950s many herders relocated to Simanjiro because of its abundant pasture and water. Elders who came to Simanjiro during this period describe how they prospered as their herds doubled, tripled, and even quadrupled. One man in particular, who was my host for much of my time in Tanzania, is rumored to have over 10,000 head of cattle. He claims to have been able to build this herd because of Simanjiro's favorable climate.

Since the 1950s, however, the reputation of Simanjiro as a great place to keep livestock has declined immensely. Most of the pasture and water that were the foundation of Simanjiro's booming herding economy have been lost to other concerns. Because of the central importance of cattle to the Maasai of Simanjiro, the decline of this herding economy has had devastating effects on their culture. The ability to live the "pure pastoralist life style," which has been a central cultural value, is now enjoyed by only a handful of wealthy herders. As the herding economy declined, so did the number of livestock available for social exchange. Local people believe that social relationships within their society have suffered accordingly. Most important, for most Maasai, the tradition of wealthy herders sharing their animals with poorer ones has been steadily disappearing. The result has been increased wealth discrepancies within Maasai society as a few wealthy men, who are now able to hire laborers for cash, accumulate large numbers of animals, while many others decline into poverty. The resentment that these poorer herders felt towards their former patrons was evident in many of my interviews.

What about Conservation?

One of the central processes that have contributed to the displacement of Maasai herders in Simanjiro is conservation. Specifically, the creation of Tarangire National Park has enclosed pasture and water resources essential to the herding economy, a process that has also contributed to ecological deterioration. Many of my informants described conservation as indistinguishable from any of the other global processes they confronted in their daily lives. Its bottom line was the alienation of traditional grazing lands for the benefit and enjoyment of other people, the majority of whom, from their perspective, were white and not even from Tanzania. As far as they were concerned, this was essentially unfair.

Of course this perspective is different from how most Americans imagine conservation. A student in my "Culture and the Environment" class once told me that for him the class had been as much about unlearning as it had been about learning. He had to unlearn things that he previously believed about conservation before he could begin to explore concepts addressed in the class. This process of unlearning is essential, because many people (myself included) hold preconceived ideas about conservation. Too often, these ideas are formed by popular notions that conceal the painful reality of how conservation affects indigenous communities around the world. . . .

Conservation and Globalization: Some Issues of Definition

Conservation

It is difficult to see what objections anyone could have to conservation. Defining this term broadly, it simply means using natural resources in ways that ensure they will be available to future generations. Conservation is also what we mean when we talk about sustainable development: cutting down a tree means planting a new one, finding alternative power sources instead of exhausting fossil fuels, and recycling or reusing the packaging of consumer goods. While these types of conservation and sustainable practice would certainly benefit the planet, they don't represent the kind of conservation that I am concerned about.

Most Western conservationists seeking to do conservation in indigenous communities also aren't talking about this kind of conservation. Almost all indigenous peoples have traditional ways of using natural resources in ways that will ensure their continued availability to future generations. In other words, they engage in sustainable resource management practices. This doesn't mean that their resource management systems are perfect, and I want to avoid popular notions of indigenous peoples living in harmony with their environment. For the most part, however, people who have used natural resources in the same area for many generations have gotten pretty good at it. If they haven't destroyed their resource base and perished as a result (and this has certainly happened to indigenous communities), they have learned from their mistakes. Through this process, they have developed resource management practices that are suited to the particular environment in which they live.

Most of people living in Western consumer culture do not face the same kinds of immediate environmental constraints as indigenous communities. The global capitalist system can destroy resources in one area and simply move to exploit the same resources in a completely different part of the world. As long as they don't use up all of a particular resource in the world, business can continue as usual. This system, and the high standards of living it provides for some, has wreaked environmental havoc from the Great Lakes to the Amazon Rainforest. It is somewhat ironic, therefore, that most Western conservationists working with indigenous peoples operate under the assumption that indigenous conservation models (if they acknowledge that such a thing exists at all) are inherently inferior to the ones of their own society. This situation is now changing somewhat, but it is changing very slowly and still has a long way to go. . . .

As a distinctly Western conservation model, parks are usually incompatible with indigenous conservation models, which aren't usually premised on the total exclusion of community members over large territories. This is the type of conservati that is usually funded by Western conservation organizatio It is also the type of conservation with which indigenous pe ples are most directly familiar. It should come as no surpri therefore, that I have heard Native Americans and indigenc Africans speak of conservation(ists) with disdain on ma occasions. While the concept is too big to define comprehe sively, certain aspects of globalization are especially releva to this study and more generally to cultural anthropology. G balization revolves around a network of institutions that ha now reached almost every part of the world. These institutic include governments and markets, as well as transnational bo ies such as the UN, the World Bank, and the International Mo etary Fund (IMF). They also include transnational conservati organizations such as the World Wildlife Fund (WWF) and t International Union for the Conservation of Nature and Natu Resources (IUCN), as well as transnational human rights org nizations such as OXFAM, Amnesty International, and Afr Watch. Among these global institutions, I also include natio parks, which link to governments and transnational bodies su as the UN and the WWF.

This global institutional network forms a system of mor and ideas. Money moves through the network, but it is a attached to certain types of ideas. Those who are able to arti late the right ideas are more likely to be able to gain acc to this global network and the money it controls. For instan the IMF operates on the idea that free markets should exist every part of the world. Third world governments that ag to promote free markets can obtain economic assistance fr the IMF; others cannot. Likewise, third world governments t promote Western conservation models can expect to get a lo economic support from groups like the IUCN, as well as fr Western governments. The problem is that the ideas attac to the money are almost always those of powerful people w run the institutions in this global network. The ideas of m ginalized people are almost never considered or implement although there are important exceptions to this rule.

Since the fall of the Soviet Union, this global network been transformed, making it more accessible to indigen communities, or at least certain community members. The of European communism also meant the end of state-cente development. Development policies began to revolve aro the idea that governments should do less. This idea was anot one to which large sums of money were attached. The inst tions that replaced governments in a variety of functions h come to be known simply as NGOs (non-governmental orga zations). NGOs have existed for a long time—they were cal charities. Since the fall of the Soviet Union, however, the nu ber of NGOs around the world has exploded. So many of th organizations came into existence in the early 1990s that so observers called it a "global associational revolution."

The Maasai, along with many other indigenous groups aro the world, have taken full advantage of this "global associatic revolution." By the late 1980s, most development aid to A can countries came with the stipulation that their governme would promote the emergence of a vibrant NGO sector. Tan nia, where I did my dissertation research, was no exception ly 1980s, only 17 registered NGOs were working in this ·. By the end of the 1990s, there were nearly 1,000 NGOs. .e development money became tied to the idea that NGOs etter than African governments at delivering services and ing democracy, Tanzania experienced its own "associa- evolution." . . .

vith other global institutions, the money Western conser- organizations offered to Maasai NGOs has been attached in ideas. In this case, these ideas revolve around Western vation models. Specifically, Western conservation orga- ns hold that it would be a good thing if indigenous groups e Maasai would embrace Western conservation models lp promote them. On an abstract level, however, these raw from certain Western fantasies about Africa in gen- d the Maasai in particular. It is important to explore these es, because they are the very kind of popular notions that n mask the painful realities of indigenous communities. le Western conservation organizations often evoke these notions in their fund raising appeals, they rarely address plications for what they are trying to achieve. These fan- herefore, are also tied to money circulating in the global onal network. Because their money gives Western conser- organizations power over Maasai NGOs, it is important to and who they are, where they come from, and what their ves are. In the following section, I address these fantasies of introduction to conservation in East Africa.

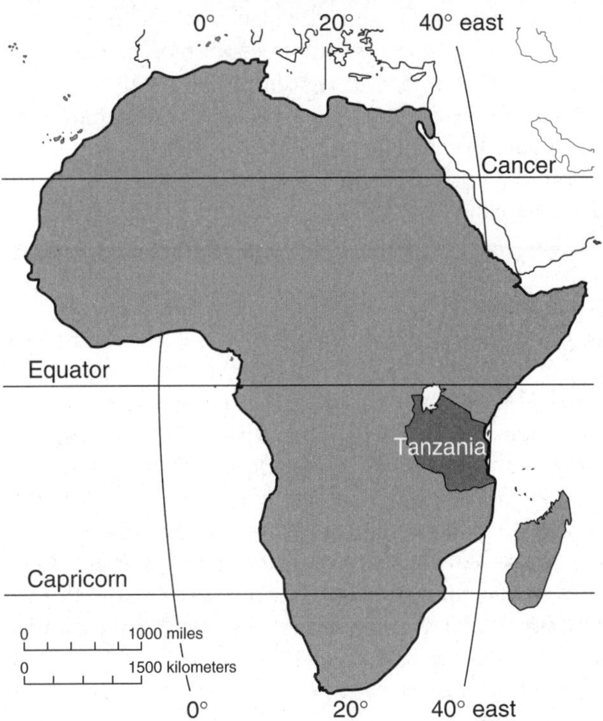

Figure 1 This map shows the relative size and location of the country of Tanzania on the continent of Africa.

t Africa as an Ecocultural me Park

tern Media Fantasies ıt Wildlife and the Maasai

gh you may not be able to find Tanzania quickly on a globe gure 1), you are probably familiar with conservation in Perhaps you have watched the *Discovery Channel* and ride of lions take down zebra on the Serengeti Plain. Or y have seen video footage of the annual wildebeest migra- ong the Great Rift Valley in Tanzania and Kenya. Tens of ds of these animals plunge into flooded rivers, apparently us to the racing current and the waiting crocodiles. Some nd some are eaten, but most survive to complete the jour- possibly you are familiar with images of machine-gunned ts, with gaping holes in their faces where poachers have extracted their tusks. These images were indispensable al highly successful fund-raising campaigns by Ameri- servation organizations in the 1980s (cf. Bonner 1993). h these popular media images, most Americans "know" servation in Africa is about animals. More specifically, ut the preservation of endangered species, most notably d elephants. While I suspect that few Americans actually nd and worry about African rhinos in their spare time, sociate Africa with wild animals.

sai are nearly as familiar to Westerners as the lions of the ti. Whether you know it or not, you probably have an idea they look like. Maasai warriors, with their flowing red d spears in hand have become a quintessential symbol for vanishing Africa. They have appeared on the *Discovery Channel*, leaping into the air in exuberant dances and (in their calmer moments) leaning on their spears gazing out over a vast African landscape of waving savanna grasses. In the movie *Out of Africa* they appear racing across the arid savanna on a mysterious mission. A lighter movie, *The Air Up There*, presents an unlikely story of a college basketball coach who goes to Kenya to recruit a Maasai warrior for his school's team. The movie climaxes with a game between the "traditional" Maasai and some "nontraditional" urban Africans. (I won't spoil the ending by telling you who wins.) A recent commercial from Nissan features a group of Maasai warriors congratulating each other on the purchase of a brand new Altima. Standing in a row outside of their mud houses, they marvel at the latest in midsize family sedans while an elephant lazily wanders by in the distant background.

This bizarre scenario captures the essence of Western fantasies about Africa, which are frequently used to market something. Both African people and African wildlife are portrayed as exotic and inhabiting an unspoiled world that no longer exists in the West. Just as important, the two are portrayed as separate from one another. People exist in one realm, and animals in another. Viewers may see lions on the *Discovery Channel*, and viewers may see Maasai on the *Discovery Channel*. It is unlikely, however, that they will ever see lions and Maasai on the *Discovery Channel* at the same time. For most Westerners this seems like a "natural" arrangement: African wildlife exists in wilderness or nature, a place untouched by the ravaging effects of human activities. This imaginary vision is difficult to resolve with the reality of a traffic jam of zebra-striped safari vans converging on a rhino that happens to be wearing a collar that allows authorities to monitor his movements with a high-tech satellite tracking system. Nevertheless, it is an idea that many hold dear: national parks equal nature and nature does not include humans. If you are fortunate enough to visit this nature, you should "take nothing but pictures and leave nothing but footprints." Westerners expect other cultures to conform to this imperative.

These expectations raise important questions for the other half of the equation: the Maasai. If they don't live in nature along with wild animals, where exactly do they live? In one respect the answer to this question is a simple: somewhere else. If you examine Western stereotypes of the Maasai closely, however, this answer doesn't make much sense. As I have already explained, the Maasai are commonly portrayed as living in a vast steppe, with nothing to see from horizon to horizon but tall savanna grasses. The reality of the situation is drastically different. A glimpse at a map of East Africa reveals that much of their rangeland has been encroached on by national parks and urban sprawl. Nairobi, a city of nearly 5 million people, sits squarely in the middle of traditional Maasai territory. I have seen Maasai herders grazing their livestock in the median of a major highway and by airport runways. In the rural areas, mechanized farms and commercial ranches have taken over much of the best grazing land outside of national parks. In short, the idea that the Maasai herd their cattle in wide-open spaces is largely inaccurate.

Disneyfication and Ecocultural Tourism in East Africa

Obviously there are some serious discrepancies between Western media fantasies about wildlife and the Maasai and the "on-the-ground" realities of life in East Africa. As long as images of African people and animals are experienced at a distance, these discrepancies are not terribly significant. As most Americans are well aware, mediums like TV, movies, and the Internet can construct "virtual realities" that are convincing to the consumer but have absolutely no relationship to the real world. But what about fantasies that are experienced as "actual reality"? Is it possible for Western fantasies about people and the environment to be imposed on the "real world" and in effect become a reality? As bizarre as this proposition may initially appear, it is something with which Americans are intimately familiar, through institutions such as subdivisions, shopping malls, and especially theme parks.

So pervasive are the effects of theme parks on the ways that Westerners look at the world that some social scientists refer to the process by which artificial realities are constructed as "Disneyfication." In his book, *The Culture of Nature* (1992), Alexander Wilson describes how the fantasy realities of Disney theme parks are created through a process known as *illusioneering* in industry-speak. He quotes one Disney *illusioneer*, who explains:

> The environments we create are more utopian, more romanticized and more like the guest imagined they would be. The negative elements are discreetly eliminated, while positive aspects are in some cases embellished to tell the story more clearly. (pp. 161–162)

Thus, riders on Disney's Jungle Cruise see pygmy villages, wild animals, and a jungle temple. They don't see lumber companies clearing the forest with bulldozers, cattle g the deforested areas to dust, local people being displa hydroelectric dams, nor any signs of poverty or malnu Of even more relevance to this book is Disney World's A Safari Ride, which simulates the African safari experie the extent of importing animals and people from Africa. board a four-wheel drive vehicle that takes them through dirt roads and swollen rivers before they finally encounte of animals listlessly grazing on an artificial savanna. An A man then runs up to the vehicle yelling, "*Bwana! Bwan* poachers are stealing the baby elephant!" The ride then be a high-speed chase, ending with the rescue of the baby ele which is a mechanical elephant's trunk sticking out of a w crate. The animals that the visitors encounter are not they were raised in captivity and descended from anima were captured somewhere in Africa like the mechanica elephant who is "saved" from such a fate over and over ag the thousands of visitors who go on the ride every day.

In an article aptly entitled "The Maasai and the Lion anthropologist Edward Bruner (2001) describes how the t fantasies produced by the "Disney dream machine" mak way back to Africa where they are repackaged and sold to ern tourists. Westerners usually go to East Africa on safar two things: animals and "traditional" Africans. To see a they go to national parks. To see "traditional" Africans the even have to leave the comfort of their luxury hotels. Most feature Maasai dancers at least a couple nights a week. Wh tourists don't realize, however, is that many of these danc not actually Maasai. Tourists will pay to see "the Maasa society with rampant unemployment, it only makes sen young men should take advantage of this opportunity by ing up like Maasai and learning "traditional" Maasai More adventurous tourists might also visit "cultural vi where they can see how the Maasai "really live" and pay some pictures for the folks back home. Unlike real Maa lages, however, cultural villages lack cows, their manure, swarms of flies they inevitably attract.

Maasai "cultural villages" are exactly the type of co experience that Western tourists pay for when they p a luxury safari. Like the rides at Disney World, luxu ris highlight the utopian and the romantic, presenting with a world that is more like they imagined it would b are met at the airport by an English-speaking guide in suit who whisks them away to the Nairobi Hilton. They the short distance from the van to the lobby with the as of porters dressed in brass-buttoned suits. The hotel sh arcade offers everything from *The New York Times* to helmet, without ever stepping outside. The same vehi brought them from the airport will transport them to a lodge inside of one of Kenya's world-famous parks. Fro they will be driven about, taking pictures of elephants and zebra. Then it's back to the Hilton, back to the airp back to the Western city from whence they came. With l only Africans they will have encountered are servants "traditional" people who danced for their entertainmen gerous animals will have been viewed from the comf safety of their safari vehicle.

lso like the riders on Jungle Cruise and the African Safari , these tourists will be spared the unpleasant realities of eal world that their "Disneyfied" experiences are modeled . If they were only to step outside the Nairobi Hilton, less a block away they would encounter 6-year-old boys sniffing on garbage heaps, shrouded lepers begging for money, and age girls forced into prostitution by poverty and despair. If were only to stop outside the national parks that they came isit, they would encounter whole communities of people have been displaced and impoverished by those very parks. use these people and their poverty are discreetly eliminated the safari experience, very few tourists will make the con- ion between the luxury hotels, where they are spared from unpleasant sights, and the vast wealth discrepancies that in countries like Tanzania and Kenya. It is one of the cen- contentions of this book, however, that the negative impacts onservation and economic development in East Africa are twined with the Western fantasies played out in African life safaris.

Western Fantasies about the asai and the Environment tually Affect Communities?

relationship between Western fantasies about Africa and oversty concealed by the luxury safari experience is by no ns simple. For one thing the illusion is never complete. ists do see poverty, even if only in fleeting glimpses. The ved wisdom, however, is that tourism generates revenues will help alleviate poverty, and that it also helps pay for the ction of valuable endangered species. These two "articles ith" make up the creed of ecotourism. That ecotourism fre- tly has the exact opposite effect is a proposition that does nesh well with these popularly held ideals.

nother important question is whether changing peoples' ptions would actually have meaningful impacts on pov- and environmental degradation in East Africa. This type estion has been hotly debated within cultural anthropol- nd other social sciences. In overly simplistic terms such es pit anthropologists influenced by the ideas of Karl Marx believed that ideas are nothing more than a superfluous by- ct of material processes), and those influenced by Michel ault (who believed that ideas are a powerful force that lly shape peoples' realities). Traditional Marxists would that it matters little how tourists imagine Africa. Poverty result of material processes, whereby Africans were dis- ssed of their land and other forms of natural wealth by ialism and international capitalism. If there was money to ade by building luxury lodges in national parks, then ideas conservation and wildlife protection were nothing more post hoc justifications for the dispossession that building lodges entailed. Foucauldians, on the other hand, would that ideas and discourses have everything to do with what ened in East Africa. Powerful ideas about wilderness and alue of wildlife, shrouded in the scientific veneer of ecol- were a driving force in the creation of national parks in this of the world.

Most anthropologists, myself included, fall somewhere in between. The enclosure of Maasai grazing lands by national parks and commercial farms is a material process with observable social and ecological impacts. It would be wrong to argue, however, that the ideas that accompanied this process were merely ideological byproducts. Notions of wilderness, wildlife, and "natural man" run deep in the Western psyche. They not only shape what Western tourists want to see when they go to East Africa, they also inform policy, science, and the formation of government agencies and NGOs. In this respect they have a much deeper impact on life in East Africa than you might initially suspect. Anthropologists' understanding of conservation in East Africa must encompass these types of ideas, as well as the historical processes of dispossession that they accompanied. For some readers this ambitious goal may seem to push the limits of cultural anthropology. Many people are attracted to this discipline for its emphasis on isolated non-Western people living in harmony with nature—an existence that seems to have been lost in the West. Ironically, these are the same ideas that inform the types of problems this book seeks to address.

The Ethnography of Conservation and Globalization

Shedding My Fantasies about Africa, or Yet Another Ethnographer's Dramatic Entrance Tale

The depth of Western fantasies about traditional Africans and pristine wildernesses are reflected in my own experience of becoming an anthropologist. I will be the first to admit that I entered the field because it offered adventure. As a child my worldview was influenced by *Dr. Doolittle* (Rex Harrison not Eddy Murphy), *Mutual of Omaha's Wild Kingdom*, a short-lived series called *Daktari* (about an American doctor living in Kenya), and a set of National Geographic books called *Peoples of the Earth.* Going to high school in suburban Detroit nearly burned this sense of adventure out of my soul, but then I went away to college and took "Introduction to Cultural Anthropology." One of the books we read in this class was *The Forest People* by Colin Turnbull. His experiences among the Mbuti of Central Africa, living in a mud house and participating in the daily life of his host community intrigued me. At the time, I was a dishwasher and selling plasma twice a week to make ends meet. Anthropological fieldwork appeared as an exciting alternative to my lifestyle of financial and intellectual impoverishment. I decided to become a cultural anthropologist. I never considered who would pay me to live among exotic people and write a book about it; I just decided it was the job for me.

As it turned out, I did get to live in a mud house. However, my experiences in the field were far more confusing and complex than those described by Turnbull. The Maasai warriors where I lived rode motorcycles, listened to reggae, and watched Jackie Chan movies on a portable video monitor. People were engaged in struggles with commercial farms and national parks that were encroaching on their land, and organizing their own NGOs. Through these NGOs, Maasai leaders were becoming active at the national and international levels. There was a great deal going on, not all of it was local, and none of it was easy to understand. Since I have left the field, Maasai warriors who have made it big as gemstone miners have begun coordinating their herding activities with cell phones (Amy Cooke, personal communication, November 2002). Tanzania also boasts a Maasai warrior rap star named Mr. Ebbo who sings about the wonders of privatization. The reality of the situation was exceedingly different from my romantic expectations of fieldwork.

In retrospect, my expectations seem rather misplaced. I didn't read *The Forest People* and rush off to Africa the next day. I went to Tanzania as a doctoral student with several years of theoretical training. Yet my ideas of social change among the Maasai were naïve. I believed that I could find communities that were essentially unaffected by modernization. I was interested in cattle markets, since many development projects for the Maasai were premised on the idea that they refused to market their livestock. It didn't take long to discover that the Maasai had been selling their animals for a long time (since probably before European contact), that some even made a living from this business, and that many considered it an important strategy for managing their herds. I also discovered that poverty was forcing many Maasai to sell off the last of their animals and out of the herding business altogether. It soon became clear that most Maasai men knew a great deal about markets and marketing, and that my assumptions about recent transformations to the Maasai herding economy were largely unfounded. Many Maasai frankly stated that my study, which was looking at the impact of cattle marketing on traditional marriage payments, wasn't very interesting.

My views of African nature and wildlife were also essentially unexamined. I knew that my intended field communities were on the borders of a national park. This concerned me, because I imagined that a lion would probably eat me. Otherwise, I didn't give the matter much thought. I was there to study social and economic change among the Maasai. What could wildlife or national parks have to do with that? The animals were inside the park, where they belonged (except for the lions that might wander out and eat me). The people, and the processes of social change that I was interested in recording, were outside the park. This seemed reasonable to me. Of course, I now realize that it doesn't make sense. Even then I had begun to acknowledge that the whole arrangement seemed kind of funny. I suspected that at some point in time the Maasai must have lived in the area that was now the park. However, these niggling doubts were overridden by my uncritical assumption that parks were nature. I didn't consider conservation as part of the economic and social transformation that I wanted to study, until people in my study area complained so loudly and frequently about it that I couldn't ignore the issue any longer.

Chance Encounters and a New Way of Looking at Things

A Change in Research Direction So how did I get from this original state of mystification and ignorance to my current analysis of conservation in East Africa? In a word: gradually. When I first went to Tanzania 1992 I had no funding for my project. I hoped to get funding, but I couldn't convince m that it was terribly important. To make matters worse, I di feel right about bothering people with lots of seemingly i evant questions. My lack of confidence was exacerbated by fear of lions, the fact that so many Maasai held my proje low-esteem, and that the local authorities seemed bent on r ing my life as difficult as possible. I also discovered that I di like smoke-filled houses, sleeping on cowhide beds, and ha goats slaughtered in my honor. My temptation was to stay in city of Arusha. Here I could go to the movies, eat Indian f and hang out by the Novotel swimming pool. Because o exchange rates that existed at the time, I could do this all few dollars a day. It would have been a perfect setup, except I couldn't relax and enjoy it. My career appeared to be g down the drain before it even got started. Besides, what w I tell my advisor? The matter was clear, I was going to to stay out of Arusha for a long time. The next day I boa an overfilled dump truck, which was listing worrisomely t left, and embarked on an extended survey of the southern M sai markets.

This survey resulted in a contact that was crucial to my rese Traveling from market to market required that I spend the in different villages. Occasionally this put me in the positi having to seek the hospitality of strangers. On one such occa I was directed to a house that turned out to be the headquarte a newly registered political party (Tanzania was a one-party until the year I started my research). The local organizer o party was a man named Saruni Ndelelya[1]. . . . Saruni was a in his thirties who had been trained as a school teacher i 1970s, and who had insisted on returning to his home vi of Orkesumet to educate another generation of Maasai. A educated member of his community he was a natural leader people constantly came to him when confronted with prob that they could not solve on their own. Saruni was also o the founders of an NGO called Pastoralists of the High (*Ilaramatak Lorkornerie*). This NGO was one of the first sai NGOs, and it received a great deal of attention from int tional donors in the mid-1990s.

Saruni taught me more in two days than I learned in the e month of my market survey. He explained that both the N and the political party were products of a local social move protesting land grabbing by European and Tanzanian inve Local people felt that the government had discriminated ag the Maasai for long enough, especially now that land grab was happening at an unprecedented rate. . . . they hoped the new NGO would promote local control of land and na resources and become a platform from which to advoca rights of cultural autonomy. This was far more exciting anything I had previously imagined. . . .

The 1993 NGO Workshop

Maasai NGO Leaders

. . . Based on my background and training, Maasai N seemed like the ultimate solution to the problem of pas ist development. No longer would misinformed outside designing socially and ecologically inappropriate develop grams. New programs could be designed by the Maasai for Maasai. What could be a better arrangement? I now know I had merely adopted a slightly more sophisticated version ıy romantic (but still largely uninformed) notion of the Maa- At the time, however, this newfound enthusiasm was just ıt I needed. I finally had a reason to be excited about my ldwork. I would make NGOs the new focus of my disserta- research! Unfortunately, I was almost completely out of ıey. I returned to the United States to write another round unding proposals. Apparently my enthusiasm for Maasai Os was convincing, because in December 1994 I returned anzania with a funded project. Aside from almost dying of aria the following year and almost cutting my arm off the after that, my research continued without a hitch. Well, 's not exactly true, but I did manage to get enough data to e my dissertation, not to mention this book.

nservation and Conflict My Research Area

ing back to the field with something important to work on ed me to overcome my apathy for research. However, my ctance to bother people with my prying questions still hin- d me. I was especially averse to bothering NGO leaders, who always exceedingly busy. With all of the environmental and al problems that they had to deal with, what possible interest d they have in a dissertation project? To make matters worse, ni was in Ireland on a development studies course. I had to e my contacts all over again. I managed to do this and began ing along to community meetings. One community meeting ırticular became a turning point in my field project. Orga- l by leaders of the Pastoralists of the Highlands, it allowed people to address representatives of several British charities, ell as a BBC reporter. Local people had lost a lot of land to a h seed company called Royal Sluis. Local people explained the seed farm had disrupted their economy as well as the ecosystem. I realized that a study of Maasai NGOs would to address the issue of land grabbing in Maasai communi- Furthermore, any data that I produced on this issue would be useful to NGOs themselves.

y research assistant, Edward Oloure, and I created an exten- land-use survey, designed to reveal the connections between grabbing and changes in Maasai resource management ices. We spent several months conducting this survey in villages. We also spent time with Maasai elders, who told bout the history of resource management in the area. These istories were indispensable, because they allowed us to see rences in past resource management practices during a time more land and water were available to herders and prac- that have emerged in the context of large-scale land loss. lso spent time "truth-testing" through independent cross- ks with Maasai elders in other villages. After we had pub- l our findings (Igoe & Brockington 1999), I learned from er researcher that they were consistent with satellite data she was analyzing for her dissertation project. While these omes do not unequivocally prove my data, they support the bility that local knowledge of the environment is frequently ate. The Maasai men and women whom I interviewed in this

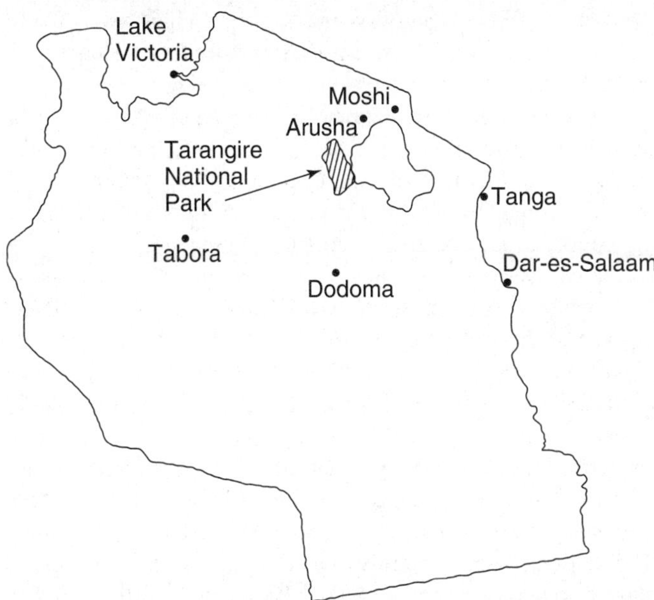

Figure 2 Map showing the relative size and location of Simanjiro District and Tarangire National Park in Tanzania.

survey presented a coherent picture of the social and environmental changes taking place in their communities. . . .

People living on the borders of Tarangire National Park complained that natural resources now inside the park were essential to the traditional economy of Simanjiro. With the enclosure of the park in 1971, followed by the arrival of commercial farms in the 1980s, herd mobility became increasingly restricted. Herders could no longer move their animals in search of pasture and water as they had done in the past. Without fallow periods in which it could recover, pasture in the area began to decline. This situation became especially tenuous during periods of drought, which happen periodically throughout East Africa. During recent drought, many herders in my research area lost all or most of their animals. Some moved away altogether; many others turned to farming in an effort to feed themselves and their families. For the most part, however, their semi-arid rangelands proved unsuitable for cultivation. The exception to this rule was the higher, wetter areas taken over by commercial farms. Herders described themselves as squeezed between the park and the commercial farms with no place left to go.

In addition to the ecological and economic stresses herders attributed to Tarangire, relationships between communities and park authorities have been consistently antagonistic. Local women expressed fear over collecting firewood in the vicinity of the park because of the danger of sexual harassment by park rangers. Men reported having their livestock confiscated, being tied up, beat up, threatened with guns, and being arrested. Fines for being arrested and retrieving confiscated livestock run into several hundreds or thousands of dollars. Local people do not view the park as a public resource, nor do they believe that those who deny them access are interested in conservation. Many were of the opinion that tourism benefited wealthy Europeans and Tanzanian elites, while bringing few benefits to the people who are forced to pay with the loss of their traditional natural resource base. This view is not entirely inaccurate; luxury lodges inside the park are highly lucrative ventures. Some lodges have already had negative environmental impacts, such as taxing local water tables (Bonner 1993).

Local concerns about Tarangire National Park came to a head in the middle 1980s, when a group of conservationists floated a proposal to extend its boundaries. Communities near the park would be incorporated into a conservation area, where agriculture would be forbidden and herding practices highly restricted. Some people would be forcefully relocated away from the park. The proposal was leaked to community leaders by a sympathetic conservationist. Alarmed by the proposal, these leaders organized the Committee to Stop Conservation in Simanjiro (translated from Swahili by the author) or the Anti-Conservation Committee for short. In fact, the proposed conservation area would probably never have materialized anyway. Nevertheless, the campaign to stop it has had a profound effect on local people's perceptions of anything called conservation. The very idea of an Anti-Conservation Committee unequivocally presents conservation as a wholly negative thing. Even when people knew little about the specific aims of Western conservation, most felt that they knew enough. To local Maasai, people who promoted conservation were outsiders who thought animals were more important than people, and who wanted to take away Maasai rangeland in order to accommodate wildlife at the Maasai's expense.

This was the prevailing view of conservation expressed by respondents to my land-use survey in 1996. During this same year a new type of conservation initiative was taking place in my research area. The European Union sponsored a group of researchers to conduct an extensive research project on the interaction of people and wildlife to the east of Tarangire National Park. One of the team members, an American economist, was conducting a community mapping project using GIS technology.[2] Towards this end, she elicited the help of local herders in identifying key resources within their communities, such as pasture, farms, water, and forests. Once completed the maps would become a resource for future resource management projects. Not surprisingly, people were suspicious. An armed park ranger accompanied the researcher, and local children had seen the project airplane flying up and down the park border. Rumors began to circulate that this was simply a more sophisticated way to expand park boundaries. By this time Saruni was back from Ireland. He and other leaders in the Pastoralists of the Highlands were instrumental in blocking the mapping project.

A New Type of Conservation?

The mapping project was part of a resource management paradigm called community-based conservation, which takes its model from Zimbabwe's Communal Areas Management Program for Indigenous Resources (CAMPFIRE) program. CAMPFIRE premised that giving local people a stake in wildlife would increase their incentive to conserve it. Wildlife would thereby become an important engine of local economic development (Kiss 1990; Murphree 1996). In other words, community-based conservation seeks to create a synthesis of conservation and development. Several local observers pointed out that this would be a bad deal. Conservation denied people access to natural resources in favor of preserving wild animals. Devel ment, during the socialist period (1967 to 1980), entailed forced resettlement of Maasai communities. Lately it appe to revolve around the transfer of community resources to str ers and outsiders. What would local people gain from progr that combined these two projects? Assertions that this w new kind of conservation were met with public skepticism one elder put it, "A warthog's tusks can be as dangerous a elephant's."

Conversations between conservationists and local pe took place in community meetings, sponsored by Tanz National Parks. The meetings were part of a pilot project ca Good Neighborliness (*Ujirani Mwema*). They were designe enroll people in the community-mapping project, and to ir duce them to the concept of community-based conservatio was immediately clear that conservationists and local pe (mostly male elders) were working at cross-purposes. Cor vationists (both Western and Tanzanian) extolled the pote values of wildlife for local communities, and encouraged pe to stop farming in wildlife migration corridors. Local pe on the other hand, demanded access to land and other na resources inside of Tarangire National Park. This was a cession that conservationists were unable (and that most unwilling) to make. At one meeting a Tanzanian official inv the ritual pageantry of Maasai celebrations saying, "When go to a feast or a party, you wear your best clothes. On days, however, you wear your regular clothes." He concl that land inside the parks was like ritual clothing and land side the parks was like regular clothes. This prompted a q tion from a young Maasai: Why weren't the people of Sima invited to the feast?

All of the community-based conservation meetings I attended during my time in the field revolved around impasse. Promoters of community-based conservation spo using tourist revenues to fund local development projects (r ing from tented safari camps to ostrich farms), which impli assumed local economic transformations. Not all local pe were opposed to economic transformation, and some were interested in the potential revenue of these projects. How most were primarily concerned about the land and na resources on which the survival of their herds depended. enue sharing and income-generating projects could not beg compensate for the resources enclosed by the national par Brockington 2002). Many pointed out the irony of a pro of good neighborliness premised on excluding people high-quality pasture. Good-neighborliness in Maasai cult closely related to a system of mutual access to land and ral resources. A Maasai elder highlighted this discrepan another community-based conservation meeting:

> Tanzania National Parks can't teach us about good neig borliness. We had good neighborliness before Tanzan National Parks ever came here. If it doesn't rain here know that I can take my cattle to Naberera [a neighbori village]. The people at Naberera won't turn me awa They will let me stay so that my cattle will not die. Th will help me, because they may need my help anoth year. This is good neighborliness. Tanzania Nation

Parks does not understand this. Their livestock [wildlife] come to graze in our villages, and we do not bother them. If it rains in the park we can't go there, even if our cattle are dying. If we do, we are beaten up and our cattle are taken away. This is not good neighborliness. I know all about Tanzania National Parks Good Neighborliness. I've seen it with my own eyes, and we don't need it here. We would all be better off if Tanzania National Parks took their Good Neighborliness and went away. . . .

onnecting the Dots: Multisited thnography and Globalization

s brief overview outlines a complex state of affairs. Stud- of this nature have become increasingly common in cul- l anthropology, as anthropologists struggle to describe the nections between specific communities and the rest of the ld. Local conflicts over land are also conflicts over mean- taking place at multiple levels. Is it traditional rangeland, a ld heritage site, or a resource to be harnessed for national elopment? The rise of the Maasai NGOs brings a new set of stions to these debates. Suddenly questions over meanings and are intertwined with questions of what it means to be isai and especially whether the Maasai have special rights ndigenous people.

The cast of players in this scene is also dauntingly complex, uding local people, Maasai NGO leaders, government offi- s (categories that often overlap), Western conservationists, ian rights advocates, missionaries, entrepreneurs, and tour- In talking about what's going on, these people mix and ch an equally confusing array of ideas: Western stereotypes it the Maasai, conservation, free trade, national sovereignty, genous rights, to name a few. To complicate matters further, scene is connected to institutions like the Tanzanian govern- t, Western governments, NGOs, and the World Bank.

In a situation like this an anthropologist struggles to understand the complexity of the local situation and the various interests and perspectives that he or she may encounter there. She or he must then try and understand the connections of this complex local situation to other institutions and places. To do this she or he will probably have to engage in what is known in anthropology as multisited ethnography. My own study, for example, began in specific Maasai communities. From what I learned at this particular ethnographic site I found it necessary to pursue additional research at meetings in workshops in the cities of Arusha and Dar-es-Salaam. I also gathered data from human rights organizations in the United Kingdom. I expect that future research along these lines might take me to Canada, Washington D.C., and maybe even Australia. Research of this nature can also take place at virtual sites on the Internet and television. I learned a great deal from visiting human rights and conservation Web sites connected to the Maasai. These virtual sites taught me a great deal about how Maasai and Western NGO leaders were representing the types of problems that I was trying to understand. As I have already mentioned, these types of representations often invoke images and stereotypes of Africa and the Maasai that have their roots in the colonial period. . . .

Notes

1. The use of first and last names in this text follows Tanzanian usage and may appear inconsistent to the Western reader—the idea of people having first and last names was brought by Europeans.
2. Geographic Information Technology (GIS) is a form of satellite technology used to make maps. Conservation biologists use it to map such things as wildebeest migration routes. Anthropologists can use it to map resource conflicts.

What Native Peoples Deserve

ROGER SANDALL

The Roosevelt Indian Reservation in the Amazon rain forest is not a happy place. Last year, the Cinta Larga Indians slaughtered 29 miners there, and in October the Brazilian who was trying to mediate the conflict was murdered at a cash machine. Neither of these events represented anything new. The reserve, located 2,100 miles northwest of Rio de Janeiro, and named for Theodore Roosevelt when he visited Brazil in 1913, is also where a notorious massacre of Cinta Larga by rubber tappers took place in 1963; only one child in the village survived.

The immediate cause of the recent violence is not rubber but diamonds. The Roosevelt Indian Reservation may be sitting on one of the world's largest deposits, and no one wants to leave it in the ground—neither the Indians, nor the itinerant diggers (*garimpeiros*), nor the government. But, under present Brazilian law, no one is free to begin digging, either. And this brings us to the deeper cause of murder and mayhem in the region.

Under Brazil's constitution, the country's Indians are not full citizens. Instead, they are legal minors, with the status of a protected species. This has one singular benefit for the Indians: the twelve Cinta Larga responsible for last year's killing of 29 wildcat prospectors may enjoy immunity from prosecution and never face jail. But there is also a downside. As wards of the state, the Indians are denied the right to mine their own land.

As for outsiders, they must apply for permits to dig, and face endless bureaucratic delays that more often than not lead nowhere. The outcome is predictable: frustrated in their own wishes, and hard-pressed by the impatient diggers, Indians make private deals, which then go sour—and the shooting starts.

At issue here is not just the law; the law is itself the product of an idea, or a set of ideas, concerning certain underlying questions. What should be done about endangered enclave societies in the midst of a modern nation? Can they, or their land, or their minerals be cut off and preserved, frozen in time, pristine and inviolate, forever? Should they be?

The massacre of the Cinta Larga in 1963 gave rise to a Brazilian state inquiry that became known as the Figueiredo Report (after the official in charge of the investigation). The inquiry was meant to find out about the shockingly grave deficiencies and abuses that were then being tolerated by the Indian Protection Service, including the use of individual Indians as slaves. Once it was completed, the old agency was closed down, and a new one created to replace it.

There the matter might have rested had not the London *Sunday Times* caught a whiff of scandal. The paper dispatched the travel writer Norman Lewis to Brazil; though he did not meet any Indians, he fo all he needed in the Figueiredo Report. "By the descriptions o who had seen them," Lewis reported, "there were no more inoffen and charming human beings on the planet than the forest Indian Brazil."

Having established a scene of primal innocence, Lewis procee to tell of the atrocities against the Cinta Larga, warning that they v being pushed to the brink of extinction and that there might not single Indian left by 1980. He concluded: "What a tragedy, wh reproach it will be for the human race if this is allowed to happ Reprinted all over the globe, his sensational article had profound lasting effects.

The first of these effects was to enshrine a form of extreme tectionism, not only as a temporary means to an end—the human cultural survival of the indigenous peoples of Brazil—but as an in itself. Soon, all those working for Indian interests were of a si opinion: the only way to protect these tribal peoples was to create olable sanctuaries where they would "live their own lives preser their own culture on their own land."

The second effect was to galvanize a number of English explo writers, and anthropologists into setting up a permanent internati lobby. The name of this flourishing body is Survival, self-describ "the world's leading organization supporting tribal peoples." Two who have been associated with it from the outset are John Hem and Robin Hanbury-Tenison.

Hemming, who served for two decades as the director of the R Geographical Society, has written a number of books about S America, among them an indispensable three volume history o impact of civilization on Brazil's indigenous peoples—*Red* (*Amazon Frontier*, and *Die If You Must,* the last of which appe in 2003.* Hanbury-Tenison, Hemming's long-time friend, was a founder of Survival and is today its president. Less well-kr but also important is the documentary filmmaker Adrian Co who has spoken up on behalf of the Amazonian Indians for n 50 years.

According to a recent article by Hemming in the British mo *Prospect,* the campaign to ensure the survival of the Amazonian ples appears to have succeeded. This is also the gist of the final ch of *Die If You Must,* where he wrote:

> The Indians will survive physically. Their populations ha grown steadily since a nadir of near-extinction in the mid-20 century. Having fallen to little more than 100,000 in the 1950 they have more than tripled to some 350,000 and are genera rising fast.

---

*Macmillan, 887 pp., $28.50 (paper)

The health of the Indians is basically good, Hemming reported in *If You Must.* The killers of yesteryear—measles, TB, pneumonia, lera, and smallpox—are rare. Their land is also secure: "a remark- 11 percent of the land-mass of Brazil is now reserved for Indi- The 587 indigenous areas total almost 260 million acres—an area ater than France, Germany, and Benelux combined." Environmen- t ideals and indigenous interests have been reconciled: "From the [one reservation] now stands out as an immense rectangle of ver- vegetation framed by the dismal brown of arid ranch-lands."

t was in the 1950's and 60's that Hemming, Hanbury-Tenison, and Cowell, three young men from Oxford and Cambridge, launched themselves on the world. They were talented and energetic, they good connections, and above all they shared a boyish taste for nture. At Eton they probably read about Lawrence of Arabia; at ord, where Hemming and Hanbury-Tenison roomed together, they ady knew that "exploring" was what they wanted to do most. They rded the rain forests of Brazil as a natural field for their endeavors, in no time they were paddling up the Amazon in canoes.

drian Cowell was a Cambridge man, and his precocity as an orer makes an impressive tale in itself. As a student in 1954 he d a university Trans-Africa Expedition. The following year he was sia. Then, as he relates in *The Heart of the Forest* (1961), "the ord and Cambridge Expedition to South America . . . brought me e Amazon forest." Thereafter he joined the Brazilian Centro Expe- n, an enterprise associated with the creation of the new national tal of Brasilia. Its purpose was "to canoe down the Xingu River and an airstrip at the exact geographical center of Brazil."

was all tremendous fun and very romantic—a word that occurs taneously in the books of Hanbury-Tenison, who has written volu- usly about his explorations and today runs a booking agency for c locations. Here, from his website, is a typical passage about an adventure in Afghanistan:

> sound like distant thunder made me look up at the rich blue oudless sky before I turned to see twenty wild horsemen in rbans and flowing robes bearing down on me. They carried ng-barreled rifles and had daggers in their belts. Beside their irited horses loped large, hairy hounds. With their Genghis han moustaches and fine, aquiline noses they were almost ricatures of the bandits we had been warned about. I should ve been frightened, but all I could think was that if I had to go ould not have found a more romantic end.

his tells us quite a bit about the attitude of all three men toward enous peoples. In light of that attitude, Hanbury-Tenison must been taken aback when, in 1971, he called on the anthropolo- Margaret Mead at the Museum of Natural History in New York l her about Survival International (as Survival was then called), he gave him a piece of her mind. Mead at the age of seventy was y different person from the idealistic young woman who had d Samoa in 1926. By 1971, she was fiercely *un*romantic, and the acle of yet another young Oxford "explorer" embarking on yet er expedition up the Amazon must have set her teeth on edge. sturdy good sense she tried to talk him out of his fantasies.

his 1973 book, *A Question of Survival,* Hanbury-Tenison ibes this "small, beady-eyed dumpling of a lady who sailed into ack as I came through the door":

> e main point that annoyed [Mead] was the concept, unstated me, that primitive peoples were any better off as they were. e said she was "maddened by antibiotic-ridden idealists who wouldn't stand three weeks in the jungle" . . . and the whole "noble savage" concept almost made her foam at the mouth. "All primitive peoples," she said, "lead miserable, unhappy, cruel lives, most of which are spent trying to kill each other." The reason they lived in the unpleasant places they did, like the middle of the Brazilian jungle, was that nobody else would.

There was much talk in those days about the pharmaceutical benefits of rain forests, and Hanbury-Tenison and his friends were sure that the Amazon was about to make a huge contribution to the world's health. (This was a little before the discovery of the supposed wonders of jojoba oil.) But Mead was having none of it:

> She said that to protect [the Indians] on the grounds that they could be useful to us or contribute anything was nonsense. "No primitive person has *ever* contributed *anything,* or ever will," she said. She had no time for suggestions of medical knowledge or the value of jungle lore.

The only grounds on which Mead relented were broadly humanitarian. For one thing, the Indians' "art, culture, dancing, music, etc. was pleasant and attractive and their grandchildren might thank us for trying to preserve or at best record it now that we have the proper technical means [i.e., tape and film] for doing so." For another thing, "it was bad for the world to let these people die, and the effort to prevent their extermination was good for mankind even if it failed."

> For the rest, however, Mead vehemently denied that the Indians had any special reasons for being protected, as she denied any advantage of one race over another. She also claimed emphatically that they all wanted one thing only, and that was to have as many material possessions and comforts as possible. Those still running away in the jungle were the ones who had encountered the most unpleasant savagery from Europeans, and even though they might be having no contact now, if they could possibly get hold of any aluminum pots they would use them.

Although faithfully recorded by Hanbury-Tenison, Mead's argument was as lost on him in 1971 as it is lost today on legions of like-minded people who teach or mouth the slogans of multiculturalism. What Mead herself failed to grasp was that, naive though he may have sounded, Hanbury-Tenison and his friends had been radicalized, and they were never going to accept her bleak view of the tribal world. It was not that they had been reading Marx; instead, they had been reading Norman Lewis's digest of the worst parts of the Figueiredo Report, including Figueiredo's judgment that "the Indians [had] suffered tortures similar to those of Treblinka and Dachau."

Torture, indeed, was too tame a word for what had taken place. In 1963, there had been massacres of the Cinta Larga tribe in Rondonia. One gunman's taped testimony describes how an employee of a rubber company named Chico Luis

> gave the chief a burst with his tommy gun to make sure, and after that he let the rest of them have it. . . . [A]ll the other guys had to do was finish off anyone still showing signs of life. . . . [T]here was a young Indian girl they didn't shoot, with a kid of about five in one hand, yelling his head off. . . . Chico shot the kid through the head with his .45 and then grabbed hold of the woman—who by the way was very pretty. "Be reasonable," I said, "why do you have to kill her?" In my view it was a waste. "What's wrong with giving her to the boys? They haven't set eyes on a woman for six weeks. Or we could give her as a present to [their boss] de Brito."

But Chico would not listen:

> He tied the Indian girl up and hung her head downward from a tree, legs apart, and chopped her in half right down the middle with his machete. Almost with a single chop I'd say. The village was like a slaughterhouse. He calmed down after he'd cut the woman up, and told us to burn down all the huts and throw the bodies into the river.

This is unbearable: but it is not essentially different from what had happened to many Indians in Latin America after 1492. The lawless frontier was for centuries a refuge for loners, criminals, and violent psychopaths who had nothing to lose and could act with impunity. Those who went searching for El Dorado in the 1540's behaved like packs of marauding wolves, seizing food from the same Indian villagers whom they then enslaved as porters, and who were tortured or killed when they failed to cooperate. As one learns from Hemming's three-volume work, this sort of thing has had a very long history indeed.

Colonial nations fashion their heroes from the timber at hand, much of which is twisted and full of knots. Australia, for example, invites its citizens to admire an unappealing Irish bandit named Ned Kelly. But the Kellys smell sweet alongside Brazil's much romanticized *bandeirantes.* What are often referred to as expeditions of "pathfinders" from São Paulo into the interior in the first half of the 17th century were mostly slave raids aimed at catching, chaining, and marching back to the coast as many Indians as a group of well-armed and ruthless men could seize.

To be sure, there was sometimes a genuinely exploratory aspect to such forays. In *Red Gold,* Hemming offers a balanced account of this phase of Brazilian expansion inland, and fairly describes the ordeals of the *bandeirantes* themselves. Since slave-raiding was a central feature of traditional Indian culture, too, the journeys engaged whites, Indians, and those of mixed ancestry (*mamelucos*) in a common enterprise:

> The Indians contributed their forest skills and geographical knowledge. They soon grasped the purpose of the mission and became expert enslavers of other natives. Although brutalized and worked hard by the captains of the *bandeiras,* the Indians probably enjoyed service on them. It was quite normal for Tupi warriors to make long marches through the forests to attack enemy tribes.

In the course of his own periodic visits to Brazil, Adrian Cowell appears to have come rather closer to the realities of Amazonian Indian life than either Hanbury-Tenison or Hemming. As a result, although aware of the horrors long endured by Indians at the hands of slavers, settlers, and frontier psychopaths, he was also more prepared to face up to the grimmer aspects of the native cultures themselves, and of the horrors Indians had long inflicted on each other.

In *The Heart of the Forest* (1961), Cowell writes in idyllic prose of the partnership he formed with an Indian hunter, carrying his friend's gun and studying his craft, teaching himself to decoy wildfowl by imitating their calls. But he also reports how, in 1958 on the Xingu River, there were continual killings of itinerant Brazilian rubber tappers (*seringueiros*) by Indians, and of Indians by *seringueiros.* A Juruna Indian told him how

> first we lived lower down the Xingu and worked for the *seringueiros,* but they killed many [Indians] with rifles. So we came up here past the great rapids and lived till the *seringueiros* say they are friends and gave us rifles. So we went downriver again and worked for the *seringueiros* till they killed more Juruna. Then we killed many *seringueiros* and came back here and killed Trumai and Kamayura Indians. Then the Txukahamae tribe came and killed almost all of us so that we are only twelve now.

That is the way things were and always had been. And this, was a seemingly ineradicable aspect of the culture that Cowell tho worthy of being saved. Back in 1967, he had joined the brothers C dio and Orlando Villas-Boas in an attempt to contact and "pacify" elusive Kreen-Akrore. But violence in the camp was making it har manage a community where different tribal groups had been bro together for their own safety. The captions on a page of photogra in Cowell's 1973 book, *The Tribe that Hides from Man,* read like list of casualties on some exotic war memorial: "*Above:* Javarit Trumai killed by Tapiokap. *Above:* Pionim, a Kayabi, killed Tapio to avenge his brother-in-law." And so on.

Much has been written about the endeavor of the Villas-Boas br ers to establish the Xingu Indian refuge and entice the tribal remn of the Kayabi or Txikao or Suya to join it. A passage from *The T that Hides from Man* offers a glimpse into the thought processe Claudio, a "Marxist philosopher" in the Latin American manner:

> Look around this camp and you will see Indians are more lovin than we are. But the expression of their love is confined to th limits of this society. They cut a hole in the wilderness to contai their family, but outside this camp is the jungle where they ki meat for food, bamboo for arrows, leaves for their beds. Killin is the essence of forest existence, and if you stopped it, the for est and the Indian would die. Within the Indian mind there is complete division between the duties within the group and th absence of duty in the land of killing outside.

At one time, Claudio suggested that Indians should feel free t white *seringueiros* or any other uninvited marauders who came the Xingu Park. While warning them of the inevitable costs of practice as a permanent way of life, he understood that, acco to the tribal code, revenge killing was natural, habitual, and i table. Nor was this the only aspect of Amazonian Indian culture was hard to reconcile with modern life. Strict rules of seclusion found among all the upper-Xingu tribes. Women were subject draconian punishments for violations of taboo. In a British te sion documentary from the 1970's, a young Mehinacu woman asked what would happen if she were to glimpse, even acciden the sacred flutes played by the men. She would be gang-raped replied, smiling sadly as if in recognition that in the genteel wo her white interviewer, such sexual punishments—culturally a rized, approved, indeed mandatory—were unthinkable.

Hemming's account of Amazonian life is hard on the effo Christian missionaries, and especially hard on Jesuits ("ical missionaries intent on replacing native society and b with their own Christian model"). One line of grudging apprec will be followed by the word "but" and ten lines of disparageme his impressive study proceeds from volume to volume, he is c tently severe, his language becomes more tendentious, and an a secularism dictates his judgment of religious matters. In his article in *Prospect,* he seems to approve wholeheartedly only politically radical priests who began to appear in the 1960's— "tı anthropologists who did not try to undermine indigenous belie ed to be aggressive proselytizers." Before that point, his view of olic missionary activity is mainly negative.

ut what exactly were the religious authorities to do when they arrived from Portugal and had to deal, for example, with the namba? Did they not have a clear obligation both to undermine to prohibit certain indigenous beliefs? In modern times, we have the rise of whole political cultures gripped by pathology, with ous consequences; so, too, sick ethnic cultures evolved histori- in the tribal world. Few quite so sick as the Tupinamba have been ded before or since.

hey loved human flesh. Prestige and power centered on the ritual htering of prisoners. In an account prepared by Alfred Métraux e Smithsonian's *Handbook of South American Indians* (1948), we that the killing and eating of these prisoners (who were fattened e purpose) "were joyful events which provided these Indians with pportunity for merrymaking, aesthetic displays, and other emo- l outlets." Métraux then describes what took place at a cannibal after the victim's skull was shattered:

> ld women rushed to drink the warm blood, and children were vited to dip their hands in it. Mothers would smear their pples with blood so that even babies could have a taste of it. he body, cut into quarters, was roasted on a barbecue, and the d women, who were the most eager for human flesh, licked e grease running along the sticks. Some portions, reputed to be licacies or sacred, such as the fingers or the grease around the er or heart, were allotted to distinguished guests.

at Portuguese settlers in the 16th century did not cope well with this aspect of the Indian tribal world is probably That the missionaries who came after them did not handle ituation as they might have done is also likely. But if they been around at the time, would John Hemming, or Robin ury-Tenison, or Adrian Cowell, or the entire staff of Survival have much better? Would any of us?

ll primitive peoples," Margaret Mead had said to her young d visitor, "lead miserable, unhappy, cruel lives, most of which ent trying to kill each other." She was overdoing it, but she had a —a point largely lost sight of in today's systematic sentimental- of the Stone Age.

f course, as we have seen, Mead also acknowledged that certain aspects of Indian culture—"their art, culture, dancing, music, etc."—deserved to survive, for the enjoyment of the themselves and for the admiration of humanity as a whole. That, l, is more or less what has happened today in the Xingu Park aces like it elsewhere. On display in such places is a pacified, ed, and somewhat feminized version of Amazonian culture, of d that middle-class travelers from the West like to see: a theatri- rld where dressing-up in feathered regalia, ritual ceremonies, mmunal dancing never stop.

mming, who welcomes the prospect of self-determination, that "modern indigenous policy seeks to empower tribes to e their own affairs." Yet both self-determination and empower- mply literacy and modern education; and here the picture is less Officially, the children are learning to read and write, and in the apter of *Die If You Must*—a chapter with the title "Present and Future" Hemming makes three rather perfunctory references to schooling. But at the same time, he strongly implies that in his vision of the future it does not matter whether the children learn to read and write or not, because others will be there to do things for them.

Who are these others? According to Hemming, the external political affairs of the Indians on the Xingu reserve are "supported by a remarkable contingent of 33 non-government organizations, a fireless band of missionaries, anthropologists, well-wishers, journalists, doctors, and lawyers, both in Brazil and abroad." As for their internal welfare, that is served by a "resident tribe of whites, composed of social scientists, doctors, teachers, nurses, biologists, and agronomists from all parts of Brazil." With friends like these, who needs self-determination?

What Hemming is describing is the fruit of the inviolable-sanctuary approach to cultural survival. This rests on what might be called fortress theory, and has two cardinal principles: that "culture" and "people" and "land" should be seen as indivisible, and that they can be kept this way forever in a suitably constructed territorial redoubt. Whatever is happening in the world around them, ethnic cultures should, insofar as possible, be preserved unchanged. With the help of an army of administrative personnel, custodially responsible for seeing to it that they go on wanting only the same things they have always wanted, their heritage will be kept alive. Social change—at least as it affects these picturesque tribal peoples—is bad, and should be stopped.

Among the Xingu Park Indians, it is in fact safe to say that the older generation remains strongly attached to its remote lands, and intends to go on living there, hunting animals and gathering fruits. But what do younger Indians want to do with their lives? If there is one thing we have learned from modern history, it is that individuals often outgrow their ethnic cultures, find life in a fortress claustrophobic, and choose to move on. In contrast to museum exhibits, real human beings have a way of developing ideas and ambitions and desires—including for aluminum pots—beyond the ken of conservators. Fortress theory, multicultural "essentialism," and the enduring cult of the noble savage are the enemies of those ambitions and human desires.

In the final paragraph of *Die If You Must*, Hemming wonders uneasily whether the pessimists might have the last laugh after all—whether the Amazon's "beautiful, ancient, and intricate cultures will be maintained only artificially as curiosities for tourists, researchers, or politically correct enthusiasts." That is quite possible. But it is hardly the only undesirable possibility. Preserving ancient cultural patterns is laudable, but it is not enough. No society in history has ever stood still, and however beautiful, and ancient, and intricate traditional cultures may be, it is wrong to lock people up inside them and throw away the key. Uprooting the dishonest and patronizing Western cult of the noble savage will be the work of generations; but as far as today's Amazonian Indians are concerned, the main priority must surely be to ensure that those among them who do not want to play the obliging role of historical curiosities, endlessly dressing up for visitors whose expectations they feel bound to fulfill, are able to find something else to do in the modern world—on the reservation or off it. In that quest we can only wish them well.

Roger Sandall taught anthropology for many years at the University of Sydney in Australia and is the author most recently of *The Culture Cult*. His essay, "Can Sudan Be Saved?," appeared in the December 2004 Commentary.

Test-Your-Knowledge Form

We encourage you to photocopy and use this page as a tool to assess how the articles in *Annual Editions* expand on the informa in your textbook. By reflecting on the articles you will gain enhanced text information. You can also access this useful form c product's book support website at *http://www.mhcls.com*.

NAME: DATE:

TITLE AND NUMBER OF ARTICLE:

BRIEFLY STATE THE MAIN IDEA OF THIS ARTICLE:

LIST THREE IMPORTANT FACTS THAT THE AUTHOR USES TO SUPPORT THE MAIN IDEA:

WHAT INFORMATION OR IDEAS DISCUSSED IN THIS ARTICLE ARE ALSO DISCUSSED IN YOUR TEXTBOOK OR OT READINGS THAT YOU HAVE DONE? LIST THE TEXTBOOK CHAPTERS AND PAGE NUMBERS:

LIST ANY EXAMPLES OF BIAS OR FAULTY REASONING THAT YOU FOUND IN THE ARTICLE:

LIST ANY NEW TERMS/CONCEPTS THAT WERE DISCUSSED IN THE ARTICLE, AND WRITE A SHORT DEFINITION:

Ve Want Your Advice

IUAL EDITIONS revisions depend on two major opinion sources: one is our Advisory Board, listed in the front of this volume, h works with us in scanning the thousands of articles published in the public press each year; the other is you—the person actu- using the book. Please help us and the users of the next edition by completing the prepaid article rating form on this page and ning it to us. Thank you for your help!

NUAL EDITIONS: Anthropology 10/11

ARTICLE RATING FORM

Here is an opportunity for you to have direct input into the next revision of this volume.
We would like you to rate each of the articles listed below, using the following scale:

1. **Excellent: should definitely be retained**
2. **Above average: should probably be retained**
3. **Below average: should probably be deleted**
4. **Poor: should definitely be deleted**

Your ratings will play a vital part in the next revision.
Please mail this prepaid form to us as soon as possible.
Thanks for your help!

'ING	ARTICLE
______	1. Before: The Sixties
______	2. Eating Christmas in the Kalahari
______	3. Tricking and Tripping: Fieldwork on Prostitution in the Era of AIDS
______	4. Yanomamo
______	5. Whose Speech Is Better?
______	6. Lost for Words
______	7. Do You Speak American?
______	8. Fighting for Our Lives
______	9. Expletive Deleted
______	10. I Can't Even Open My Mouth: Separating Messages from Metamessages in Family Talk
______	11. Shakespeare in the Bush
______	12. At a Loss for Words
______	13. The Inuit Paradox
______	14. Ties That Bind
______	15. Playing Indian at Halftime: The Controversy over American Indian Mascots, Logos, and Nicknames in School-Related Events
______	16. Sick of Poverty
	17. When Brothers Share a Wife: Among Tibetans, the Good Life Relegates Many Women to Spinsterhood

RATING	ARTICLE
______	18. Death without Weeping
______	19. Arranging a Marriage in India
______	20. Who Needs Love!: In Japan, Many Couples Don't
______	21. The Berdache Tradition
______	22. Where Fat Is a Mark of Beauty
______	23. . . . but What If It's a Girl?
______	24. Rising Number of Dowry Deaths in India
______	25. Shamanisms: Past and Present
______	26. The Adaptive Value of Religious Ritual
______	27. Understanding Islam
______	28. The Secrets of Haiti's Living Dead
______	29. Body Ritual among the Nacirema
______	30. Baseball Magic
______	31. Why Can't People Feed Themselves?
______	32. The Arrow of Disease
______	33. The Price of Progress
______	34. Of Ice and Men
______	35. Inundation
______	36. Isolation
______	37. Seeing Conservation through the Global Lens
______	38. What Native Peoples Deserve

NO POSTAG
NECESSAR
IF MAILED
IN THE
UNITED STAT

BUSINESS REPLY MAIL
FIRST CLASS MAIL PERMIT NO. 551 DUBUQUE IA

POSTAGE WILL BE PAID BY ADDRESSEE

McGraw-Hill Contemporary Learning Series
501 BELL STREET
DUBUQUE, IA 52001

ABOUT YOU

Name Date

Are you a teacher? ❒ A student? ☒
Your school's name

Department

Address City State Zip

School telephone #

YOUR COMMENTS ARE IMPORTANT TO US!

Please fill in the following information:
For which course did you use this book?

Did you use a text with this ANNUAL EDITION? ❒ yes ❒ no
What was the title of the text?

What are your general reactions to the Annual Editions concept?

Have you read any pertinent articles recently that you think should be included in the next edition? Explain.

Are there any articles that you feel should be replaced in the next edition? Why?

Are there any World Wide Websites that you feel should be included in the next edition? Please annotate.

May we contact you for editorial input? ❒ yes ❒ no
May we quote your comments? ❒ yes ❒ no

VOLUMES AVAILABLE

Adolescent Psychology
Aging
American Foreign Policy
American Government
Anthropology
Archaeology
Assessment and Evaluation
Biological Psychology
Business Ethics
Child Growth and Development
Comparative Politics
Computers in Education
Computers in Society
Criminal Justice
Developing World
Drugs, Society, and Behavior
Dying, Death, and Bereavement
Early Childhood Education
Economics
Educating Children with Exceptionalities
Education
Educational Psychology
Entrepreneurship
Environment
The Family
Film
Gender
Geography
Global Issues
Health
Homeland Security
Human Development
Human Resources
Human Sexualities
International Business
Management
Marketing
Mass Media
Microbiology
Multicultural Education
Nutrition
Personal Growth and Behavior
Physical Anthropology
Psychology
Public Policy and Administration
Race and Ethnic Relations
Social Problems
Social Psychology
Sociology
State and Local Government
United States History, Volume 1
United States History, Volume 2
Urban Society
Violence and Terrorism
Western Civilization, Volume 1
Western Civilization, Volume 2
World History, Volume 1
World History, Volume 2
World Politics

The Annual Editions Series

ANNUAL EDITIONS

Anthropology 10/11 is one in a series of over sixty-five volumes, each designed to provide convenient, inexpensive access to a wide range of current, carefully selected articles from some of the most respected magazines, newspapers, and journals published today. Within the pages of this volume are interesting, well-illustrated articles by anthropologists, educators, researchers, and writers providing effective and useful perspectives on today's important topics in the study of anthropology.

CORRELATION GUIDE INSIDE. *Instructor prep time just got easier!*
It's easy to use this reader in conjunction with other best-selling McGraw-Hill titles. You'll find the helpful Correlation Guide following the Table of Contents.

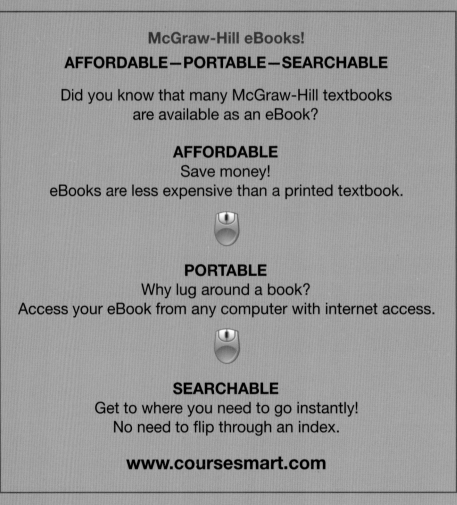

www.mhhe.com/cls

The McGraw·Hill Companies

ISBN 978-0-07-812782-3
MHID 0-07-812782-3